JOURNAL FOR THE STUDY OF THE NEW TESTAMENT
SUPPLEMENT SERIES
53

Executive Editor, Supplement Series
David Hill

Publishing Editor
David E. Orton

JSOT Press
Sheffield

REVELATION
and
REDEMPTION
at
COLOSSAE

Thomas J. Sappington

Journal for the Study of the New Testament
Supplement Series 53

To Katy

Copyright © 1991 Sheffield Academic Press

Published by JSOT Press
JSOT Press is an imprint of
Sheffield Academic Press Ltd
The University of Sheffield
343 Fulwood Road
Sheffield S10 3BP
England

Printed in Great Britain
by Billing & Sons Ltd
Worcester

British Library Cataloguing in Publication Data

Sappington, Thomas J.
   Revelation and redemption at Colossae.
   1. Christianity. Scriptures
   I. Title   II. Series
   227

ISSN 0143-5108
ISBN 1-85075-307-5

CONTENTS

PART I. THE ASCETIC-MYSTICAL PIETY
OF JEWISH APOCALYPTICISM

Chapter 1
INTRODUCTION TO THE LITERATURE
OF JEWISH APOCALYPTICISM

ACKNOWLEDGMENTS

This study consists of a revised version of my doctoral dissertation. Accordingly, I would like to express my appreciation to those who have assisted in bringing it to completion and publication. I am especially indebted to Professor Richard N. Longenecker of Wycliffe College, Toronto, for his guidance in the study of Jewish apocalyptic literature, his many helpful suggestions and criticisms with regard to the style and presentation of this work, and his support and encouragement at critical points in my doctoral programme. I am also grateful to Professors Joseph Plevnik, John Hurd, Abraham Rotstein and Alan Segal for the comments and criticisms they provided during the examination process. Many thanks are due as well to Professor Joseph L. Trafton of Western Kentucky University for taking time to read a rough draft and to offer a number of helpful suggestions. I am, however, ultimately responsible for the form and content of this study.

Special thanks are due to the staff of the Inter-Library Loan department of Robarts Library. Their assistance at many points during my time in Toronto was invaluable.

Without the financial support provided by my in-laws, Roger and Elinor Tompkins, and my late father, George Sappington, this study would never have been completed. Also, I am indebted to Wycliffe College for the generous bursaries they provided during the first few years of my studies.

I would like to thank the elders and the congregation of Westminster Bible Church, Bowling Green, Kentucky, for encouraging my research and writing and for providing some time off from pastoral work in order for me to give attention to these matters.

I have appreciated so much the encouragement and help provided by Dr David Hill, Dr David Orton and Ms Elizabeth Lye of Sheffield Academic Press. It has been a privilege to work with them toward the publication of this book. My thanks go also to Professor David J.A. Clines at the Press for his meticulous reading of the text.

Finally, I would like to thank my wife, Katy, for her encouragement and support throughout my studies. She has helped me in more ways than she will ever know.

ABBREVIATIONS

ANRW	*Aufstieg und Niedergang der römischen Welt* (ed. H. Temporini and W. Haase; Berlin and New York: de Gruyter, 1972–).
APAT	*Die Apokryphen und Pseudepigraphen des Alten Testaments* (2 vols.; ed. E. Kautzsch; Tübingen: Mohr, 1900).
Apocalypticism	*Apocalypticism in the Mediterranean World and the Near East: Proceedings of the International Colloquium on Apocalypticism, Uppsala, August 12–17, 1979* (ed. D. Hellholm; Tübingen: Mohr, 1983).
APOT	*Apocrypha and Pseudepigrapha of the Old Testament* (2 vols.; ed. R.H. Charles; Oxford: Clarendon Press, 1913).
ARW	*Archiv für Religionswissenschaft*
AUSS	*Andrews University Seminary Studies*
BAGD	W. Bauer, W.F. Arndt, F.W. Gingrich and F.W. Danker, *A Greek–English Lexicon of the New Testament* (Chicago: University of Chicago Press, 1979).
BASOR	*Bulletin of the American Schools of Oriental Research*
BDF	F. Blass, A. Debrunner and R.W. Funk, *A Greek Grammar of the New Testament* (Chicago: University of Chicago Press, 1961).
Bib	*Biblica*
BibLeb	*Bibel und Leben*
Biblical Greek	M. Zerwick, *Biblical Greek* (English edn adapted from the fourth Latin edn by J. Smith; Rome: Biblical Institute Press, 1963).
BibSac	*Bibliotheca Sacra*
BLit	*Bibel und Liturgie*
CBQ	*Catholic Biblical Quarterly*
Conflict	*Conflict at Colossae* (trans. and ed. F.O. Francis and W.A. Meeks; Missoula, MT: Scholars Press, 1975).
CTJ	*Calvin Theological Journal*
DBSup	*Dictionnaire de la Bible, Suppléments* (ed. L. Pirot *et al.*; Paris: Letouzey & Ané, 1928–).
EJ	*Encyclopedia Judaica* (16 vols.; ed., C. Roth *et al.*; New York: Macmillan, 1971–).
EQ	*Evangelical Quarterly*
EvT	*Evangelische Theologie*
ExpTim	*The Expository Times*

FO	*Folia Orientalia*
HTR	*Harvard Theological Review*
HUCA	*Hebrew Union College Annual*
Ideal Figures	*Ideal Figures in Ancient Judaism* (ed. G.W.E. Nickelsburg and J.J. Collins; Missoula, MT: Scholars Press, 1980).
Idiom Book	C.F.D. Moule, *An Idiom Book of New Testament Greek* (Cambridge: Cambridge University Press, 1959).
Int	*Interpretation*
IOS	*Israel Oriental Studies*
JAOS	*Journal of the American Oriental Society*
JBL	*Journal of Biblical Literature*
JE	*The Jewish Encyclopedia* (12 vols.; ed. I. Singer *et al.*; New York and London: Funk & Wagnalls, 1901–1906).
JETS	*Journal of the Evangelical Theological Society*
JJS	*Journal of Jewish Studies*
JQR	*Jewish Quarterly Review*
JSHRZ	*Jüdische Schriften aus hellenistisch-römischer Zeit* (ed. W.G. Kümmel *et al.*; Gütersloh: Gütersloher Verlagshaus, 1973–).
JSJ	*Journal for the Study of Judaism*
JSNT	*Journal for the Study of the New Testament*
JSP	*Journal for the Study of the Pseudepigrapha*
JSS	*Journal of Semitic Studies*
JTC	*Journal for Theology and the Church*
JTS	*Journal of Theological Studies*
JWSTP	*Jewish Writings of the Second Temple Period* (ed. M.E. Stone; Compendia Rerum Iudaicarum ad Novum Testamentum 2.2; Philadelphia: Fortress Press, 1984).
LSJ	J.G. Liddell, R. Scott and H.S. Jones, *A Greek–English Lexicon* (Oxford: Clarendon, 1968).
LTQ	*Lexington Theological Quarterly*
MM	J.H. Moulton and G. Milligan, *The Vocabulary of the Greek Testament* (Grand Rapids: Eerdmans, 1930).
Neot	*Neotestamentica*
NIDNTT	*The New International Dictionary of New Testament Theology* (3 vols.; ed. C. Brown; Grand Rapids: Zondervan, 1975–78).
NovT	*Novum Testamentum*
NTS	*New Testament Studies*
OTP	*The Old Testament Pseudepigrapha* (2 vols.; ed. J.H. Charlesworth; Garden City, NY: Doubleday, 1983–85).
RB	*Revue biblique*
REJ	*Revue des études juives*
RechBib	*Recherches bibliques*
RevExp	*Review and Expositor*
RGG³	*Die Religion in Geschichte und Gegenwart* (6 vols.; ed. K. Galling *et al.*; Tübingen: Mohr, 1957–65).

RelSRev	*Religious Studies Review*
ResQ	*Restoration Quarterly*
RevQ	*Revue de Qumran*
RSR	*Recherches de science religieuse*
RTR	*Reformed Theological Review*
SEÅ	*Svensk exegetisk årsbok*
ST	*Studia Theologica*
Syntax	N. Turner, 'Syntax', in J.H. Moulton, *A Grammar of New Testament Greek*, Vol. III (Edinburgh: T. & T. Clark, 1963).
TDNT	*Theological Dictionary of the New Testament* (10 vols.; ed. G. Kittel and G. Friedrich; trans. G.W. Bromiley; Grand Rapids: Eerdmans, 1964–74).
TLZ	*Theologische Literaturzeitung*
Trad	*Traditio*
TRu	*Theologische Rundschau*
TV	*Theologia Viatorum*
Visionaries	*Visionaries and their Apocalypses* (ed. P.D. Hanson; Philadelphia: Fortress Press, 1983).
VT	*Vetus Testamentum*
ZAW	*Zeitschrift für die alttestamentliche Wissenschaft*
ZKT	*Zeitschrift für katholische Theologie*
ZTK	*Zeitschrift für Theologie und Kirche*

INTRODUCTION

1. The Problem of the Colossian 'Philosophy'

The nature of the error that occasioned the writing of Colossians has been a source of much controversy.[1] Lightfoot's classic work generally set the parameters of the debate when it described the 'heresy' as a kind of Gnostic Judaism that stood in the line of development from the Essenes to Cerinthus.[2] The general characterization of the error as 'gnosticizing Judaism' has been adopted by many,[3] though some writ-

---

1. That the argument of the letter was directed against a specific 'error' is almost universally agreed; *contra* M.D. Hooker, 'Were There False Teachers in Colossae?', in *Christ and Spirit in the New Testament* (ed. B. Lindars and S.S. Smalley; Cambridge: Cambridge University Press, 1973), pp. 315-31. By using the term 'error' to describe the Colossian 'philosophy', our intention is to reflect the perspective of the Colossian letter itself, and to stand in continuity with most previous research.

2. J.B. Lightfoot, *Saint Paul's Epistles to the Colossians and to Philemon* (London: Macmillan, 1879; Grand Rapids: Zondervan, 1959 reprint), pp. 73-113. E.W. Saunders ('The Colossian Heresy and Qumran Theology', in *Studies in the History and Text of the New Testament* [ed. B.L. Daniels and M.J. Suggs; Salt Lake City: University of Utah Press, 1967], pp. 133-45) argues that the Qumran texts corroborate Lightfoot's hypothesis based on the descriptive accounts of Philo and Josephus.

3. F.F. Bruce (with E.K. Simpson), *Commentary on the Epistles to the Ephesians and Colossians* (Grand Rapids: Eerdmans, 1957), p. 166, and *idem*, *Paul: Apostle of the Heart Set Free* (Grand Rapids: Eerdmans, 1977), pp. 412-17. This stands in contrast, however, with the approach taken in the 1984 revision of his commentary on Colossians, where he adopts the view that the error is a form of ascetic-mystical piety. For other examples of writers who view the error as 'gnosticizing Judaism', see H.C.G. Moule, *The Epistles to the Colossians and to Philemon* (Cambridge: Cambridge University Press, 1894), pp. 30-37; C.F.D. Moule, *The Epistles to the Colossians and to Philemor* (Cambridge: Cambridge University Press, 1957), p. 31; and H.M. Carson, *The Epistles of Paul to the Colossians and Philemon* (Grand Rapids: Eerdmans, 1960), pp. 15-18. T.H. Olbricht ('Colossians and Gnostic Theology', *ResQ* 14 [1971], 67, 69, 78) emphasizes the other side of the description of the error. In his opinion, it is best described as 'incipient gnosticism' that contains Jewish elements. Cf., however, H. Koester, *Introduction to the New Testament* (Philadelphia: Fortress, 1982), 2.265, who stops short of the characterization

ers have stressed that it is highly syncretistic and contains 'pagan' elements of various sorts.[1] On the other hand, some have argued that the 'philosophy' confronted is essentially like the faith and piety one encounters in the Dead Sea Scrolls, which can be described at most as 'pre-gnostic'.[2]

Several writers have suggested models of interpretation that are primarily 'pagan' in their focus. Most significant of these was Dibelius, who argued that Christians at Colossae were seeking initiation into a gnostic or pre-gnostic mystery cult.[3] His basic approach has been very influential, though some have introduced modifications.[4] A

'Jewish-Christian gnostics', preferring rather to speak of the errorists as 'Jewish-Christian syncretists'.

1. G. Bornkamm ('The Heresy of Colossians', in *Conflict*, pp. 123-45) argues that it is a 'Jewish or Judaizing gnosticism that is deeply infected by Iranian views'. It also includes Chaldean astrological beliefs and involves the practice of a mystery within the congregation. Bornkamm's general approach is followed by H. Conzelmann, 'Der Brief an die Kolosser', in *Die kleineren Briefe des Apostels Paulus* (Göttingen: Vandenhoeck & Ruprecht, 1962), p. 147, and H.M. Schenke, 'Der Widerstreit gnostischer und kirchlicher Christologie im Spiegel des Kolosserbriefes', *ZTK* 61 (1964), pp. 391-403. Unfortunately, such treatments tend to multiply the number of different influences which are operative at Colossae in an effort to explain various aspects of the argument of Colossians.

2. W.D. Davies, 'Paul and the Dead Sea Scrolls: Flesh and Spirit', in *Christian Origins and Judaism* (London: Darton, Longman & Todd, 1962), pp. 157-59; P. Bénoit, 'Qumran and the New Testament', in *Paul and Qumran* (ed. J. Murphy-O'Connor; Chicago: Priory, 1968), pp. 16-17; F.M. Cross, Jr, *The Ancient Library of Qumran and Modern Biblical Studies* (Garden City, NY: Doubleday, 1958), p. 150; A.R.C. Leaney, '"Conformed to the Image of His Son" (Rom. VIII 29)', *NTS* 10 (1964), p. 478. Cf. also W. Foerster, 'Die Irrlehrer des Kolosserbriefes', in *Studia Biblica et Semitica* (ed. W.C. van Unnik and A.S. van der Woude; Wageningen: Veenman & Zonen, 1966), p. 80, who refers to the false teachers as 'Juden den Essenern verwandter Richtung', though his description of the error closely resembles the ascetic-mystical piety described by Francis and others, and N. Kehl, 'Erniedrigung und Erhöhung in Qumran und Kolossä', *ZKT* 91 (1969), pp. 364-94. For a critique of this position, see E. Yamauchi, 'Sectarian Parallels: Qumran and Colosse', *BibSac* 121 (1964), pp. 141-52.

3. M. Dibelius, 'The Isis Initiation in Apuleius and Related Initiatory Rites', in *Conflict*, pp. 61-121; cf. *idem*, *An die Kolosser, Epheser, an Philemon* (3rd edn, revised by H. Greeven; Tübingen: Mohr, 1953), p. 35.

4. E. Lohse, *Colossians and Philemon* (trans. W.R. Pöhlmann and R.J. Karris; Philadelphia: Fortress Press, 1971), pp. 127-31, though he admits that 'an important contribution to this philosophy has also been made by the Jewish tradition'. Similar are the treatments by G.H.P. Thompson, *The Letters of Paul to the Ephesians, to the Colossians and to Philemon* (Cambridge: Cambridge University Press, 1967), pp. 120-21, and R.A. Argall, 'The Source of a Religious Error in Colossae', *CTJ*

very different construction is set forth by Schweizer, who contends that the false teaching is a form of Jewish Pythagoreanism.[1] The Jewish element is included to account for the fact that Sabbath observance is mentioned in 2.16, but it is clear that the error is basically 'pagan' in nature.[2]

This brief survey of interpretations, which is by no means exhaustive, illustrates the tremendous diversity of opinion that exists with regard to the nature of the Colossian 'philosophy'. There is at present simply no consensus on this question.[3]

2. *Ascetic-Mystical Piety and the Colossian 'Philosophy'*

In his 1965 dissertation, Fred Francis focused on ascetic-mystical piety as a possible background to the problem at Colossae.[4] Building on a suggestion by his supervisor, Nils Dahl, Francis utilized a number of Jewish, Christian and Gnostic sources (including *1, 2* and *3 Enoch*; *4 Ezra*; *Testament of Levi*; *2* and *3 Baruch*; *Apocalypse of Abraham*; *Testament of Job*; *Testament of Isaac*; *Testament of Jacob*; *Joseph and Aseneth*; *Ascension of Isaiah*; Philo; Tertullian; the *Shepherd of Hermas*; the *Corpus Hermeticum*; also he alludes to the later documents of Merkabah mysticism) to argue that the Colossian 'philosophy' conforms closely to the ascetic-mystical piety that 'obtained generally in

22 (1987), pp. 6-20. J. Lähnemann, *Der Kolosserbrief* (Gütersloh: Gütersloher Verlagshaus, 1971), pp. 76-100, also sets forth the view that the false teachers promoted a mystery cult, though in his opinion the challenge to the congregation is also Jewish and highly syncretistic. The problem with these studies is that ἃ ἑόρακεν ἐμβατεύων of Col. 2.18 by no means necessarily refers to entrance into a mystery. In fact, there are serious problems with this interpretation which will be discussed below.

1. E. Schweizer, *The Letter to the Colossians* (trans. A. Chester; Minneapolis: Augsburg, 1982), pp. 125-33, as well as his numerous articles on matters related to Colossians. His position is best described as idiosyncratic.

2. Schweizer, *Colossians*, pp. 132-33.

3. Telling is the fact that J.J. Gunther, *St. Paul's Opponents and their Background* (Leiden: Brill, 1973), pp. 3-4, lists some forty-four diverse opinions with regard to the nature of the Colossian 'philosophy', though many of these could be consolidated under broader headings.

4. F.O. Francis, 'A Re-examination of the Colossian Controversy' (PhD dissertation, Yale University, 1965). The main lines of argumentation were published earlier in summary form in 'Humility and Angelic Worship in Col 2:18', *ST* 16 (1962), pp. 109-34, and reprinted in *Conflict*, pp. 163-95.

the Hellenistic world'.[1] In his view, the problem at Colossae was not directly christological, but centered around matters of *praxis*. It was no cult of angels that threatened the faith and life of the congregation. Rather, Christians at Colossae were attempting to gain a visionary experience of heaven and to participate in the heavenly worship that the angels offer to God. Such mystical experiences resulted from various ascetic practices, some of which are mentioned in Colossians 2. This form of piety was highly destructive since it created divisions in the church, with some Christians standing in judgment over others who did not follow this practice.

Francis followed up his dissertation with several articles, all of which develop this basic position.[2] Nevertheless, for some fifteen years his model of interpretation received little notice in the scholarly literature. In fact, only Andrew Bandstra adopted his fundamental interpretation of Col. 2.18.[3] More recently, however, support for this interpretation has increased significantly, particularly in the writings of Wesley Carr,[4] Andrew Lincoln,[5] Craig Evans,[6] Patrick O'Brien,[7]

---

1. Francis, 'Humility and Angelic Worship', p. 185.
2. 'Visionary Discipline and Scriptural Tradition at Colossae', *LTQ* 2 (1967), pp. 71-81; 'The Background of EMBATEUEIN in Legal Papyri and Oracle Inscriptions', in *Conflict*, pp. 197-207, and 'The Christological Argument of Colossians', in *God's Christ and His People* (ed. J. Jervell and W.A. Meeks; Oslo: Universitetsforlaget, 1977), pp. 192-208. The 1967 article presents in popular form the theory of scriptural tradition at Colossae that was developed in his dissertation. While this is related to his general argument, the model of ascetic-mysticism does not necessarily include this factor and so should be handled separately.
3. His support is mentioned briefly in *The Law and the Elements of the World* (Kampen: Kok, 1964), p. 160, and developed in detail in 'Did the Colossian Errorists Need a Mediator?', in *New Dimensions in New Testament Study* (ed. R.N. Longenecker and M. Tenney; Grand Rapids: Zondervan, 1974), pp. 329-43, where he ties in the notion of a polemic against a mediator.
4. *Angels and Principalities* (Cambridge: Cambridge University Press, 1981), pp. 66-85.
5. *Paradise Now and Not Yet* (Cambridge: Cambridge University Press, 1981), pp. 110-13.
6. 'The Colossian Mystics', *Bib* 63 (1982), pp. 188-205.
7. *Colossians and Philemon* (Waco, TX: Word, 1982), pp. xxxvi-xxxviii.

Christopher Rowland,[1] F.F. Bruce,[2] Roy Yates,[3] and John Levison.[4] While these writers differ as to details, with several narrowing the background of the error significantly,[5] for the most part their analyses of the problem at Colossae agree with that set forth by Francis. Little is added to his discussion. In fact, several appear to base their discussions on his summary articles alone, being evidently unaware of the many linguistic and exegetical problems that emerge in Francis's lengthy analysis of the polemical passages of Colossians 2. The cogency of this type of analysis, however, is coming to be recognized increasingly. Still, there is a danger that research will not push ahead to gain a clearer picture of the problem that threatened the life of the church at Colossae.

3. *The Ascetic-Mystical Piety of Jewish Apocalypticism and the Colossian 'Philosophy'*

There is need for a thorough re-examination of ascetic-mystical piety, particularly as it comes to expression in Jewish apocalypticism, as a possible explanation for the problems that faced the church at Colossae. This is so, first of all, because of the nature of Francis's work. It was a pioneering work, and, as such, it was incumbent on him to devote much of his time to basic lexical and syntactical matters.[6]

---

1. 'Apocalyptic Visions and the Exaltation of Christ in the Letter to the Colossians', *JSNT* 19 (1983), pp. 73-83.
2. *The Epistles to the Colossians, to Philemon, and to the Ephesians* (Grand Rapids: Eerdmans, 1984), pp. 17-26.
3. ' "The Worship of Angels" (Col 2:18)', *ExpTim* 97 (1985), pp. 12-15.
4. '2 Apoc. Bar. 48:42–52:7 and the Apocalyptic Dimension of Colossians 3:1-6', *JBL* 108 (1989), pp. 93-108.
5. Evans, pp. 203-204, Rowland, p. 74, Bruce (1984), pp. 22-26, and Yates, p. 14, all focus exclusively on Jewish apocalypticism and Jewish mysticism, while Carr (p. 71) refers only to 'Christian traditions'. Lincoln (p. 223) evidently misunderstands Francis's work. He writes that it 'is probably too one-sided' since it treats the problem 'almost solely from a Jewish background'. Of course, this is exactly what Francis was attempting to avoid. Of these writers, only O'Brien, pp. xxxvi-xxxviii, speaks of the broad religious pattern with which Francis was concerned.
6. Some more important examples of this type of analysis can be found in 'Reexamination', pp. 28-38 (his analysis of ταπεινοφροσύνη), pp. 39-76 (his study of the meaning and connotations of ἐμβατεύειν, in which he argues that its primary background is to be found in legal papyri dealing with the possession of property rather than the Clarian oracle, *contra* M. Dibelius, 'Isis Initiation', pp. 61-121), and

Therefore, it is not surprising that his analysis of ascetic mysticism in the various documents is sketchy at many points. Nevertheless, we are now in a position to build on his research, and so to clarify our perceptions of the situation significantly.

Second, and of far greater importance, are the numerous advances that have been made during the last twenty-five years in the study of the literature of Jewish non-conformity. We are now, for example, in a much better position to assess with some precision the role of the heavenly dimension at Qumran.[1] While this is helpful to our task, of even greater significance are the advances in understanding that have been made of late in the area of Jewish apocalyptic literature. Important here is (1) the interest in the influence of the wisdom tradition on Jewish apocalyptic as sparked by the works of Gerhard von Rad,[2] as well as (2) the analysis of the relation between various sections of the Jewish apocalypses (esp. chs. 1–36 of *1 Enoch*) and the later writings of Jewish mysticism as set forth by Gershom Scholem.[3]

The concepts sketched out in these studies, together with the greater understanding of the characteristics of the genre 'apocalypse' that has been obtained in recent years,[4] have generated some interest in the

pp. 13-100 (his survey and evaluation of the syntax of Col. 2.18). Francis's work in these areas merits close attention.

1. An important recent work in this area is C. Newsom, *Songs of the Sabbath Sacrifice: A Critical Edition* (Atlanta: Scholars Press, 1985). Significant as well is S.F. Noll, 'Angelology in the Qumran Texts' (PhD dissertation, Manchester, 1979). Also, the subject is discussed in virtually all of the more recent studies on the theology and piety of the community at Qumran. Cf. also the older studies by J.A. Fitzmyer, 'A Feature of Qumran Angelology and the New Testament', *NTS* 4 (1957), pp. 48-58, and J.T. Milik, *Ten Years of Discovery in the Wilderness of Judaea* (trans. J. Strugnell; London: SCM, 1959), p. 114.

2. This argument was published originally in *Theologie des Alten Testaments* (Munich: Chr. Kaiser Verlag, 1960), and revised and supplemented in his later works. Generally, von Rad's thesis has not been received with open arms; cf., e.g., J.L. Crenshaw, review of *Wisdom in Israel* by G. von Rad, in *RelSRev* 2 (1976), p. 10, and E.W. Nicholson, 'Apocalyptic', in *Tradition and Interpretation* (ed. G.W. Anderson; Oxford: Clarendon, 1979), pp. 207-11. Nevertheless, it was precisely as scholars evaluated his thesis that they came to a more balanced appreciation of Jewish apocalyptic.

3. *Major Trends in Jewish Mysticism* (London: Thames & Hudson, 1955), and *Jewish Gnosticism, Merkabah Mysticism and Talmudic Tradition* (New York: Jewish Seminary of America, 1960).

4. See esp. the articles contained within the section entitled 'The Literary Genre of Apocalypses' in *Apocalypticism*, pp. 327-637.

vertical axis of the apocalyptic writings.[1] This dimension of apocalyptic thought has traditionally been neglected in favor of the horizontal axis. But scholars are increasingly coming to recognize that there is much more to apocalyptic than *ex eventu* surveys of history and an imminent expectation of judgment. John Collins, for example, argues that the crucial factor in Jewish apocalyptic is 'the transcendence of death' through heavenly revelation in the present or the experience of the new age,[2] while Ithamar Gruenwald lays stress on supernatural revelation and the mystical character of early Jewish apocalyptic and develops the line of thought introduced by Scholem.[3] It is Christopher Rowland, however, who lays particular stress on revelation through visions or heavenly ascent as central in Jewish apocalyptic literature. He writes, with regard to Daniel and the Revelation of John as representative of the Jewish apocalypses, that 'the unifying factor which joins both these apocalypses and separates them from other contemporary literature is the conviction that runs through both, that man is able to know about the divine mysteries by means of revelation, so that God's eternal purposes may be disclosed, and man, as a result, may see history in a totally new light'.[4]

Since the particular model of interpretation that I propose to follow views the error at Colossae as involving the attempt to achieve supernatural experiences and to gain heavenly revelation or 'wisdom' through certain ascetic practices, these new trends in apocalyptic research are highly relevant for my purposes. They suggest that a detailed analysis of Jewish apocalypticism as a possible 'background' for Colossians could yield significant results.[5] And my research con-

---

1. See J.J. Collins, 'Introduction: Towards the Morphology of a Genre', *Semeia* 14 (1979), pp. 1-19, and *idem*, 'The Jewish Apocalypses', Semeia 14 (1979), pp. 21-59. He stresses the importance of the vertical dimension in the Jewish apocalypses in his careful analysis of the genre.

2. 'Apocalyptic Eschatology as the Transcendence of Death', in *Visionaries*, pp. 61-84.

3. *Apocalyptic and Merkavah Mysticism* (Leiden: Brill, 1980), pp. 3-72; cf. *idem*, 'Knowledge and Vision', *IOS* (1973), pp. 63-107.

4. C. Rowland, *The Open Heaven* (New York: Crossroad, 1982), p. 13. This work is a revision of his 'The Influence of the First Chapter of Ezekiel on Judaism and Early Christianity' (PhD dissertation, Cambridge University, 1975).

5. This involves, of course, a significant narrowing of Francis's original investigation. This seems proper given the developments in the field of Jewish apocalypticism and the specific parallels that can now be drawn between the faith and piety of

firms this hypothesis, as I shall argue in detail in the following chapters.

4. *The Authorship of Colossians*

Before turning to the documents themselves, a brief explanation is necessary as to my position on the authorship of Colossians. Several recent studies have sided against Pauline authorship. Significant here are the multi-level stylistic analysis of Bujard[1] and (building on Bujard's work) the more comprehensive study by Kiley.[2] So convincing, in fact, is Bujard's work that Wayne Meeks writes, 'Walter Bujard's thorough stylistic analysis ought to put to rest the long debate whether Paul himself could have written the letter: he did not'.[3] The argument that the style of the Colossian letter differs from that of the undisputed Pauline letters cannot be taken lightly. Neither can the differences in teaching on certain themes and issues.

Still, it is important to keep in mind the broader picture, for several considerations suggest that the issue is still open to debate. The impact of the stylistic differences is lessened by two factors: (1) the possibility that Paul made extensive use of traditional material in the Colossian letter, and (2) the probable use of an amanuensis in its composition.

George Cannon has argued in favor of Pauline authorship on the basis of the use of traditional material in the letter.[4] In his view, arguments from style and theology are confounded by the presence of hymnic and liturgical materials, such as those found in 1.12(15)-20 and 2.9(13)-15. One should not, therefore, expect stylistic analyses of Colossians to agree with those of other Pauline letters, since Colossians contains a high percentage of material that is pre-Pauline.

the Jewish apocalyptists and that of the errorists at Colossae as it is described in Col. 2.

1. W. Bujard, *Stilanalytische Untersuchungen zum Kolosserbrief als Beitrag zur Methodik von Sprachvergleichen* (Göttingen: Vandenhoeck & Ruprecht, 1973).

2. M.C. Kiley, 'Colossians as Pseudepigraphy' (PhD dissertation, Harvard University, 1983), published as *Colossians as Pseudepigraphy* (Sheffield: JSOT Press, 1986).

3. W.A. Meeks, *The First Urban Christians* (New Haven: Yale University Press, 1983), p. 125. Cf. W. Schenk, 'Der Kolosserbrief in der neueren Forschung (1945–1985)', in *ANRW* II.25.4, pp. 3326-38.

4. G.E. Cannon, *The Use of Traditional Materials in Colossians* (Macon, GA: Mercer University Press, 1983).

Cannon's arguments on the question of authorship are thought-provoking. Nevertheless, caution is in order. For the stylistic characteristics uncovered by Bujard are present in 'non-traditional' as well as allegedly 'traditional' passages. Also, the presence of traditional material, I would argue, is not as securely documented as many maintain. However, I shall reserve my evaluation of 1.12(15)-20 and 2.9(13)-15 for Part II of my study.

The question of the role of an amanuensis is more telling with regard to arguments from style. The words of 4.18, 'I, Paul, write this greeting in my own hand', point unmistakably to the use of an amanuensis in the composition of the letter. Beyond that, however, we know virtually nothing about the process of composition. The letter may have been dictated verbatim, or an amanuensis (Timothy?, see Col. 1.1) may have 'fleshed out' the general line of thought suggested by the author himself, who then approved the content of the letter and added his own signature and greeting.[1] A change in amanuensis and/or a change in the degree of freedom given the amanuensis (due to a change in circumstances?) would readily account for differences in style between Colossians and the undisputed letters of Paul.[2]

The differences in teaching and emphasis between the undisputed Pauline letters and Colossians have been assigned varying degrees of significance. For some, the distinctive christology, ecclesiology, eschatology, and soteriology of Colossians tell decisively against

---

1. On these customs, see R.N. Longenecker, 'Ancient Amanuenses and the Pauline Epistles', in *New Dimensions in New Testament Study*, pp. 281-97; *idem*, 'On the Form, Function, and Authority of the New Testament Letters', in *Scripture and Truth* (ed. D.A. Carson and J.D. Woodbridge; Grand Rapids: Zondervan, 1983), pp. 106-109. Cf. O. Roller, *Das Formular der paulinischen Briefe* (Stuttgart: Kohlhammer, 1933), p. 333.

2. Note the explanation given by E. Schweizer, 'The Letter to the Colossians—Neither Pauline nor Post-Pauline?', in *Pluralisme et oecuménisme en recherches théologiques: mélanges offerts au R.P. Dockx* (ed. Y. Congar *et al.*; Paris: Duculot, 1976), p. 14: 'Let us suppose that Paul's imprisonment was stricter at the time of writing to the Colossians than it was when he wrote to the Philippians. Let us suppose that he was not able to dictate or write personally more than a sentence or two at the end (and, may be, a short letter like that to Philemon). If so, would not Timothy write the letter that was needed in the usual style of a letter from "Paul. . . and Timothy. . . to the. . . Colossians"?' Cf. P. Bénoit, 'Rapports littéraires entre les épîtres aux Colossiens et aux Éphésiens', in *Neutestamentliche Aufsätze. Festschrift für Prof. Josef Schmid* (ed. J. Blinzler, O. Kuss and F. Mussner; Regensburg: Pustet, 1963), pp. 21-22.

Pauline authorship.[1] For others, however, these differences are simply further evidence of development in Pauline thought, as is also evident in the undisputed letters.[2] And then there is always the difficult question of the extent to which the distinctive presentation of Colossians resulted from the particular situation that was addressed. Needless to say, there remains much work to be done in defining the parameters of Paul's thought and teaching.

Many questions remain as to the authorship of Colossians. So I shall simply proceed with the traditional designation of the author as 'Paul', with the understanding that this could imply authorship in an 'extended' sense as we have suggested above. Fortunately, however, determination of author is peripheral to my concerns in this study, for none of my conclusions depend on a particular view of authorship. My goal is simply to understand how the letter's distinctive views as to revelation and redemption grew out of the situation addressed in the congregation at Colossae.

Conclusion

In what follows I shall consider, first, the ascetic-mystical piety of Jewish apocalypticism (Part I, Chapters 1–4). Then I shall turn to the soteriology of Colossians as a response to the ideas and practices of those who adopted this religious pattern (Part II, Chapters 5–8). My description of the concept of revelation in Jewish apocalypticism will prove useful not only in my reconstruction of the Colossian error (Chapter 6), but also as I seek to understand Paul's response to the situation that threatened the church at Colossae (Chapters 7 and 8).

---

1. E.g. G. Bornkamm, 'Die Hoffnung im Kolosserbriefe—zugleich ein Beitrag zur Frage der Echtheit des Briefes', in *Studien zum Neuen Testament und zur Patristik, Festschrift für Erich Klostermann* (ed. Kommission für spätantike Religionsgeschichte; Berlin: Akademie Verlag, 1961), pp. 56-64, and E. Lohse, 'Pauline Theology in the Letter to the Colossians', *NTS* 15 (1968-69), pp. 211-20.

2. E.g. C.H. Dodd, 'The Mind of Paul: II', *BJRL* 18 (1934), pp. 68-110; C.H. Buck and G. Taylor, *St. Paul: A Study of the Development of his Thought* (New York: Scribner's, 1969). Cf. L. Cerfaux, 'En faveur de l'authenticité des épîtres de la captivité', *RechBib* 5 (1960), pp. 60-71.

PART I

THE ASCETIC-MYSTICAL PIETY OF
JEWISH APOCALYPTICISM

Chapter 1

INTRODUCTION TO THE LITERATURE OF
JEWISH APOCALYPTICISM

The field of Jewish apocalyptic has, in recent years, blossomed;
indeed, there has appeared in the last ten years a staggering number of
articles, commentaries and monographs in this area of research.[1]
Many of these studies are concerned with critical issues of individual
writings, with results often running contrary to traditional formulations. Recent apocalyptic research has also expanded its vision to
include writings that received little attention in the past, such as *2
Enoch* and the *Apocalypse of Zephaniah*. There is in the present state
of research, in fact, little that can be taken for granted. It is, therefore, incumbent on any researcher to spell out one's own critical
assumptions. So I devote the first chapter of my investigation to this
task. My intention is not to provide an exhaustive introduction to all
eleven documents with which I am concerned, but to set out in a rea-
soned manner the critical assumptions that underlie the following
analysis.

---

1. It is now customary to distinguish carefully between related yet somewhat distinct terminology in this field. I use 'apocalypse' to refer to the literary genre, 'apocalyptists' to refer to the writers and practitioners of the faith and piety portrayed in the
apocalypses, and 'apocalypticism' to refer to the broad movement itself. 'Apocalyptic' is used here in the more general, traditional sense to include all of these. See
M.E. Stone ('Lists of Revealed Things in the Apocalyptic Literature', in *Magnalia
Dei: The Mighty Acts of God* [ed. F.M. Cross *et al.*; Garden City, NY: Doubleday,
1976], pp. 439-43), who distinguishes between 'apocalyptic' or 'apocalypticism'
and 'apocalypses', while P.D. Hanson (*The Dawn of Apocalyptic* [Philadelphia:
Fortress Press, 1979]) makes use of the three-fold distinction between 'apocalypticism' (the sociological life-setting), 'apocalyptic eschatology' (the dominant theme,
according to many) and 'apocalypses' (the literary genre). Cf., however, M.A.
Knibb, 'Prophecy and the Emergence of the Jewish Apocalypses', in *Israel's
Prophetic Tradition* (ed. R. Coggins, A. Phillips and M. Knibb; Cambridge: Cambridge University Press, 1982), p. 161.

1. *Daniel*

Scholars are unanimous in their designation of Daniel 7–12 as an apocalypse. Chapters 1–6, however, have been variously classified as 'court tales, popular romances, martyr legends, aretalogies, paradigmatic stories or dramatized wisdom or belonging to the haggadic genre'.[1] Such designations, of course, lay stress on certain aspects of these chapters in a manner that is entirely legitimate. Yet it needs to be noted (1) that apocalyptic is a complex genre and so can encompass various components,[2] and (2) that, at least in its present form, the two main sections of Daniel are interlocked on the basis of both form[3] and content.[4] In view of these considerations, I shall be utilizing material from the whole of Daniel in my analysis.

Most scholars are inclined to assign the two halves of Daniel to different periods. Indeed, it has become one of the 'assured results' of critical scholarship that chs. 7–12 originated during 167–164 BC,[5] while chs. 1–6 are to be dated to the third century or the beginning of the second century BC.[6] Furthermore, just as the two parts of Daniel are usually assigned to different periods, so also they are usually said to have originated in different locales.[7] Still, a good case can be made

1. J.G. Gammie, 'The Classification, Stages of Growth, and Changing Intentions in the Book of Daniel', *JBL* 95 (1976), pp. 191-92, who provides bibliography for each of these suggestions.
2. K. Koch, *The Rediscovery of Apocalyptic* (trans. M. Kohl; London: SCM Press, 1972), pp. 27-28.
3. J.J. Collins, *The Apocalyptic Vision of the Book of Daniel* (Missoula, MT: Scholars Press, 1977), pp. 11-19. According to his analysis, ch. 7 links together the two halves of the book. It is grouped with chs. 1–6 on the basis of the symmetrical arrangement set forth by A. Lenglet ('La structure littéraire de Daniel 2–7', *Bib* 53 [1972], pp. 169-90), and by the fact that the Aramaic section begins in ch. 2 and ends in ch. 7, yet the traditional sequence of the four kingdoms links it with chs. 8–12.
4. Several points of contact between the two sections are evident, including the references to the *maśkîlîm* in 1.4; 11.35 and 12.3, 10, and the correspondences between the four kingdoms in the visions of Nebuchadnezzar (ch. 2) and Daniel (ch. 7).
5. For a survey of research, see O. Eissfeldt, *The Old Testament: An Introduction* (trans. P.R. Ackroyd; Oxford: Blackwell, 1965), pp. 517-19.
6. A. Mertens, *Das Buch Daniel im Lichte der Texte vom Toten Meer* (Würzburg: Echter Verlag, 1971), p. 19.
7. Interest in the Gentile court and its wisdom in chs. 1–6 suggests to many an Eastern diaspora provenance, while the emphasis given to the persecutions under Antiochus IV points to Palestine as the locale where chs. 7–12 were written. On this

both for the unity of the work[1] and for an earlier date.[2] Fortunately, however, these critical problems do not negate my primary concern, to examine Daniel in its extant form as a primary witness to the phenomenon of Jewish apocalypticism.

The precise nature of the group(s) represented by the author(s) remains uncertain. Clearly they were committed to a rigorous observance of the Jewish law and to non-violence, even if this resulted in martyrdom.[3] As well, they were learned wise men who were open to 'mantic wisdom' and revelation through dreams and visions (unlike Ben Sirach).

2. *1 Enoch (Ethiopic Enoch)*

1 Enoch is perhaps the most significant of the extant Jewish apocalypses. It is also, however, the most complex due to its composite nature and the tremendous variety of material it contains. Since the discovery of Aramaic MSS of parts of *1 Enoch* in cave 4 of Qumran, it is virtually certain that the original documents (with the possible exception of chs. 37–71) were written principally in Aramaic.[4] Other critical problems are best considered in dealing with the individual sections of the work below.

question, see J.J. Collins, 'The Court Tales in Daniel and the Development of Apocalyptic', *JBL* 94 (1975), pp. 218-34. He argues that the group in which the writing originated brought the 'court-tales' from the Eastern diaspora to Palestine, where they were combined with the visions.

1. The most vigorous proponent of the unity of Daniel was H.H. Rowley ('The Unity of the Book of Daniel', in *The Servant of the Lord and other Essays on the Old Testament* [2nd edn; Oxford: Blackwell, 1965], pp. 249-80), though he allowed that the writer used various oral and written sources. On the possibility that mainly oral traditions underlie chs. 1-6, see F. Dexinger, *Das Buch Daniel und seine Probleme* (Stuttgart: Katholisches Bibelwerk, 1969), p. 28.

2. See esp. R.K. Harrison, *Introduction to the Old Testament* (Grand Rapids: Eerdmans, 1969), pp. 1110-27.

3. While many, including O. Plöger (*Das Buch Daniel* [Gütersloh: Mohn, 1965], pp. 27-28), ascribe the final redaction to one of the Hasidim, Collins (*Apocalyptic Vision*, pp. 201-14) argues that the author's evident commitment to non-violence tells against such a sweeping identification.

4. M. Black (ed.), *Apocalypsis Henochi Graece* (Leiden: Brill, 1970), p. 6; M.A. Knibb, in consultation with E. Ullendorff, *The Ethiopic Book of Enoch* (2 vols.; Oxford: Clarendon, 1978), II, p. 7; and E. Isaac, '1 (Ethiopic Apocalypse of) Enoch', in *OTP*, I, p. 6. These more recent writers regard the possible Hebrew sections of the work as minor, in contrast to R.H. Charles, 'Book of Enoch', in *APOT*, II, pp. 171-77.

The Book of the Watchers (Book 1, chs. 1–36)

Along with chs. 72–82, the Book of the Watchers (= BW) is probably the earliest section of *1 Enoch*, going back to the third century BC, possibly between the years 250 and 200.[1] In fact, chs. 6–11 appear to be a compilation of traditions that may date back as far as the fourth century BC.[2] To this 'traditional unit'[3] chs. 12–16 were added as a kind of commentary,[4] though both sections seem to have undergone some internal redaction at a later point.[5] A redactor also seems to have appended chs. 17–19, probably 'a pre-existing piece of Enochic tradition excerpted from another context and pressed into service here'.[6] Chapters 20–36 are best attributed to the author of the existing BW,[7] as appears to be the case as well with chs. 1–5.[8]

---

1. The Qumran MSS are especially important here. J.T. Milik (*The Books of Enoch: Aramaic Fragments of Qumrân Cave 4* [Oxford: Clarendon Press, 1976], p. 5) dates 4QEn[a] to the first half of the second century BC on the basis of firmly established paleographical criteria, though unfortunately he has not published a photograph of the MS. Since it is logical to assume that some time elapsed between the composition and the earliest extant copies, a third-century date seems likely; see M.E. Stone, 'The Book of Enoch and Judaism in the Third Century B.C.E.', *CBQ* 40 (1978), pp. 479-92; *idem*, 'Enoch, Aramaic Levi and Sectarian Origins', *JSJ* 19 (1988), pp. 159-70. Milik (*Books of Enoch*, p. 24), promises to set forth evidence for an even earlier dating in a future edition of the *Testament of Levi*, but this has not yet appeared.

2. G.W.E. Nickelsburg, 'Enoch, Levi, and Peter: Recipients of Revelation in Upper Galilee', *JBL* 100 (1981), p. 575.

3. See J.C. VanderKam, *Enoch and the Growth of an Apocalyptic Tradition* (Washington, DC: Catholic Biblical Association, 1984), p. 110.

4. The view that chs. 12–16 were added as a commentary on chs. 6–11 is common in recent studies; e.g. D. Suter, 'Fallen Angel, Fallen Priest: The Problem of Family Purity in *1 Enoch* 6–16', *HUCA* 50 (1979), p. 115.

5. C.A. Newsom ('The Development of *1 Enoch* 6–19: Cosmology and Judgment', *CBQ* 42 [1980], p. 319), suggests that the material containing the teaching motif was later added both to chs. 6–11 and to chs. 12–16.

6. Newsom, p. 323. The difficulty of these chapters in their present context has been noted previously; see P. Grelot, 'La géographie mythique d'Hénoch et ses sources orientales', *RB* 65 (1958), p. 38.

7. Milik (*Books of Enoch*, p. 25) argues that the author revised his source in chs. 20–25, and then set forth what amounts to his own composition in chs. 26–36. We would here concur, though, as Newsom (p. 312) points out, 'the relationship of chs 20–36 to the rest of *The Book of the Watchers* needs further clarification'.

8. While older writers such as G. Beer ('Das Buch Henoch', in *APAT*, I, p. 224) generally viewed these chapters as a later introduction to the whole work, the fact that chs. 5 and 6 are linked together in 4QEn[b] suggests that chs. 1–5 are earlier than some other parts of *1 Enoch*; cf. L. Hartman, *Asking for a Meaning* (Lund: Gleerup,

With regard to the precise setting of embedded traditions, individual sub-sections and the BW as a whole, there is much uncertainty. Several diverse suggestions have been set forth with regard to chs. 6–11 and the various traditions contained therein, yet these are not particularly relevant for our purposes and must remain uncertain. Even the setting of the final redaction of the work is problematic, precisely because of 'the essential polyvalence of apocalyptic symbolism'.[1] Nevertheless, a setting in Judea in the second half of the third century BC seems most plausible.[2]

The Book of the Similitudes (Book 2, chs. 37–71)

While much could be said concerning the Similitudes of Enoch (= BP or Book of the Parables), it is the question of date and provenance that is most important. There has, of course, never been a consensus with regard to the precise date of the Similitudes, though until recently most scholars were prepared to place the work some time in the first century BC.[3] With the publication of the Qumran Enochian materials, however, a much wider range of possibilities has been considered.

J.T. Milik proposed that the BP is a Christian writing from about the year AD 270, but his view has not found widespread acceptance.[4] His arguments based on the absence of the BP from Qumran,[5] as well as on its historical allusions,[6] kinship of literary genre,[7] alleged liter-

1979), p. 138, though it is important to note that the connection between 5.9 and 6.1 is not as secure as one might desire (as is evident from the text as given in Milik, *Books of Enoch*, p. 165).

1. J.J. Collins, 'The Apocalyptic Technique: Setting and Function in the Book of Watchers', *CBQ* 44 (1982), p. 98.

2. Milik, *Books of Enoch*, p. 25, bases his view of the provenance of the work on the author's view of Jerusalem and his thorough knowledge of the Holy City; cf. Isaac, p. 8.

3. See R.H. Charles, *The Book of Enoch* (Oxford: Clarendon Press, 1912), p. 67 (94–79 BC); cf. also F. Martin, *Le Livre d'Hénoch* (Paris: Letouzey et Ané, 1906), p. xcvii, who dates the work to the years 95–78 BC.

4. J.H. Charlesworth, 'The SNTS Pseudepigrapha Seminars at Tübingen and Paris on the Books of Enoch', *NTS* 25 (1979), p. 322, found that no one accepted Milik's late date at the 1978 SNTS seminar in Paris.

5. Milik, *Books of Enoch*, p. 91. See J.C. Greenfield and M.E. Stone, 'The Enochic Pentateuch and the Date of the Similitudes', *HTR* 70 (1977), pp. 51-56, 63.

6. Milik (*Books of Enoch*, pp. 95-96) argues that *1 En.* 56.5-7 refers to the wars between the Parthians and the Romans in the mid-third century AD. More plausible historical interpretations of this passage are set forth by E. Sjöberg (*Der Menschensohn im äthiopischen Henochbuch* [Lund: Gleerup, 1946], pp. 38-39 (40–38 BC),

ary dependence,[1] absence of early citations, and other more minor points are all exceedingly tenuous. That the work is Jewish is now almost universally acknowledged.[2] The main area of disagreement is whether the BP is to be dated before or after the fall of Jerusalem in AD 70. The total absence of allusions to this event is a strong argument in favor of an earlier dating,[3] though arguments from alleged relationships to other Jewish writings and the New Testament[4]—as well as the absence from Qumran—are more subjective.[5] I therefore date the work in the mid-first century AD, and will consider it as being highly relevant for my purposes.[6]

With the exception of Milik, virtually all authorities believe that the original language of the BP was Semitic, though there is disagreement

and J.C. Hindley ('Toward a Date for the Similitudes of Enoch: An Historical Approach', *NTS* 14 [1968], pp. 551-65 [113–117 AD]); though, as D.W. Suter ('Weighed in the Balance: The Similitudes of Enoch in Recent Research', *RelSRev* 7 [1981], p. 218) notes, this passage may reflect 'an apocalyptic version of the ancient Zion motif' rather than an historical allusion.

7. See Milik (*Books of Enoch*, p. 92) who argues that the Similitudes are closely akin to the *Sibylline Oracles*; cf., however, G.W.E. Nickelsburg, review of J.T. Milik (ed.), *The Books of Enoch: Aramaic Fragments of Qumrân Cave 4*, in *CBQ* 40 (1978), p. 418.

1. Milik (*Books of Enoch*, 95) writes that *1 En.* 56.5-7 was 'obviously inspired' by *Sib.* 3.663ff.; cf., however, Suter, 'Weighed in the Balance', p. 218.

2. See Charlesworth, p. 322. Decisive here are two observations. First, the total absence of references to Christ, his death or his resurrection is highly significant, especially in view of the subject matter of the Similitudes and the explicit nature of such references in the *Testaments of the Twelve Patriarchs* and the Christian portions of the *Ascension of Isaiah*; cf. M.A. Knibb, 'The Date of the Parables of Enoch: A Critical Review', *NTS* 25 (1979), p. 350. Second, the 'life world' of the Similitudes is obviously Jewish rather than Christian; see the evidence adduced by Suter, 'Weighed in the Balance', p. 218.

3. Sjöberg, p. 38; against Knibb, 'Date of the Parables', p. 358. While it is true that 'not every work written after that time must automatically refer to the Fall of Jerusalem', one must take care not to underestimate the significance of this national tragedy.

4. It is absurd to adduce parallels between the BP and *4 Ezra* and *2 Baruch* in support of a later date (see Knibb, 'Date of the Parables', p. 358), when the overriding concern of these two latter documents is completely absent from the former.

5. On the absence of the BP from the Qumran discoveries, see Greenfield and Stone, p. 56.

6. So D.W. Suter, *Tradition and Composition in the Parables of Enoch* (Missoula, MT: Scholars Press, 1979), p. 32; cf. also M. Black, *The Book of Enoch or I Enoch* (Leiden: Brill, 1985), p. 188, who proposes a pre-AD 70 date for the Hebrew *Urschrift*.

as to whether it was Hebrew or Aramaic.[1] Older writers on *1 Enoch* often attempted to identify written sources behind the BP.[2] More recent investigators have seen in it an oral style of composition that relies on living traditions rather than literary deposits,[3] and with that approach I tend to agree.

The Astronomical Book (Book 3, chs. 72–82)

Care is required in the interpretation of the Astronomical Book (= AB), since the Greek and Ethiopic texts probably represent abbreviated versions of an original Aramaic corpus of such texts.[4] Furthermore, the question of the relationship of chs. 80–81(82) to the remaining chapters of the AB is problematic.[5] Nevertheless, it is clear that this text, along with the BW, provides a 'window' through which we can obtain glimpses of the Judaism of the third century BC. It is, therefore, highly significant.[6] With regard to the provenance of the

1. This question has been debated for years, though more recent scholars favor an Aramaic original, against Milik (*Books of Enoch*, 92); cf. Knibb (*Ethiopic Enoch*, II, pp. 38-42), who takes up the old argument that the Similitudes are a direct translation from Aramaic. Black (*Book of Enoch*, pp. 187) may be correct in his suggestion that 'the Grundschrift was itself the *mixtum compositum*'.

2. Beer, pp. 227; Charles, *Book of Enoch*, pp. 64-65.

3. Suter, *Tradition and Composition*, pp. 153-55; cf. earlier Sjöberg, pp. 13-35.

4. The table of the phases of the moon (4QEnastr[a] and 4QEnastr[b] 1-22) is absent in Ethiopic, as are other significant sections of the Aramaic. Even where a relationship exists between the two versions there are substantial differences. In view of the lengthy nature of the Aramaic version it is most likely that the Ethiopic represents an abbreviation of the original document, though the question is a difficult one; cf. Knibb, *Ethiopic Enoch*, II, p. 13, and Milik, *Books of Enoch*, p. 7.

5. These chapters have been viewed by many writers, both earlier and more recent, as a later addition; cf. Martin, p. lxxxiv, and Charles, *Book of Enoch*, pp. 147-49; more recently VanderKam, pp. 76-79. There is, however, some debate as to the date and the exact limits of the 'addition', since O. Neugebauer (with additional notes on the Aramaic Fragments by M. Black), *The 'Astronomical' Chapters of the Ethiopic Book of Enoch (72 to 82). Translation and Commentary* [Copenhagen: Munksgaard, 1981], p. 5), refers to 80.2–82.3 as an 'apocalyptic intrusion', and G.W.E. Nickelsburg (*Jewish Literature Between the Bible and the Mishnah* [Philadelphia: Fortress Press, 1981], pp. 150-51, 158), views chs. 81–82 as a part of the framework into which the AB was later inserted. Milik's late date for ch. 81 (after the Book of Dreams but before the composition of *Jubilees*) is difficult to sustain; see *Books of Enoch*, pp. 13-14.

6. The crucial piece of evidence here is the dating of the earliest MS of 4QEnastr[a], to the end of the third or the beginning of the second century BC on paleographical grounds. Further support is found in the allusion to the AB in Pseudo-Eupolemus's book about the Jews; see VanderKam, pp. 84-88. Milik (*Books of Enoch*, p. 8),

work there is some debate. Yet while the work shows clear borrowings from Mesopotamian traditions, there is no solid evidence for attributing the actual composition of the AB to the Babylonian exile.[1] The presentation of calendrical data is consistent with what we know of later Palestinian Jewish non-conformity.[2]

The Dream Visions (Book 4, chs. 83–90)
Charles wrote of Book 4, the Enochian Dream Visions, 'it is the most complete and self-consistent of all the Sections, and has suffered least from the hand of the interpolator'.[3] It is composed of two visions: the first is a simple description of cosmic destruction (chs. 83–84); the second (the Animal Apocalypse [= AA], chs. 85–90) a lengthy *ex eventu* prophecy of history. The first vision may have circulated independently. It is apparently of semitic origin and is perhaps earlier than the AA.[4] The two visions, however, are complementary, and it appears that the date of composition for the AA is also the time when the two were joined.[5] The general date for the composition of the AA seems clear enough. The paleographical evidence[6] and the symbolic reference of 90.9-16 point to the time of Judas Maccabeus.[7] And since

argues for a date in the Persian era, but his position is at present untenable. See also the literature cited in my discussion of *1 En.* 1–36.

1. J.C. VanderKam, 'The 364-Day Calendar in the Enochic Literature', in *The Society of Biblical Literature 1983 Seminar Papers* (ed. K.H. Richards; Chico, CA: Scholars Press, 1983), pp. 164-65.

2. Milik's contention (*Book of Enoch*, pp. 8-10) that the AB is of Samaritan origin is without merit; cf. the evidence set forth by R.T. Beckwith, 'The Earliest Enoch Literature and its Calendar: Marks of their Origin, Date and Motivation', *RevQ* 10 (1981), p. 370.

3. Charles, *Book of Enoch*, p. 179.

4. The published MSS from Qumran contain no evidence of the first vision, but this is of little significance in view of the fragmentary nature of the texts. Furthermore, 84.2-4 and 84.6 (Eth.) may bear some relationship to 4QEnGiants[a] 9 and 4QEnGiants[a] 10, respectively, though at present it is not clear what this might be. In any case, the Semitic origin of the vision is clear; cf. Black, *Book of Enoch*, p. 20.

5. VanderKam (*Enoch*, p. 161) suggests not only that they date to the same period, but that they were written by the same author. It is clear, however, that extrabiblical stories of the Flood were circulating at this time, and it is likely that one of these is incorporated here.

6. Since the earliest MS (4QEn[f]) dates to the third quarter of the second century BC, a date prior to about 125 BC is required; cf. Milik, *Books of Enoch*, p. 41.

7. The identification of the Horned Ram as John Hyrcanus (134–104 BC), as advanced by Beer (p. 296) and A. Dillmann (*Das Buch Henoch* [Leipzig: Vogel, 1853], p. 278), is now generally rejected; see Milik, *Books of Enoch*, p. 44, who

Judas is still fighting when the apocalypse shifts to prediction in 90.17, a date somewhere around 165–161 BC seems reasonably secure.

The Epistle of Enoch (Book 5, chs. 91–105/108)
The extent of the final section of *1 Enoch* in its original form is a disputed question. Chapter 108 is certainly a later addition,[1] and it is probable that chs. 106–107 stem from an independent Noah tradition.[2] There has also been some debate with regard to ch. 105, though its presence in the Qumran materials suggests that it belongs with the rest of this section.[3] The beginning of this fifth section, however, is less problematic, for while the 'Epistle' proper begins at 92.1, ch. 91 introduces this section and clearly stands in its proper position.[4]

In general, the work is composed of many traditional forms—such as woes, exhortations, descriptions and revelatory formulae. The Apocalypse of Weeks (= AW) is clearly an independent traditional unit,[5] with a date just prior to the Maccabean revolt (c. 170 BC) being most probable.[6] Unfortunately, the remaining portions of the Epistle are extremely difficult to date. Nickelsburg argues that the work was

dates the AA too precisely, and VanderKam, *Enoch*, p. 161. For a similar view among older scholars, cf. Martin, p. 226, and Charles, *Book of Enoch*, p. 208.

1. It is absent in both Greek and Aramaic versions; cf. Black, *Book of Enoch*, p. 323.

2. Cf. the earlier studies by Martin, p. lxxxviii, and Charles, *Book of Enoch*, pp. xlvii, 244. These chapters are attested among the Qumran fragments, though they are separated from the preceding text by one and a half lines (4QEn^c 5.i.24-25). This peculiar fact, along with some discrepancies with regard to content, has led more recent writers to separate these chapters from the remaining portions of the 'Epistle'; cf. Milik, *Books of Enoch*, pp. 55-57.

3. The evidence from Qumran overturns the impression given by the Greek that ch. 105 was a later interpolation; see Milik, *Books of Enoch*, p. 54, and Black, *Book of Enoch*, p. 318.

4. Charles (*Book of Enoch*, p. 224), suggested that ch. 92 originally preceded ch. 91, but 4QEn^g 1.ii.2 supports the order of the Ethiopic.

5. While Milik (*Books of Enoch*, pp. 255-56) denies that there is 'serious evidence' that places the Apocalypse of Weeks before the rest of chs. 91–105, it is clear that the AW was inserted as an independent unit in ch. 93; cf. the evidence in F. Dexinger, *Henochs Zehnwochenapokalypse und offene Probleme der Apokalyptikforschung* (Leiden: Brill, 1977), pp. 103-104.

6. J.C. VanderKam ('Studies in the Apocalypse of Weeks [*1 Enoch* 93.1-10; 91.11-17]', *CBQ* 46 [1984], pp. 511-23) makes a good case for this earlier dating based on an analysis of the structure of the AW; cf., however, Dexinger (*Zehnwochenapokalypse*, pp. 139-40) and the scholars he lists who support a date of 166 BC.

composed 'in circles ancestral to the Essenes'. If he is correct, then these sections may be virtually contemporaneous with the AW.[1]

3. 2 Enoch (Slavonic Enoch)

It is best to begin my discussion of 2 *Enoch* by considering the relationship between the 'shorter' and the 'longer' recensions, since our conclusions here will affect the discussion of several important issues. While Charles's preference for the 'longer' recension has been influential,[2] others have come down on the side of the 'shorter' recension, arguing that the 'longer' text contains many late expansions and interpolations.[3] More recent studies, however, suggest that both of these positions somewhat oversimplify the question. Specialists cannot agree, for example, on which manuscripts are really 'long' and which are 'short', and it is possible that a twofold classification is far too simple.[4] It is clear that all recensions have been reworked by later scribes, at least to some degree;[5] and one must bear in mind that abbreviation (as in the 'shorter' recension) as well as expansion (as in the 'longer' recension) are both reasonable possibilities. We do not as yet, it seems, possess an adequate methodology for deciding the originality of disputed passages, and so it is best 'to present all the evidence

1. G.W.E. Nickelsburg, 'The Epistle of Enoch and the Qumran Literature', *JJS* 33 (1982), pp. 347-48.

2. R.H. Charles, with W.R. Morfill, *The Book of the Secrets of Enoch* (Oxford: Clarendon, 1896), pp. xv-xvi. Of course, the 'shorter' version is viewed as 'a short résumé' of the longer text. Cf. G.N. Bonwetsch, *Die Bücher der Geheimnisse Henochs* (Leipzig: Hinrichs, 1922), pp. xiii.

3. N. Schmidt, 'The Two Recensions of Slavonic Enoch', *JAOS* 41 (1921), pp. 307-12, and, more recently, A. Vaillant, *Le Livre des Secrets d'Hénoch* (2nd edn; Paris: Institut d'Etudes Slaves, 1976), pp. iv-viii; Milik, *Books of Enoch*, pp. 107-108, and A. Rubinstein, 'Observations on the Slavonic Book of Enoch', *JJS* 13 (1962), p. 1.

4. F.I. Andersen ('2 [Slavonic Apocalypse of] Enoch', in *OTP*, I, p. 93), proposes a more precise division of the MSS into four recensions; cf. his report to the 1977 SNTS Pseudepigrapha Seminar, summarized in J.H. Charlesworth, *The Old Testament Pseudepigrapha and the New Testament* (Cambridge: Cambridge University Press, 1985), p. 104.

5. J.H. Charlesworth (*The Pseudepigrapha and Modern Research with a Supplement* [Chico, CA: Scholars Press, 1981], p. 104) states, nonetheless, that it is especially the longer recension that was reworked in this manner.

and suspend judgment'—at least for the present.[1] This is not, however, a major problem for my study, since I plan to consider broad patterns present in both recensions rather than deal extensively with detailed textual points.

Problems of date and provenance for *2 Enoch* are also exceedingly complex, and many diverse suggestions have been made. Charles viewed it as a Jewish work from the first half of the first century AD,[2] though many have followed A.S.D. Maunder in her contention that *2 Enoch* is 'a specimen of Bogomil propaganda composed in the "Middle Bulgarian" period—i.e., between the 12th and 15th centuries'.[3] In spite, however, of such a tremendous range of opinion, it is probable that at least the core of the work is both ancient and Jewish, since arguments for its late date and Christian character lack substance. The arguments from the calendar described in the work[4] and the portrayal of Melchizedek in chs. 71–72[5] are double-edged in their force. Fur-

1. Andersen, pp. 93-94; cf. also R. Bauckham, 'The Apocalypses in the New Pseudepigrapha', *JSNT* 26 (1986), p. 99.

2. Charles and Morfill, p. xxvi.

3. A.S.D. Maunder, 'The Date and Place of Writing of the Slavonic Book of Enoch', *TO* 41 (1918), p. 316; J.K. Fotheringham, 'The Date and Place of Writing of the Slavonic Enoch', *JTS* 20 (1919), p. 252; *idem*, 'The Easter Calendar and the Slavonic Enoch', *JTS* 23 (1922), pp. 49, 54-55; and K. Lake, 'The Date of the Slavonic Enoch', *HTR* 16 (1923), p. 398, who states, on the basis of Maunder's argument, that *2 Enoch* is 'not earlier than the seventh century'. Cf. also Milik, *Books of Enoch*, pp. 109, 112, who dates the long form to the seventh century and the short form to the ninth or tenth centuries, and Vaillant, pp. viii-xiii. It is virtually certain, however, that the work did not originate among the purely dualistic Bogomils; see R.H. Charles, 'The Date and Place of Writing of the Slavonic Enoch', *JTS* 22 (1921), pp. 162-63.

4. The references to the 532 year cycle (16.5) and the lunar epacts are confined to the 'longer' recension and should not be used as the basis for dating the document unless new evidence points in this direction. Furthermore, the fact that certain sections of the 'shorter' recension contain apologetics for a solar calendar and polemics against a lunar calendar, an approach that is both typical of Second Temple Judaism and atypical of medieval dualism, tells in favor of an early Jewish provenance; see Charlesworth (*Pseudepigrapha and the New Testament*, p. 34), who bases his argument on the Russian work of Meshchersky, and J. van Goudoever, *Biblical Calendars* (2nd edn; Leiden: Brill, 1961), p. 115.

5. While Melchizedek might be thought to prefigure Christ in his supernatural birth (71.17-19) and the description of him as 'the priest of all holy priests' and 'the head of the priests of the future' (71.29-30, though only in the 'longer' recension), as Vaillant (p. xi), and Rubinstein (pp. 14-15), maintain, it is difficult to understand how a Christian could write thus of Melchizedek without even mentioning Christ. Furthermore, one must also reckon with two additional possibilities: (1) that this sec-

thermore, alleged Christian language or phraseology is for the most part confined to the 'longer' form, and so can be set aside for the moment.[1] On the other hand, the argument that the Temple is still standing is difficult to assess since the sacrifices mentioned are quite unlike the levitical cultus as practiced in the Temple.[2] Nevertheless, a number of studies have detected a development in the Jewish mystical tradition from *1 Enoch* (especially chs. 1–36) through *2 Enoch* to the later Hekhalot writings,[3] and so in view of *2 Enoch's* place in this trajectory a date in the first or second century BC seems most likely. As for the place of composition, that is even more uncertain, though many have suggested that the work originated in the Jewish diaspora. The original language was probably Greek, though one must allow for the possibility of Hebrew sources or sections.

4. Jubilees

The relationship of *Jubilees* to the genre 'apocalypse' is problematic. On the one hand, it contains certain features characteristic of the Jewish apocalypses, including the manner of revelation (chs. 1–2), pseudonymity, *ex eventu* prophecy, judgment and destruction of the wicked, etc.[4] On the other hand, most of these traits are located in ch. 23.[5] Furthermore, *Jubilees* bears striking resemblance to several other types of literature. Indeed, Testuz is probably correct when he speaks of *Jubilees* as a work of composite genre, sharing characteristics with historical writings, legislation, chronology, apocalypses and testa-

---

tion is intended as a polemic against the kind of approach found in Hebrews, and (2) that this section is a later appendix, as Charles and Morfill (p. 85) argued.

1. G. Scholem ('Die Lehre vom "Gerechten" in der Jüdischen Mystik', *Eranos-Jahrbuch* 27 [1959], p. 251) argues that these references contain nothing that a contemporary Jew could not equally well have written.

2. Rubinstein, pp. 13-14.

3. H. Odeberg, with a prolegomenon by J.C. Greenfield, *3 Enoch or The Hebrew Book of Enoch* (New York: Ktav, 1973), pp. 60-63, and P. Alexander, '3 (Hebrew Apocalypse of) Enoch', in *OTP*, I, pp. 247-48.

4. Collins, 'Jewish Apocalypses', pp. 28, 32.

5. Collins, p. 32. Collins writes that 'the content of the angelic revelation has little apocalyptic or eschatological material', with the obvious exception of ch. 23. This line of argumentation is somewhat strange in view of the recent trend in apocalyptic research (of which Collins is a leading proponent) away from viewing apocalyptic eschatology as the essence of the Jewish apocalypses.

ments.[1] More recently, *Jubilees'* relationship to Jewish Midrash has also been explored, though this genre is at present the subject of much debate.[2] Perhaps, therefore, it is best to reserve the designation 'apocalypse' for ch. 23—though there is no evidence to suggest that this chapter was composed independently of the remaining chapters of Jubilees. The writing as a whole, however, yields material that is helpful for my discussion, for its connection with circles responsible for the composition and preservation of certain apocalyptic writings is evident.[3] And so I shall take it as a whole into consideration.

Apart from the question of genre, other introductory questions concerning *Jubilees* are relatively straightforward. The ancient Jewish character of the work is now universally accepted, and the fragments at Qumran confirm the opinion of a majority of scholars that the original language was Hebrew. Many have dated the work to the time of John Hyrcanus.[4] There has, however, been a trend in recent research toward an earlier date for the writing,[5] before the establishment of the Hasmonaean high priesthood.[6] This earlier date, before the sectarians left for Qumran, would account for the similarities and

1. M. Testuz, *Les idées religieuses du Livre des Jubilés* (Geneva: Droz, 1960), p. 12.

2. For a discussion of the affinities between *Jubilees* and the Jewish Midrashim, see O.S. Wintermute, 'Jubilees', in *OTP*, II, pp. 39-40.

3. The fact that ch. 23 is included suggests some connection with Jewish apocalypticism, and 'the apocalyptic eschatology and world view are presupposed throughout' (Collins, 'Jewish Apocalypses', p. 33). The connection with *1 Enoch* is suggested by the calendrical interest common to both writings, and by the fact that both were preserved at Qumran.

4. R.H. Charles, *The Book of Jubilees* (London: Black, 1902), pp. lviii-lxvi. He is more specific in his later work, 'The Book of Jubilees', *APOT*, II, p. 6, dating *Jubilees* between 109 and 105 BC. Cf. also Testuz, p. 35, who dates the work at 110 BC.

5. The thesis of G.L. Davenport (*The Eschatology of the Book of Jubilees* [Leiden: Brill, 1971], pp. 10-18), that there were three stages in the composition of *Jubilees* (the angelic discourse, 200 BC; the second edition, 166–160 BC, and the 'sanctuary-oriented redaction', 140–104 BC) is set forth without even minimal support; cf. the critique of G.W.E. Nickelsburg, 'The Bible Rewritten and Expanded', in *JWSTP*, p. 102.

6. Especially significant here is J.C. VanderKam, *Textual and Historical Studies in the Book of Jubilees* (Missoula, MT: Scholars Press, 1977), pp. 214-85, for a date between 161 and 152 BC; cf. Wintermute, p. 44, (161–140 BC), and K. Berger, 'Das Buch der Jubiläen', in *JSHRZ* II.3, p. 300 (145–140 BC). The earliest dating proposed in recent times for the work as a whole is c. 168 BC; see Nickelsburg, 'Bible Rewritten and Expanded', p. 103.

differences between the doctrines and practices of *Jubilees* and the writings from Qumran.[1] So it seems likely, in view of the totality of the evidence, that *Jubilees* emanated from circles ancestral to the Essenes, and that it was taken along with them when they left Jerusalem and its illegitimate High Priest to form their own religious community on the shores of the Dead Sea.

5. *4 Ezra*

The date and language of '*4 Ezra*'[2] are matters on which there is considerable scholarly agreement. There is solid evidence that the original language was Semitic, most probably Hebrew.[3] The Eagle Vision, the pseudonymous setting (3.1), and the fact that the work was preserved in Christian circles indicate a date sometime between AD 100 and 120.[4] Various suggestions have been made with regard to provenance (Rome, Egypt, etc.), but the Semitic character of the text points to Palestine as the most likely place of origin.[5]

Important for the interpretation of *4 Ezra* is source criticism. R. Kabisch first proposed a division into several sources.[6] It was G.H. Box and W.O.E. Oesterley, however, who popularized this approach among English-speaking scholars.[7] On the basis of inconsistencies

1. For discussions of the similarities and differences that point to a date for *Jubilees* before the formation of the community at Qumran, see VanderKam, *Textual and Historical Studies*, pp. 280-83; Berger, pp. 295-96, and Wintermute, p. 44.

2. By this designation I refer to chs. 3–14 of 2 Esdras, omitting from my discussion the Christian additions of chs. 1–2 and 15–16.

3. See J. Schreiner, 'Das 4. Buch Esra', in *JSHRZ* V.4, pp. 294-95.

4. See the excellent discussion in B.M. Metzger, 'The Fourth Book of Ezra', in *OTP*, II, p. 520; cf. also Schreiner, p. 301, and J.M. Myers, *I and II Esdras* (Garden City, NY: Doubleday, 1974), pp. 115-19. Of course, sources or traditions contained within the work might go back earlier. For a recent study that regards a date before AD 70 or even in the first century BC as a reasonable possibility, see W. Harnisch, 'Der Prophet als Widerpart und Zeuge der Offenbarung. Erwägungen zur Interdependenz von Form und Sache im IV. Buch Esra', in *Apocalypticism*, p. 486. The hypothesis that the Eagle Vision and the Vision of the Man from the Sea are secondary additions, however, is unlikely, and Harnisch fails to account for the work's pseudonymous setting (3.1).

5. Metzger, p. 520; cf. Schreiner, p. 302, who gives a useful survey of views.

6. R. Kabisch, *Das vierte Buch Esra auf seine Quellen untersucht* (Göttingen: Vandenhoeck & Ruprecht, 1889).

7. G.H. Box, 'IV Ezra', in *APOT*, II, p. 549-53, and, more succinctly, *idem, The Apocalypse of Ezra* (London: SPCK, 1917), pp. vii-viii; cf. W.O.E. Oesterley, *II Esdras* (London: Methuen, 1933), pp. xi-xix.

between sections or passages within the work, these writers distinguished between (1) the primary document, (2) a Salathiel-apocalypse
(most of chs. 3–10, with pieces misplaced in 12.40-48 and 14.28-35),
(3) several traditional pieces, and (4) the material created by the final
redactor himself.[1] Assuming such an approach, it is difficult to speak
of the message of *4 Ezra* as a whole in any meaningful way; one can
only examine the individual units and consider the ideas expressed in
each of these in relation to the broader conceptual movements of the
day.

Such source-critical analyses, however, are subject to several criticisms. First, one must ask whether sufficient consideration has been
given to the fact that apocalyptic writers in general are not overly
concerned with logical consistency.[2] Second, it is appropriate to ask
whether enough attention has been given to the possibility that the
author's message emerges out of a dialogue set up between opposing
viewpoints. Recent critical studies have demonstrated that *4 Ezra* is
very carefully structured, with a close relationship existing between
form and content.[3] The trend of late, in fact, is toward the recognition
of the compositional integrity of *4 Ezra*.[4] Thus, while acknowledging
the author's use of traditions and sources, I shall view *4 Ezra* as a literary unit and seek to interpret each part in light of the whole.

1. Oesterley differs from Box in that he views the primary document as an Ezra
apocalypse.
2. See the excellent discussion by Oesterley, p. xii, who still, however, advocates
a division hypothesis. P. Vielhauer ('Apocalypses and Related Subjects', in *New
Testament Apocrypha* [ed. E. Hennecke and W. Schneemelcher; Philadelphia:
Westminster Press, 1965], II, p. 549) lists 'lack of uniformity' as a basic characteristic of apocalypses.
3. Building on the suggestion of G. Volkmar (*Das vierte Buch Esra und apokalyptische Geheimnisse überhaupt* [Zürich: Meyer & Zeller, 1858], pp. 11-18), that *4
Ezra* is divided into seven episodes, E. Breech ('These Fragments I have Shored
against my Ruins: The Form and Function of 4 Ezra', *JBL* 92 [1973], pp. 267-74),
has argued convincingly that 3.1–9.22 form a triptych made up of three panels, each
of which is organized in exactly the same manner. Carefully structured as well in
parallel fashion are the climactic visions (11.1–13.58).
4. E.g. Breech, pp. 267-68, and A.P. Hayman, 'The Problem of Pseudonymity
in the Ezra Apocalypse', *JSJ* 6 (1975), p. 48. That this is the direction of more
recent research is recognized by Harnisch (p. 470), though his own studies take a
different direction. For an earlier study that argues, similarly, for the essential unity
of the work, see L. Gry, *Les dires prophétiques d'Esdras* (2 vols.; Paris: Paul
Geuthner, 1938), I, pp. xciv-xcviii.

A major problem in any analysis of *4 Ezra* is the question of where the author's voice is to be found. Several authorities have argued that the author presents his arguments through the angel Uriel. Indeed, Brandenburger and Harnisch have argued that Ezra is the spokesman for a skeptical, gnosticizing viewpoint against which the author is contending.[1] Several cogent objections against such a view, however, have been set forth by A.P. Hayman: (1) Why should the author 'choose as the mouthpiece of an heretical viewpoint the venerable Ezra'?; (2) There is, in fact, a good deal of overlap between the views of Ezra and the position espoused by Uriel, so that it is unlikely that the author intends to represent two positions radically opposed to each other; (3) The view set forth by Ezra is not heretical, but is within the range of Jewish orthodoxy; and (4) Ezra never 'breaks down and confesses the error of his ways', as one might expect if he is the representative of a heretical position.[2]

A number of recent writers have adopted an approach to the interpretation of *4 Ezra* that sees the author's message emerging out of the dialogue between Ezra and Uriel, in light of the visions that follow. Building on Gunkel's psychological approach, yet moving beyond it in many significant respects,[3] recent interpreters have emphasized the traditional nature of Ezra's expressions of doubt and despair[4] and have stressed the experiential rather than the rational side of the work's theodicy.[5] This kind of interpretation allows each section of the work

---

1. E. Brandenburger, *Adam und Christus: Exegetisch-religions-geschichtliche Untersuchung zu Röm. 5.12-21* (Neukirchen: Neukirchener Verlag, 1962), p. 30; W. Harnisch, *Verhängnis und Verheissung der Geschichte: Untersuchungen zum Zeit- und Geschichtsverständnis im 4. Esra und in der syr. Baruchapokalypse* (Göttingen: Vandenhoeck & Ruprecht, 1969), pp. 63-66; and *idem*, 'Prophet als Widerpart', pp. 472-78. Cf. also the older work by W. Mundle, 'Das religiöse Problem des IV. Esrabuches', *ZAW* 47 (1929), pp. 222-49. Mundle, of course, regarded both participants in the dialogues as representing acceptable Jewish teaching, and so differs from those who later developed this view.

2. Hayman, pp. 50-53.

3. H. Gunkel, 'Das vierte Buch Esra', in *APAT*, II, pp. 35-52. He viewed the dialogue between Ezra and Uriel as corresponding to the author's own inner struggle.

4. Hayman (pp. 55-56) appeals to a 'Hebrew tradition of troubled questioning'; cf. Breech (pp. 27-28), who compares Ezra's role with the lament psalms.

5. M.E. Stone ('Reactions to Destructions of the Second Temple', *JSJ* 12 [1981], p. 203), argues persuasively that the problems set forth in the dialogues 'are not solved merely by the knowledge of eschatological reward of which he has been repeatedly assured in the first three dialogues. They are resolved by an experience of

to play a significant part in the overall presentation. And it is this understanding that will be followed in my analysis.

6. *2 Baruch*

While *2 Baruch* is extant in complete form only in Syriac, it is clearly a translation from a Greek version, which is, itself, according to most authorities, a translation of a Hebrew original.[1] Furthermore, it is probable that it was composed in Palestine,[2] though its stance vis-à-vis other Jewish movements is rendered problematic by the fact that it utilizes several diverse traditions.[3] A more difficult question is the date of the work, though only in specifics. A clear *terminus a quo* is AD 70, since the destruction of Jerusalem is assumed.[4] The *terminus ad quem* is certainly the second Jewish revolt in AD 132–135, since the events surrounding this period are nowhere mentioned or implied in the work. A more precise dating within this period, however, is difficult. Determinations of date on the basis of historical references[5] or literary relationships[6] are indecisive. Since, however, it is likely

---

overpowering strength.' See also A.L. Thompson, *Responsibility for Evil in the Theodicy of IV Ezra* (Missoula, MT: Scholars Press, 1977), p. 340.

1. So R.H. Charles, 'II Baruch', in *APOT*, II, pp. 472-74; V. Ryssel, 'Die Syrische Baruchapokalypse', *APAT*, II, p. 411; A.F.J. Klijn, 'Die syrische Baruch-Apokalypse', in *JSHRZ*, V.2, pp. 110-11. The one major recent exception is P. Bogaert (*Apocalypse de Baruch* [2 vols.; Paris: Cerf, 1969], I, p. 380) who considers both Hebrew and Greek as equally possible.

2. Klijn, pp. 107, 114. The original language, of course, points to this conclusion.

3. Charles ('II Baruch', p. 470) argued that the work is Pharisaic, but more recent scholars have recognized that pre-Jamnia Judaism was far more complex than earlier imagined, so that this kind of simple categorization is inappropriate. G.B. Sayler (*Have the Promises Failed? A Literary Analysis of 2 Baruch* [Chico, CA: Scholars Press, 1984], pp. 115-18) makes the attractive suggestion that the author was from a sectarian group that viewed its leaders as scribal/prophetic figures in the turbulent times following AD 70.

4. Virtually all authorities date the work after AD 70, though J. Hadot ('La datation de l'apocalypse syriaque de Baruch', *Semitica* 15 [1965], pp. 94-95) revives an old view that the work is a response to Pompey's entrance in 63 BC. The majority view does not exclude the possibility that the author utilized traditions going back prior to AD 70.

5. See the discussion of various suggestions in Sayler, pp. 104-107.

6. While older writers tended to assume a literary relationship between *4 Ezra* and *2 Baruch*, recent writers acknowledge that both documents may be dependent on a common apocalyptic tradition; cf. Klijn, p. 113. Equally problematic is the relation-

that a few years elapsed between the destruction of Jerusalem and the composition of *2 Baruch*, a date at the end of the first century or the beginning of the second century AD seems highly probable.

More significant for our study here is the question of unity. Older scholars tended to emphasize the diversity of the materials embedded in *2 Baruch* without considering whether there was an underlying unity. Charles, for example, proposed a very elaborate source-critical analysis, classifying blocks of material according to their attitudes toward Israel's future, the presence or absence of a Messiah figure, and their chronological relationships to the fall of Jerusalem.[1] His conclusion was that the author utilized at least six sources. Recent scholars, however, have stressed the fact that apocalyptic writers are not overly concerned with logical consistency, and so argue that such divisions on the grounds of content are illegitimate.[2] In addition, the seven-fold structure of *2 Baruch* and the interrelationship of its form and content have recently been discovered.[3] Thus, it seems best to approach *2 Baruch* as the work of one author in the fullest sense, seeking to interpret the message of its parts in light of the interplay of its form and content as a whole—without, however, denying its inclusion of various sources, which differ at times in respect to details.[4]

ship between *2 Baruch* and the *Paralipomena of Jeremiah*. Literary dependence is possible, but this could run either way and it is more likely that they drew on a common tradition, as G.W.E. Nickelsburg ('Narrative Traditions in the Paralipomena of Jeremiah and 2 Baruch', *CBQ* 35 [1973], pp. 60-68) argues.

1. R.H. Charles, *The Apocalypse of Baruch, Translated from the Syriac* (London: Black, 1896), pp. liii-lxv; cf., however, the introduction by W.O.E. Oesterley in R.H. Charles, *The Apocalypse of Baruch* (London: SPCK, 1917), pp. x-xii. Oesterley stresses the unity of the work on the grounds that the apocalyptists were not concerned to harmonize discrepancies.

2. Especially significant here are the comments of Bogaert, I, pp. 58-91, and Sayler, pp. 4-6.

3. Sayler, pp. 11-39; cf. also Harnisch, *Verhängnis*, p. 14. Sayler builds on the structural observations of Bogaert, I, pp. 58-67. Unfortunately, she excludes the Epistle of Baruch from her analysis, though her arguments from content and terminology are subject to the same objections that she sets forth against the division hypotheses of Charles and others. On the unity of letter and apocalypse, see Bogaert, I, pp. 67-78.

4. See A.F.J. Klijn, 'The Sources and the Redaction of the Syriac Apocalypse of Baruch', *JSJ* 1 (1970), pp. 65-76.

7. 3 Baruch

The apocalypse called *3 Baruch* is extant in both Greek, which is almost certainly its original language,[1] and Slavonic. Critical for the interpretation of the work is the relationship between the Greek and the Slavonic texts, though such a study is complicated by the prior need for a detailed investigation of the relationship between the two Slavonic versions, namely the South Slavonic and the Russian.[2] While the Slavonic has traditionally been viewed as a mere abbreviation of the Greek text,[3] such a view underestimates the systematic transformation to which the work was subjected, at least as found in the South Slavonic version.[4] There are, in fact, instances where the priority of the Slavonic over the Greek is probable.[5] Further research is necessary on these matters, for detailed reconstruction of the original text can only be undertaken after there has been a thorough analysis of the pattern of the 'series of systematic transformations' to which each version was subjected.[6] For our purposes here, however, it is sufficient to note the broad patterns that are common to the two versions.

As for the provenance of *3 Baruch*, though James referred to it as 'a Christian Apocalypse of the second century',[7] recent authorities are agreed that the writing is essentially Jewish[8]—though obviously reworked by a Christian scribe. The extent of this Christian 'redaction', however, is a matter on which there is some debate. Christian interpolations are evident in 4.15, 13.4 and 15.4. But many

---

1. H.E. Gaylord, Jr, '3 (Greek Apocalypse of) Baruch', in *OTP*, I, p. 655: 'There is no convincing argument that the Greek is a translation from another language'.

2. J.-C. Picard, *Apocalypsis Baruchi Graece* (Leiden: Brill, 1967), pp. 69-71.

3. M.R. James, *Apocrypha Anecdota* (Cambridge: Cambridge University Press, 1897), p. lii, who has been followed by others.

4. Picard, pp. 72-73.

5. Gaylord (p. 655) mentions that explicit NT citations (4.15; 5.3; 15.4; 16.2) and the phrase 'through Jesus Christ Emmanuel' at 4.15 are absent in the Slavonic, as are the possible dependencies on *4 Baruch* in the introduction and first chapter.

6. Picard, p. 72.

7. James, p. lxxi.

8. Charlesworth (*Pseudepigrapha and Modern Research*, p. 87) writes, 'the Jewish character of chapters 1–17 is now widely accepted'.

see the remaining verses of 4.9-15[1] and the whole of chs. 11–17 as
being Christian as well.[2] Picard, I believe, has made a good case for
the composite character of ch. 4 (thus limiting the interpolation to
4.15).[3]

The question as to the end of the writing, however, is more
difficult. Christian features are minimal in the Greek version and
could reasonably be explained as self-contained interpolations. The
promises that Baruch will see 'the glory of God' (4.2; 6.12; 7.2; 11.2;
16.4 [Sl]), viewed in light of the fact that Jewish mystical writings
often focus on the divine throne and the surrounding glory, perhaps
tell in favor of the suggestion, however impossible to prove, that the
work has been abbreviated from the more usual scheme of seven
heavens. Nevertheless, apart from such relatively obvious interpolations, there is no evidence to suggest that the fundamentally Jewish
character of the work has been altered.

A more precise description of *3 Baruch* as a whole is problematic.
Certainly it belongs to the tradition of Jewish mysticism, of which the
earliest representative is *1 Enoch* 1–36 (cf. also *2 Enoch*). While not
gnostic in any proper sense,[4] it incorporates many hellenistic and
oriental ideas.[5] Possibly it originated in Egypt.[6] A date in the second
century AD is widely accepted.

1. E.g. L. Rost, *Einleitung in die alttestamentlichen Apokryphen und Pseudepigraphen einschliesslich der grossen Qumran-Handschriften* (Heidelberg: Quelle &
Meyer, 1971), p. 87.

2. James (pp. lxx-lxxi) suggests we do not have the end of the apocalypse in its
original form, yet he makes no definite suggestions with regard to its relation to the
Apocalypse of Paul. Cf. V. Ryssel, 'Die griechische Baruchapokalypse', in *APAT*,
II, p. 447, who argues that a piece of the original work from which the Apocalypse
of Paul was composed is substituted, and H.M. Hughes, 'The Greek Apocalypse of
Baruch or III Baruch', in *APOT*, II, pp. 529-30, who argues vigorously in support
of the Christian character of these chapters.

3. Picard, p. 76.

4. *Contra* L. Ginzberg, 'Baruch, Apocalypse of (Greek)', in *JE*, II, p. 551, and
O. Eissfeldt, *Einleitung in das Alte Testament* (3rd edn; Tübingen: Mohr, 1964),
p. 854.

5. A.-M. Denis, *Introduction aux pseudépigraphes grecs d'Ancien Testament*
(Leiden: Brill, 1970), p. 82.

6. J.-C. Picard, 'Observations sur l'apocalypse grecque de Baruch', *Semitica* 20
(1970), p. 103; cf. Nickelsburg, *Jewish Literature*, p. 303, who cites parallels with
Jewish mythology and *2 Enoch* in support of this position. For a different view, see
Rost, p. 88, who favors Syria.

8. *The Apocalypse of Abraham*

The *Apocalypse of Abraham* is certainly a Jewish document.[1] It was originally written in Hebrew, though it possibly came into Slavonic through a Greek translation.[2] The first part of the work (chs. 1–8, which contain haggadic legend) seems to have existed prior to and independently of the second part (chs. 9–31, the apocalypse proper), though the latter section appears to have been composed as a complement to the earlier chapters (cf. 10.13; 25.1 and 26.2-3).[3] While written after AD 70, since it mentions the destruction of Jerusalem (ch. 27), the exact date of composition is uncertain. It shares with *2 Baruch* and *4 Ezra* 'a common apocalyptic tradition that was crystallized after 70 C.E. in response to that crisis',[4] and so probably dates to the first half of the second century AD.[5] Its language of composition suggests that it originated in Palestine.

There are points of contact between the *Apocalypse of Abraham* and the Jewish mystical tradition that stretches from sections of *1 Enoch* to the medieval mystical texts.[6] There are also certain affinities with the doctrines of the Qumran sect, but there is no reason to postulate that the work originated in that community. Rather, it is more probable that the *Apocalypse of Abraham* and certain of the Qumran writings

1. Recent studies are unanimous in viewing the *Apocalypse of Abraham* as a Jewish document. Bauckham, p. 108, writes that 'there can be no real doubt about the Apocalypse of Abraham's place among the ancient Jewish apocalypses'; cf. J. Licht, 'Abraham, Apocalypse of', in *EJ*, II, p. 127: 'The Jewish origin of the book cannot be doubted'.

2. Cf. the detailed studies by A. Rubinstein, 'Hebraisms in the Slavonic "Apocalypse of Abraham"', *JJS* 4 (1953), pp. 108-15; *idem*, 'Hebraisms in the "Apocalypse of Abraham"', *JJS* 5 (1954), pp. 132-35; R. Rubinkiewicz, 'Les sémitismes dans l'Apocalypse d'Abraham', *FO* 21 (1980), pp. 141-48. The numerous examples of obvious Semitisms listed in these studies, along with the absence of Aramaisms, points to Hebrew as the language of composition.

3. Persuasive here is B. Philonenko-Sayar and M. Philonenko, 'Die Apokalypse Abrahams', in *JSHRZ*, V.5, p. 417. This analysis is confirmed by the fact that the first part is found alone in some manuscripts.

4. Nickelsburg, *Jewish Literature*, p. 298; cf. M. Stone, 'Apocalyptic Literature', in *JWSTP*, p. 416.

5. This view is commonly held today; cf., e.g., R. Meyer, 'Abraham-Apokalypse', in *RGG*[3], I, p. 72, and R. Rubinkiewicz, 'Apocalypse of Abraham', *OTP*, I, p. 683, who argued that the second-century text of *Recognitiones* alludes to this writing (33.1f.).

6. See esp. Nickelsburg, *Jewish Literature*, p. 299, and Stone, 'Apocalyptic Literature', p. 417.

contain traces of the mystical currents that were present in the Judaism of the day.

While the Jewish character of the original work is relatively secure, the fact that it is preserved only in Slavonic renders appeal to details of the text somewhat problematic, for there is always the possibility of influence by the Bogomils.[1] Indeed, Rubinkiewicz argues that the doctrines of this medieval dualistic sect can be found in certain glosses (viz. 20.5, 7; 22.5), as well as in the interpolation of 29.3-13.[2] Caution, however, is in order here, for vv. 5 and 7 of ch. 20 are very difficult to comprehend on any interpretation, and 22.5 fits well with the ethical dualism of the Qumran writings. Furthermore, while portions of ch. 29 are often regarded as Christian interpolations,[3] the text is difficult whether viewed as Jewish, Christian or Gnostic.[4] Further research is necessary on such matters before we can set forth any firm conclusions. Until that time we must use the material from the Apocalypse of Abraham critically, especially in these passages. Overall, however, 'most of the contents of the apocalypse have sufficient parallels in other early Jewish documents to give us confidence in their originality'.[5]

9. *The Testament of Abraham*

While the form of the *Testament of Abraham* is unique in many respects, chs. 10–15 (rec. A; chs. 8–12 in rec. B) contain many features characteristic of Jewish apocalypses; in fact, this section fits well the type of apocalypse that combines an other-worldly journey with

---

1. This is, of course, a problem for any work that has been preserved only in Slavonic; see Charlesworth, *Pseudepigrapha and the New Testament*, pp. 32-36.

2. Rubinkiewicz, 'Apocalypse of Abraham', p. 684. H. Weinel ('Die spätere christliche Apokalyptik', in *EUXAPISTHPION: Studien zur Religion und Literatur des Alten und Neuen Testaments, für Hermann Gunkel* [ed. H. Schmidt; Göttingen: Vandenhoeck & Ruprecht, 1923], II, p. 169) argued many years earlier that the work was made up of three components, Jewish, Christian and Gnostic.

3. G.N. Bonwetsch, *Die Apokalypse Abrahams* (Leipzig, 1897; Aalen: Scientia, 1972 reprint), p. 64; J.B. Frey, 'Abraham (Apocalypse d')', in *DBSup*, I, p. 32.

4. Philonenko-Sayar and Philonenko, p. 417. See also R.G. Hall, 'The "Christian Interpolation" in the Apocalypse of Abraham', *JBL* 107 (1988), pp. 107-12, who argues that the figure of *Apoc. Abr.* 29.3-13 is not Christ but a 'man of sin'.

5. Bauckham, p. 109.

personal eschatology.[1] On matters of date and provenance, however, there is significant disagreement among scholars. Most reject the view that the work is Jewish-Christian.[2] The Christian elements are not essential to the work, but are probably the result of transmission by Christian scribes.[3] Crucial in this matter are three considerations: (1) that in both form and content the work is essentially Jewish,[4] (2) that the Christian elements are only superficial, with the work not even containing an elementary christology,[5] and (3) that many 'Christian' features can with equal probability be traced to Jewish traditions.[6]

A more precise determination of provenance, however, is problematic. There is nothing particularly Essene about the work.[7] Sanders is probably correct in his contention that it represents 'lowest-common-denominator Judaism'.[8] There are some features that may suggest that the work originated in Egypt,[9] though it has been argued that our

1. See Collins, 'Jewish Apocalypses', pp. 23, 28.

2. M.R. James, *The Testament of Abraham* (Cambridge: Cambridge University Press, 1892), pp. 23, 52-55; Weinel, p. 170. Most suggest that the Christian author is building on Jewish legends or a Hebrew 'Grundschrift'; cf. J. Schreiner, *Alttestamentlich-jüdische Apokalyptik* (München: Kösel, 1969), p. 71.

3. Virtually every modern work is decisive in this regard; e.g. Stone, 'Apocalyptic Literature', p. 420.

4. Especially important here is the study of K. Kohler ('The Pre-Talmudic Haggada. II. C. The Apocalypse of Abraham and its Kindred', *JQR* 7 [1895], pp. 581-606), who demonstrated many points of contact between this writing and the rabbinic traditions.

5. M. Delcor, *Le Testament d'Abraham* (Leiden: Brill, 1973), p. 66.

6. On the doctrine of the 'two ways' and the 'two gates', see G.H. Box, *The Testament of Abraham* (London: SPCK, 1927), p. xvii.

7. An Essene origin for the work has been suggested by Kohler, (p. 594), and F. Schmidt ('Le Testament d'Abraham: Introduction, édition de la recension courte, traduction et notes' [2 vols.; unpublished doctoral dissertation, University of Strasbourg, 1971], I, p. 120. Delcor (p. 72) points out differences as well as similarities with the beliefs and practices of the Essenes, though his own contention that the work stems from the Therapeutae is without foundation. These writers have failed to show that there is anything *distinctively* Essene about the *Testament of Abraham*; cf. E. Janssen, 'Testament Abrahams', in *JSHRZ*, III.2, p. 200.

8. E.P. Sanders, 'Testament of Abraham', *OTP*, I, p. 876, though I should not wish to imply by this that I regard it as representative of the 'essence' of the Jewish religion, which was far too diverse to permit such a judgment; cf. Charlesworth, *Pseudepigrapha and the New Testament*, pp. 47-58. I mean only that the work is without distinguishing characteristics.

9. For Egypt as the place of composition, see Nickelsburg (*Jewish Literature*, p. 253) and Denis (p. 36). Delcor (pp. 67-73) sets forth a list of Egyptian characteristics.

Greek text represents a revision of an original Palestinian work.[1] The original language and date, however, remain uncertain, although a Greek original[2] sometime in the first two centuries AD is reasonably probable.[3]

In studying the *Testament of Abraham*, one must consider the problem of relations between the recensions. At present, however, the question cannot be addressed with confidence. Many have followed James in his contention that the longer recension (rec. A) best represents the original narrative while the shorter recension (rec. B) at times contains archaic language.[4] Yet proponents of the priority of rec. B have made a good case for their position.[5] Several recent studies, in fact, have argued that neither recension is dependent on the other, and that both contain useful material from an earlier text.[6] Therefore, I shall utilize material from both recensions critically, attempting to ascertain the original text in important cases on an individual basis.

10. *The Apocalypse of Zephaniah*

A significant preliminary question concerning the *Apocalypse of Zephaniah* is the relations between (1) the portion cited as from the *Apocalypse of Zephaniah* by Clement of Alexandria (in *Stromata*, 5.11.77), (2) the Sahidic fragment where the seer identifies himself as Zephaniah, and (3) the fuller Akhmimic text which, at least in its surviving portions, lacks reference to the identity of the seer. Several

---

1. Box, *Testament of Abraham*, pp. xxviii-xxix. Janssen (p. 199) argues simply that the writing was composed in Palestine.

2. Sanders (pp. 873-74) argues convincingly that the author attempted to imitate classical Hebrew style, a technique practiced in Greek rather than Hebrew literature; cf. Delcor, p. 34.

3. Dates range from the first half of the first century AD (so Box, *Testament of Abraham*, pp. xxviii-xxix) to the second century AD (James, *Testament of Abraham*, p. 55). While the *Testament* gives every appearance of being an early Jewish apocalyptic work, solid evidence for a precise date is lacking.

4. James, *Testament of Abraham*, p. 49; Box, *Testament of Abraham*, pp. xiii-xv; Denis, p. 36, and Sanders, p. 872.

5. N. Turner, 'The "Testament of Abraham": Problems in Biblical Greek', *NTS* 1 (1955), pp. 221-22, and F. Schmidt, 'The Two Recensions of the Testament of Abraham: In which Direction did the Transformation take Place?' in *Studies on the Testament of Abraham* (ed. G.W.E. Nickelsburg; Missoula, MT: Scholars Press, 1976), pp. 65-83. This collection of essays contains several relevant articles.

6. Delcor, pp. 5-15, and Janssen, pp. 195-96.

writers have urged caution with regard to the equation of the apoca-
lypse(s) represented by these three sources.[1] Yet a majority of
authorities have followed Schürer in his contention that all three represent the same work.[2]

Several factors favor Schürer's view. First, the connection between
the Sahidic fragment and the Akhmimic texts is suggested by the
striking similarities of wording found in Sahidic ln. 4 and Akhmimic
7.9; 9.1-2,[3] with that suggestion strengthened by the fact that both are
associated with the *Apocalypse of Elijah* in the manuscripts in which
they are extant.[4] Second, the equation of the work cited by Clement
and that represented in the Sahidic fragment seems secure enough, for
both are identified explicitly with Zephaniah, and Zephaniah seems
somewhat of an unusual choice for an apocalyptic seer. Nevertheless,
significant problems remain.[5] It is, in fact, possible that we are here
dealing with different recensions of some common source.[6]

With regard to date and provenance, one is struck by an almost
complete lack of solid data. That the work in its present form is

1. Significant here is the discussion of G. Steindorff (*Die Apokalypse des Elias,
eine unbekannte Apokalypse und Bruchstücke der Sophonias-Apokalypse* [Leipzig:
Hinrichs, 1899], pp. 14-16), who argues that the Sahidic fragment would not make
sense in any lacunae of the Akhmimic text; cf. Bauckham (p. 101), who points out
that in 6.10 the Babylonian exile is referred to as a past event, a blatant anachronism
if the seer is indeed Zephaniah.

2. E. Schürer, review of *Die Apokalypse des Elias, eine unbekannte Apokalypse
und Bruchstücke der Sophonias-Apokalypse* by Georg Steindorff, in *TLZ* 24 (1899),
col. 8. Cf. e.g. M.R. James, *The Lost Apocrypha of the Old Testament* (London:
SPCK, 1920), p. 73; A. Lods, *Histoire de la littérature hébraïque et juive* (Paris:
Payot, 1950), p. 944; and, most recently, O.S. Wintermute, 'Apocalypse of Zephaniah', *OTP*, I, pp. 499-500.

3. On the verbal connections between the two manuscripts as grounds for establishing their identity, see R. Meyer, 'Zephanja-Apokalypse', in *RGG*³, VI, p. 1900.

4. The close association between these two works is also suggested by the
stichometry appended to the chronography of Nicephorus, Patriarch of Constan-
tinople (806-15), by the *Synopsis scripturae sacrae* of Pseudo-Athanasius (perhaps
6th cent.), and by the anonymous *Catalogue of the Sixty Canonical Books*; see
Denis, p. 192, and Wintermute, 'Apocalypse of Zephaniah', pp. 499-500.

5. One major problem is the reference to the fifth heaven in Clement's citation, for
neither the Sahidic nor the Akhmimic texts contain any trace of a belief in a multiplic-
ity of heavens. It is possible that such an ascent through the heavens was placed
before the beginning of the Akhmimic text (so Schürer, p. 8); yet, even so, one
would expect to find some trace of this belief in the surviving pages.

6. M. Himmelfarb, *Tours of Hell* (Philadelphia: University of Pennsylvania
Press, 1983), p. 158.

Christian is suggested by the fact that it is extant in Coptic. Yet with the possible exception of two relatively minor embellishments,[1] there is nothing obviously Christian about the book.[2] Rather, there are numerous points of contact with the Jewish mystical tradition. Indeed, the *Apocalypse of Zephaniah* seems to bear a close relationship to the Book of the Watchers—which suggests that it is not only a Jewish document, but a relatively ancient one at that.[3]

A precise date for the work, however, is problematic. The manuscript evidence as well as its use by the *Apocalypse of Paul* puts the date of the *Apocalypse of Zephaniah* before the fourth or fifth century AD.[4] If this is the work cited by Clement, then we can move the *terminus ad quem* back to the last quarter of the second century AD. In view of its connections with the Book of the Watchers, it may be even earlier. Most believe that the book was originally written in Greek, probably by a Jew of the Diaspora.

11. *The Testament of Levi 2–5*

With regard to the *Testament of Levi*, it is most helpful, for my purposes, to begin with the question of genre. Though 'testament' is perhaps the best description of the genre of this writing (if indeed we can speak generally of a 'testament' genre[5]), there exists a close relation

1. Possible Christian touches are found at 2.2-4 (cf. Mt. 24.40-41 and Lk. 17.34-35; so Weinel, II, p. 163) and 10.9 (so Bauckham, p. 102), though these may simply be parts of a common Jewish-Christian heritage (Wintermute, 'Apocalypse of Zephaniah', p. 501).

2. While the present form of the book was taken over by Christians, there is no evidence to support the claim of Weinel (p. 162), and A. Harnack *(Geschichte der altchristlichen Literatur bis Eusebius* [2nd edn; Leipzig: Hinrichs, 1958], pt. 2, I, p. 573) that the text is a Christian reworking of 'eine jüdische Grundschrift'.

3. For a list of close links between the Book of the Watchers and the *Apocalypse of Zephaniah*, see Himmelfarb, pp. 151-53.

4. While the precise nature of relations between these two documents remains open, it seems clear enough that the *Apocalypse of Paul* represents a later phase of the tradition; cf. Himmelfarb, p. 151: 'the incidents in the *Apocalypse of Zephaniah* that are without parallel in the *Apocalypse of Paul* are precisely the ones that one would expect to trouble later Christians'.

5. This assumption is called into question by H.W. Hollander and M. de Jonge *(The Testaments of the Twelve Patriarchs: A Commentary* [Leiden: Brill, 1985], pp. 32-33), who argue that the *Testaments of the Twelve Patriarchs* stands by itself in many respects. They classify this work as 'a collection of farewell discourses'.

between the *Testament of Levi* and Jewish apocalypses.[1] Hence, while the *Testament of Levi* manifests many of the fundamental characteristics of a discourse delivered in anticipation of death,[2] it focuses on two visions (2.3–6.2; 8) granted to the patriarch just prior to his death.[3] In fact, the authority of the writing is based on the fact that it is 'revealed' in this manner rather than on the prestige of the speaker or that it is his farewell address. This is, in Collins's judgment, precisely what distinguishes an apocalypse from a testament.[4] Furthermore, the *Testament of Levi* contains many features that distinguish an apocalypse from other writings—especially with regard to the manner of revelation[5] and the material being presented from the perspective of the imminent expectation of judgment as well as death (1.1).[6] So I shall include this important writing in my discussion, though I shall focus on chs. 2–5 in view of their close relationship to other Jewish apocalypses and their obvious relevance for our topic.

Along with the question of genre, the issue of provenance is of great significance. The issue is whether the *Testaments of the Twelve Patriarchs* is (1) a thoroughly Jewish document,[7] (2) a basically Jewish document with Christian interpolations that can be isolated and removed,[8] or (3) a Christian writing that has utilized Jewish sources in

---

1. I do not intend by this to prejudge the difficult question of origin, but to suggest a marked similarity of form and content.

2. Collins, 'Testaments', in *JWSTP*, p. 325.

3. On differences between the structure and content of the Testament of Levi, see Hollander and de Jonge, p. 129.

4. Collins, 'Jewish Apocalypses', p. 44.

5. *Ibid.*, p. 28.

6. H.C. Kee, 'Testaments of the Twelve Patriarchs', in *OTP*, I, p. 788: 'The real writer of *TLevi* obviously thinks that he is standing near the day of judgment; hence his eagerness to convey his warnings and promises'.

7. M. Philonenko (*Les interpolations chrétiennes des Testaments des Douze Patriarches et les manuscrits de Qoumrân* [Paris: Presses Universitaires de France, 1960]) virtually eliminates Christian interpolations by interpreting the significant messianic passages as references to the Teacher of Qumran, but his theory is idiosyncratic and almost universally rejected. Scholars today are ready to grant the 'Christian' character of at least certain sections of the work.

8. This approach was made popular by R.H. Charles (*The Testaments of the Twelve Patriarchs* [London: Black, 1908], pp. liv-lvi, lxi-lxv), and was dominant until at least 1951; see H.D. Slingerland, *The Testaments of the Twelve Patriarchs: A Critical History of Research* (Missoula, MT: Scholars Press, 1977), pp. 34-43. In recent times it has been re-introduced, albeit with certain modifications; e.g. J. Becker, *Untersuchungen zur Entstehungsgeschichte der Testamente der Zwölf Patriarchen* (Leiden: Brill, 1970), pp. 373-77, and A. Hultgard, *L'eschatologie des Tes-*

such a way that it is impossible to distinguish between what is Jewish and what is Christian.[1] Using critical methods presently available, scholars have been unable to come to a consensus; indeed, the many hypotheses set forth with respect to the origin and composition of the writing are varied and contradictory, and the problem appears to be insoluble. Slingerland even goes so far as to suggest that we abandon an 'either–or' approach to this question and consider the Testaments from the perspective of *both* Judaism *and* Christianity.[2] Where the work originated and the date of its composition are, of course, linked to this prior question, with suggested locations including Palestine and Egypt. The work has been dated variously between the first part of the second century BC (for the basic Jewish document, exclusive of Christian additions) and the beginning of the third century AD (for the extant Christian work).

In light of the present state of research on the *Testaments*, caution is called for in using materials from *Testament of Levi* 2–5. There appears to be an 'organic' relation between the Greek *Testament of Levi* and the Aramaic *Levi* materials discovered at Qumran.[3] But the precise nature of this relation remains uncertain.[4] We cannot determine with any precision, in fact, the extent to which the Greek *Testament of Levi* is dependent on a Jewish 'Vorlage'. It is therefore necessary to utilize material from the *Testament of Levi* critically, using it only where it supports or illumines conclusions arrived at on the basis of more secure evidence.

Conclusion

The preceding survey has uncovered a number of introductory issues that must remain somewhat uncertain. Furthermore, it is clear that the *Testament of Levi* can only be used to support conclusions derived

taments des Douze Patriarches (Uppsala: Almqvist & Wiksell, 1981), II, pp. 223-38.

1. This view was dominant from about 1700 to 1884 (see Slingerland, pp. 6-18), and has been revived in recent times by M. de Jonge, *The Testaments of the Twelve Patriarchs: A Study of their Text, Composition and Origin* (Assen: Van Gorcum, 1953), esp. pp. 117-21. For a list of authorities who view the Testaments as a Christian writing, see Becker, pp. 146-47.

2. Slingerland, pp. 106-15, though his discussion is weighted toward the Christian perspective.

3. Charlesworth, *Pseudepigrapha and Modern Research*, p. 38.

4. Hollander and de Jonge, pp. 23-24.

from other documents. Nevertheless, apart from this one major exception, the fundamentally Jewish character of the writings enumerated above seems probable, though we must take care in certain cases to avoid materials that appear to have been reworked by early Christians or medieval dualists. Other introductory issues of a less pressing nature will be addressed at appropriate points in the analysis that follows. For the most part, however, I shall take for granted the major introductory conclusions set forth above. This will allow me to shift my focus from these problems to more relevant matters—namely, the fundamental teachings in these Jewish apocalypses on the themes of revelation and redemption.

Chapter 2

REVELATORY EXPERIENCES IN JEWISH APOCALYPTICISM

To understand the revelatory experiences depicted in the literature of Jewish apocalypticism, it is necessary to consider first of all the conceptual world of the apocalyptists themselves,[1] particularly their views as to (1) the need for heavenly revelations, (2) the achievement of heavenly revelations, and (3) the media of heavenly revelations. In addition, we must ask as to whether genuine visionary experience actually underlies at least some of the Jewish apocalypses, or whether the visionary activities described are to be understood as merely literary conventions. Thus prior to dealing with matters concerning the content of revelation (Chapter 3) and the functions of revelation (Chapter 4) in Jewish apocalypticism, this chapter will be concerned with certain crucial introductory issues having to do with the apocalyptists' self-understanding as recipients of revelation. I shall avoid making judgments regarding the validity of the apocalyptists' experiences. My goal is simply to understand how they viewed the revelations described in the Jewish apocalypses.

1. The Need for Heavenly Revelations

One of the most significant components of an apocalyptic world view is the idea that it is necessary to obtain special revelation from heaven. Several factors reinforce this notion.

---

1. J.J. Collins (*The Apocalyptic Imagination* [New York: Crossroad, 1984], p. 7) argues that the Jewish apocalypses have a shared 'conceptual structure' and express their disagreements within this structure. In his view, the basic presupposition as to how the world works is this: 'human life is bounded in the present by the supernatural world of angels and demons and in the future by the inevitability of a final judgment'. Cf. O. Plöger, *Theocracy and Eschatology* (trans. S. Rudman; Oxford: Basil Blackwell, 1968), pp. 26-27.

a. *The Transcendence of God*
A common feature in the Jewish apocalypses is the concept of the transcendence of God, which manifests itself in a variety of ways.[1] The God of the apocalypses does not occupy an earthly Temple; his throne is located in a celestial palace and so the seer must ascend through numerous heavenly spheres in order to reach his goal.[2] Conversely, revelation, for the most part, no longer comes directly from God,[3] but is mediated through such angelic figures as Gabriel (Daniel), Uriel (*1 Enoch, 4 Ezra*), Ramael (*2 Baruch*), Iaoel (*Apocalypse of Abraham*) and others.[4] These angelic figures fulfill a variety of roles, from interceding on behalf of the righteous (Dan. 10.13, 21; 12.1; *1 En.* 89.76; 90.14; *T. Levi* 5.5-6)[5] and 'shepherding' the nation Israel (*1 En.* 89.59-67)[6] to overseeing many aspects of the day to day operation of the cosmos (esp. *1 Enoch* 72–80). In fact, the overall impression one gains from these writings is that God is little involved in his world, which for the duration of this age is under the control of angelic powers—many of which are satanic or demonic.[7]

Several factors undoubtedly contributed to the development of such a transcendent view of God. Probably most significant was the fact that the Jewish people had not observed God's saving activity on their

---

1. On the transcendence of God in the apocalypses and other OT pseudepigrapha, see J.M. Charlesworth, 'A History of Pseudepigrapha Research', *ANRW*, II.19.1, pp. 81-84.
2. See the discussion in I. Gruenwald, 'Jewish Apocalyptic Literature', *ANRW*, II.19.1, p. 96.
3. Some exceptions are *1 En.* 14–15; *4 Ezra* 14.1-26; *2 Bar.* 1.2–5.4; 10.1-3; 13.2–20.6; 22.2–30.5; 41.1–43.3; 48.1–52.7.
4. See Collins, *Apocalyptic Vision*, pp. 75-76, and S. Niditch, *The Symbolic Vision in Biblical Tradition* (Chico, CA: Scholars Press, 1980), p. 244. In many cases, of course, the revelation is no longer straightforward, but involves a symbolic vision that requires the ministry of the *angelus interpres*; cf. Dan. 7.2-14, with interpretation in 7.16-27; Dan. 8.2-14, with interpretation in 8.16-26; *4 Ezra* 9.38–10.28, with interpretation in 10.38-54; *4 Ezra* 13.1-13, with interpretation in 13.21-56; *2 Bar.* 53, with interpretation in 55–74, etc. See further below, §2.3.b.1.
5. See Kee, I, p. 790; cf. Black, *Book of Enoch*, p. 304.
6. Note esp. 89.59, 'He then summoned seventy shepherds and surrendered those sheep to them. . .'
7. There is, however, no true cosmological dualism, for God simply allows others to have control during the present age; see esp. *Apoc. Abr.* 23.12-14; cf. G.H. Box and J.I. Landsman, *The Apocalypse of Abraham* (London: SPCK, 1918), pp. 65-66; Philonenko-Sayar and Philonenko, 5.5, p. 446; M. Hengel, *Judaism and Hellenism* (trans. J. Bowden; Philadelphia: Fortress Press, 1974), I, p. 190, and Rowland, *Open Heaven*, pp. 90-92, 143-44.

behalf in any meaningful way from the time of the Babylonian conquest until the fall of Jerusalem to the Romans.[1] The apocalyptists, in fact, began not with a dogma of the transcendence of God, but with the 'empirical observation' of his relative absence from their immediate experience.[2] This development also corresponds to broader religious trends in the hellenistic world which tended to conceptualize deity more abstractly.[3] Indeed, one must not underestimate the significance of the hellenistic Zeitgeist in the development of Jewish apocalyptic thought regarding the relations of God with his people.

b. *Spatial Dualism*

Closely related to a stress on the transcendence of God is the spatial dualism of the Jewish apocalypses. This was by no means a new conception in the history of Israel. What is significant here, however, is the emphasis that is placed in the apocalypses on the contrast between the things above (the heavenly world) and the things below (the earthly world). This is evident especially in apocalypses that contain otherworldly journeys (*1 Enoch* 1–36; 37–71; 72–82; *2 Enoch*; *Apocalypse of Abraham*; *Testament of Levi*; *3 Baruch*; *Testament of Abraham*; and *Apocalypse of Zephaniah*),[4] though it is also present to some degree in virtually all the Jewish apocalypses.[5]

The notion is especially clear in certain of the Enochic materials. In chs. 1–36 of *1 Enoch* 'the heavens' refers to the dwelling place of

---

1. A notable exception here is *Jubilees* (23.26-31), since the author of this work views the messianic age as inaugurated by the Hasidim and the Maccabees; see also 1 Macc. 14.4-15 (an ode to Simon that celebrates the 'Golden Age' of Hasmonean dominance) and, possibly, *Testament of Levi* 18, if it is not the result of Christian influence. R. Bauckham ('The Rise of Apocalyptic', *Themelios* 3 [1978], p. 20) is correct to say that for the most part the apocalyptists refused as spurious the 'solution of a realized eschatology accommodated to Gentile rule and the cult of the second temple: they insisted on believing that the prophecies meant what they said'. If God acted on their behalf, they believed, it would be to establish Jerusalem in a manner that was both dramatic and cataclysmic.

2. Bauckham, 'Rise', p. 20, though he speaks primarily of the negative view of history commonly attributed to the apocalyptists.

3. Hengel, I, p. 233.

4. Collins, 'Introduction', pp. 14-15.

5. J.J. Collins ('The Genre Apocalypse in Hellenistic Judaism', *Apocalypticism*, pp. 544-45) notes that this feature is prevalent among apocalypses that originated in the Jewish Diaspora, though it is also an emphasis in certain Palestinian apocalypses. The distinction between Palestinian and diaspora apocalypses, however, should not be pressed too far.

God and of 'the children of heaven' (6.2), who are the angels, while
humans are confined to existence 'on the earth', and so subject to
oppression and wickedness (9.1-11). Special emphasis is placed on the
holy character of the angelic realm (1.2; 12.4; 15.3), with no one,
except the seer, being able to penetrate the barrier that separates
heaven and earth (12.1-2; 19.3). The Book of the Watchers is particularly preoccupied with the heavenly realms,[1] while The Book of the
Similitudes is more balanced in its tension between a temporal and a
spatial dualism. For our purposes, it is the contrast between heaven
and earth that is significant. Living human beings are consistently
referred to as 'those who dwell on the earth' (37.2, 5; 38.2; 40.6;
43.4; 53.1; 55.1; 60.5, 22; 64.12; 66.2; 68.7; 70.1). Furthermore, the
earthly realm is characterized by 'darkness' (58.5), at least for the
present, and is contrasted with the heavenly sphere of light. The two
realms are thus separate and the barrier between them generally
impenetrable (55.2).

Spatial dualism appears frequently throughout most of the other
works as well. In *2 Baruch*, for example, the idea is set forth in various ways,[2] though it is perhaps best expressed in ch. 51. There the
righteous look forward to a time of divine intervention when they will
experience the blessings of heaven in the age to come:

> For they shall see that world which is now invisible to them, and they will see
> a time which is now hidden to them. And time will no longer make them
> older. For they will live in the heights of that world and they will be like the
> angels and be equal to the stars (51.8-10).

Somewhat more explicit as to the limitations placed on humans as
earthly creatures in the present age is the *Apocalypse of Abraham*.
There Abraham, after his ascent, sees not only the mysteries of
heaven, but also looks down on 'the earth and its fruit, and its moving
things and its things that had souls, and its host of men and the impiety
of their souls and their justification' (21.3). Yet in spite of the privilege granted to him, Abraham is still a child of the earth, and Azazel's
threat rings in his ears:

> What are you doing, Abraham, on the holy heights, where no one eats or
> drinks, nor is there upon them food for men. But these all will be consumed

---

1. J.G. Gammie, 'Spatial and Ethical Dualism in Jewish Wisdom and Apocalyptic
Literature', *JBL* 93 (1974), pp. 367-68.
   2. *Ibid.*, p. 371.

by fire and they will burn you up. Leave the man who is with you and flee!
For if you ascend to the height, they will destroy you (13.4-5).

Abraham, of course, overcomes the opposition of Azazel, but only
because he receives the garment of incorruptibility that formerly
belonged to Azazel (13.14). He is thus the exception that proves the
rule. Humanity's 'lot' is to be on the earth, and it is only through a
special revelation from heaven that it can transcend the limitations of
the earthly realm.[1]

c. *The Heavenly Nature of Wisdom*
Another feature that reinforces the need for special revelation in the
Jewish apocalypses is the notion—familiar as well from several wisdom writings (Job 28; Sir. 1.1-10; Prov. 1.20-33)—that wisdom is
hidden away in heaven.[2] Especially significant here are several passages among the apocalypses, including *1 Enoch* 42, *4 Ezra* 4.5–5.13
and *2 Bar.* 48.33-36,[3] though the concept that wisdom belongs to the
heavenly realm literally permeates these writings.

Numerous passages express this view of wisdom. We must confine
ourselves, however, to but a few of the more significant ones. *1 Enoch*
is especially clear in this respect. The work opens by identifying the
revelation that is to follow as 'a holy vision from the heavens which

---

1. On spatial dualism as one of several forms of dualism in this work, see R.
Rubinkiewicz, 'La vision de l'histoire dans l'Apocalypse d'Abraham', *ANRW*,
II.19.1, p. 149.

2. Useful here is the distinction proposed by H. Conzelmann ('Paulus und die
Weisheit', *NTS* 12 [1966], pp. 236, 242) between 'near' wisdom (Deut. 30.12-14;
Ps. 70.20; Prov. 30.4; etc.), 'hidden' wisdom (Job 28; Sir. 1.1-10), and 'vanished'
wisdom (*1 Enoch* 42). This distinction is picked up as the basis for analysis in B.L.
Mack, *Logos und Sophia* (Göttingen: Vandenhoeck & Ruprecht, 1973), pp. 34-62;
cf. P.S. Fiddes, 'The Hiddenness of Wisdom in the Old Testament and Later Judaism' (PhD dissertation, Oxford University, 1976), p. 84. It is primarily 'vanished'
wisdom with which we are here concerned, though these various forms of wisdom
are certainly related (even if we do not trace them back to an original Ur-myth).

3. These references differ in their portrayal of the heavenly nature of wisdom. *1
Enoch* 42 is often viewed as the most complete statement of an underlying gnostic
myth that consists of the descent of wisdom, together with her rejection, withdrawal
and revelation to the elect; see e.g. R. Bultmann, *Exegetica* (ed. E. Dinkler; Tübingen: Mohr, 1967), p. 16, and U. Wilckens, *Weisheit und Torheit* (Tübingen: Mohr,
1959), pp. 124-25, 160-62. Many apocalyptic passages, it is argued, presuppose
this myth even if they contain only one or two elements. My concern, however, is
not so much with alleged mythical backgrounds as it is with the function of these
passages within the Jewish apocalypses.

the angels showed me'. This description is especially significant in view of the fact that the introduction to the Book of the Watchers characterizes the material that follows as a 'Weisheitsrede'.[1] So wisdom, it is suggested, necessitates a revelation from heaven. Equally emphatic is The Book of the Similitudes. For it is only after Enoch is 'carried off' from the earth (39.3) that he is able to see 'all the secrets in heaven' (41.1).[2] Also in chs. 37–71, wisdom is said to abound before the divine throne and the angelic beings which surround it (48.1; 49.1). So it is not surprising that 'the Elect One', in whom 'dwells the spirit of wisdom', now stands before 'the Lord of the Spirits' (49.2-3) and awaits the time of his appearing to those who dwell 'on the earth'. For the present, however, perfect wisdom is something that belongs to the heavenly sphere and to those who dwell therein. Thus, while ch. 42 is generally viewed as a foreign intrusion in its context,[3] it is in harmony at this point with the general attitude of the Similitudes as a whole.[4]

Similarly, in Epistle of Enoch the heavenly character of wisdom is clearly seen through a series of rhetorical questions in 93.11-14, which, in view of their position in the Ethiopic text, function not 'as a total denial of the possibility of such knowledge, but only of its availability to ordinary men under ordinary circumstances'.[5] Immediately preceding these questions is the prediction that at the close of the sev-

---

1. E. Rau, 'Kosmologie, Eschatologie und die Lehrautorität Henochs' (Doctoral dissertation, Hamburg, 1974), p. 40. On the other hand BW is also a 'Prophetenbuch'; see below, §2.4.b.

2. Though a heavenly ascent is mentioned only in 39.3, it appears to be essential to the pattern of revelation in 39.3–40.10 and is likely presumed in chs. 60–63; see D.W. Suter, 'Apocalyptic Patterns in the Similitudes of Enoch', in *Society of Biblical Literature 1978 Seminar Papers* (ed. P.J. Achtemeier; Missoula, MT: Scholars Press, 1978), I, pp. 1-2.

3. Charles, *Book of Enoch*, p. 123.

4. So J.J. Collins, 'The Heavenly Representative. The "Son of Man" in the Similitudes of Enoch', in *Ideal Figures*, pp. 112-13.

5. M.E. Stone, 'Revealed Things', p. 425. Of course, its place in the Apocalypse of Weeks has been frequently questioned. Charles (*Book of Enoch*, p. 274) suggests that it belonged originally to chs. 72–82, and more recently the evidence from Qumran has confirmed its status as an interpolation; cf. Milik, *Books of Enoch*, p. 247, and VanderKam, 'Apocalypse of Weeks', p. 517. Dexinger (*Zehnwochenapokalypse*, p. 108) suggests that the longer Aramaic text is the work of a first redactor, and that a second redactor abbreviated these verses to form what is essentially the Ethiopic text. In any case, our concern is primarily with the text in its present form.

enth week the elect will 'receive sevenfold instruction concerning all his creation'.[1] So the writer not only affirms the ignorance of earthly creatures in this present age, but also confidently predicts 'the eschatological reversal of this ordinary situation'.[2] All five sections of *1 Enoch*, in fact, predict such an eschatological revelation of wisdom, in contrast to the darkness and folly that characterize the earthly sphere in the present age.[3]

The notion that wisdom belongs to the heavenly sphere in the present age is also clear in *4 Ezra* and *2 Baruch*. In *4 Ezra* several passages that emphasize the hiddenness of wisdom from humans are placed in emphatic positions, particularly 4.1-11c, 4.11d-21 and 5.31-40. These lay stress on the hiddenness of two matters, namely the way of God and the evil heart.[4] Both of these are related to the author's concern with theodicy. Furthermore, several passages suggest that wisdom will be withdrawn just before the eschatological consummation (5.1-2, 9-10; 14.17-18),[5] while the revelation of perfect wisdom will come only with the inauguration of the new age (6.25-28; 8.51-54; cf. 13.52).

Such statements, however, do not tell the whole story, for they stand in juxtaposition with statements that lay emphasis on the greatness of God's revelation to the seer (10.38; cf. esp. 14.40, 47). This scheme, therefore, (1) rejects earthly wisdom, yet (2) suggests that true wisdom comes through the revelation of mysteries from heaven.[6] The pattern is much the same in *2 Baruch*, where wisdom is hidden from humans in the present (14.8-12; 48.3), though the seer is granted a measure of insight into the divine mysteries. Temporarily, wisdom withdraws and folly increases just prior to the inauguration of the new age (48.32, 36; 77.12-14), when wisdom will be poured out upon all creation. *2 Baruch* differs somewhat from the other Jewish apocalypses in that it identifies wisdom with the law more closely (38.1-4;

---

1. So B and C, though there is some variation among the texts with respect to the content of that revelation; see Isaac, I, p. 74.

2. Stone, 'Revealed Things', p. 425.

3. *1 En.* 5.7-8; 38.1-4 (related to the appearance of 'the Son of Man' = 'the Righteous One'); 82.1-2; 89.32-33, 41, 51-54, 74; 90.6-7, 34-35; 91.10; 93.10.

4. E. Brandenburger, *Die Verborgenheit Gottes im Weltgeschehen* (Zürich: Theologischer Verlag, 1981), pp. 198-99.

5. This corresponds to a theme that is common in the apocalypses, namely the moral and religious decline that will precede the end of this age; see Vielhauer, p. 589 (Dan. 2; *4 Ezra* 5.55; 14.10; *2 Bar.* 85.10).

6. Vielhauer, p. 589.

44.14; 48.24; 51.3-4; 77.15-16), and so views the present age slightly
more optimistically. Nevertheless, the need for heavenly revelation in
this age is still a major theme even in *2 Baruch*.

d. *Heavenly Revelation and the Hellenistic Zeitgeist*

The features listed above all reinforce the need for heavenly revelations as viewed by the Jewish apocalypses. Since, however, these
apocalyptic writings are by no means unique in setting forth the need
for the revelation of wisdom, our discussion needs to be set in a
broader religio-cultural cor.text. That 'higher wisdom through revelation' was a general characteristic of religion from the beginning of the
second century BC has been competently argued by Martin Hengel,
who has gathered numerous examples of analogous phenomena from a
variety of religious movements of the hellenistic period.[1] As Hengel
contends, Jewish apocalypses stand 'in a wider cultural context as a
counter-movement to "Greek alienation"'. As such, they can be truly
called 'a fruit of the Hellenistic period'.[2]

Still, it is important to highlight the fundamentally Jewish character
of these writings. While not denying that there was, in numerous particulars, direct influence on Jewish apocalypticism by hellenistic
thought, the combined emphasis on (1) the transcendence of God, (2)
the heaven–earth dualism, and (3) the hiddenness of wisdom, in the
context of Jewish notions of election and covenant, is particular to the
Jewish apocalypses. Furthermore, as we shall observe in the following
chapters, the function of revelation as set forth in these writings stands
generally within the range of expression of the other major Jewish
writings of this period. So we are dealing here not primarily with a
phenomenon that was taken over directly from an alien culture—
though, again, one can hardly dispute the fact that there was extensive
borrowing with respect to details. Rather, it seems we have to do pri-

---

1. Hengel, I, pp. 210-18.
2. Hengel, I, p. 212. Similar is the argument of J.J. Collins, 'Jewish Apocalyptic
against its Hellenistic Near Eastern Environment', *BASOR* 220 (1975), pp. 27-36.
Collins (p. 27) offers the following explanation: 'The similarities which we find
throughout the Hellenistic Near East are due primarily to the fact that traditions which
had much in common to begin with. . . were subjected to the same new
circumstances'.

marily with an inner-Jewish development that was analogous to what transpired in many religious movements of the hellenistic age.[1]

2. *The Achievement of Heavenly Revelations*

The Jewish apocalypses emphasize the need for special revelations from heaven. But how could one achieve such a revelatory experience? Two factors are of importance here: (1) the moral and spiritual qualifications of those who would receive special heavenly revelations, and (2) the variety of practices regularly associated with revelatory experiences. I shall direct most of my attention to the latter, though the former is not insignificant for my purposes and merits at least brief consideration.

a. *Qualifications for Heavenly Revelations*
Throughout the Jewish apocalypses reference is made to the righteous character of the seer. In many cases, in fact, it is precisely these traits that enable him to receive revelations from heaven. In Daniel it is stated at the outset that the hero 'resolved not to defile himself with the royal food and wine' (1.8); and as the writing progresses, we are informed that God gives true wisdom only to those who are 'wise' (2.21; cf. 12.10).[2] Numerous references to the righteousness of the seer are present as well in both *1 Enoch* (1.2; 10.17; 12.4; 15.1; 19.3; 92.1) and *2 Enoch* (64.5, both rec. but esp. J; 68.7, rec. J) with the seer being portrayed in the former as the prototype of the righteous wise man.[3] *4 Ezra* also makes explicit the connection between a righteous life and heavenly revelations in a number of passages; for example:

1. My position diverges significantly from that of H.D. Betz ('On the Problem of the Religio-Historical Understanding of Apocalypticism', *JTC* 6 [1969], pp. 134-56) who argues that Jewish (as well as Christian) apocalypticism 'must be seen and presented as peculiar expressions within the entire development of Hellenistic syncretism'. In contrast to Betz, I would emphasize the fundamentally Jewish nature of these writings. Cf. Stone, 'Revealed Things', p. 438.

2. Dan. 9.23 links the revelation explicitly with God's judgment of Daniel, 'As soon as you began to pray, an answer was given, which I have come to tell you, for you are highly esteemed'.

3. Rau, p. 88. Also S. Uhlig, 'Das äthiopische Henochbuch', *JSHRZ*, 5.6, p. 493, who lists many references. For broader Jewish parallels with respect to the righteousness of Enoch, see Uhlig, p. 466.

I will again declare to you greater things than these, because your voice has surely been heard before the Most High; for the Mighty One has seen your uprightness and has also observed the purity which you have maintained from your youth (6.31-32).[1]

And the same is the case in *2 Baruch*,[2] *3 Baruch*,[3] the *Apocalypse of Abraham*[4] and the *Testament of Abraham*.[5]

Such references to the righteousness and wisdom of the seer perform a variety of functions in the Jewish apocalypses.[6] In certain cases, they are almost mandatory given the reputation of the ascribed authors.[7] Yet it is probable that in some cases such statements also

---

1. See Box, *Apocalypse of Ezra*, p. 43, and M.A. Knibb (with R.J. Coggins), *The First and Second Books of Esdras* (Cambridge: Cambridge University Press, 1979), p. 153. These writers recognize the connection between a righteous life and the experience of revelation, and both translate the latter (*pudicitiam*) as 'chastity'. Cf. 10.38-39; 12.7, 9, 36; 13.14, 53-56. Also, see Brandenburger, *Verborgenheit Gottes*, p. 122, for a catalogue of the various ways the concepts are connected in *4 Ezra*. Knibb (*Second Esdras*, p. 153) writes, 'Behind these statements we should perhaps see the author's convictions about his own standing before God'.

2. *2 Bar.* 54.5; cf., however, 54.9, though such exclamations of humility only serve to reinforce the overall impression that Baruch is righteous in character.

3. *3 Bar.* 17.3 (Gk); cf. 1.3, 6 (both versions). In *3 Bar.* 11.7 (Gk) Michael addresses the angelic guide as the 'interpreter of revelations to those who pass through life rightly'. Contrast those who pass through their lives badly and are judged (4.5, Gk version); Gaylord, '3 Baruch', p. 674. Picard ('Observations', p. 92) refers to *3 Bar.* 1.6 (Gk), the command to 'cease irritating God', as the 'épreuve qualifiante' for the revelation of divine mysteries.

4. 23.3; cf. 9.6; 10.7, 15. Cf. Box and Landsman, p. 45. Nickelsburg (*Jewish Literature*, pp. 297-98) notes that the primary emphasis here is on the fact that Abraham forsook idolatry.

5. The *Testament of Abraham* is more difficult in this respect, since Abraham clearly resists God's summons through the angelic figure Death. Nevertheless, great stress is placed on Abraham's righteous character in this work; cf. rec. A, 2.3; 4.6; 8.2, 4; 15.13-15; 16.5, 9, 11, 15; 17.7, 10, 19; 18.1, 6, 11; 19.7; 20.3, 14; and rec. B, 1.2; 2.4, 10, 13; 4.10; 6.6; 8.2; 9.4; 13.1, 5, 9, 13. Box (*Testament of Abraham*, p. 1) argues that the writer placed special emphasis on Abraham's hospitality. Nickelsburg ('Eschatology in the Testament of Abraham', in *Studies on the Testament of Abraham*, p. 25) may be correct, however, when he suggests that the tour of creation may have been cut short by Abraham's actions; see 9.6, which suggests a trip of greater scope than we find in this work.

6. E.g. in *1 Enoch* certain references (19.3; 37.4; cf. 10.17) function to reinforce the greatness and the uniqueness of the revelation, thus securing the reader's attention.

7. For a collection of evidence that demonstrates that Enoch's reputation as a wise man was widely known, see Uhlig, pp. 466, 493-94, and Janssen, p. 235. On the

represent the self-conception of the apocalyptists. In their view, it seems, revelations come only to those who are wise and righteous; conversely, such experiences and the teaching they convey lead those who are receptive into a deeper experience of wisdom and righteousness. It is, therefore, only for those who are so qualified that the various practices associated with heavenly revelations are effective.[1]

b. *Practices Associated with Heavenly Revelations*
There is no practice, or cluster of practices, that is viewed as normative for heavenly revelations in the Jewish apocalypses. Yet several practices are commonly associated with revelatory experiences. In some cases the association between practice and revelation is loose; in others, the revelation is explicitly said to come in response to the actions of the seer. There are also several cases in the apocalypses in which the revelation appears to be spontaneous, with such practices lacking.[2] It is better, however, to focus on general patterns instead of exceptions, and so to consider briefly the types of practices commonly associated with heavenly revelations in the Jewish apocalypses.

1. Prayer is one of the most basic activities associated with heavenly revelations. The revelations attributed to Daniel come only after he seeks God's help in prayer (Dan. 2.18-19).[3] Very similar are the accounts in *4 Ezra*, *2 Baruch* and *3 Baruch*.[4] Most of these prayers are straightforward requests for revelation, though Dan. 9.3-19 is a prayer of confession and supplication that Daniel might see the completion of the 'desolations of Jerusalem' (9.1).[5]

2. Another practice connected with revelatory experiences in the Jewish apocalypses is fasting. Such fasts can be partial[6] or com-

wide use of the designation 'Scribe of righteousness' for Enoch, see F. Schmidt, 'Le Testament d'Abraham', I, pp. 65, 69.
1. Note Ezra's prayer for revelation: 'If I have found favor in your sight, and if it is possible, and if I am worthy, show me this also' (*4 Ezra* 4.44).
2. *1 En.* 1.2; 37.1 (presumably similar to the first, since it is 'the vision which Enoch saw the second time').
3. Cf. Dan. 9.3, 20, where prayer is combined with fasting, the wearing of sackcloth and ashes, and confession.
4. *4 Ezra* 5.13; 6.31, 35 (with weeping and fasting); 9.23-28 (with a partial fast); *2 Bar.* 54.6-7; 56.1; 76.1; *3 Bar.* 1.4-5 (both rec.); 4.13-15 (Gk, with crying; Slav., with fasting and crying).
5. See Hengel, I, p. 203.
6. Dan. 10.2-3 (no 'choice food', i.e. meat or wine); *4 Ezra* 9.23-28 (no meat or wine, but only flowers; linked with prayer); 12.51 (only flowers); *Apoc. Abr.* 9.7

plete,[1] varying significantly in their duration.[2] Despite their frequency of mention, however, the precise significance of these fasts and the way in which they were believed to bring about revelations from heaven are extremely difficult to pinpoint. With the possible exception of *2 Enoch*,[3] one finds no ascetic ideal in the Jewish apocalypses—though such tendencies were certainly widespread in the hellenistic age and seem to have come to expression at Qumran.[4] Fasting in the Jewish apocalypses is often connected with prayer and mourning, and its significance appears to be related intrinsically to these experiences. For the moment, however, it is sufficient to note that fasting is viewed as 'the usual preparation for the reception of supernatural communications'.[5]

3. Confession, mourning and the contemplation of God's judgment are also integral to the experience of receiving revelation in several Jewish apocalypses. Such is the case in Daniel 9, where, in addition to prayer and fasting, Daniel seeks God by taking on

(no wine or food cooked by fire). Knibb (*Second Esdras*, p. 218) suggests, 'Ezra's diet also corresponds to the diet of man in the period before the flood' (cf. Gen. 1.29; 9.3).

1. *4 Ezra* 5.13, 20 (with prayer and mourning); 6.31, 35-37 (with prayer and mourning); *2 Bar.* 9.2 (with mourning); 12.5; 20.5-6 (no bread or water); 21.1-2; 43.3; 47.2; *Apoc. Abr.* 12.1-2. Since *4 Ezra* 6.35-38 mentions three weeks of fasting, several authorities have argued that the introduction to the first dialogue (3.1-3) also contained a fast of one week's duration; cf. Box, *Apocalypse of Ezra*, p. 44, and Knibb, *Second Esdras*, p. 155.

2. The fasts run (a) until evening (*2 Bar.* 5.6-7), (b) for seven days (*4 Ezra* 5.13, 20; 6.31, 35-37; 9.23-28; 12.39, 51; *2 Bar.* 9.2; 12.5; 20.5-6; 21.1-2; 43.3) and (c) for forty days (*Apoc. Abr.* 9.7; 12.1-2). On the seven day interval, see Bogaert, II, p. 26. A.Y. Collins ('Numerical Symbolism in Jewish and Early Christian Apocalyptic Literature', *ANRW*, II.21.2, pp. 1247-49) argues that this use of numerical symbolism indicates that there is 'a certain orderliness in revelatory experience'.

3. *2 En.* 56.2 (both recensions) states that Enoch did not eat after he ascended to heaven and was there anointed (22.7-8).

4. Cf. Hengel (I, pp. 213, 247), who connects the ideal of asceticism at Qumran with the movement toward the 'fundamental superiority of the "prophets of the East"' in the hellenistic age.

5. Charles, *Apocalypse of Baruch*, p. 13. Fasting is, of course, associated with prophetic activity in a variety of sources, whether pagan or Christian; see P.R. Arbesmann, *Das Fasten bei Griechen und Römern* (Berlin: Töpelmann, 1929), pp. 97-102, and, more extensively, *idem*, 'Fasting and Prophecy in Pagan and Christian Antiquity', *Trad* 7 (1949-51), pp. 1-71. Fasting in order to produce visions is not unknown in Talmudic sources; cf. S. Lowy, 'The Motivation of Fasting in Talmudic Literature', *JJS* 9 (1958), pp. 19-38.

sackcloth and ashes and confessing his sins and those of the people (vv. 3-4, 20). The fact that he refrains from anointing himself (10.3) is also a sign of mourning (cf. v. 2). And in both Daniel 9 and 10 this self-humiliation and mourning provides the immediate occasion for the reception of revelation.[1] Furthermore, the cause of Daniel's mourning is clearly related to God's judgment on his people in the exile (9.1-3). Such mourning is also present in *4 Ezra*, *2 Baruch* and *3 Baruch*, where the occasion bears a close resemblance to that of Daniel.

4. Meditation is another practice associated with heavenly revelations in the Jewish apocalypses. In several cases the seer receives a revelation while he meditates on a passage of Scripture, as in Daniel 9 where Daniel's vision of Gabriel is predicated on his meditation on Jer. 25.11-12.[2] More important for my purposes, however, are the cases where a revelation is related specifically to a meditation on the Merkabah of Ezekiel 1 and Isaiah 6,[3] since an association between reflections on these chapters and mystical experiences was well established in the Merkabah tradition.[4]

5. One also notes an emphasis on time and place in the Jewish apocalypses.[5] In some writings revelations are explicitly associated with nighttime (*T. Abr.* 6.1 [rec. B]; 5.7 [rec. A];[6] *T. Levi* 2.4-5),

---

1. See Dan. 9.23 and 10.12. D. Satran ('Daniel: Seer, Philosopher, Holy Man', in *Ideal Figures*, pp. 35-36) argues that chs. 9 and 10 represent 'two distinct stages in the development of the figure of the seer', since, in his opinion, the connection between 'self-affliction' and revelation is only made explicit in 10.12. Unfortunately, he misses the significance of Dan. 9.23. Anointing the body with oil was a mark of joy often associated with feasting (Eccl. 9.8; Ps. 23.5; Amos 6.6), and so to avoid this practice was an outward sign of grief and mourning (*Apoc. Abr.* 9.7; 2 Sam. 14.2); see Box and Landsman, p. 45.

2. Rowland (*Open Heaven*, pp. 214-17) points to a number of other examples, including *4 Ezra* 6.38-59 where the seer meditates on his own version of the account of creation in Genesis 1.

3. *1 En.* 14.8-23 is certainly the earliest example of this specific activity, though we should mention as well *1 Enoch* 71; *2 Enoch* 22 (both recensions) and context; *Apocalypse of Abraham* 17–18 and context. Cf. the Christian use of this tradition in Rev. 4. For a reasonably comprehensive discussion of examples, see Gruenwald, *Apocalyptic and Merkavah Mysticism*, pp. 32-72.

4. On Merkabah mysticism as one of the heirs of Jewish apocalypticism, see below, §2.4.b.

5. Brandenburger, *Verborgenheit Gottes*, p. 115.

6. Box (*Testament of Abraham*, p. 44) argues that the shorter recension is the original here, and that the seventh hour, immediately after midnight, was 'the time most congenial for the reception of divine revelation'; cf. *b. Ber.* 3b.

which is hardly surprising in view of the fact that apocalyptic revelations often come while the seer sleeps (*1 En.* 13.7-8; *2 En.* 1.2-3;[1] *4 Ezra* 3.1-3; 10.58–11.1; *2 Bar.* 52.7–53.1).[2] Closely connected with this is the importance given to solitude in several writings (*1 En.* 10.2;[3] *2 Bar.* 20.5; 43.3). There are, as well, numerous references to specific places of revelation, such as rivers,[4] fields,[5] mountains,[6] trees[7] and the Holy of Holies.[8] So there is, on the one hand, some relationship between the state of sleep and revelatory experiences in the apocalypses, though apart from *4 Ezra* we find no explicit statements that people go to sleep in hopes of receiving a revelation.[9] On the other hand, revelations often come to those who spend lengthy periods of time meditating at sites that are sacred or that have some association with revelatory experiences.

   6. One final factor possibly associated with the reception of revelations, at least in two of the writings, is sexual abstinence. Absti-

---

1. On the differences between the recensions here, see Andersen, p. 106.

2. Dreams can also come before sleep (Dan. 10.9) or after sleep (*2 En.* 1.6-10, both recensions). In any case, as Niditch (p. 236) writes, 'Dream-night-sleep-time is the liminal time'. The association between sleep and revelation is especially clear in *4 Ezra* 10.59, where 'The seer is actually told to sleep in order to receive a vision. His motivation for sleeping is the hope for divine revelation' (Niditch, p. 236); cf. D.S. Russell, *The Method and Message of Jewish Apocalyptic* (Philadelphia: Westminster Press, 1964), pp. 164-66.

3. Here we have an injunction to Noah, who is to withdraw to receive the angelic revelations; cf. Dillmann, *Das Buch Henoch*, p. 99; Charles, *Book of Enoch*, p. 193; Black, *Book of Enoch*, p. 133.

4. Dan. 10.4; 12.5; *1 En.* 13.7-8; cf. Ezek. 1 and the Slavonic introduction to *3 Baruch*. M.E. Stone (*Scriptures, Sects and Visions* [Philadelphia: Fortress Press, 1980], p. 85) suggests that behind such visions may lie 'a magical, meditative technique known from the Graeco-Roman sphere which involved contemplation of a body of water until visions were seen in it'.

5. *4 Ezra* 9.23-26; 10.58; 12.51; 14.37.

6. Mount Horeb is the place of revelation in the *Apocalypse of Abraham* (9.8; 12.3-10), while the revelatory site in *2 Baruch* is Mount Zion (*2 Bar.* 13.1; 20.5-6; 21.1-2; 47.2; 76.3; cf. the Slavonic introduction to *3 Baruch*).

7. *4 Ezra* 14.1 and *2 Bar.* 6.1; 55.1-2. On the first passage, Oesterley (*II Esdras*, p. 165) argues that 'some special, well-known oak is meant', somewhere in the neighborhood of Jerusalem. Cf. Box, *Apocalypse of Ezra*, p. 108.

8. *2 Bar.* 34.1; 35.1.

9. Niditch, p. 236; E.L. Ehrlich (*Der Traum im Alten Testament* [Berlin: Töpelmann, 1953], pp. 13-15) argues that there are clear examples of incubation in the OT, but as in most of the Jewish apocalypses there is no explicit statement that the seers lie down in certain places specifically to receive a revelation.

nence from sex is perhaps implied in *2 Enoch*, where Nir the priest is said not to have slept with his wife Sothonim 'from the day that the Lord had appointed him in front of the face of the people' (71.2).[1] In this case, however, the revelation occurs only after her death (71.9-11 [rec. A]), so the link between sexual abstinence and revelation is by no means explicit. Much discussion has been generated by the statement in *1 En.* 83.2, 'I saw two [visions] before I got married'. On the basis of this passage, Beer argued that virginity was viewed as a necessary condition of the prophetic office,[2] though such a position creates certain problems because elsewhere in *1 Enoch* it is not said that the visions occurred before the seer was married.[3] Yet we must be prepared to allow for differences between the views of the various authors represented in *1 Enoch*.[4] We must also reckon with the possibility that sexual abstinence, at least on a temporary basis, is assumed by the authors of the other sections.[5] The ideal of celibacy was certainly strong at Qumran.[6] And while it does not seem to have been a major concern for the majority of the writers of Jewish apocalypses, it is possible that it was a factor in the thinking of at least two of the authors with which we are concerned—namely, the authors of *2 Enoch* and chs. 83–90 of *1 Enoch*.

There is in the Jewish apocalypses no sequence of steps that leads consistently to a revelation from heaven. Rather, various activities and practices are associated with revelatory experiences. Yet while the evidence by no means suggests that the apocalyptists viewed rigid theurgic methods as necessary prerequisites to receiving revelation, the similarities of practice and the commonalities of various revelatory experiences are striking and should not be overlooked. The

---

1. Both recensions, though recension J contains the additional words 'nor had he touched her'.

2. Beer (p. 288), who cites Mt. 19.12 and Jer. 16.2; cf. Black, *Book of Enoch*, p. 254.

3. See Martin, pp. 193-94.

4. Charles (*Book of Enoch*, p. 182) argues on the basis of this point that chs. 83–90 came from a different hand than the other sections of *1 Enoch*.

5. Milik (p. 42) sees an allusion, not to an 'ascetic' tendency, but to 'the rites of incubation which demanded temporary continence'.

6. M. Black, 'The Tradition of Hasidaean-Essene Asceticism: Its Origins and Influence', in *Aspects du Judéo-Christianisme: Colloque de Strasbourg* (Paris: Presses Universitaires de France, 1965), pp. 19-33.

judgment of Adela Collins seems most accurate in this regard: 'Divine revelation cannot be controlled, but it can be encouraged and there are orderly and appropriate ways to invite it'.[1]

3. *The Media of Heavenly Revelations*

An understanding of the media of heavenly revelations in the Jewish apocalypses is integral to any study of the revelatory experiences in these writings. Yet in view of the scope of the material, we must limit our discussion to matters that relate closely to our overall purpose. Our concern in this section, therefore, is not to provide an exhaustive form-critical analysis of the materials,[2] but to survey the means by which revelation comes to the apocalyptic seers. In this way we hope to illumine the kinds of revelatory experiences characteristic of Jewish apocalypticism.

a. *Diverse Kinds of Revelation*
A number of references to diverse forms of revelation occur in the Jewish apocalypses, and it is best to begin by mentioning these. There are several cases where 'the word of the Lord' comes to Baruch in a manner that closely resembles the OT prophets, and which often results in a dialogue between the seer and God (see *2 Bar.* 10.1, and the opening of the book). These experiences appear to be non-visionary, though the dialogue in *2 Bar.* 22.2–30.5 is introduced by a statement that 'the heaven was opened, and I saw, and strength was given to me, and a voice was heard from on high' (22.1).[3] A similar dialogue between Ezra and the Most High is found in *4 Ezra* 14.1-26, where God speaks out of a bush in a manner reminiscent of the experience of Moses in Exodus 3. A somewhat different revelatory experience is presented in *4 Ezra* 14.37-48, where Ezra drinks from a cup and gains understanding and wisdom, which enable him to dictate

---

1. A.Y. Collins, p. 1249.
2. This kind of analysis is available in J.J. Collins, *Daniel, with an Introduction to Apocalyptic Literature* (Grand Rapids: Eerdmans, 1984), pp. 6-11, 14-17.
3. The voice is clearly the voice of God. In non-visionary contexts, cf. the dialogues in *2 Bar.* 1.2–5.4; 13.2–20.6; 41.1–43.3; and 48.1–52.7, where it is initiated by Baruch's prayer. The 'word of the Lord' produces no dialogue in *2 Bar.* 10.1-3. Of course, 22.1 may imply that these other dialogues were themselves visionary in nature, but this is uncertain, and there are no contextual references to support such an interpretation.

Scripture as well as the seventy apocalyptic writings. Such instances suggest that ideas as to the media of revelation in the Jewish apocalypses were somewhat fluid.

b. *Revelation through Dream Visions*
The dominant mode of revelation in the Jewish apocalypses, however, is that of the dream vision. It is impossible to insist on a rigid distinction between 'dreams' and 'visions', since the writers themselves refer to these experiences interchangeably.[1] Furthermore, since the majority of heavenly ascents take place in a dream vision,[2] there is no reason to distinguish sharply between heavenly ascents and other varieties of dream visions— though, for purposes of analysis, it may be helpful to deal with them separately. So I shall include under my discussion of dream visions several phenomena: (1) symbolic dream visions, (2) angelic disclosures and dialogues, which form dominates the 'historical' or 'horizontal' apocalypses, and (3) heavenly ascents, the standard mode of revelation in the 'vertical' apocalypses.[3]

1. *Symbolic Dream Visions*. The symbolic dream vision is a development of a form of revelation that can be traced back to the symbolic

1. J. Lindblom (*Gesichte und Offenbarungen* [Lund: Gleerup, 1968], pp. 32-33) argues that dreams come during sleep, while visions come during waking hours when the visionary is sure that he is not asleep—but he also acknowledges that visions in the apocalypses are often designated as 'dream visions' (p. 27); see also *idem*, 'Die Vorstellung vom Sprechen Jahwes zu den Menschen im Alten Testament', *ZAW* 75 (1963), p. 273: 'Traum und Nachtgesicht (oder Gesicht) promiscue gebraucht wurden. . .', with many examples from the Jewish apocalypses. Cf. J.S. Hanson, 'Dreams and Visions in the Graeco-Roman World and Early Christianity', in *ANRW*, II.23.2, p. 1408, and VanderKam, *Enoch*, pp. 134-35. W. Bousset (*Die Offenbarung Johannis* [6th edn; Göttingen: Vandenhoeck & Ruprecht, 1906], p. 4) argues that the apocalypses moved from dream visions to ecstatic visions; see also Vielhauer, p. 583.
2. The one exception is the *Testament of Abraham* (9.6-8 [rec. A] and esp. 7.18–8.3 [rec. B]), where Abraham is taken up 'in the body'. M. Dean-Otting (*Heavenly Journeys: A Study of the Motif in Hellenistic Jewish Literature* [Frankfurt: Lang, 1984], p. 196) correctly observes that in rec. A (9.8), 'the idea that bodily weight must actually be carried has taken hold and Abraham is conveyed by means of a chariot'. Of course, as Russell (p. 162) notes, our modern distinction between 'subjective' and 'objective' would have meant very little to these writers.
3. I do not dispute J.J. Collins's decision to list these items separately (*Daniel*, pp. 6-19), since this is proper from a form-critical perspective. My concerns, however, center around the phenomenology of revelation in Jewish apocalypticism, and so his concerns and mine are not identical.

visions of Amos (chs. 7 and 8) and Jeremiah (chs. 1 and 24).[1] With the exception of *1 Enoch* 83–90,[2] the symbolic visions of Jewish apocalypticism follow a common pattern:

1. Indication of the circumstances.
2. Description of the vision, introduced by a term such as 'behold'.
3. Request for interpretation, often because of fear.
4. Interpretation by an angel.
5. Variable concluding material.[3]

While a number of these visions can be traced back to Daniel,[4] several are certainly independent of Daniel. Consequently, we cannot speak of a single stream of tradition.[5] Nevertheless, symbolic visions are a common form of revelation in the Jewish apocalypses, and it is helpful to understand their use in these writings.

Later I shall discuss the function of heavenly revelations (see Chapter 3). Here, however, my concern is with the purpose of this mode of revelation in the Jewish apocalypses, answering the question: 'What is gained by the use of this particular form to communicate the heavenly revelations?'

It seems that the use of symbolic dream visions reinforces certain fundamental notions of the Jewish apocalypses. Clearly, the apocalyptic visions are highly symbolic; and while the roots of this type of symbolism are present in the OT prophets, the apocalypses have developed the foliage. As Koch notes, 'what is plain in the prophets—a transparently simple image—is heightened into the grotesque by the

1. Niditch traces in detail the development of this form; cf. K. Koch, 'Vom profetischen zum apokalyptischen Visionsbericht', in *Apocalypticism*, pp. 413-46.

2. The vision of 83.2-5 is very brief and a correspondingly brief interpretation is provided by Mahalalel in 83.7-9, while the animal apocalypse (chs. 85–90) is a lengthy symbolic vision without interpretation.

3. I am indebted to J.J. Collins, *Daniel*, p. 6, for this outline. My only problem with it is at (4), since in *2 Bar.* 39.2–40.4 and *4 Ezra* 13.21-56 the interpretations are provided by God himself; cf. *4 Ezra* 12.10, where the giver of the interpretation appears to be the Most High (12.6) and the 'sovereign Lord' (12.7), though 12.39 seems to imply that an angel was responsible. Other examples of symbolic dream visions are to be found in Dan. 7.2-27; 8.2-26; *2 Bar.* 53.1–76.5; *4 Ezra* 9.38–10.59.

4. See G.K. Beale, *The Use of Daniel in Jewish Apocalyptic and in the Revelation of St. John* (Lanham, MD: University Press of America, 1984).

5. J.J. Collins (*Daniel*, p. 8) notes that the dream visions of *1 Enoch* and the vision of the cloud and the waters in *2 Baruch* (53.1-12; interpretation in 55.3–76.5) are clearly independent of Daniel.

apocalyptic writers and is now incomprehensible without interpretation'.[1] Revelation in the Jewish apocalypses, therefore, is no longer given directly, at least as a rule. When it comes it is cloaked in symbolism and is intelligible only with the help of a heavenly figure.

2. *Angelic Disclosures and Dialogues.* Angels, as we have seen, are generally involved in the symbolic dream visions of Jewish apocalypticism. They also, however, function independently to communicate revelation to the seers. This mode of revelation, which like the dream visions is also visionary in character,[2] is evident especially in *4 Ezra* 4.1–9.25, as well as in Daniel 10–11. Also bordering on this category is *Jubilees* 2–50, where an angel dictates to Moses from the heavenly tablets (cf. 1.29; 6.35).

The purpose of angelic disclosures appears to be twofold: (1) to reinforce the indirect nature of revelation in line with the apocalyptists' views of divine transcendence, and (2) to guarantee the trustworthiness of the communication, since truth resides primarily in heaven and the revelation has come via a prominent figure from there.[3] The purpose of the angelic dialogues, particularly those of *4 Ezra*, is not to refute heresy, but to set the stage for the primarily experiential theodicy that follows.[4]

3. *Heavenly Ascents.* Characteristic of the 'vertical' apocalypses is the theme of heavenly ascent,[5] a mode of revelation particularly significant for our purposes. Reports of such experiences are common

1. Koch, *Rediscovery*, p. 26; cf. Russell, pp. 122-27.
2. See *4 Ezra* 4.1–5.13, where the seer is sleeping; possibly also *4 Ezra* 7.1–9.25. See, however, *4 Ezra* 5.31–6.28, where Ezra is standing during the dialogue. J.J. Collins (*Daniel*, p. 9) points out that dialogue in dream reports was rare in the Near East, though in the prophets of Israel it had long been used to supplement vision reports.
3. This is especially clear in *Jubilees*, where it is the 'Angel of the Presence' who is the agent of revelation, the same figure who wrote 'the book of the first law'; see Davenport, p. 12, and Charles, *Jubilees*, p. 7.
4. On the purpose of *4 Ezra*, see the discussion in Chapter 1.
5. There is, however, some overlap with the 'horizontal' apocalypses in this respect. In *2 Bar.* 22.1 the new series of revelations come after 'the heaven was opened'; cf. W.C. van Unnik, 'Die "geöffneten Himmel" in der Offenbarungsvision des Apokryphons des Johannes', in *Apophoreta: Festschrift für Ernst Haenchen* (ed. W. Eltester; Berlin: Töpelmann, 1964), p. 272. Whether an apocalypse contains an ascent to heaven or not, it is clear, of course, that true revelation comes only from heaven.

in various cultures and religions. And Alan Segal is probably correct to speak of heavenly ascent as 'a deep structure of Hellenistic thought'.[1]

It is necessary, however, here to introduce two distinctions. First, we must differentiate between permanent and temporary ascents. As Bousset long ago argued:

> Und zwar handelt es sich um eine eigentlich eschatologische Gedankenreihe, nämlich um die Lehre, dass die Seele nach ihrer Loslösung vom Leibe durch den Tod die Himmelsregionen durchwandert, um vor den Thron Gottes zu gelangen, zweitens aber auch um eine mystisch ekstatische Lehre, dass dem Gläubigen und Frommen der Aufstieg zum höchsten Gott schon in diesem Leben möglich sei, und eine daran sich anschliessende bestimmte Praxis der Ekstase.[2]

In the Jewish apocalypses we are dealing primarily with temporary ascents—though *1 Enoch* 70–71 describes the permanent ascent of Enoch to heaven (esp. 70.1-2; 71.15-17), the *Apocalypse of Zephaniah* is unclear in this regard,[3] and in the *Testament of Abraham* a temporary ascent in the body precedes the permanent ascent of the soul in death (*T. Abr.* 20.9-15, rec. A; 14.7-9, rec. B). A second distinction to be made when considering heavenly ascents in the Jewish apocalypses is that between ascents that take the form of a tour (*1 Enoch*, chs. 1–82; *Testament of Abraham*) and those where the seer proceeds more directly through a series of heavens (*Testament of Levi; 2 Enoch; Apocalypse of Abraham*), even though these two types of ascents may have similar functions.[4]

---

1. A.F. Segal, 'Heavenly Ascent in Hellenistic Judaism, Early Christianity and their Environment', *ANRW*, II.23.2, p. 1337. He concludes his article by suggesting that 'it is possible to see the heavenly journey of the soul, its consequent promise of immortality and the corollary necessity of periodic ecstatic journeys to heaven as the dominant mythical constellation of late classical antiquity' (p. 1388).

2. W. Bousset, 'Die Himmelsreise der Seele', *ARW* 4 (1901), p. 136; cf. M. Smith, *Clement of Alexandria and a Secret Gospel of Mark* (Cambridge, MA: Harvard University Press, 1973), p. 238.

3. M.R. James (*The Apocryphal New Testament* [Oxford: Clarendon Press, 1924], p. 530) argues that the opening described the death of a righteous man, though there are also indications that Zephaniah's role closely resembles that of Paul in the *Apocalypse of Paul*; see the parallels in Himmelfarb, pp. 147-48.

4. J.J. Collins, *Daniel*, pp. 16-17.

As with other media of revelation in the Jewish apocalypses, heavenly ascents are generally visionary in character.[1] One cannot, however, distinguish sharply between such visions and accounts of literal bodily ascensions.[2] The heavenly realm, which is hidden from humans, is opened to the seer. Yet the emphasis is not so much on the spectacular nature of the seer's experience as on the greatness of the revelation that is communicated.[3] This impression of greatness is reinforced by the use of a number of devices within the ascent accounts— for example, revelations by angels,[4] visions, and heavenly books and tablets.[5]

All this multiplication of various means of revelation functions to authenticate the revelation. This is evident especially in Enoch's exhortations to his descendants, where the seer highlights a number of items associated with the heavenly ascent itself:

> Concerning the children of righteousness, concerning the elect ones of the world, and concerning the plant of truth, I will speak these things, my children, verily I, Enoch, myself, and let you know (about it) according to that which was revealed to me from the heavenly vision, that which I have learned from the words of the holy angels, and understood from the heavenly tablets (*1 En.* 93.2).[6]

1. The only exception is the *Testament of Abraham*, where the ascent is clearly 'in the body'; *T. Abr.* 9.6, rec. A; 7.18 and 8.3, rec. B. In several apocalypses (*1 En.* 13.7-8; *T. Levi* 2.5-6) the seer is sleeping, while in *2 Enoch* the vision begins while he is asleep (1.3-5, both recensions) and the ascent occurs after he awakens (1.6-7; 3.1-3, both recensions).

2. A.F. Segal ('Paul and Ecstasy', in *Society of Biblical Literature 1986 Seminar Papers* [ed. K.H. Richards; Atlanta: Scholars Press, 1986], p. 558) notes that in Merkabah mysticism the adept often speaks of traveling from place to place in heaven, while it is clear that his body is stationary on earth.

3. F. Lentzen-Deis ('Das Motiv der "Himmelsöffnung" in verschiedenen Gattungen der Umweltliteratur des Neuen Testaments', *Bib* 50 [1969], p. 310) notes that 'Die Himmelsöffnung hat also. . . die Funktion, die Überschreitung der Schwelle der "Transzendenz", die Eröffnung der himmlischen Sphäre zu markieren'.

4. The overlap between angelic disclosures and angelic dialogues is so extensive that we cannot begin to list all of the relevant texts. We can, however, mention a few texts from *1 Enoch*: 21.5; 33.4; 40.2; 43.3; 46.2; 72.1; 74.2; 75.3, 4; 79.6; 80.1; cf. Charles, *Book of Enoch*, p. 174.

5. Visions are used in *Apoc. Abr.* 21.7; 23.1, 4; 24.3; 26.7; 29.4, 17 (the 'picture of creation'); heavenly books and tablets are referred to in *1 En.* 39.2; 81.1; 82.7; etc.

6. This function is also explicit in *1 En.* 82.7, though implicit throughout the apocalypses.

There is, therefore, significant overlap between the various modes of revelation in the Jewish apocalypses. All are basically visionary in character. Yet they can be classified for purposes of analysis as symbolic dream visions, or as angelic disclosures and discourses, or as heavenly ascents. All three classes must be taken into consideration if we are to come to an understanding of the media of revelation in Jewish apocalypticism.

4. *Genuine Visionary Experience or Literary Convention?*

Involved in any discussion of the revelations depicted in the Jewish apocalypses is the question: Do genuine visionary experiences actually underlie the presentations of these documents, or are the visions described merely literary conventions? While this question may have surfaced to some extent earlier in my study, it is appropriate here to consider it directly and in some detail. I shall do this by (1) sketching out some of the positions that have been taken with respect to the question, (2) examining positive evidences for genuine visionary experiences among the apocalyptists, (3) considering problems that arise from such a view, and, finally, offering my own working hypothesis in the conclusion to this chapter. My goal throughout is not to comment on the validity of the experiences, but to inquire as to the self-understanding of the Jewish apocalyptists themselves.

a. *A Sketch of Various Views*
There have always been those who have insisted, for one apocalyptic writing or another, that the visionary experience described was merely a literary convention used by an author to convey a message to his or her readers.[1] Among those who discuss the problem, however, this has always been a minority position.[2] Most twentieth-century writers on the subject allow that actual visionary experiences among the apocalyptic seers is a reasonable possibility, though they acknowledge that the content of these visions has been expanded and reworked

---

1. E.g. A. Sabatier, 'L'apocalypse juive et la philosophie de l'histoire', *REJ* 14 (1900), p. 67; cf. Eissfeldt, *Introduction*, p. 528, and A. Oepke, 'ἔκστασις, ἐξίστημι', *TDNT*, II, p. 455.
2. For a discussion of various scholars and their views on this issue, see J.M. Schmidt, *Die jüdische Apokalyptik* (Neukirchen-Vluyn: Neukirchener Verlag, 1969), pp. 218-19, 279-81.

through extensive literary activity.[1] Several modern writers, in fact, argue strongly that the Jewish apocalypses were the product of no mere literary activity, with a few proposing that in certain cases we can even determine the parameters of the materials that were generated by their actual visionary experiences with a reasonable degree of confidence.[2] So while there is some disagreement with respect to the extent of actual 'visionary' materials and our ability to distinguish these from their literary framework, a majority of modern authorities take seriously the hypothesis that Jewish apocalyptists were involved, at least to some extent, in actual visionary praxes.[3]

1. See e.g. J. Kaufmann, 'Apokalyptik', *EJ*, II, pp. 1142-61; W.O.E. Oesterley, *The Jews and Judaism during the Greek Period* (London: SPCK, 1941), pp. 71-72, 196; W. Bousset and H. Gressmann, *Die Religion des Judentums im späthellenistischen Zeitalter* (4th edn; Tübingen: Mohr, 1966), pp. 395-99; M.E. Stone, 'Apocalyptic—Vision or Hallucination', *Milla wa-Milla* 14 (1974), pp. 47-56; and E. Jacob, 'Aux sources bibliques de l'apocalyptique', in *Apocalypses et théologie de l'espérance* (ed. L. Monloubou; Paris: Cerf, 1977), p. 47. With respect to individual works, see Gunkel, II, pp. 34-43; F.C. Burkitt, *Jewish and Christian Apocalypses* (London: Oxford University Press, 1914), pp. 40-41 (both on *4 Ezra*); W.O.E. Oesterley, Foreword to Charles, *Apocalypse of Baruch*, pp. xi-xii; G. Widengren, *Literary and Psychological Aspects of the Hebrew Prophets* (Uppsala: Lundeqvist, 1948), pp. 108-10 (on *1 Enoch*). A number of authorities are open to the possibility of real visionary experiences, but decline to commit themselves; cf. L. Hartman, *Prophecy Interpreted* (trans. N. Tomkinson; Uppsala: Gleerup, 1966), p. 108, and Beale, pp. 8-9.
2. A strong believer in genuine visionary experiences is Russell (pp. 158-73). On criteria for distinguishing genuine visionary material from its literary framework, see Rowland (*Open Heaven*, pp. 235-40), who expands and refines the criteria suggested by Lindblom (*Gesichte*, pp. 218-39). Rowland is positive with regard to genuine visionary experiences in the apocalypses, both Jewish and Christian, though I believe he is mistaken in his impression that this is a minority position among scholars of apocalyptic (p. 235). Most writers do not focus attention on the question (as does Rowland), but they appear to be open to the presence of genuine visionary experiences, and many affirm that such phenomena were probable among the Jewish apocalyptists.
3. Some suggest that the contrast between genuine visionary experience and literary convention is overdone; cf. the older study by J.A. Montgomery, *A Critical and Exegetical Commentary on the Book of Daniel* (New York: Scribner's, 1927), pp. 102-104; also J.J. Collins (*Apocalyptic Imagination*, p. 31), who writes, 'The composition of highly symbolic literature involves a vivid use of the imagination, which may be difficult to distinguish from visionary experience in any case'.

b. *Positive Evidences for Genuine Visionary Experiences*

Several considerations render probable the hypothesis that actual visionary experiences underlie the Jewish apocalypses. One of the most significant of these is found in the antecedents of these writings, the most important being the Hebrew prophets.[1] That there were ecstatic visions and auditions, even among the classical prophets, is a matter on which there is general agreement, though there can be little doubt that there was also significant literary activity.[2] Given the fact that the Jewish apocalypses are a development from this earlier form of religion, it is not unlikely that similar visionary experiences were involved in the developed phenomenon as well. The probability that we have continuity between prophecy and apocalyptic in this area is heightened by the fact that the apocalyptists manifest, in many cases, a prophetic consciousness.

In *1 Enoch*, for example, there are numerous clues that point to a prophetic consciousness on the part of the author(s). The introduction (chs. 1–5) is especially revealing. There the author, under the guise of Enoch, 'sets himself in the line of the prophets' through various means related to both form and content.[3] Much the same can be said with

---

1. As S. de Vries observes, regardless of the identity of the father of Jewish apocalypticism, 'prophecy is its true mother' ('Observations on Quantitative and Qualitative Time in Wisdom and Apocalyptic', in *Israelite Wisdom: Festschrift for Samuel Terrien* [ed. J.G. Gammie *et al.*; Missoula, MT: Scholars Press, 1978], p. 266). Still, there is some disagreement with respect to the manner in which the development from prophecy to apocalyptic took place. For a survey of different views, see Nicholson, pp. 189-213.

2. E.g. A.R. Johnson, *The Cultic Prophet in Ancient Israel* (Cardiff: University of Wales Press, 1962), pp. 31-46; J. Lindblom, *Prophecy in Ancient Israel* (Oxford: Blackwell, 1963), pp. 105-48, 173-82, 423-24, and D.E. Aune, *Prophecy in Early Christianity and the Ancient Mediterranean World* (Grand Rapids: Eerdmans, 1983), pp. 86-87. For specific cases, see R.B.Y. Scott, 'Isaiah xxi 1-10; The Inside of a Prophet's Mind', *VT* 2 (1952), pp. 278-82, and W. Zimmerli, 'Visionary Experience in Jeremiah', in *Israel's Prophetic Tradition*, pp. 95-118.

3. Nickelsburg, *Jewish Literature*, p. 49. Rau (pp. 34-40) is especially helpful. He argues that 1.1-9 is constructed by analogy to the introduction to OT prophetic books. Several of his points are relevant: (1) The reference to 'a holy vision from the heavens which the angels showed me' (1.2) is an allusion to the visions of the heavens and of God's throne. This visionary introduction is thus comparable to chs. 1–3 of Ezekiel. (2) The juxtaposition of *logos* and *orasis* in 1.1-2 is similar to the use of terms in a number of prophetic books (Amos 1.1; Mic. 1.1; Hab. 1.1; Obad. 1.1; Zech. 1.7-8; Ezek. 1.1, 3). (3) The description of the eschatological judgment-theodicy in 1.3-9 is also present in the introductions to Amos (1.2), Micah (1.2-4)

regard to the introduction to chs. 37–71, where 'The vision which Enoch... son of Jared... saw' is reminiscent of Isa. 1.1.[1] The prophetic consciousness of the writer(s) comes through in a somewhat different way in chs. 91–105/108. There we find a significant concentration of 'prophetic' speech forms and formulas such as woes (94.6-8; 95.4-7; 96.4-8; 97.7-10; 98.9, 11-16; 99.1-2, 11-16; 100.7-9; 103.5-8) and descriptions of the future (97.3-6; 99.3-5; 100.1-3, 4-6, 10-13; 102.1-3). Furthermore, the revelatory claims of the author(s) (93.1-3) are analogous to the prophets' claims to have access to the divine council.[2]

The prophetic consciousness is somewhat less prominent in *2 Baruch*, though the introduction closely parallels the opening words of several prophetic books (Jer. 1.1-3; Ezek. 1.1-3; Hos. 1.1) and this is no isolated occurrence within the work (cf. 10.1). It is, however, in *4 Ezra* that connections with prophecy are particularly marked. For not only is the parallel between Ezra and Moses as eschatological prophets a major theme in the work (7.127-31; 12.36-38; 13.38-47; 14.6-8),[3] but the people are represented as crying out to Ezra, 'For of all the prophets you alone are left to us' (13.42). Furthermore, there is some evidence to suggest that the revelation communicated by the venerable Ezra was held in higher honor than the OT Scriptures themselves (14.45-47; cf. 14.3-6).[4] This attitude, of course, is unusual within the Jewish apocalypses, but it serves to demonstrate our point—that the apocalyptists were no mere interpreters of the canonical prophets, though at times they took up this role (e.g. Dan. 9).[5] On the contrary,

and Nahum (1.2-8). On the theophany and its biblical foundations, see VanderKam, *Enoch*, p. 119.

1. Rau, p. 40. There is, of course, a wisdom flavor to this introduction as well as to the opening chapters of the Book of the Watchers, but this does not reduce the significance of the prophetic element for our purposes.

2. See G.W.E. Nickelsburg, 'The Apocalyptic Message of 1 Enoch 92–105', *CBQ* 39 (1977), pp. 309-28, to whom I am indebted in this section; cf. Aune, p. 114, who argues that the evidence presented by Nickelsburg provides 'some confirmation' of the view that some of the reports of visions were based on genuine experience.

3. See Brandenburger, *Verborgenheit Gottes*, p. 159; cf. pp. 118-20. See also M.A. Knibb, 'Apocalyptic and Wisdom in 4 Ezra', *JSJ* 13 (1982), pp. 62-63.

4. This interpretation of these unusual verses is suggested by Gunkel, p. 401, and Oesterley, *II Esdras*, pp. 173-74.

5. Unfortunately, this has been the emphasis of many recent studies. See e.g., Bauckham, ('Rise', p. 18), who writes, 'The authority of the apocalyptists' message is only derivative from that of the prophets'.

they viewed themselves as true prophets of the end times, holding out the message of life and death to their readers. The comments of Nickelsburg are especially significant in this regard:

> it is clear that the question of the 'cessation' of prophecy cannot be answered simply on the basis of statements from 'establishment' documents such as 1 Maccabees. The evidence of writings like *Enoch* 92–105 indicates that there were people in the late Hellenistic period who claimed revelation and expressed themselves in the forms of older prophecy. The self-understanding evidenced in the use of these forms should not be obscured by our author's lack of accreditation among many of his contemporaries (shades of the prophets?) nor by the *Sachkritik* of the modern exegete or theologian.[1]

Recent studies, however, argue that Hebrew prophecy was not the only factor that contributed to the development of the Jewish apocalypses and the world view they represent. Significant as well was the phenomenon known as mantic wisdom, which was widespread in the Near East and which appears to have been a constant undercurrent in Israel, though it became more familiar in the exilic and post-exilic periods (cf. Gen. 41.8; Est. 1.13; Isa. 44.25; 47.10, 13; Wis. 8.8).[2] This type of wisdom involves the divination of 'the secrets of the future by various methods including the interpretation of dreams, omens, mysterious oracles, and the stars'.[3] There is little doubt that the practitioners of mantic wisdom sought after subjective revelatory experiences. Theirs was no mere literary work, though their visionary experiences were issued in literary documents of various forms.[4]

In Daniel and chs. 1–36 of *1 Enoch* the seer is portrayed as the ideal mantic wise man. In both cases the identity of the group that

---

1. Nickelsburg, 'Apocalyptic Message', p. 327. For historical manifestations of prophetic activity during this period, see R. Meyer, 'προφήτης', *TDNT*, VI, pp. 819-27. Thus, the unqualified argument that the Revelation of John 'marks a return of apocalyptic to its prophetic origins' is misleading; for this view, see e.g. B. Vawter, 'Apocalyptic: Its Relation to Prophecy', *CBQ* 22 (1960), pp. 45-46.

2. See H.-P. Müller, 'Mantische Weisheit und Apokalyptik', in *Congress Volume, Uppsala 1971* (Leiden: Brill, 1972), pp. 268-93; J.J. Collins, 'Court-Tales', pp. 229-34, and Bauckham, 'Rise', pp. 13-15. VanderKam (*Enoch*, pp. 52-75) states that the significance of mantic wisdom as a contributing factor in the development of Jewish apocalypticism is 'one of the major theses' of his work. On divination and mantic activity in Israel, see also B.O. Long, 'The Effect of Divination upon Israelite Literature', *JBL* 92 (1973), pp. 489-97.

3. Bauckham, 'Rise', p. 13.

4. See the survey of Mesopotamian divination, its practices, its literature, and its relationship to Jewish apocalypticism in VanderKam, *Enoch*, pp. 52-75.

stands behind the writing is bound up with the visionary hero of the apocalypse.[1] Thus, it is evident that another of the antecedents of Jewish apocalypticism involved what was believed to be actual visionary experiences,[2] and that at least some apocalyptists identified closely with the practitioners of this type of wisdom. Such considerations suggest that genuine visionary experiences were not unusual among the circles that produced (at least some of) the Jewish apocalypses.

But not only do the antecedents of Jewish apocalypticism render probable the hypothesis of genuine visionary experiences among the writers of these documents, the connections between the Jewish apocalypses and Jewish mysticism also point in this direction. Since the pioneering work of Gershom Scholem, who demonstrated many points of contact between several Jewish apocalypses and Merkabah mysticism of the later Hekhalot writings,[3] a majority of writers have concluded that an early stage of this kind of mysticism can be detected in several Jewish apocalypses. The earliest of these is *1 Enoch* 14, but there are also close parallels in the *Similitudes of Enoch* (39.9-14; 47.2; 61.9-12; 71.14),[4] *2 Enoch* (8.1-8; ch. 31 [rec. A only]; ch. 37),

---

1. Daniel is especially clear in this regard; see J.J. Collins, *Apocalyptic Vision*, p. 29: 'Even as the visionary took over the name of Daniel, so he adopted one of the terms applied to the wise men of the exile as the primary designation for the group to which he belonged. His primary interest in the court-tales would therefore appear to derive from the fact that he saw himself and his companions as wise men after the model of Daniel and his companions' (cf. pp. 27-28, 73). On chs. 1–36 of *1 Enoch*, see VanderKam (*Enoch*, pp. 115-19) who observes that the introduction to the work (1.2-3a) contains several phrases borrowed from the Balaam stories in Num. 22–24. Thus, Enoch is presented, in effect, as another Balaam, the diviner (mantic wise man) known from the accounts in these chapters. VanderKam sees mantic wisdom as standing behind several portions of *1 Enoch*. Cf. Rau, p. 38, and J.C.H. Lebram, 'The Piety of the Jewish Apocalyptists', in *Apocalypticism*, p. 180.

2. The interpretation of dreams is also a common element in mantic circles, and, as we have observed, this cannot be sharply distinguished from visionary experiences in the Jewish apocalypses. VanderKam (*Enoch*, pp. 60-61) observes that in one sort of dream omen 'the dreamer either descends to the netherworld or rises to the heavens, and depending upon his experiences in either place, consequences are predicted'. This kind of experience is reasonably close to the ascent visions in the Jewish apocalypses, though in the dream omina the consequences are personal, rather than national or cosmic.

3. Scholem, *Major Trends*, pp. 40-79, esp. pp. 40, 43 and 73; *idem*, *Jewish Gnosticism*, pp. 14-19.

4. J.C. Greenfield, Foreword to Odeberg, *3 Enoch*, pp. xvi-xviii, xxxii-xxxv; cf. Suter, *Tradition and Composition*, pp. 14-23, though he prefers to classify the

the *Apocalypse of Abraham* (chs. 9–29), the *Apocalypse of Zephaniah*, and the *Testament of Levi* (5.1).[1] Nevertheless, while most are pre-pared to acknowledge that there are significant points of contact between Jewish apocalypticism and Merkabah mysticism, and that the latter movement issued from the former,[2] there is less agreement with respect to the question of genuine visionary experiences at certain stages in the trajectory.[3] Still, the evident connections between Jewish apocalypticism and Merkabah mysticism are significant for our pur-poses. For since genuine visionary experiences were common among both the ancestors (Hebrew prophecy) and the descendants (Merkabah mysticism) of Jewish apocalypticism, the burden of proof must rest

Similitudes as 'proto-Merkabah', and Nickelsburg, 'Enoch, Levi, and Peter', pp. 578-82.

1. For discussions of the parallels in these various works, see Scholem, *Major Trends*, pp. 40-79, and Gruenwald, *Apocalyptic and Merkavah Mysticism*, pp. 32-69.

2. In addition to the works already mentioned, see A.J. Saldarini, 'Apocalypses and "Apocalyptic" in Rabbinic Literature and Mysticism', *Semeia* 14 (1979), p. 189: 'The presence of the genre "apocalypse" within mystical literature validates Scholem's thesis that Jewish mysticism is the heir to the older Jewish apocalypses'; cf. Bauckham ('Apocalypses', pp. 112-13), who points out that not only the Mer-kabah texts, but also Christian apocalypses and Hebrew apocalypses, issued from the older tradition of Jewish apocalypticism. P.S. Alexander ('Comparing Merkavah Mysticism and Gnosticism: An Essay in Method', *JJS* 35 [1984], pp. 10-12) sug-gests that Jewish apocalypticism is a common ancestor for both Merkabah mysticism and Gnosticism.

3. E.g. M. Smith ('Observations on Hekhalot Rabbati', in *Biblical and Other Studies* [ed. A. Altmann; Cambridge, MA: Harvard University Press, 1963], pp. 155-58), who sets the *terminus ante quem* for the development of mystical praxis at the beginning of the second century; J.W. Bowker, '"Merkabah" Visions and the Visions of Paul', *JSS* 16 (1971), pp. 157-59; Alexander, '3 Enoch', pp. 229-39; and J. Neusner, *A Life of Yohanan ben Zakkai* (2nd edn; Leiden: Brill, 1970), pp. 134-41, who argues that this major figure (c. 1–80 AD) was involved in definite mystical experiences.

Those who question the continuity between earlier sources and the Hekhalot writ-ings argue that the problems of pseudonymity, dating and redaction confound the study of the Palestinian evidence, particularly from the tannaitic period; see particu-larly D.J. Halperin (*The Merkabah in Rabbinic Literature* [New Haven: American Oriental Society, 1980], pp. 176-77, 181-85), who argues that the conception of Merkabah mysticism entered rabbinic circles only in Amoraic Babylonia, and that ecstatic mysticism may not have been practiced even at that time. More balanced is I. Chernus, *Mysticism in Rabbinic Judaism* [Berlin: de Gruyter, 1982], pp. vi-ix, who notes that 'a preponderance of the evidence' is on Scholem's side, though he believes that the tannaitic evidence is the weakest link in the trajectory.

with those who would argue that the visions depicted in Jewish apocalyptic writings are to be understood as only literary conventions in service of an author's message.

Moreover, the fact of genuine visionary experience in the NT is also relevant to our discussion. Alan Segal has emphasized the importance of Paul's mystical report in 2 Cor. 12.1-9 as evidence that ecstatic experiences were known among Jews in the first century AD.[1] And this evidence is all the more significant in view of the similarities between Paul's experience and the visions of Merkabah mysticism.[2]

Furthermore, it is important to note the similarities between the Jewish apocalypses and the Christian Apocalypse of John. Since the experiences of the Johannine apocalypse are narrated in the first person, many authorities are inclined to accept the hypothesis that genuine visionary experiences underlie at least some parts of the work, though the final product is certainly the result of conscious literary activity.[3]

The connections between the Apocalypse of John and the Jewish apocalypses are all the more significant in light of the following three considerations. First, apart from the obvious commitment of the Apocalypse of John to the lordship of Christ, the differences between this writing and the Jewish apocalypses are largely superficial, and do

---

1. Segal, 'Paul and Ecstasy', pp. 555-80. Segal even writes that 'Paul's conversion experience and his mystical ascension forms the basis of his theology'. I would affirm, with Segal, the importance of the NT as a source for the study of first-century Judaism; see A.F. Segal, *The Other Judaisms of Late Antiquity* (Atlanta: Scholars Press, 1987), pp. xvi-xvii. Several other writers lay stress on the importance of ecstatic experiences in Paul's life and experience; e.g. W. Baird, 'Visions, Revelation, and Ministry: Reflections on 2 Cor. 12.1-5 and Gal. 1.11-17', *JBL* 104 (1985), pp. 651-62. Lincoln, p. 72, observes that 'lack of frequent references does not necessarily mean lack of frequent experience'. See, however, H.D. Betz, *Der Apostel Paulus und die sokratische Tradition* (Tübingen: Mohr, 1972), p. 84: '2 Kor 12,2-4 ist die Parodie eines Himmelfahrtsberichtes'. In this case he appears to subordinate content to rhetorical form too rigorously.

2. Bowker, pp. 157-73. Cf., however, P. Schäfer ('New Testament and Hekhalot Literature: The Journey into Heaven in Paul and in Merkavah Mysticism', *JJS* 35 [1984], pp. 19-35) who argues that an 'arbitrary verbal comparison' fails to support the conclusion that Paul's ecstatic experience is linked to Merkabah mysticism.

3. E.g., Bousset, *Offenbarung Johannis*, pp. 3-14. For a review of the older discussions, see E. Lohmeyer, 'Die Offenbarung des Johannes 1920-34', *TR* 7 (1935), pp. 38-43. Most significant of these is C. Schneider, *Die Erlebnisechtheit der Apocalypse des Johannes* (Leipzig: Dörffling & Franke, 1930). More recently, see the review and detailed argumentation in Lindblom, *Gesichte*, pp. 206-39.

not reflect a significant shift in perspective.[1] Second, there are striking similarities between the self-consciousness of the author of the Johannine apocalypse and a number of the Jewish apocalyptists, particularly in that both combine a prophetic consciousness with the use of the genre apocalypse to express their message.[2] And, third, the Apocalypse of John evidently shares with the Jewish apocalypses some relation to the tradition of Merkabah mysticism,[3] and this common relationship suggests that the affinity between the Jewish apocalypses and this Jewish Christian work are closer than one might initially think. So while Christianity brought with it an increase in ecstatic activity, it seems also that the Apocalypse of John carries over at least some of this ecstatic activity from the circles that produced the Jewish apocalypses.

One other consideration merits attention here as well—that the descriptions of visionary experiences in the Jewish apocalypses have many parallels with ecstatic experiences observed in various other cultures and societies. The work of Susan Niditch is especially helpful here.[4] Building on the studies of shamans, ecstatics and mystics in a variety of cultures by M. Eliade and others,[5] Niditch demonstrates close parallels with respect to the motivations or reasons for undergoing visions, the ritual patterns, the descriptions of the emotional and physical state of the seer, the descriptions of contact with spirits and visionary travel, and even the actual content of the visions.[6] In light of the impressive nature of these parallels, she writes:

> What I can say with assurance is that comparison with non-Jewish material leads me to conclude that these writers have at least a genuine notion of that

1. J.J. Collins, 'Pseudonymity, Historical Reviews and the Genre of the Apocalypse of John', *CBQ* 39 (1977), pp. 41-42.
2. See Rev. 1.1-3; 10.7; 11.18; 19.10; 22.6, 9; cf. G.R. Beasley-Murray, *The Book of Revelation* (Grand Rapids: Eerdmans, 1981), pp. 19-29.
3. See Gruenwald, *Apocalyptic and Merkabah Mysticism*, pp. 62-69, though L.W. Hurtado ('Revelation 4–5 in the Light of Jewish Apocalyptic Analogies', *JSNT* 25 [1985], pp. 105-24) argues correctly that there is a significant shift toward a Christian perspective even in these chapters.
4. S. Niditch, 'The Visionary', in *Ideal Figures*, pp. 153-79.
5. She utilizes, among others, the major work by M. Eliade, *Shamanism: Archaic Techniques of Ecstasy* (Princeton: Princeton University Press, 1964). See Niditch, 'Visionary', pp. 175-79; cf. S.B. Reid, '1 Enoch: The Rising Elite of the Apocalyptic Movement', in *Society of Biblical Literature 1983 Seminar Papers* (ed. K.H. Richards; Chico, CA: Scholars Press, 1983), p. 150.
6. Niditch, 'Visionary', pp. 158-63.

which visionaries do, how they experience visions, the sorts of things they see and so on.[1]

I concur with Niditch in the general thrust of her comments. Yet I would also argue that these close parallels suggest more than she is prepared to acknowledge. Certainly visions and other pneumatic phenomena, some of which included an ascent to the heavens, were broadly diffused throughout the hellenistic world.[2] As well, they are attested by the historical sources relating to Judaism of this period.[3] Given this situation, an understanding of visionary experiences could have been available to Jewish writers who desired to make use of such descriptions for their own literary purposes. Yet the fact that the writers of the Jewish apocalypses devoted considerable space and energy to detail for their readers the precise nature of such visionary experiences, coupled with the fact that their descriptions parallel those of genuine mystics and ecstatics,[4] suggest that they had more than a casual acquaintance with genuine visionary experiences. The simplest and most probable explanation is that genuine visionary experiences were reasonably common within at least some circles of Jewish apocalypticism.[5]

1. *Ibid.*, p. 158.

2. See J.S. Hanson, 'Dreams and Visions', pp. 1395-96; cf. Segal ('Heavenly Ascent', p. 1388), who argues that the preoccupation with heavenly ascent is rooted in 'a deep structure of Hellenistic thought which indeed pre-dates Christianity'; E.R. Dodds, *The Greeks and the Irrational* (Berkeley: University of California Press, 1951), pp. 102-34, and Hengel, I, p. 207.

3. Stone, 'Apocalyptic Literature', p. 429. See Josephus, *Ant.*, 13.282, 299, 311-13, 345-46; 14.22; 15.373-79; *War* 1.68-69, 78-80; 2.112-17.

4. Contrast the Jewish apocalypses with the Qumran Sabbath Shirot on this point. As C.A. Newsom ('Merkabah Exegesis in the Qumran Sabbath Shirot', *JJS* 38 [1987], p. 29) observes, 'the Sabbath songs do not associate the merkabah with a scene of revelatory disclosure'. Still, this text represents an exegesis of Ezekiel which served 'as the vehicle by which the human worshipping community shares in the experience of heavenly praise'.

5. Several writers emphasize the importance of *4 Ezra* 10.55-56 for this issue. Gunkel (p. 390) argues that this reference tells in favor of true visionary activity since it shows that the seer saw and heard much more than he reports. He also draws parallels between this and Paul's reticence to speak of the ἄρρητα ῥήματα that he heard during his ecstatic ascent (2 Cor. 12.4); cf. Box, *Apocalypse of Ezra*, p. 89; Oesterley, *II Esdras*, p. 127, and Gry, II, p. 325. For my purposes, it may suggest that experiences of 'heavenly revelation' were common in apocalyptic circles, though this is supported primarily by the consistent testimony of the writings to visionary experiences as the mode of revelation most familiar to them.

c. *Problems with the Hypothesis*

The considerations mentioned above give reasonable support to the hypothesis that genuine visionary experiences underlie the Jewish apocalypses. Yet this view is not without its problems. Two points merit discussion: (1) the problem of pseudonymity, and (2) the presence of traditional and pseudo-scientific material in the documents.

Most prominent in discussions that call into question the hypothesis of genuine visionary experiences in Jewish apocalypticism is the problem of pseudonymity and its implications. The following questions are unavoidable. If genuine visionary experiences were common among the Jewish apocalyptists, why did they present their message through the medium of pseudonymity? Would not the account be in the first person if it was backed by actual visionary experiences? Such questions are entirely proper. And they require that we consider the function of pseudonymity within the Jewish apocalypses.

Numerous explanations have been offered for the pseudonymous nature of these writings, with most recent treatments acknowledging that the answer probably involves a number of factors.[1] Certainly the device functioned to augment the prestige and authority of the works.[2] Furthermore, it enabled the authors to achieve several of their purposes, including the communication of a deterministic view of history through *ex eventu* prophecy[3] and the development of a correspon-

---

1. A survey of views is provided by J.M. Schmidt, pp. 46-47, 77-78, 171, 219-20 and 277-78. On the need to take into account a number of factors, see J.J. Collins, *Apocalyptic Vision*, pp. 71-74.

2. This is partly, though not exclusively, related to the decline of prophecy after the Persian period, as R.H. Charles ('Introduction', in *APCT*, II, p. ix) argued influentially; cf. also I. Willi-Plein, 'Das Geheimnis der Apokalyptik', *VT* 27 (1977), pp. 64-66. More recent studies have pointed out that certain figures from Israel's past were counted among the great savants of antiquity and that this notion attracted many and varied traditions of knowledge. This living and fluid 'tradition of speculative wisdom' whose 'source and father' was said to be Enoch or Daniel or any one of several figures of old led naturally to the pseudonymous framework of the apocalypses, since the apocalyptists could easily include their material within this broader framework and so take advantage of the prestige of the figure and the fluidity of the tradition; see Stone, 'Vision or Hallucination', p. 55, and Gruenwald, 'Jewish Apocalyptic Literature', pp. 105-106. In any case, the function of the device is not to indicate that the apocalyptists were mere interpreters of the prophets of old, as Bauckham ('Rise', p. 18) argues.

3. Without the device of pseudonymity this feature of apocalyptic would not have been possible; see J.J. Collins, 'Pseudonymity', pp. 332-33.

dence between primal time and end time (*Endzeit wird Urzeit*).[1]
Given these functions within the documents, however, it is important
to observe that the pseudonymity of the apocalypses is completely
unrelated to the question of the genuineness of the visionary experiences. The device performs significant functions within the apocalypses as literary documents, since it gains a hearing for the works
and, in some cases, it enables the writer to express the content of the
message. There is little reason to suppose that a visionary would be
hesitant to make use of this helpful device in the literary expression of
what he or she has seen; in fact, the frustration of believing that one
had received a true vision analogous to those of the prophets and wise
men of old, yet recognizing that such a claim would fall upon deaf
ears, provides the strongest motivation for the pseudonymous nature
of the writings.

A second observation, many would argue, tells against the hypothesis of genuine visionary experiences in the Jewish apocalypses. As
Michael Stone argues, 'they were definitely not written as the immediate, intimate, auto-biographic records of experiences which
visionaries have undergone'.[2] This observation is supported by the
tremendous amount of traditional and pseudo-scientific material that is
evident throughout the Jewish apocalypses.

To such an objection, however, several points need to be made.
First, the fact that traditional material appears within the final form of
a writing tells us nothing about its original setting, especially since
certain of the Jewish apocalypses, most notably *1 Enoch*, are known to
have taken shape over some period of time. Second, the fact that the
content of the visions includes ideas that were traditional or that were
common in that day is not surprising, since visionaries commonly
interiorize the mythology or cosmology of their society, which then
becomes 'the itinerary for ecstatic journeys'.[3] Third, such an objection
is relevant only if one attempts to deny that a large part of the content
of the Jewish apocalypses is the result, not of visionary activity, but of
literary activity in the truest sense. The fact that the writings contain
much that is literary in origin is consistent, however, with the hypo-

---

1. Hengel, I, p. 205, points out that the revelation 'to the spirit-possessed pious
of primal times' was now made known to the pious in the last days.
2. Stone, 'Vision or Hallucination', p. 49.
3. Eliade, *Shamanism*, p. 266; cf. Niditch, 'Visionary', p. 162. On the interaction between intermediaries and their respective societies, see R.R. Wilson, *Prophecy
and Society in Ancient Israel* (Philadelphia: Fortress Press, 1980), pp. 28-88.

thesis that visionary practitioners expressed their visions as well as their conceptions of the world through literary means.

Conclusion

My working hypothesis is that there were genuine visionary experiences among at least some of the writers of the Jewish apocalypses. This does not mean, however, that scholarship today can delineate the parameters of such visionary materials. Such attempts are extremely hypothetical, since the materials generated by genuine visionary experiences have been reworked and greatly expanded. I acknowledge that the bulk of the material in the Jewish apocalypses stems from the literary efforts of their authors. Yet this in no way undermines the view that at least some of the apocalyptists experienced genuine visions. Neither is it a hindrance to my primary concerns, to explore the nature of their visionary praxes and to lay out the conceptual framework or world view of Jewish apocalypticism.

Chapter 3

THE CONTENT OF REVELATION IN JEWISH APOCALYPTICISM

Recent studies of Jewish apocalypticism have pointed to the comprehensive nature of revelation in these writings.[1] The tremendous diversity of content in the apocalypses is evident both from a study of the writings themselves and from the ways in which the writers refer to the revelations that purportedly came to them. In Dan. 1.17, for example, it is said that 'God gave knowledge and understanding of all kinds of literature and learning' (cf. 1.20); in *1 En.* 52.1 Enoch claims to have seen 'all the secret things of heaven and the future things';[2] and in *3 Bar.* 1.4 (Gk) the angel promises to disclose to Baruch 'all things of God'.[3] Such statements lead one to expect revelations of an extremely complex nature, and that is certainly what these writings present. I am here, however, primarily concerned with those features relevant to the mystical praxis at Colossae. So I shall limit myself to two major areas of content: (1) the visions of the Merkabah, along with angelic worship that is a part of those scenes; and (2) the judgment scenes, along with such attendant motifs as the angelic witnesses, the heavenly book(s), the post-mortem judgment, and the consequences of judgment, which include, of course, the blessedness of the righteous and the condemnation of the wicked.

---

1. Cf. particularly M.E. Stone, 'Enoch and Apocalyptic Origins', in *Visionaries and their Apocalypses*, pp. 99-100, and Rowland, *Open Heaven*, p. 76; see also J.J. Collins, *Apocalyptic Imagination*, p. 9. For an example of the older approach that focused almost exclusively on the theme of eschatology in the Jewish apocalypses, see Vielhauer, II, pp. 584, 587. This new approach is related in part to the earlier dates assigned in recent years to chs. 1–36 and 72–82 of *1 Enoch*, since it is now evident that the earliest non-canonical apocalypses are concerned with cosmology and other matters, and not exclusively with eschatology.

2. See also *1 En.* 1.2; 25.2; 41.1; 60.10.

3. The Slavonic reads 'all the mysteries of God', and may conflate v. 4 and v. 8 (cf. Gaylord, p. 663).

1. *The Visions of God and the Angelic Praise*

In Chapter 2 it was noted that visions of the Merkabah were common in the vertical apocalypses. There I cited numerous examples from *1 Enoch*, *2 Enoch*, the *Apocalypse of Abraham*, the *Apocalypse of Zephaniah*, and the *Testament of Levi*.[1] The characteristics of these visions have been discussed in detail by Gershom Scholem, Ithamar Gruenwald, Christopher Rowland, and others, and so there is no need to attempt here a comprehensive analysis of these texts ourselves. Instead, my study will focus on those features of relevance to a reconstruction of the ascetic-mystical piety that occasioned Paul's letter to the Colossians.

These Merkabah visions, based on Ezekiel 1, Isaiah 6 and other passages from the OT,[2] are especially significant since they appear, in most cases, as the climax of an ascent or tour.[3] The earliest of these is found in *1 Enoch* 14, a text especially worth noting since it demonstrates the antiquity of this tradition.[4] In this passage, which may originally have been independent of its present context,[5] Enoch passes through the various precincts of the heavenly temple until he enters the holy of holies, and so gains a vision of God himself.[6] The influence of Ezekiel is evident in the description of the 'lofty throne' with wheels that have an appearance 'like the shining sun'; also, the theme

1. While *3 Baruch* may have contained a Throne-vision in its original form, the gates to the fifth heaven remain closed to Baruch in the present text. In spite of repeated promises that he will see 'the glory of God' (4.2 [Sl]; 6.12; 7.2; 11.2; 16.4 [Sl]), the seer is not granted such a privilege (cf. Gaylord, pp. 657, 678).

2. See H. Bietenhard, *Die himmlische Welt im Urchristentum und Spätjudentum* (Tübingen: Mohr, 1951), pp. 53-54.

3. Among the significant developments over against the mystical visions of the OT, however, is the fact that the visionary experience occurs during the course of an ascent to heaven; see Gruenwald, *Apocalyptic and Merkavah Mysticism*, p. 32.

4. Scholem, *Major Trends*, p. 43.

5. Dean-Otting, p. 46.

6. On the OT background of a 'House of God' in heaven, see Black, *Book of Enoch*, p. 148. Nickelsburg ('Enoch, Levi, and Peter', p. 580) writes, 'The similarities to Ezek. 40–48, together with other evidence, indicate that Enoch is describing his ascent to the heavenly temple and his progress through its *temenos* to the door of the holy of holies, where the chariot throne of God is set'; cf. Uhlig, p. 539. Similarly, Dean-Otting (p. 49) argues, 'This fantastic description is not merely an imaginary creation, but it rests concretely on the layout of the Temple in Jerusalem'. On pp. 49-50 she explores the various aspects of the Temple described in this passage.

of the glory of God receives extensive attention.[1] Enoch, the right-eous, in fact, is granted the privilege of penetrating 'into the presence of the inaccessible God'.[2]

There is, however, no explicit mention of angelic singing or wor-ship, which characterizes many of these visions in the apocalypses and later Hekhalot writings,[3] but *1 Enoch* 14 speaks of 'the tens of millions [that stood] before him' (v. 22) and of 'the most holy ones' who 'are near to him' and who 'neither go far away at night nor move away from him' (v. 23). There are, therefore, some indications that the angels may be viewed as offering praise[4] as well as performing priestly service in the heavenly temple.[5] They may also, in fact, be members of the divine council.[6]

While *1 Enoch* 14 contains the most important Merkabah vision in the collection of writings called *1 Enoch*, it is not the only text in that collection that has connections with the Merkabah tradition. Also significant is the vision of ch. 71, which Enoch responds to as follows:

> I fell on my face, my whole body mollified and my spirit transformed. Then I cried with a great voice by the spirit of the power, blessing, glorifying, and extolling. And those are the blessings which went forth out of my mouth, being well-pleasing in the presence of that Antecedent of Time (vv. 11-12).[7]

Multitudes of angels are included in the vision (vv. 7-9, 13), but again, as in ch. 14, their worship is not mentioned explicitly—though

---

1. God is referred to as 'the Great Glory' and 'the Glorious One', and his appear-ance is so bright that 'no one of the flesh can see him'. On the glory theme and its background, see Dean-Otting, pp. 50-58.

2. Nickelsburg, 'Enoch, Levi, and Peter', p. 581.

3. See Bietenhard (pp. 137-42), who suggests that the basis for this conception is found in certain OT passages.

4. On the significance of their presence at night, see Gruenwald, *Apocalyptic and Merkavah Mysticism*, pp. 54-55; cf. M. Himmelfarb, 'From Prophecy to Apoca-lypse: The Book of the Watchers and Tours of Heaven', in *Jewish Spirituality: From the Bible through the Middle Ages* (ed. A. Green; New York: Crossroad, 1986), p. 152.

5. Nickelsburg ('Enoch, Levi, and Peter', p. 585) argues on the basis of Ezek. 44.13, 15, 16; 45.4 that the term 'approach' in *1 En.* 14.23 (Isaac, p. 21, translates 'to be near', while Charles, *Book of Enoch*, p. 82, renders 'to draw nigh') has 'technical cultic connotations'; cf. *T. Levi* 3.5 and R.H. Charles, 'The Testaments of the XII Patriarchs', in *APOT*, II, p. 306.

6. Himmelfarb, 'From Prophecy to Apocalypse', p. 150.

7. Charles (*Book of Enoch*, p. 34) suggests that the author of ch. 71 used *1 En.* 14.18-22 as a model.

it may also be implicit in this passage.[1] More important from my perspective is the fact that this text could be 'one of the earliest references
to a Merkavah hymn recited not by the angels but by the visionary
himself!'[2] And if this be true, then it is possible that the notion of the
participation of a seer in the heavenly liturgy antedates the *Apocalypse
of Abraham* 17, which will be considered below.

There are also several other texts in *1 Enoch*, particularly the
Similitudes, that are relevant here. *1 Enoch* 39–40 does not mention
the throne explicitly, but the seer certainly encounters God himself.
The 'Elect One' is closely associated with God in this vision,[3] though
the heavenly praise, which comes from the seer (39.9-11) as well as
the angelic hosts (39.12–40.5), is directed only to 'the Lord of the
Spirits'. Interestingly enough, special attention is paid to 'a dwelling
place underneath the wings of the Lord of the Spirits' (39.7), and
Enoch claims that his 'portion' is there, reserved for him 'before the
Lord of the Spirits'. Also significant is *1 En.* 47.3 in that it contains
(1) the notion of the opening of the heavenly books, which I will discuss below, and (2) a reference to the heavenly praise of 'the holy
ones' (v. 2). We also find a Merkabah vision in a similar context of
judgment and angelic praise in *1 En.* 61.6-13. And there is a vision of
the Merkabah in a context of judgment, but without reference to
angelic worship, in *1 En.* 60.1-4; also in the Book of the Watchers, *1
En.* 25.3 (cf. 28.8-9).

Such visions are not confined to *1 Enoch*, for the vision of the
Merkabah and the theme of angelic praise are significant elements in
other apocalyptic writings as well. Worthy of special attention are
several passages in *2 Enoch*, particularly the vision of God in the seventh heaven (chs. 20–22) that stands within a context rich with angelic
praise (20.3–21.1; 22.2-3).[4] Reference to the dwelling place of God is
also combined with the motif of angelic worship in ch. 8, which con-

1. The connection between the passages is very close. In fact, Charles (*Book of
Enoch*, p. 34) suggests that the author of ch. 71 used *1 En.* 14.18-22 as a model.

2. Gruenwald, *Apocalyptic and Merkavah Mysticism*, p. 45.

3. Cf. also *1 En.* 46 for a vision, apparently rooted in the vision of Dan. 7, that
also includes 'the Son of Man'. Gruenwald (*Apocalyptic and Merkavah Mysticism*,
pp. 38-39) notes that the Messiah is included in some Hekhalot literature.

4. According to the preface to this work, Enoch is taken away to see 'the very
great many-eyed and immovable throne of the Lord' and the 'indescribable singing of
the army of the cherubim' (rec. A; rec. J is only slightly different). Consequently,
chs. 20–22 are the focal point of the revelation, at least to the writer of this introductory section.

tains a description of Paradise, the place prepared for the righteous (9.1).[1] In fact, references to the heavenly liturgy are particularly evident throughout this work (8.8; 17.1; 19.3, 6; 31.2 [only rec. J];[2] 42.4 [rec. J]), so much so that the absence of praise in the fifth heaven calls for special comment (18.2 [rec. A], 8). So Enoch exhorts the angelic Grigori:

> Why don't you perform the liturgy before the face of the Lord? Start up the former liturgy. Perform the liturgy in the name of fire, lest you annoy the Lord your God (so that) he throws you down from this place (18.8, rec. A; rec. J has only minor variations).

Thus the vision of the fifth heaven closes with Enoch telling the reader that the Grigori responded to his exhortation by offering praise in unison (18.9).

These visions of God and of angelic worship are also found in apocalypses not associated with the name of Enoch. In *T. Levi* 3.8 we read, 'There with him [i.e. God] are thrones and authorities; there praises to God are offered eternally'.[3] Furthermore, in Clement of Alexandria's quotation from the *Apocalypse of Zephaniah* the visionary runs across a group of angels called 'lords' who sing hymns to God (*Strom.* 5.11.77), while in the Akhmimic manuscript he joins the angelic praise after he triumphs over the accuser and embarks on a journey out of Hades:

> Thousands of thousands and myriads of myriads of angels gave praise before me. I, myself, put on an angelic garment. I saw all of those angels praying. I, myself, prayed together with them, I knew their language, which they spoke with me (8.2-4).

The participation of the seer in angelic worship is here explicit. Yet this theme, which has been observed in *1 Enoch* 39 and 71, is most fully developed in the *Apocalypse of Abraham*. For in *Apoc. Abr.* 17.8-21, not only is the association between angelic worship and the

---

1. Gruenwald (*Apocalyptic and Merkavah Mysticism*, p. 50) observes, 'Wherever this Paradise is located, either on earth or in heaven, the Tree of Life could be the place on which God rests, and God's theophany on the Tree of Life is, thus, a counterpart to His theophanies in the Temple or on His Throne of Glory'.

2. It is also mentioned prior to v. 1 in ch. 31 (rec. J).

3. This is, of course, not connected immediately with the Throne-vision (5.1); nevertheless, the description of the Throne is exceedingly brief, and the words 'with him' suggest that the angels who offer praise are also those who surround his Throne. Cf. 3.7.

vision of the Throne set forth explicitly,[1] but the seer even learns a
song of praise in a manner that closely resembles the writings of
Merkabah mysticism.[2]

This survey is sufficient to demonstrate that in Jewish apocalypticism there is an interest in the worship offered by angels in heaven,
and that visions of the Merkabah are closely associated with the angels'
praise and liturgy. This connection is most prominent in the *Apocalypse of Abraham* (and is considerably developed in the later writings
of Jewish mysticism), but is by no means absent from the majority of
the vertical apocalypses. The pattern is clear: when a seer ascends to
receive a vision of the Merkabah, he also receives a vision of the
angelic hosts and their worship—and in certain cases he is constrained
to join them in giving praise to the Most High.

2. *The Scenes of Judgment and Related Elements*

While eschatological judgment no longer dominates the study of the
Jewish apocalypses to the extent that it did some years ago, there can
be little doubt that the expectation of this event played a major role in
shaping the outlook of the writers of these documents. The notion of a
coming judgment is obviously a central concern in many parts of the
apocalypses. It is set forth, however, most dramatically in the judgment scenes themselves, which are embedded in the writings at various
points. I am indebted to George Nickelsburg for his detailed form-
critical study of these passages,[3] and his observations provide an excellent starting point for my own analysis.

Nickelsburg argues that 'in intertestamental Jewish theology the
beliefs in resurrection, immortality, and eternal life are carried
mainly within the framework of three forms',[4] viz.(1) the story of the
righteous man and the Isaianic exaltation tradition, (2) the judgment

---

1. Immediately after Abraham obeys the command to 'Recite without ceasing', he
sees the Throne itself (18.3). The sequence of events suggests that the song brings
on the actual vision of the Merkabah, as in the Hekhalot writings; Dean-Otting,
pp. 252-53.

2. Box and Landsman, pp. xxix-xxx; Scholem, *Major Trends*, pp. 57-61; Dean-
Otting, pp. 252-53; Gruenwald, *Apocalyptic and Merkabah Mysticism*, p. 55;
Philonenko-Sayar and Philonenko, p. 419.

3. G.W.E. Nickelsburg, *Resurrection, Immortality, and Eternal Life in Intertestamental Judaism* (Cambridge, MA: Harvard University Press, 1972), esp. pp. 11-
42.

4. *Ibid.*, p. 170.

scene, and (3) two-way theology. Of these forms, it is the judgment scene itself that I am primarily concerned with—though it is important to note, as Nickelsburg acknowledges, that the forms become mixed at certain points. So it is not surprising that features of the judgment scene appear as well in passages that can be categorized in terms of the other two forms.

Beginning with Dan. 12.1-3 and moving on from there to consider the *Assumption of Moses* 10, *Jub.* 23.27-31 and *Testament of Judah* 25, Nickelsburg isolates the following common features found in an apocalyptic judgment scene:[1]

1. The angelic witnesses, both good and bad;
2. The heavenly book of deeds;
3. The post-mortem judgment, which includes both the good and the evil;
4. The consequences of judgment, which includes the vindication of the righteous and the condemnation of the wicked.

It is of little consequence for the present analysis how the writers of these apocalypses viewed certain specifics of the post-mortem judgment, that is, whether their conceptions involved resurrection, immortality or some combination of the two. There were, in fact, many views among the apocalyptists on this subject.[2] Three of these features, however, are of importance to the present study, and I shall consider these separately—my concern being in each case to begin with the particular feature as it appears in the judgment scenes themselves, and then to consider how it appears more widely in the Jewish apocalypses.

a. *The Angelic Witnesses*
The biblical basis for the concept of angelic witnesses is found in Job 1.6-12, 2.1-7 and Zechariah 3, with features found in these passages being related more broadly to the notion of the 'council of Yahweh' as found in such passages as 1 Kgs 22.19-22; Isaiah 6 and Jer. 15.17.[3] In

---

1. Several other texts, of course, contain features relevant to the judgment scene, as has been mentioned, but these passages provide an excellent starting point for Nickelsburg's analysis of this tradition.
2. For a discussion of the various views, see H.C.C. Cavallin, *Life after Death* (Lund: Gleerup, 1974), esp. pp. 197-215.
3. On this see H.W. Robinson, 'The Council of Yahweh', *JTS* 45 (1944), pp. 151-57.

both Job and Zechariah the context is judicial: the accuser (the Satan) points to the sin of the righteous man, or to his potential to sin as a result of testing. The angelic figure in both of these cases is a negative witness, though his function is by no means demonic. He is the official prosecutor and appears to belong to 'the sons of God'.[1] This is evident especially in Job, where God permits the testing of his 'blameless and upright' servant, and so, in a real sense, bears the ultimate responsibility for the calamities that befall him. In the vision of Zechariah 3, however, Satan's accusation against Joshua is abruptly declared out of order:

> The Lord said to Satan, 'The Lord rebuke you, Satan! The Lord, who has chosen Jerusalem, rebuke you! Is not this man a burning stick snatched from the fire?' (v. 2)

Thus the function of the Satan in this scene contains implicitly

> elements which later produce a more sinister conception. The authorization which he receives from Yahweh gives him control over such hostile factors as sickness, natural disasters, robbery etc. *De facto*, then, he is more than a prosecutor. He has powers which go beyond his purely legal function.[2]

As well as depicting a heavenly accuser, these texts are also concerned to present a heavenly advocate or counsel for the defense. In both Job and Zechariah it is Yahweh himself who takes the side of the accused. This is clearest in Zechariah 3 where reference is made to 'the angel of the Lord' (v. 1) whose words are the words of Yahweh himself (v. 2). He appeals to the election of Jerusalem and argues that Joshua is a part of the remnant of his people.[3] So his sin is 'taken away' and he receives garments that are rich and clean (vv. 4-5).

In the Jewish apocalypses a variety of features come to the fore. In Dan. 12.1-3 Michael's function is primarily military, i.e. he fights on behalf of Israel against 'the angelic princes of Persia and Greece' (cf.

---

1. Cf. Bietenhard, p. 209; also M. Ziegler, *Engel und Dämon im Lichte der Bibel, mit Einschluss der ausserkanonischen Schriftums* (Zürich: Origo, 1957), pp. 122-23.

2. G. von Rad and W. Foerster, 'διαβάλλω, διάβολος', *TDNT*, II, p. 74.

3. This is surely the meaning of the question, 'Is not this man a burning stick snatched from the fire?' See particularly the discussion of H.G. Mitchell, *A Critical and Exegetical Commentary on Haggai and Zechariah* (Edinburgh: T. & T. Clark, 1912), p. 150: 'It is probable that the high priest here represents the survivors from the overthrow of Judah, and that the question. . . is an expression of sympathy with them in their excessive suffering'.

10.13, 21), yet a judicial function is also present.[1] This passage, in fact, suggests that an attempt to distinguish sharply between military and judicial functions in judgment scenes is misguided. The former is evident in *Ass. Mos.* 10.1-2, where the great angelic figure wreaks vengeance on the enemies of Israel, and in Rev. 12.7, where Michael and his angels wage war against the dragon and his angels. The latter, however, is more common in Jewish apocalyptic writings. It appears in *T. Judah* 20.5 and *1 Enoch* 104.1. And it is most clearly present in the judgment scenes embedded in *Testament of Abraham* 12–13 (rec. A; ch. 10, rec. B) and *Apocalypse of Zephaniah* 7–8 (Akhmimic text).

Among the apocalypses in which the angelic witnesses are judicial in their function, we still observe varying degrees of involvement in the process of judgment. In the *Testament of Abraham* (rec. A), for example, the function of the angels is primarily to act as scribes of human deeds, whether good or bad, and so to provide the evidence on which a judgment is made.[2] In other passages, however, they adopt a more active role vis-à-vis the individual who stands under judgment, as in the *Apocalypse of Zephaniah* where a negative witness 'accuses men in the presence of the Lord' (6.17), but where (in spite of the break in the Akhmimic text after 7.11) 'the angel of the Lord' produces a manuscript containing the good deeds of the seer and so functions as counsel for the defense.[3]

Diversity is evident as well with regard to the character of the negative witnesses in the judgment scenes. The angel who records the sinful actions of humans is viewed as an angelic servant of God in *T. Abr.* 11.12 and 12.9 (rec. A), and in *T. Judah* 20.5 as 'the spirit of truth' who 'testifies to all things and brings all accusations'. In the *Apocalypse of Zephaniah*, however, the character of the angelic witness is ambiguous. And in *Jubilees* 23 and *Assumption of Moses* 10 the malevolent nature of this satanic figure is obvious, with its elimination being a feature in the eschatological intervention of God.[4]

---

1. Nickelsburg, *Resurrection*, pp. 11-12. He notes that the verb עמד occurs in the OT in judicial contexts; cf. also A. Lacocque, *Le Livre de Daniel* (Neuchâtel: Delachaux et Niestlé, 1976), p. 177.

2. In rec. B the scribal role is confined to Enoch (though the plural in 11.4 of MS B is confusing); see James, *Testament of Abraham*, p. 124; Delcor, pp. 138-39, and Sanders, p. 900.

3. See Wintermute, 'Apocalypse of Zephaniah', pp. 513-14.

4. See Berger, p. 445. On the figure of Satan in Jubilees, see Testuz, pp. 82-86.

As we move from the judgment scenes themselves to the other sections of the Jewish apocalypses, a similar impression of diversity in function and character is obtained. In several Jewish apocalypses the angelic witnesses, even when giving negative evidence, act as the servants of God. This point is made explicitly in *1 Enoch* 89 and 90, which culminate in a scene of judgment on the basis of the contents of the books (see 89.61-65; 90.17, 20). Of course, here they are recording the misdeeds of the angelic shepherds rather than of humans. But the principle is much the same, as note the *Epistle of Enoch* (see particularly *1 En.* 99.16 and 100.10),[1] *2 Enoch* (19.5, rec. J)[2] and the *Testament of Abraham* where they act in similar fashion with respect to humans.[3]

Not all the apocalyptic writings, however, portray the angels' witness in such a positive manner. The ambiguous nature of accusing angels in the *Apocalypse of Zephaniah*, while not evident in the judgment scene itself, is suggested in ch. 3 of the Akhmimic text:

> Then I saw two other angels weeping over the three sons of Joatham, the priest. I said, 'O angel, who are these?' He said, 'These are the angels of the Lord Almighty. They write down all the good deeds of the righteous upon their manuscript as they watch at the gate of heaven. . . Also the angels of the accuser who is upon the earth, they also write down all of the sins of men upon their manuscript. They also sit at the gate of heaven. They tell the accuser and he writes them upon his manuscript so that he might accuse them when they come out of the world (and) down there (vv. 5-9).

1. There is some ambiguity in the Ethiopic text of 100.10 as to the precise role of the angels and the stars, but this does not affect our point; cf. Knibb, *Ethiopic Enoch*, II, p. 235, and Black, *Book of Enoch*, p. 378. The writing of sins is mentioned several times in the Epistle, but these are the only passages that mention the recording agents; cf. 98.7-8 and 104.7, where the passive is used, presumably with reference to the angelic scribes. In any case, the function is obviously positive throughout this section.

2. The positive nature of this task is suggested by the fact that elsewhere Enoch is said to write down the deeds of humans (53.2); cf. P. Volz, *Die Eschatologie der jüdischen Gemeinde im neutestamentlichen Zeitalter* (Tübingen: Mohr, 1934), p. 291, and Andersen, p. 133. This writing contains, of course, a figure called Satanail who is prince of the Grigori, the angels who rebelled against God and who are consequently under divine judgment (7.3, rec. J; 18.3, 7; 29.3-5, rec. J; 31.3-6, rec. J). Nevertheless, neither Satanail nor his followers are said to fulfill the function of a negative witness. See Charles and Morfill, pp. 21-22.

3. The negative witness is mentioned only in the judgment scene itself.

Especially significant here is the contrast between 'the angels of the Lord Almighty', who witness to the good deeds of 'the righteous', and the 'angels of the accuser who is upon the earth'. This reference suggests that the accusing angel and his followers perform a more sinister function than some writers are prepared to admit.[1]

Jubilees is, in this regard, also somewhat confusing. At certain points the writing of the deeds of humans is presented unambiguously as a positive function, as in 4.23 where Enoch is said to reside in the garden of Eden 'writing condemnation and judgment of the world, and all of the evils of the children of men' (cf. also 4.6; 10.17; 28.6; 30.17 and 39.6).[2] Yet we must also reckon with the prominent place accorded the figure of Mastema or Satan in this document,[3] who is chief of the demons. Together with his followers, he tempts and leads humans astray (10.2, 8; 48.12, 17),[4] accuses them of sin (1.20; 17.16; 48.15, 18) and participates in their destruction (10.2, 6).[5] He tempts in order to accuse, and he accuses in order to destroy. Consequently, while his activity may serve God's sovereign purpose, i.e. the condemnation of the wicked, his intention is malevolent throughout.[6]

When we turn our attention to the Similitudes of Enoch, we find that the figure of the negative witness is consistently demonic. Satan

1. Wintermute ('Apocalypse of Zephaniah', p. 503) denies that the accuser and his angels are evil. Yet the reference to 'the servants of all creation' in 4.6, to which he refers, points to the angels who take the soul of ungodly men to the place of judgment, not the accuser or his followers.

2. In the last three references the scribal agent is unclear, since 'they' or the passive form is used to indicate the action of writing. Nevertheless, the positive nature of this work is certainly implied.

3. The two figures are clearly identical in *Jubilees*, as is evident from 10.7, 11. See Charles (*Jubilees*, p. 81); *contra* Davenport (p. 39), who appears to misread this text. In 1.20 he is also referred to as 'the spirit of Beliar'.

4. In 15.31 it is said that God caused these spirits to rule over the nations 'so that they might lead them astray from following him'.

5. See Charles, *Jubilees*, p. 80; cf. also K. Schubert, 'Versuchung oder Versucher? Der Teufel als Begriff oder Person in den biblischen und ausserbiblischen Texten', *BLit* 50 (1977), p. 108.

6. Clearly he is opposed to the purposes of God in every form, though it would seem that, albeit unwittingly, he is still a servant of the Almighty. This is perhaps most evident in 48.3, 'Did he [i.e. Prince Mastema] not desire to kill you with all of his might and save the Egyptians from your hand because he saw that you were sent to execute judgment and vengeance upon the Egyptians?' Thus we would take issue with Nickelsburg (*Resurrection*, p. 12) who argues that Mastema's function 'fluctuates between outright malevolence and the accusatory activity attributed to *has-satan* in the O.T.'

and his subordinates tempt in order to lead humans astray (54.6; 69.4, 6), and they accuse (40.7) in order to achieve destruction (53.3).[1] The sin of the Watchers, in fact, consists in their becoming subjects of Satan (54.6), whose evil nature is here presupposed.[2]

In the Jewish apocalypses, therefore, the angelic witnesses perform a variety of functions. The judicial side of their role comes to the fore in a number of writings, yet there are also several writings where their military function predominates. The ambiguity of the statements in Job and Zechariah has, it appears, influenced the thought-world of the Jewish apocalypses. Consequently the witness of the angels is variously portrayed, in accordance with the views of the respective writers, as that of an angel who acts as a servant of God, or as that of a figure with an ambiguous status, or as that of a decidedly demonic entity. There are, in fact, even contradictory views within some of the writings, a state of affairs not uncommon in the apocalypses.

b. *The Heavenly Book(s)*
In addition to the function and character of the angelic witnesses, we need to consider a feature closely linked to the scenes of judgment in the Jewish apocalypses—the heavenly book(s), a feature that appears in the apocalypses in several forms.[3] I am particularly interested here in books that contain the deeds of humans, whether good or evil, since these are of immediate concern to my study.

The idea of heavenly book(s) that contain a record of human deeds appears in such OT writings as Ps. 56.8 and Isa. 65.6,[4] though it is far

1. It is on the basis of this verse that several writers identify Satan and his subordinates with the 'angels of punishment' in 53.3; 56.1; 62.11; 63.1 and 66.1; cf. Dillmann, p. 147, and Martin, p. 86. Black (*Book of Enoch*, p. 200) notes, however, that this role is also performed by the archangels (54.6; cf. 10.4 and 90.21). Cf. also Bousset and Gressmann, p. 333.

2. Certainly there is no reference to a 'fall' of Satan in the Similitudes, though the significance of this omission is unclear; see Dillmann, pp. 147-48, and Charles, *Book of Enoch*, p. 66.

3. On these various writings, see Volz, pp. 290-92; L. Koep, *Das himmlische Buch in Antike und Christentum* (Bonn: Hanstein, 1952), pp. 231-43; Bousset and Gressmann, p. 258.

4. Cf. F. Nötscher ('Himmlische Bücher und Schicksalglaube in Qumran', in *Vom Alten zum Neuen Testament* [ed. F. Nötscher; Bonn: Hanstein, 1962], p. 75), who includes Mal. 3.16 (and possibly Ps. 139.16) among passages that refer to the record of deeds; see also G. Schrenk, 'βίβλος, βιβλίον', *TDNT*, I, p. 620. Yet Ps. 139.16 is definitely a reference to the book of the fate of individuals, and the 'scroll of remembrance' in Mal. 3.16 may be seen to represent this idea as well. The motif

less frequent in the OT than in the documents with which we are presently concerned. Three points in particular need be made regarding this motif in what follows: (1) that the motif of heavenly book(s) of deeds, especially sinful deeds, is common in the apocalypses; (2) that it is usually the content of this book(s) that determines the eschatological fate of individuals,[1] and (3) that this motif is not just one feature of the apocalyptic judgment scenes, but it is a major and important feature in the Jewish apocalypses that consistently draws the reader's attention back to the judgment scenes themselves as described in these writings.[2] It is this final point that is the most significant for our purposes. Hans Bietenhard says regarding the motif of the heavenly books or tablets in Jewish apocalypticism:

> Alle diese Vorstellungen und Lehren bekommen ihre Wichtigkeit und ihre Ausrichtung durch den Gerichtsgedanken. Beim Gericht—entweder gleich nach dem Tode oder dann am jüngsten Tage—werden die Bücher geöffnet, Schulden und Verdienste kommen ans Licht, und auf Grund der Schlussabrechnung wird über das endgültige ewige Los des Menschen bestimmt.[3]

As we shall see, the book(s) of deeds stands as the basis for judgment even apart from the scenes of judgment. In fact, the apocalyptists made use of this image as a kind of 'shorthand' for the judgment scene itself. With this motif they sought to evoke in their readers a mental image of the event of judgment, and so to produce a certain response.

The book of Daniel provides a starting point for the study of the apocalyptic judgment scenes. Two references are important here. First, Dan. 12.1 is highly significant since it contains not only mention of an angelic witness, but also the notion of a heavenly book:

> Now at that time Michael, the great prince who stands guard over the sons of your people, will arise. And there will be a time of distress such as never

---

of a book of the fate of individuals is also common in rabbinic materials; see Bietenhard, pp. 232-40.

1. We should not be surprised, therefore, that there is some interaction between the notion of the book(s) of deeds and the book of life, as we will point out below.

2. The motif of the 'book of deeds', we would argue, is consistently set forth against the 'referential background' of the judgment scene in the Jewish apocalypses. I have borrowed this terminology from L. Hartman, *Asking for a Meaning*, pp. 123-24.

3. Bietenhard, p. 234; cf. Bousset and Gressmann, p. 256, where the discussion of the heavenly book(s) is included in the section on 'das grosse Gericht'.

occurred since there was a nation until that time; and at that time your people, everyone who is found written in the book, will be rescued.

Most see here a reference not to a book of the *deeds* of humans, but rather to a book that contains the *names* of the righteous within Israel. Consequently, in its present form this text is to be related to another group of passages that make reference to a different, though related, image—the Book of Life.[1] Yet since (1) the book(s) of deeds is clearly the more common apocalyptic motif, especially in scenes of judgment, and (2) the book(s) of deeds is the motif that one would most naturally expect in the context of a judgment scene, Nickelsburg suggests that an original book of deeds has attracted a piece of tradition that mentions the Book of Life. The latter motif lays stress on the reconstitution of the new Israel, and so fits well with Daniel's purpose and emphasis— with the result that a secondary tradition of the Book of Life has supplanted a book of deeds present in the earlier form of the judgment scene.[2] This suggestion is possible, but highly speculative.

Dan. 7.10 also is pertinent here, for the opening of the books in this passage—which is also set in the context of a scene of judgment—is probably a reference to the books of the deeds of humans, though this is not mentioned explicitly.[3] In Dan. 7.10 and 12.1 it is not stated explicitly that the opening of the books is the basis for judgment, though that is certainly implied.

---

1. In the OT, see Exod. 32.32-33; Ps. 69.28; Isa. 56.5. In the apocalypses, see *1 En.* 47.3; 104.1; 108.3; *Jub.* 36.10; Rev. 20.12; *Apoc. Zeph.* 9.2 (Akhmimic text). A related idea is the book of those who are friends (*Jub.* 19.8-9; 30.19-21) or enemies (*Jub.* 30.21-23; 36.10). See Volz, p. 291.

2. Nickelsburg, *Resurrection*, p. 40. Rau (pp. 312-15) suggests that the secondary motif of the Book of Life has also displaced the book(s) of deeds in the judgment scene of *1 En.* 47.3. The motif still has a forensic flavor, but now indicates 'that God's judgment is being passed in favor of the saints and against their persecutors' (Beale, p. 103).

3. The plural 'books' perhaps suggests this interpretation, though the content of the books is not stated explicitly; cf. *4 Ezra* 6.20, and, on this passage, the comments of Nötscher (p. 79). Most authorities are in accord with this view of Dan. 7.10, though Volz (p. 292) argues that this verse refers to the books that contain divine decisions. Against this view, see particularly Rau (pp. c-ci), who notes (1) that such an interpretation requires a 'Überlieferungsbruch' between the vision of the thrones and the actual scene of judgment, and (2) that later visions of judgment scenes tend to indicate that the books of deeds are meant; see also Schrenk, p. 620.

The idea of the heavenly book(s) of deeds plays a significant role as well in writings associated with the name of Enoch.[1] In *1 En.* 81.2 the seer describes his experience as follows:

> And I looked at everything in the tablets of heaven, and I read everything which was written, and I noted everything. And I read the book and everything which was written in it, all the deeds of men, and all who will be born of flesh on the earth for the generations of eternity.[2]

This vision leads the seer to praise 'the Great Lord, the King of Glory', after which he sets forth a beatitude that is of particular relevance for our study:

> Blessed is the man who dies righteous and upright, against whom no record [lit. 'book'] of oppression has been written, and who received no judgment on that day (81.4).

There is, of course, some tension between the traditions included here, for Enoch's vision is of a book of 'all the deeds of men'[3] while the beatitude speaks more narrowly of a 'book of oppression'. Nevertheless, the connection with the event of judgment is evident enough. And it is obvious, as well, that it is the content of the heavenly book that determines the eschatological fate of individuals.

1 Enoch 91–105/108 also contains significant passages in this regard. Nickelsburg speaks here of the creative 're-use' of the traditional judgment scene as 'the refutation part of a structured apologetic argument'.[4] Admittedly, the image of a book of deeds is not explicitly mentioned; nevertheless, it is clearly implied in several passages. In each case the reference is oriented toward the eschatological judgment of sinners:

> Woe unto you who carry out oppression, deceit, and blasphemy! There shall be a record of evil against you (96.7).

---

1. P. Schäfer, *Rivalität zwischen Engeln und Menschen* (Berlin: de Gruyter, 1975), pp. 30-31.

2. We have here followed the translation of Knibb, *Ethiopic Enoch*, II, p. 186, which is very close to that of Black, *Book of Enoch*, p. 70. The translation of Isaac, p. 59, is confused at this point.

3. It is also difficult to determine whether the book contains only the deeds of humans or some other information such as names or fates as well. The latter interpretation, however, would be surprising since no other references to the heavenly book suggest that the content is mixed.

4. Nickelsburg, *Resurrection*, pp. 120-22.

In those days, the prayers of the righteous ones shall reach unto the Lord; but for all of you, your days shall arrive. He shall read aloud regarding every aspect of your mischief, in the presence of the Great Holy One. Then your faces shall be covered with shame, and he will cast out every deed which is built upon oppression. Woe unto you, sinners, who are in the midst of the sea and on the dry land; (you) whose records are (both) evil (and) against you (97.5-7).

I swear to you, sinners, by the Holy Great One, that all your evil deeds are revealed in the heavens. None of your (deeds of injustice are covered and hidden. Think not in your spirit, nor say in your hearts)[1] that you neither know nor see all our sins being written down every day in the presence of the Most High. From now on do know that all your injustices which you have committed unjustly are written down every day *until the day of your judgment* (98.6-8).

Now, you sinners, even if you say, 'All our sins shall not be investigated or written down,' nevertheless, all your sins are being written down every day (104.7).

That the record of evil deeds will serve as the basis for eschatological judgment is explicit in 98.6 and implied in 96.7, 97.5-7 and 104.7. Especially important in this regard are the woes of 96.7c-8, 97.8 and 98.9-16, which are eschatologically oriented,[2] while the context of 104.7 contrasts the fate of 'the righteous' and 'the sinners' in view of 'the great judgment' (104.5). Furthermore, the writing of the deeds of humans seems to be linked to another motif, namely the idea that angels 'remind' God, presumably in connection with the judgment, about the sufferings of 'the righteous' as a result of the evils performed by 'the sinners' (99.3; cf. 104.1).[3]

The notion of a heavenly book of deeds is also present in the Enochian Animal Apocalypse, where again the writing of deeds is the basis for eschatological judgment (89.61-62, 64, 70-71, 76-77; 90.17, 20).[4] Yet in these passages it is the oppressive deeds of angelic shep-

---

1. Isaac (p. 78) notes, 'The whole passage in parentheses is missing from A, most probably due to homoeoteleuton'.

2. See Rau (pp. 339-41), who notes that 98.1-8 is framed by two preceding woes (97.7-10) and a concluding series of woes (98.8–99.5), and that the dominant point, namely the threat of judgment, is strengthened through three oaths in 98.1, 4, 6.

3. Nickelsburg, *Resurrection*, pp. 120-21.

4. There is clearly some relation between the scene of judgment in *1 En.* 90 and the similar scene in Dan. 7. In fact, Beale argues (pp. 81-88) on the basis of his overview of the basic components and the order in which they are presented, that *1*

herds rather than the deeds of humans that are recorded, so the idea is somewhat different.

In *2 Enoch* it is the book(s) of the 'achievements' of humans (50.1; 65.4-5, rec. J) or their 'deeds' (19.5; 43.1, rec. J; 44.5, rec. A; 52.15; 53.2-3) that receives considerable attention. In spite of the fact that *2 Enoch* contains no scene of judgment, the association between the heavenly writing(s) and the event of judgment seems secure enough. *2 En.* 44.5-7 (rec. A) reads:

> Happy is he who directs |his heart| toward every person, such as bringing help to him who has been condemned, and by giving support to him who has been broken, and by giving to the needy. Because on |the day of| the great judgment every deed of mankind will be restored by means of the written record. Happy is he whose measure will prove to be just and whose weight just and scales just! Because on the day of the great judgment every measure and every weight and every scale will be exposed.

The reference to a 'written record' is both preceded and followed by a beatitude, with the 'happiness' of which the writer speaks having an eschatological orientation—that is, it results from an appropriate decision at the last judgment. And, of course, the 'written record' stands as the basis for that decision. Equally clear is the connection of the heavenly book(s) with the eschatological judgment in several other passages from *2 Enoch*, including 50.1 (cf. the reference to judgment in v. 4), 52.15 and 53.2-3. *2 En.* 52.15 and 53.2-3 follow an alternating list of blessings and curses, with the eschatological orientation of this list—as well as the reference to the writing of deeds—being set forth explicitly in 52.15.[1]

There are also a number of similar passages in *Jubilees*. In *Jub.* 4.23 Enoch, who now resides in the garden of Eden, 'is there writing condemnation and judgment of the world, and all of the evils of the children of men'. It is interesting to note that the idea of the writing of the fates of humans (here expressed negatively, i.e. 'condemnation and judgment') and the writing of their deeds—which, it may be postulated, were originally two separate traditions—are here juxtaposed. Yet the connection with judgment (and here condemnation as well) seems secure enough in this passage.

En. 90.9-27 is an 'apocalyptic midrash' on Dan. 7. One of the common elements, of course, is the opening of the books.

1. The recensions differ slightly, but both make reference to 'the great judgment day'.

A similar situation is evident in the statement concerning the consequences of adultery in *Jub*. 39.6:

> There is a judgment of death which is decreed for him in heaven before the Lord Most High. And the sin is written (on high) concerning him in the eternal books always before the Lord.

There is a difference, of course, between the teaching of this passage and that of *Jub*. 4.23, for here the sin recorded is not merely one of many but itself sufficient to merit 'the judgment of death'.[1] Nevertheless, the association between the writing of deeds and judgment is clear. It is implied as well in the other two references to the writing of deeds in *Jubilees*, in 28.6 and 30.17.

The heavenly book(s) of deeds is also present in the judgment scene of ch. 12 of the *Testament of Abraham* (recension A), though it is not found elsewhere in that writing. The text speaks of a book 'whose thickness was six cubits, while its breadth was ten cubits' (v. 7). Alongside were two angels, 'the one on the right recorded righteous deeds, while the one on the left (recorded) sins' (v. 12). Later, as the scene unfolds, the judge calls for the book in order to render a judgment:

> And the judge told one of the angels who served him, 'Open for me this book and find for me the sins of this soul.' And when he opened the book he found its sins and righteous deeds to be equally balanced, and he neither turned it over to the torturers nor (placed it among) those who were being saved, but he set it in the middle (vv. 17-18).

The sequence of events, as Nickelsburg observes, is complicated by the fact that the author appears to have fleshed out a traditional Jewish judgment scene with details from an Egyptian tradition, and so it is difficult to determine with precision the relationship between the various motifs that are utilized in this passage.[2] Particularly puzzling is the interaction between the book, the recording angels, and the concept of 'weighing' deeds.[3] Nickelsburg suggests a couple of ways in which one could integrate these various images:

---

1. On this question, see E.P. Sanders, *Paul and Palestinian Judaism* (Philadelphia: Fortress Press, 1977), pp. 366-74.

2. Nickelsburg, 'Eschatology in the Testament of Abraham', pp. 39-40; *contra* Rau (pp. 320-21), who suggests that the conception of the book and the writing of deeds were added later to the judgment scene.

3. The Egyptian concept of the weighing of 'souls' is also introduced in v. 13; see F. Schmidt, I, pp. 72-76, and Sanders, 'Testament of Abraham', p. 889.

What is the relationship between the paper on which they record the sins and righteous deeds and the book that contains the record of deeds? In the passage under consideration, the record found in the book fits into the judgment process. Perhaps the author intends to say that the two angels copy out the record of the sins and righteous deeds and lay the two sheets in the two pans of the balance. A less likely explanation is that the angels' records are entered as loose leaves into the book and are taken out and weighed at the time of judgment.[1]

Regardless of what position one takes on this question, it is evident enough that the record of deeds stands as the basis for judgment. It is the content of the book that determines the fate of individuals, at least in many cases.[2]

The book(s) of deeds plays a significant role as well in the *Apocalypse of Zephaniah*. The writing of the deeds of humans is mentioned, first, in ch. 3 of the Akhmimic text:

These are the angels of the Lord Almighty. They write down all the good deeds of the righteous upon their manuscript as they watch at the gate of heaven. And I take them from their hands and bring them up before the Lord Almighty; he writes their name in the Book of the Living. Also the angels of the accuser who is upon the earth, they also write down all of the sins of men upon their manuscript. They also sit at the gate of heaven. They tell the accuser and he writes them upon his manuscript so that he might accuse them when they come out of the world (and) down there (vv. 6-9).

The parallelisms between good and evil angels and good and evil deeds that appear in some earlier apocalyptic writings are also present here, albeit in modified form. The scope of the content of the 'manuscripts' is varied, so that 'the angels of the Lord Almighty' write down 'all the good deeds *of the righteous*', while 'the angels of the accuser' record 'all of the sins *of men*'. Furthermore, it is the record of the good deeds of the righteous that is connected with the image of 'the Book of the Living', with the implication being that the 'manuscript' of good

---

1. Nickelsburg, 'Eschatology in the Testament of Abraham', p. 30. James (*Testament of Abraham*, pp. 124-25) offers a similar interpretation: 'The idea seems to be that these latter [i.e. the recording angels] register what is happening on earth for future insertion in the book'. As a result, 'the great book on the table contains a transcript of the sins and good deeds of men made from the record of the angels in front of the table'.

2. In the case of the soul whose deeds were balanced (12.16-18), however, it is the mercy of God in response to the supplication of Abraham and Michael that leads to its salvation (14.1-8). Nevertheless, it is the content of the book that leads the angel to place the soul 'in the middle'.

deeds is the basis for enrollment in the book of those who are saved. There is, however, no book of those who are condemned or who are recorded as 'enemies' of God.

The interpretation of *Apocalypse of Zephaniah* 7, which is the judgment scene itself, is hindered by a lacuna of two pages in the Akhmimic text. Still, it seems from what we have that the motif of the books is used in a manner entirely consistent with the earlier references in ch. 3: the righteous seer must face the accuser, who is armed with a manuscript containing the record of all his sins. There is also another manuscript, however, and while the text breaks off before describing the content of this writing, it is probable that it contains the record of the good deeds of the righteous. The text picks up again after the seer has triumphed over the accuser, and 'a great angel' says to him, 'You will now cross over the crossing place. For your name is written in the Book of the Living' (9.2). It seems, therefore, that the seer's victory over the accuser, which is certainly tied in with the content of the 'manuscripts', is the basis for writing his name in the Book of the Living. And it is the inclusion of the seer's name in this Book of the Living that is the condition for his salvation.

This survey of references to the book(s) or writing(s) of the deeds of humans supports the thesis that the motif is common in the Jewish apocalypses—which is not surprising since it is closely associated with the event of judgment, a major theme or preoccupation in these writings. It occurs in traditional judgment scenes, but is also present in a number of passages outside of these sections. The image of a book(s) of deeds always points the reader to the coming day of judgment, and so elicits particular responses. Indeed, the record of deeds stands as the basis for the eschatological judgment and so determines the fate of individuals. The writing(s) of the deeds of humans also interacts in various ways with the Book of Life,[1] though the two images represent separate traditions and must not be confused.

c. *The Consequences of Judgment*

The final element of the judgment tradition to be considered here is the consequences of judgment, which include both the vindication of the righteous and the condemnation of the wicked. While the condem-

---

1. The interaction between the two images is also seen in Rev. 20.11-15, where they are simply juxtaposed; see Rau, p. 314. Nevertheless, our primary concern is with the Jewish apocalypses.

nation of the wicked is certainly prominent in the apocalypses, it is the theme of the vindication of the righteous that is more significant for my purposes. Nickelsburg has noted that the notion of the vindication of the righteous is often associated in the judgment tradition with two particular themes, the exaltation or ascension of the righteous and the association of the righteous with stars and angels in all their brilliance and glory.[1] And these concepts, indeed, are closely linked, since they both express in slightly different ways the confident expectation that the righteous will enjoy the blessings of the heavenly world.

In Daniel 12 the brilliance of the righteous, as well as their association with the stars of heaven, is set forth explicitly:

> Those who are wise will shine like the brightness of the heavens, and those who lead many to righteousness, like the stars for ever and ever (v. 3).

There is no suggestion here of a literal exaltation to heaven; rather, the language of simile is used to highlight the transcendent glory of the righteous following their resurrection and the event of judgment.[2] Comparable similes appear in *1 En.* 104.2, 'But now you shall shine like the lights of heaven, and you shall be seen; and the windows of heaven shall be opened for you'. Then in v. 4 the fate of the righteous is further described: 'You are about to be making a great rejoicing like the angels of heaven'. It is difficult to determine whether the concluding clause of v. 2, 'the windows of heaven shall be opened for you', implies some kind of literal ascension or exaltation; nevertheless, the future glory of the righteous and their association with the life of the angels in heaven is secure.[3]

4 Ezra 7.97 also looks forward to a time when those who are obedient to the Law will 'shine like the sun' and 'be made like the light of the stars, being incorruptible from then on'. In fact, in 7.125 it is even said that 'those who practiced self-control shall shine *more than* the stars'. The association of the righteous with the angels is most clearly expressed, however, in *Apoc. Zeph.* 8.2-4, where, as a result of his

---

1. *Resurrection*, p. 38.
2. Cf. *ibid.*, p. 26.
3. See P.B. Decock, 'Holy Ones, Sons of God, and the Transcendent Future of the Righteous in 1 Enoch and the New Testament', *Neot* 17 (1983), pp. 70-82, for a discussion, not only of this passage, but also of other possible evidence for the association of the righteous with the life of the angels in *1 Enoch*. As in Dan. 12.3, it is the language of simile that is utilized: the righteous rejoice 'like the angels of heaven'. Cf. Cavallin, p. 44.

triumph over the accuser in the previous chapter, the seer is enabled
to participate in the heavenly chorus of praise:

> Thousands of thousands and myriads of myriads of angels gave praise before
> me. I, myself, put on an angelic garment. I saw all of those angels praying. I,
> myself, prayed together with them, I knew their language, which they spoke
> with me (8.2-4).

These references to the consequences of judgment for the righteous
stand, of course, in sharp contrast to the references to the condemnation of the wicked. Furthermore, while the references we have surveyed are, in each case, a part of a traditional judgment scene, it is
important to recognize that descriptions of the consequences of judgment are present as well in many other sections of the Jewish apocalypses.[1] As one might expect, there is little consistency with respect to
details—even within individual writings. The apocalyptic writers were
not concerned so much with giving a precise and detailed description
of the post-judgment condition of the righteous as they were with
insisting (1) that a separation between the righteous and the wicked
will take place, and (2) that the righteous will enjoy the transcendent
blessings of the heavenly sphere. The Jewish apocalypses repeatedly
set out 'the association between the immortal blessed and stars, angels,
and other heavenly bodies or beings' and repeatedly emphasize the
'assumption or glorification' of the righteous.[2] These emphases are
consistent with what we have observed in the judgment scenes, though
the transcendent post-judgment condition is a major concern of the
apocalyptists even apart from the judgment tradition (Dan. 12.2-3; *1
En.* 91.17; *Jub.* 23.26-30; *4 Ezra* 7.78, 97, 113-14, 125; 8.52-54; *2
Bar.* 51.3-12).[3] Balanced with these concerns for the fate of the righteous, of course, are similar concerns for the fate of the wicked (*4
Ezra* 7.36; 9.9;[4] *2 Bar.* 30.4-5; 51.1-5).[5]

---

1. Unlike the Merkabah visions and references to the accusing angels and the
heavenly books, descriptions of the consequences of judgment are too widespread in
these writings to permit a survey of the material in individual works. For such an
analysis, see Cavallin, pp. 26-215.

2. Cf. Cavallin, pp. 203-206.

3. See the many examples in H.C. Cavallin, 'Leben nach dem Tode im Spätjudentum und im frühen Christentum. I. Spätjudentum', in *ANRW*, II.19.1,
pp. 266-69.

4. *4 Ezra* does not dwell on this extensively. In fact, in 9.13 Ezra is exhorted: 'Do
not continue to be curious as to how the ungodly will be punished; but inquire how
the righteous will be saved'.

Conclusion

The preceding survey of the content of revelation in the Jewish apocalypses has been by no means exhaustive. It is intended only to highlight those features of relevance for an analysis of the problem encountered in the church at Colossae. For the features of the one bear a certain relation to the features of the other—particularly the idea of a throne of glory that is associated with the event of eschatological judgment.

It is, of course, impossible to say whether any or all of the themes surveyed were rooted in actual visionary experiences. In view of apocalypticism's connections with later Merkabah mysticism, I would argue that this is probable, especially in the case of the visions of God and the heavenly worship. Yet, as was observed in Chapter 2, distinctions between an actual vision and a literary convention should probably not be pressed too rigorously since the writers of these materials viewed their own inspiration as including both the content of their visions and the literary conventions used to convey that content. In any case, the intention here has been primarily to lay the groundwork for an analysis of the functions of revelation in this body of literature, and it is to that topic we must now turn in order to understand the impact of the apocalyptists' message on the lives of those they addressed.

5.   Detailed descriptions of the final state of the wicked are rare in the apocalypses, though the fact that judgment will take place is a major concern.

Chapter 4

THE FUNCTIONS OF REVELATION IN JEWISH APOCALYPTICISM

Contemporary research no longer treats the Jewish apocalyptic writings as mere containers of doctrine. Instead, scholarship today adopts a literary approach that seeks to integrate three significant factors: form, content and function. Having dealt with form and content in Chapters 2 and 3, it is the function of revelation in Jewish apocalypticism that I am concerned with here.

As John Collins points out, in Jewish apocalypticism 'the communication with the heavenly world is never an end in itself'.[1] Indeed, it is precisely through such transcendent revelations that the readers are called on to 'live justly, responding in a free and uninhibited manner to the demands of righteousness, and so attain the experience of the approval of God'.[2] There can, in fact, be little doubt that the Jewish apocalypses are hortatory in nature. Even where explicit exhortations are lacking, such a goal is implied.[3] So David Hellholm, for one, proposes the following addition to the standard definition of 'apocalypse' as set forth by John Collins: that it was 'intended for a group in crisis with the purpose of exhortation and/or consolation by means of divine authority'.[4] And this realization of the hortatory nature of Jewish

1. J.J. Collins, 'Jewish Apocalypses', p. 26. Collins's formulations in this article stem from the Apocalypse Group of the SBL Genres Project.
2. J.J. Collins, 'Apocalyptic Eschatology', p. 77; cf. *idem*, 'Morphology', pp. 9, 11; 'Jewish Apocalypses', pp. 26-27.
3. Koch (*Rediscovery*, p. 25) lists 'paraenetic discourses' as one of the significant features of the apocalypses, while Rowland (*Open Heaven*, p. 50) argues that the apocalypses are characterized by a tripartite structure of legends, visions and admonitions. Such formulations are problematic, but they serve to illustrate the significance of exhortation in these writings.
4. D. Hellholm, 'The Problem of Apocalyptic Genre and the Apocalypse of John', in *Society of Biblical Literature 1982 Seminar Papers* (ed. K.H. Richards; Chico, CA: Scholars Press, 1982) p. 168.

apocalypticism, whether explicit or implied, has been growing among several other contemporary scholars.[1]

While the importance of 'function' in the study of Jewish apocalyptic writings is evident, the analysis of these documents in terms of their function is fraught with difficulties. Despite the fact that these writings share a common religious outlook, and so certain functions may therefore be considered characteristic, the Jewish apocalypses by no means constitute a unified corpus.[2] Consequently, analysis must be sufficiently flexible to allow for various permutations. One must, in fact, take care not to flatten out the evidence.

Nevertheless, with such a caution in mind, it is appropriate (1) to categorize the various kinds of functions that are represented in the apocalypses, and (2) to study the ways in which these functions came to expression in writings with diverse settings.[3] In what follows, therefore, I shall take into account both general functions and specific formulations, seeking to understand better the relationship between content and function in the Jewish apocalypses.

The scope of the material requires that my analysis be somewhat selective. Thus I shall focus my attention on those functions that are particularly significant for an analysis of the problems reflected in the Letter to the Colossians: (1) exhortations of the godly for the purpose of continued obedience, and (2) admonitions and rebukes of the unrighteous to repent and obey the teachings of God.

---

1. E.g. Rowland, *Open Heaven*, pp. 29-30; also J.J. Collins, *Apocalyptic Imagination*, pp. 31-32, though with certain caveats.

2. Cf. J.J. Collins, *Apocalyptic Imagination*, p. 29, with particular reference to the variety of social settings represented by the Jewish apocalypses; see also Stone, 'Apocalyptic Literature', pp. 433-35, and E.J.C. Tigchelaar, 'More on Apocalyptic and Apocalypses', *JSJ* 18 (1987), pp. 137-44. Consequently, definitions must operate at a fairly high level of abstraction. This is a major problem for any 'essentialist' definition, e.g. that of E.P. Sanders, 'The Genre of Palestinian Jewish Apocalypticism', in *Apocalypticism*, pp. 447-59. Recent research has emphasized both the diversity of Second Temple Judaism and the problem of defining its 'essence'; see G.G. Porton, 'Diversity in Postbiblical Judaism', in *Early Judaism and its Modern Interpreters* (ed. R.A. Kraft and G.W.E. Nickelsburg; Philadelphia: Fortress Press, 1986), pp. 57-80, and Charlesworth, *The Old Testament Pseudepigrapha and the New Testament*, pp. 47-58.

3. F.J. Murphy (*The Structure and Meaning of Second Baruch* [Atlanta: Scholars Press, 1985], p. 32) observes correctly that the way in which 'transcendence is expressed within each apocalypse is very important and could change our idea of precisely what function this transcendence serves in each work'.

Two caveats at the start, however, are necessary. First, it is important to recognize that the consolation of the righteous in crisis settings is central to the Jewish apocalypses, particularly to such writings as Daniel and the Similitudes of Enoch. I shall be unable to devote any extensive attention to this broad topic since it is not directly related to the error at Colossae, but I intend in no way to minimize its significance in the Jewish apocalyptic literature.[1] In fact, in many cases the consolation of the righteous lays the groundwork for an exhortation to continued obedience. Second, the distinction between exhortation and admonition, which I shall use in what follows, is utilized primarily to facilitate clarity of analysis, and does not always reflect the consciousness of the apocalyptic writers themselves. In certain of these writings, in fact, the status of the audience is unclear, and may include those considered both righteous and unrighteous. Nevertheless, since the distinction is helpful in several cases, I shall proceed to survey the evidence in terms of these categories.

1. *Exhortations of the Righteous*

One of the most obvious functions of revelation in the Jewish apocalypses is to exhort the righteous to continued obedience in spite of their present trials and temptations. Though there have been arguments to the contrary by some scholars of a previous generation,[2] the ethical concern of the Jewish apocalyptic writers has been generally vindicated, especially of late.[3]

---

1. For a discussion of the consolation of the righteous as a major function in Jewish apocalyptic literature, see T.J. Sappington, 'The Factor of Function in Defining Jewish Apocalyptic Literature', *JSP* (forthcoming).

2. E.g. R.T. Herford, *Talmud and Apocrypha* (London: Soncino, 1933), pp. 263-69. Far more balanced is H.M. Hughes, *The Ethics of Jewish Apocryphal Literature* (London: Culley, n.d.), though see pp. 103-105.

3. Such a point was argued earlier by R.H. Charles, *Eschatology: The Doctrine of the Future Life in Israel, Judaism and Christianity* (reprint edn; New York: Schocken, 1963), p. 173; Oesterley, *Jews and Judaism*, p. 72; W.D. Davies, *Torah in the Messianic Age and/or the Age to Come* (Philadelphia: Society of Biblical Literature, 1952), p. 3; *idem*, 'Apocalyptic and Pharisaism', in *Christian Origins and Judaism*, pp. 22-23; Vielhauer, p. 587; Russell, pp. 100-103. Most recently, see J.J. Collins (*Apocalyptic Imagination*, p. 5), who writes, 'Paraenesis occupies a prominent place in a few apocalypses (e.g. *2 Enoch, 2 Baruch*), but all the apocalypses have a hortatory aspect, whether or not it is spelled out in specific exhortations and admonitions'. A.N. Wilder (*Eschatology and Ethics* [rev. edn; New York: Harper, 1950], p. 32) argues, 'From first to last we should draw our contrasts not

Because of the degree of diversity within this corpus of literature, it will be helpful to consider the various authors' exhortations to the righteous under two headings. First, the content of the paraeneses. My focus here will be to note the range of legal and ethical concerns that are present in these writings. Second, I shall consider the way in which the revelation of eschatological judgment serves as the basis for the apocalyptists' exhortations. Studying the material under these two headings will not only clarify the relationship between the revelatory materials in the apocalypses and the exhortations to obedience (whether explicit or implicit), but will also reveal the surprising extent of the apocalyptists' concerns.

a. *The Content of the Paraeneses*
For the Jewish apocalyptic writers, a proper Jewish lifestyle involves obedience to the Mosaic law, taking into account all its specific commands and injunctions. Dietrich Rössler argued that references to 'the law' in the apocalypses are general and non-specific—that the apocalyptists had no interest in the detailed particulars of the Mosaic law but were only concerned with one's overall stance in relation to that law, since that was what demonstrated whether or not one belonged to the people of God.[1] And so Rössler, on this basis, contrasted the Jewish apocalypses and the writings of rabbinic Judaism. More recently, however, such a position has been decisively refuted by Andreas Nissen. Today, in fact, there can be little doubt that the apocalyptists were concerned with specific acts of obedience as prescribed in the Law of Moses and not merely one's general attitude toward the law.[2]

---

between ethics and apocalyptic. . . But we should draw our contrast between an ethical and a non-ethical apocalyptic.' This is true, in part, but my research has failed to uncover even one example of the latter category; *contra* G.E. Ladd, 'Why Not Prophetic-Apocalyptic?', *JBL* 76 (1956), pp. 192-200.

1. D. Rössler, *Gesetz und Geschichte, Untersuchungen zur Theologie der jüdischen Apokalyptik und der pharisäischen Orthodoxie* (Neukirchen: Neukirchener Verlag, 1960), pp. 45-54, 78, 101-102. Cf. W. Schmithals, *The Apocalyptic Movement* (trans. J.E. Steely; Nashville: Abingdon Press, 1973), p. 46; also Herford (p. 218), who says with regard to *1 Enoch*: 'The ordinary distinctions of ethics between the several virtues and vices are lost sight of, as they are merged in the one broad distinction between the righteous and the wicked. Of ethic in the sense of the right conduct of life in the service of God, the writers of Enoch have hardly anything to say.'

2. A. Nissen, 'Tora und Geschichte im Spätjudentum', *NovT* 9 (1967), pp. 260-69. He argues, for example, that obedience and disobedience are often referred to in

It is not difficult to produce from the apocalyptic writings a list of specific sins that are to be avoided, even in works such as *1 Enoch, 4 Ezra* and *2 Baruch*.[1] It would, however, be a mistake, at least at the outset, to focus on the tremendous variety of concerns expressed. What is important, rather, is to note that it is whole-hearted obedience to the commands of Torah that is the basis for salvation in these writings. This is clear particularly in *1 Enoch* 1–5,[2] where the 'referential background' is the Mosaic covenant—as indicated by the allusion to Mount Sinai, the terminology of the denouncement speech, and the echoes of the last chapters of Deuteronomy.[3]

the plural (i.e. acts of obedience or disobedience, pp. 260-61), cites numerous examples of specific ethical concerns (pp. 262-63), and sets forth evidence that the writers of the apocalypses were interested not only in what sinners are but also in what they do (pp. 264-65). Cf. Koch, *Rediscovery*, 40-41, 86-88; also Sanders, *Paul*, pp. 409-10, 423-24, who sees both the apocalypses and the rabbinic writings as representatives of 'covenantal nomism'; C. Münchow, *Ethik und Eschatologie: Ein Beitrag zum Verständnis der frühjüdischen Apokalyptik* (Göttingen: Vandenhoeck & Ruprecht, 1982), p. 40; J.J. Collins, 'Apocalyptic Literature', in *Early Judaism*, p. 359.

1. See the detailed lists of specific concerns in Nissen, pp. 262-63, and Münchow, pp. 134-37.

2. Münchow (p. 40) makes an important observation that applies not only to chs. 1–5, but also to the whole of *1 Enoch*: 'Die Mahnungen (sieht man von den begründenden Erweiterungen ab) können wohl nur deshalb so "allgemein" gehalten sein, weil sie sich auf Vorgegebenes und Bekanntes, d.h. auf die Mosetora, beziehen, ohne diese expressis verbis anzuführen'. Lebram (pp. 176-77) assumes that the apocalyptic paraenesis refers to the fulfillment of the traditional Jewish law, but notes that we cannot tell whether 'they refer to the Pentateuch or to a special collection of Halakhot'. While certain of the apocalypses, which will be discussed below, include specific items of legal interpretation in their paraenesis, there is in this group of writings no evident concern to list detailed Halakah; consequently, the evidence points decisively toward Lebram's former conclusion.

3. Cf. Hartman, *Asking for a Meaning*, pp. 123-24. The impression of the orderliness of nature (creation) given in *1 En.* 1–5 only serves to support this conclusion, since it demonstrates that the forces of the cosmos regularly submit to the will of the creator in a way that is paradigmatic for those who are truly the people of God. The law of creation and the law of Moses are thus in agreement; neither is subordinated to the other (*contra* M. Limbeck, *Die Ordnung des Heils: Untersuchungen zum Gesetzesverständnis des Frühjudentums* [Düsseldorf: Patmos, 1971], pp. 71-72), nor do they stand in conflict with one another. Certainly it is true that the law is placed in a wider context in these chapters and that 'the ultimate authority is older than Moses and applies not only to Israel but to all humanity' (J.J. Collins, *Apocalyptic Imagination*, pp. 37-38). But it is inaccurate to argue from this that the writer is not vitally concerned with obedience to the Mosaic law. These conclusions apply as well to other sections of *1 Enoch*, which will be treated below.

Worth noting also is the centrality of the commands and requirements of the Torah in *4 Ezra* and *2 Baruch*. The dialogues of *4 Ezra* set out two differing viewpoints: Ezra consistently lays stress on God's election as the basis for salvation (see esp. 5.23-28 and 6.54-59), while Uriel argues that obedience to the law is the condition for acceptance before God (7.20-24, 72, 77, 89, 92, and 105).[1] The latter episodes of consolation also link salvation to obedience, though here mercy plays a role as well (12.34; 14.34). Consequently, there is a tension in *4 Ezra*, though ultimately obedience to the law is the only sure basis for salvation.[2] Indeed, the final word of *4 Ezra* seems to come in ch. 14 when Ezra admonishes the people, 'If you, then, will rule over your minds and discipline your hearts, you shall be kept alive, and after death you shall obtain mercy' (v. 34). So it is not perfect adherence to the details of the Mosaic law, but wholehearted obedience to its requirements that is the condition for salvation.[3]

The situation is even clearer when we turn to *2 Baruch*, which, while not eliminating the concept of divine election,[4] clearly subordinates this theme to that of keeping the requirements of the Mosaic law. Some stress on the observance of sabbaths and festivals is evident in 66.4 and 84.8, and there may be some special concern in this regard. Yet *2 Baruch* is primarily concerned to stimulate its readers to a more general obedience to all of the divine commandments.[5] Many times, in fact, the work states that obedience is the condition for a person to be saved (14.12; 46.5-6; 51.3) or, if it is lacking, to be condemned (15.5-8; 48.40, 46-47; 77.4)—though, as in *4 Ezra*, there are indications that

---

1. Cf. A.L. Thompson, pp. 312-13.

2. *Ibid.*, p. 317; Thompson, however, sees this emphasis as more prevalent in the consolation episodes than we would be prepared to acknowledge.

3. Contrary to Sanders (*Paul*, p. 418), this work fits roughly into the pattern he calls 'covenantal nomism'. G.W.E. Nickelsburg ('Revealed Wisdom as a Criterion for Inclusion and Exclusion', in *'To See Ourselves as Others See Us'* [ed. J. Neusner and E.S. Frerichs; Chico, CA: Scholars Press, 1985], pp. 81-82) argues that 'Ezra' 'esteems the Torah as the source of the wisdom that leads to salvation'.

4. Cf. 13.9-10, 44.13-15, and 54.5. Certainly a special relationship between God and Israel is implied here on the basis of election and covenant, and this is not surprising in view of the fact that the major question of the book is whether God has nullified the covenants made with Abraham and Moses; see Sayler, p. 131.

5. The emphasis on the calendar is by no means as strong as in *Jubilees*, and we find no apology for a particular calendrical scheme.

it is a wholehearted obedience rather than a perfect obedience that is required.[1]

The content of the exhortations is slightly different in those Jewish apocalypses that have their origins in the hellenistic diaspora vis-à-vis those that likely originated in Palestine.[2] They are, of course, still oriented toward the law of Moses. Nevertheless, there is a tendency in Diaspora Jewry 'to bypass the distinctive laws of Judaism and concentrate on monotheism and matters of social and sexual morality'.[3]

One thinks in this regard immediately of *2 Enoch* with its humanistic emphasis, evident especially in 44.1-2:

> The Lord with his own two hands created mankind; and in a facsimile of his own face. Small and great the Lord created. Whoever insults a person's face insults the face of the Lord; whoever treats a person's face with repugnance treats the face of the Lord with repugnance. Whoever treats with contempt the face of any person treats the face of the Lord with contempt.[4]

The exhortations of *2 Enoch* lay stress on such particulars as kindness to widows, orphans and others who are helpless (9.1; 43.8-10; 44.4; 63.1; etc.) and dealing with others in a manner that is truthful, just and compassionate (9.1; 42.12-13). There is, however, an even more fundamental principle at work in *2 Enoch*, which stands, ultimately, as

---

1. In chs. 41–42 there is a discussion of the punishments that await those who 'separated themselves from your statutes and who have cast away from the yoke of your Law' (41.3). Such a description applies not to individuals who have generally followed the law with the exception of a few details; rather, it refers to apostates, those who do not love God's law (54.14) and even despise it (51.4). This group stands in contrast to those who have 'not withdrawn from mercy' and who have 'preserved the truth of the Law' (44.14). These have not forgotten God's law (44.7-8); indeed, they have subjected themselves to its demands (54.5).

2. In making this statement I do not intend to downplay the great diversity of Diaspora Jewry; cf. A.T. Kraabel, 'The Roman Diaspora: Six Questionable Assumptions', *JJS* 33 (1982), pp. 445-64, esp. 457. Nevertheless, the tendency we describe is evident in several of the apocalypses.

3. J.J. Collins, *Between Athens and Jerusalem* (New York: Crossroad, 1983), p. 162. Of course, circumcision was one element often downplayed. Such an approach was almost certainly intended to attract learned Gentiles. But it seems also to reflect the practice of certain more liberal strands of Diaspora Judaism. We cannot, of course, assume that they observed only those commandments that are mentioned explicitly, but it is certainly these that they emphasized (*ibid.*, p. 167).

4. The longer recension differs somewhat in its wording, but the thrust is the same—one must treat other human beings with respect in spite of their social class, since God created them in his own likeness; cf. 52.6 and 60.1, as well as the comments of J.J. Collins, *Apocalyptic Imagination*, pp. 196-97.

the basis for its humanistic ethic—the fear of God, which is listed as the highest virtue in 43.3 (cf. 48.6-9).[1] 2 *Enoch* also stresses the need for obedience to its own particular version of the solar calendar, but this does not receive the emphasis that it does in certain other writings to be discussed below.[2]

Similar ethical viewpoints are also present in other writings from the Jewish diaspora. E.P. Sanders has labeled the *Testament of Abraham* as representative of 'a kind of lowest-common-denominator Judaism',[3] in part because of the fact that the sins mentioned are not at all distinctive to Judaism. Among those receiving explicit mention are burglary (10.10), robbery (10.5), murder (10.5; cf. the different account in ch. 10 of rec. B; 12.9 [rec. B]), sexual immorality (10.8; cf. 10.13 and 12.2 of rec. B) and slander (12.6 [rec. B]), while 'righteousness' would appear to include hospitality (1.1-2, 5; 17.7) and love for God (17.7). Much the same is the case with 3 *Baruch*, where the writer mentions murder, adultery, fornication, perjury, theft, idol worship and other sins that would be heinous to many Gentiles as well as to Jews (4.17; 13.4 [Gk]). There is also some evidence of an ascetic tendency (see 4.8-9, 16-17),[4] and perhaps one allusion to the 364-day calendar.[5] Likewise, though the evidence is fragmentary, such a stance seems maintained in the *Apocalypse of Zephaniah*. For this work lays special emphasis on acts of mercy to those who are helpless (7.4-5) and other social concerns (10.5-7), while also mentioning fasting and observance of the times of prayer (7.6).

Yet there is another group of writings that evidence a more specific basis for their exhortations, namely the law of Moses *as properly interpreted*. For the authors of these writings, a general obedience to the law is not enough. One's actions must conform, as well, to the proper interpretation of that law as advocated by the writer and his community. One of the clearest examples of this kind of approach is

1. Cf. Andersen, p. 96. The fear of God, of course, leads one to worship him and to abstain from idolatry (33.8; 36.1-2, both recensions; cf. 35.1-3).

2. Andersen (p. 124) notes both similarities and differences between the calendar set forth in 2 *Enoch* and that which is advocated in *Jubilees* and at Qumran. He points out, 'It has no interest in a seven-day week nor in sabbath observance'. This is consistent with its general attitude toward the law described above.

3. Sanders, 'Testament of Abraham', pp. 876-77.

4. Cf. J.J. Collins, *Apocalyptic Imagination*, p. 199. The sins listed above are said to arise from the drinking of wine.

5. There may be a reference to the 364-day calendar in 6.13 (Greek version), so Gaylord, p. 630; but this issue receives no emphasis.

found in chs. 91–105/108 of *1 Enoch*. For, though it may be difficult to determine with any degree of precision the points at issue,[1] it is evident that in these chapters the group of Jews for whom the author speaks made exclusive claims for their interpretation of the Torah. Those who adhered to this inspired interpretation would be saved (99.10), while those whose interpretation differed would not escape the coming judgment (98.9-10, 14-16; 99.2; 104.9-10). Correct interpretation, according to the Epistle of Enoch, is essential to salvation.[2]

Somewhat more obvious as to the importance of a correct interpretation for salvation are those writings that propose a distinctive view of calendrical matters. The interpretation of these writings is made difficult by a lack of scholarly consensus about the status of the 364-day solar calendar in the period with which I am concerned.[3] Certain observations, however, are nonetheless possible. For while a concern with calendrical matters may be evident in Dan 7.25,[4] it is particularly

1. Nickelsburg ('Epistle of Enoch', p. 343) writes: 'Perhaps the author refers to his own exhortations to righteousness in general, or to other Enochic books about the right calendar for the observance of feasts, or to yet other Enochic literature that we no longer possess. Perhaps he refers to all of these.' In the context of the work as a whole, of course, the calendrical matters come to mind. But there are no explicit references to this in the Epistle, where the emphasis is on the violence of the rich who oppress them.

2. Nickelsburg, 'Epistle of Enoch', pp. 334-43; *idem*, 'Revealed Wisdom', pp. 74-75.

3. Several recent studies have supported the thesis of A. Jaubert (*The Date of the Last Supper* [trans. I. Rafferty; Staten Island, NY: Alba House, 1965], pp. 31-38) and others with regard to the antiquity of the solar calendar; cf. e.g. J.C. Vander-Kam, 'The Origin, Character, and Early History of the 364-Day Calendar: A Reassessment of Jaubert's Hypothesis', *CBQ* 41 (1979), pp. 398-99, and P.R. Davies, 'Calendrical Change and Qumran Origins: An Assessment of VanderKam's Theory', *CBQ* 45 (1983), pp. 81-82; contrast, however, J.M. Baumgarten, 'The Calendar of the Book of Jubilees and the Bible', in *Studies in Qumran Law* (Leiden: Brill, 1977), pp. 101-14, and M.D. Herr, 'The Calendar', in *The Jewish People in the First Century* (ed. S. Safrai and M. Stern; Assen: Van Gorcum, 1976), II, pp. 834-35. Nevertheless, even among those who acknowledge the probable antiquity of the solar calendar, there is significant disagreement with regard to the time when this calendar was abandoned in cultic use. Jaubert (pp. 43-51) and P.R. Davies (p. 83) argue that it was modified prior to the second century BC; VanderKam ('Early History of the 364-Day Calendar', p. 411) suggests it was not abandoned in cultic use until the time of Antiochus IV. Thus while it seems that a solar calendar was dominant at an early time, we simply cannot say with any degree of confidence how widely it was used in the early Second Temple period.

4. Jaubert, p. 46; Rau, pp. 92-93; Lacocque, pp. 115-16; Lebram, p. 189; cf. P.R. Davies, p. 87.

in *1 Enoch* 72–82, *Jubilees*, and the writings from Qumran that such matters play a critical role.

In the Enochian Astronomical Book, at least in its present form,[1] the calendar is clearly a major concern to the author/ redactor, though there is no converse polemic against a lunar calendar.[2] The author's primary opponents appear to be those who omit the four epagomenal days and so follow a calendar of 360 days (75.1-3; 82.4-7).[3] One also suspects that such calendrical concerns are implied in chs. 1–36 of *1 Enoch*, though that is difficult to establish with any degree of confidence since there is no explicit statement to this effect.[4] In *1 Enoch* 72–82, however, the solar calendar is certainly a major item in the saving wisdom that is revealed to the seer.[5]

> Blessed are all the righteous ones; blessed are those who walk in the street of righteousness and have no sin like the sinners in the computation of the days in which the sun goes its course in the sky (82.4).

Those who omit the four epagomenal days are described not only as 'sinners' but also as 'people that err' (82.5). Rau's tradition-historical analysis is helpful in understanding this passage. He argues persuasively that 81.5–82.3 is an inserted piece, and that 82.4-8 explains the nature of the unrighteousness that is presupposed in 81.4 as having to

---

1. On the problems related to chs. 80 and 81, see VanderKam, *Enoch*, pp. 106-109. The parting address to Methuselah in ch. 82 'underlines the primary purpose of the Astronomical Book: to prevent sin by calendrical error' (J.J. Collins, *Apocalyptic Imagination*, p. 48; cf. Uhlig, p. 572).

2. It is helpful to contrast the Astronomical Book, which includes a description of the course of the moon (chs. 73–74) as well as the course of the sun, with *Jubilees*, which has a description only of the latter phenomenon; see J. Maier, 'Die Sonne im religiösen Denken des antiken Judentums', in *ANRW*, II.19.1, p. 354, and Wintermute, 'Jubilees', p. 39.

3. VanderKam, '364-Day Calendar in the Enochic Literature', pp. 163-64; *idem*, *Enoch*, p. 91; and J.J. Collins, *Apocalyptic Imagination*, p. 47; cf. Charles, *Book of Enoch*, p. 161.

4. Rau (p. 28) argues that in these chapters 'das in Hen 72–82 entfaltete astronomisch-kalendarische System vorausgesetzt, nicht aber als solches dargestellt wird'. Cf. Rau, pp. 92-93; Nickelsburg, 'Revealed Wisdom', p. 77, and R. Murray, '"Disaffected Judaism" and Early Christianity: Some Predisposing Factors', in *'To See Ourselves as Others See Us'*, p. 267; *contra* Lebram, pp. 189-90. VanderKam ('The 364-Day Calendar in the Enochic Literature', p. 161) is non-committal.

5. Here I make reference to the final form of the book (including all of chs. 72–82), since it is particularly in ch. 82 that the significance of proper calendrical observance becomes evident.

do with the 364-day year. Consequently, the traditions of the heavenly books and the astronomical materials are brought together to reinforce the importance of proper calendrical observance.[1]

The 364-day solar calendar was also a major issue for the writer of *Jubilees*.[2] James VanderKam comments helpfully as follows:

> The Book of Jubilees, which contains a succinct summary of an extensive cycle of lore about Enoch, supports the same calendar. It refers to astronomical and calendrical revelations that were granted to Enoch (4.17-18, 21), and, when one considers the author's stance on these matters, it is fair to infer that he included the 364-day system in his understanding of these disclosures.[3]

In *Jubilees* the primary concern is with the fixed position of the sacred days within each week, so that sacred feasts are observed only on days that are clean and not profane.[4] Such precision, of course, is impossible if one utilizes the lunar calendar. Thus the author's concern with the solar calendar is related to his broader theological approach to special times.

Even more clearly than in *1 Enoch*,[5] the observance of the 364-day calendar is a fundamental matter of Torah to the author of *Jubilees*. Those who abandon this calendar 'forget the feasts of the covenant and walk in the feasts of the Gentiles, after their errors and after their ignorance' (6.32-38, esp. v. 35). While it is not explicitly stated that such people will be 'cut off' or 'rooted out',[6] there can be little doubt that the language of ch. 6 implies just that. This is evident especially

---

1. Rau, pp. 309-11.

2. Obedience to the requirements of the covenant involved, of course, much more than observance of the correct calendar. But this matter was critical and is significant for my purposes. For a survey of other legal concerns in *Jubilees*, see Sanders, *Paul*, pp. 364-66. The author lays stress especially on 'commandments between man and God', presumably as a part of his concern to separate between Israel and the Gentiles.

3. VanderKam, 'The 364-Day Calendar in the Enochic Literature', p. 161; cf. W.A. Meeks, 'Moses as God and King', in *Religions in Antiquity: Essays in Memory of Erwin Ramsdell Goodenough* (ed. J. Neusner; Leiden: Brill, 1968), pp. 367-68.

4. Jaubert, pp. 49-50; Wintermute, 'Jubilees', pp. 38-39.

5. Enoch is referred to as the revealer of calendrical secrets in *Jub.* 4.16-19. Thus there is a sense in which *Jubilees* builds on the earlier work.

6. Sanders, *Paul*, p. 385, though he comes to a different conclusion with regard to the significance of the calendar in *Jubilees*.

from the use of the scheme of deuteronomic history in ch. 1,[1] where it is said that 'they [presumably a significant portion of the people of Israel] will err concerning new moons, sabbaths, festivals, jubilees, and ordinances' (v. 14). This statement concludes a lengthy description of Israel's rebellion that includes idolatry (vv. 8-9, 11) and forsaking 'my ordinances and my commandments and the feasts of my covenant and my sabbaths and my sacred place' (v. 10). As a result of this behavior, they fall into the hand of the enemies of Israel (v. 10) and are removed 'from the midst of the land' (v. 13). They are, in short, subject to divine judgment. Nevertheless, the author holds before his readers the opportunity of repentance, forgiveness and the resultant experience of the blessing of God (vv. 15-18; see also 23.26). His perspective is optimistic. He expects to find a favorable response to his writing of the 'second law'.

It is clear from the nature of this description in *Jubilees* 1 that the author is not concerned with minor sins through error. Rather, he presents to his readers a graphic portrayal of a people who have abandoned the covenant of their God and its requirements, and who are consequently subject to God's judgment. What is particularly striking for present purposes, however, is the fact that at the climax of this description of apostasy is the prediction of calendrical error (v. 14)! Such a view is not surprising in view of the fact that the violation of the sabbath is a sin that results in death (cf. 2.27). For it is only as one follows the solar calendar that the feasts fall on fixed days, thereby avoiding the sabbath.

In *Jubilees* 6 the calendrical discussion concludes as follows:

> Your sons will be corrupted so that they will not make a year only three hundred and sixty-four days. And therefore, they will set awry the months and the (appointed) times and the sabbaths and the feasts, *and they will eat all of the blood with all flesh* (v. 38).

Since those who eat meat with the blood in it are explicitly described as those who 'shall be rooted out of the land' (6.12), the similarity of 6.38 to ch. 1 is obvious—in both cases calendrical error is attributed to those who deny and repudiate the covenant of their God. Those who abandon the 364-day calendar are thus clearly presented as apostates who, if they continue on their present path, will face future judgment

---

1. See O.H. Steck (*Israel und das gewaltsame Geschick der Propheten* [Neukirchen-Vluyn: Neukirchener Verlag, 1967], pp. 157-64) on this pattern in *Jubilees*.

and condemnation (cf. 23.19-25). Yet the author's intent is not merely
to set forth a message of condemnation, but to offer a message of
judgment that will lead to repentance and restoration.[1]

While a solar calendar is highlighted in parts of *1 Enoch* and in
Jubilees, it is by no means the only issue that receives attention in the
Jewish apocalypses. In Daniel, for example, special attention is
devoted to food laws and the observance of times of prayer; while in *3
Baruch*, as we have seen, there is evidence of an ascetic tendency.
These special features do not receive the same kind of attention that
the calendar receives in such works as *1 Enoch* and *Jubilees*, yet my
primary contention is clear enough: some of the writings exhort their
readers to obey the commandments of the Torah in a general sense,
while others lay stress on a specific revealed interpretation of the law.
In this latter group of documents, one's obedience must be directed in
a specific way that is in accord with the revelation set forth in these
writings; otherwise, one cannot enjoy the blessings of the covenant and
look forward to eschatological salvation.

b. *Eschatological Judgment as the Basis for the Paraenesis*
Amidst all of the diversity within this great mass of material, one
basic principle stands out with astonishing clarity: that the revelation
of the event of judgment, with its attendant blessedness for the righteous and condemnation for the wicked, is the basis for the exhortations to obedience in the Jewish apocalypses. Christoph Münchow,
basing his investigation on *1 Enoch*, *Jubilees*, the *Testament of Moses*,
4 Ezra and *2 Baruch*, argues persuasively that there is a fundamental
connection between ethics and eschatology in the Jewish apocalypses.
He refers, in fact, to the perspective of these writings as a 'Gerichts-
ethik' since judgment is the foundation of the admonitions.[2]

While the connection between judgment and obedience is implicit in
the Book of Daniel, the Enochic materials set forth this relationship in
an explicit manner. Eschatological judgment and its consequences as
the basis for exhortation is clear in the *Epistle of Enoch* where, as
noted earlier, the Apocalypse of Weeks forms the basis for the intense
expectation of judgment that pervades this section. The connection is

---

1. I differ here from Sanders (*Paul*, pp. 383-85) and suggest that the outlook of
Jubilees is far more like that of the Qumran community than Sanders is prepared to
admit.
2. Münchow, pp. 127-29.

explicit in 91.3-11, 18-19, 94.1-5 and 99.10, with two of these being especially significant in light of their proximity to the Apocalypse of Weeks:

> Now I shall speak unto you, my children, and show you the ways of right-eousness and the ways of wickedness. Moreover, I shall make a revelation to you so that you may know that which is going to take place. Now listen to me, my children, and walk in the way of righteousness, and do not walk in the way of wickedness, *for all those who walk in the ways of injustice shall perish* (91.18-19).

> Now to you, those righteous ones, I say: Do not walk in the evil way, or in the way of death! Do not draw near to them lest you be destroyed! But seek for yourselves and choose righteousness and the elect life! Walk in the way of peace *so that you shall have life and be worthy!* (94.3-4).

The point that Enoch makes is simple: judgment is coming, and his readers are faced with the two options of continued obedience that will lead to blessedness or disobedience that will result in condemnation. So they should obey the commandments that they might escape the divine wrath and enjoy God's blessedness!

While the connection between blessedness or condemnation and exhortation is implicit throughout *1 Enoch*,[1] it is set forth in an instructive manner in the final chapter of the present form of the Astronomical Book. We have already suggested that probably 81.5–82.3 is an inserted piece, and that originally 82.4-8 followed directly after 81.4.[2] The result of this analysis is that 82.4-8 explains the unrighteousness presupposed in 81.4 as that which relates to the viola-tion of the 364-day solar calendar. Those who are righteous, particu-larly in this matter, are said to be 'blessed', because no record of transgression has been written against them (81.4). Indeed, it is significant to note that the heavenly book of deeds (cf. vv. 1-2), which was considered earlier in this study, stands as the basis for the exhor-tation to obedience in calendrical matters. Consequently, in the present text it is important for one generation to pass on this revelation to the next, that they too might receive and obey it (81.5-6; 82.1-3) and so enjoy the blessedness of which the author/redactor speaks—particu-larly as they face the time of judgment.

---

1. On the eschatological theophany in *1 En.* 1 as encouraging obedience, see Rowland, *Open Heaven*, p. 161.
2. Cf. Rau, pp. 309-11.

Even more explicit is *2 Enoch*. For though the connection between blessedness or condemnation and exhortation is evident throughout that writing, it is clearest in the description of the places of salvation (8.1–9.1) and condemnation (10.1-6). These graphic descriptions provide the occasion for the portrayals of virtues and vices:

> This place has been prepared, Enoch, for the righteous, who suffer every kind of tribulation in this life and who afflict their souls, and who avert their eyes from injustice, and who carry out righteous judgment, to give bread to the hungry, and to cover the naked with clothing, and to lift up the fallen, and to help the injured, who walk before the face of the Lord, and who worship him only—for them this [place] has been prepared as an eternal inheritance (9.1, rec. A).

The description of the place of condemnation and the list of vices that characterize those for whom it is prepared (10.1-6) closely parallels this arrangement. And in both descriptions the paraenetic intent is obvious.

A similar connection is evident in *2 Enoch* 42 and 44, where the descriptions of Hell (40.13–42.2) and of Paradise (42.3-5) immediately precede a series of beatitudes that has a strong eschatological thrust.[1] In both chs. 8–10 and chs. 42–44, then, the revelations of the terrible nature of the condemnation faced by sinners and the glory that the righteous shall enjoy clearly function to support the specific ethical concerns of the writer.[2]

It is also instructive to note how the writer makes use of the heavenly book of deeds to bolster his exhortation to obedience. In ch. 52 there is a series of beatitudes similar to those in chs. 42 and 44, though they alternate with statements that run 'Cursed is he who. . .' Here the blessedness of the righteous and the condemnation of the wicked are brought together. Furthermore, the context is clearly paraenetic, for Enoch hopes to discourage his children from sin. He begins in 50.1 by mentioning the heavenly record of one's 'achievements', moves on in 50.2–51.4 to 'eine Gebotsparänese', and then concludes the series of beatitudes and curses (52.1-14) with a ref-

---

1. Andersen, p. 168: 'It relates the form of the eternal reward to a person's temporal behaviour. The same pattern applies to punishment. The golden rule is turned around; what you did to others (good or bad) will be done to you.'

2. On the transformation of Enoch so that he becomes 'like one of the glorious ones' (22.8-10) as paradigmatic for those who obey, see Collins, *From Athens to Jerusalem*, pp. 231-32.

erence to 'the book on the great judgment day' (52.15).[1] The reference to this heavenly writing is then picked up again in ch. 53:

> Now, *therefore*, my children, keep your hearts from every injustice in the balance; inherit the light for eternity. You will not say, my children, '(Our) father is with the Lord, and by his prayers he will keep us free from sin'. You see that the works of every person, I, even I, am writing them down. And no one will destroy my handwriting, because the Lord sees everything. (And) now, *therefore*, my children, pay close attention to all your father's sayings, whatever I say to you. . . (vv. 1-4).

It is clear from the connectives (as italicized) that the exhortation refers back to the allusion to the heavenly book of 52.15. Thus the author utilized this tradition of the heavenly book of deeds in order to strengthen his exhortation, so making reference to a motif that was intimately associated with the event of judgment. In this way his readers were compelled to consider the consequences of their actions in light of the imminent expectation of judgment.[2]

Much the same perspective is evident in *Jubilees*, though this work is in many ways a very different kind of writing. *Jubilees* is less interested in eschatology than many other apocalypses.[3] Its focus is on the near future. It expects God to act quickly to bring about a change of heart so that 'children will begin to search the law, and to search the commandments and to return to the way of righteousness'.[4] Nevertheless, like the Enochic writers, the author of *Jubilees* too utilizes the blessedness or condemnation theme to support his exhortations and admonitions. He provides a number of examples from the history of Israel of punishment for those who disobeyed (7.20-25; 16.5-9) and blessing for those who were obedient (17.17-18; 18.14-16; 39.6-7; 40.8-10),[5] with it being clear that such consequences could be expected in his day. Furthermore, the pattern of sin–judgment–restoration appears at the beginning, and, in fact, serves as a key for the work (1.7-18).[6] The author, of course, is optimistic with regard to the restoration of God's people. Yet it is possible to sin in such a way that

---

1. Rau, p. 338. The longer recension of 52.15 is more explicit, '[For] all these things (will be weighed) in the balances and exposed in the books on the great judgment day'.

2. Rau, p. 338.

3. Cf. Wintermute, 'Jubilees', pp. 46-47; Davenport, pp. 72-79.

4. Wintermute, 'Jubilees', p. 48.

5. Wintermute, 'Jubilees', p. 38.

6. Steck, pp. 157-64.

one is left without the possibility of forgiveness (cf. 15.34). So he points out to his readers the seriousness of sin and disobedience.

In *Jubilees* the motif of the heavenly writings supports the paraenesis in much the same way as it does in the Enochian materials.[1] The record of sins is mentioned in 28.6 and 39.6-7; the writing of righteous deeds is alluded to in 30.20, 23. The context of 39.6-7 is especially informative for our purposes, for here reference is made to the words Jacob used to read that forbid fornication. This kind of transgression 'is written (on high) concerning him in the eternal books always before the Lord'. The writer then gets to the point of this section, 'And Joseph remembered these words and he did not want to lie with her' (v. 7). The paraenetic intent is obvious—the writer desires his readers to follow Joseph's example!

A related idea is that those who practice righteousness are written down 'as a friend and a righteous one in the heavenly tablets' (30.20), while those who 'transgress and act in all the ways of defilement. . . will be recorded in the heavenly tablets as enemies' (30.22). The paraenetic intent is evident in 30.21: 'I have commanded you to speak to the children of Israel that they might not commit sin or transgress the ordinances or break the covenant which was ordained for them *so that they might do it and be written down as friends*'. The author also mentions a 'book of life' and a 'book of those who will be destroyed', again in the context of exhortation (30.23; 36.10).[2] Various devices, therefore, are used, but the import of them all is the same: one must obey God's law in view of the coming judgment, which will distinguish between the righteous and the sinners on the basis of the content of the heavenly records.

This kind of perspective is by no means unique to apocalypses that can be dated before the fall of Jerusalem; it plays a significant role, as well, in the writings written after the destruction of the Second Temple. A few of the more striking examples from the apocalyptic writings of post-destruction Judaism will suffice as illustrative.

Ezra's exhortations in *4 Ezra* 14 set before the people a choice between life and death—a choice that amounts to a life of obedience or a life given over to disobedience:

---

1. On Enoch as the heavenly scribe of the deeds of humans, see Berger, p. 345; cf. Rau, p. 407.

2. On these passages, see Rau, pp. 336-37. In the latter text the point is to exhort the readers to love their brothers and to refrain from desiring evil against them.

If you, then, will rule over your minds and discipline your hearts, you shall be kept alive, and after death you shall obtain mercy. For after death the judgment will come, when we shall live again; and then the names of the righteous will become manifest, and *the deeds of the ungodly will be disclosed* (vv. 34-35).

Here, then, at the paraenetic climax of *4 Ezra*,[1] the revelation of both the blessedness of the righteous and the condemnation of the wicked (as predicted in the preceding visions) stands clearly as the basis for the exhortation.[2] It is interesting to note as well that, while there is no mention of the heavenly writings in this passage, disclosure of 'the deeds of the ungodly' is referred to explicitly.[3] Reference to such a disclosure serves the same purpose as reference to the heavenly book(s)—to reinforce the exhortation to obedience by bringing to mind the event of judgment and its consequences in a vivid and graphic manner.

Even more explicit than *4 Ezra* in relating blessedness or condemnation to exhortation is *2 Baruch*. The relevant passages are numerous, and we can only make reference to a few of the more important texts. One clear example is particularly intelligible if we compress several verses from ch. 44:

You, however, do not withdraw from the way of the Law, but guard and admonish the people who are left lest they withdraw from the commandments of the Mighty One. . . For when you endure and persevere in his fear and do not forget his Law, the time again will take a turn for the better for you. And they will participate in the consolation of Zion. . . These are they who prepared for themselves treasures of wisdom. And stores of insight are found with them. And they have not withdrawn from mercy and they have preserved the truth of the Law. For the coming world will be given to these, but the habitation of the many others will be in the fire (vv. 3, 7, 14-15).

A similar connection is evident in 46.4, where the author stresses the salvation of the obedient rather than the condemnation of the wicked:

But Israel will not be in want of a wise man, nor the tribe of Jacob, a son of the Law. But only prepare your heart so that you obey the Law, and be subject to those who are wise and understanding with fear. And prepare your

---

1. J.J. Collins (*Apocalyptic Imagination*, p. 168) regards this passage as giving a summary of the author's message, though the overall impact of the work is much broader.
2. For other passages that make this connection, see Rowland, *Open Heaven*, p. 168.
3. Cf. *4 Ezra* 6.20, though the immediate context is not paraenetic.

soul that you shall not depart from them. If you do this, those good tidings
will come to you of which I spoke to you earlier.

The use of the blessedness or condemnation theme to support the
author's paraenetic concerns can also be found in 31.1-8; 51.3, 7;
59.2; 76.5; 83.8; 84.6, and 85.8-11.

The connection of blessedness or condemnation and exhortation also
appears in *3 Baruch*, the *Apocalypse of Abraham* and the *Apocalypse
of Zephaniah*, though less explicitly so. The cosmic dimension, which
will be discussed below, provides the primary support for the exhortations of *3 Baruch*. Still, the blessedness of the righteous and the condemnation of the wicked is described in some detail in chs. 15 and 16,
and the relationship of these depictions to the ethical concerns of the
author seems probable, at least in the Greek version (16.4). The connection between judgment and paraenesis is only implicit in the
Apocalypse of Abraham (see 9.10 and 29.17). The *Apocalypse of
Zephaniah*, however, which dwells on the theme of judgment and
provides graphic descriptions of Hades, is more direct in its
connections. For its author sets forth several detailed lists of offenses
that the readers are presumably urged to avoid, with several of these
offenses being mentioned as recorded in the 'manuscript' wielded by
the accusing angel over whom the righteous seer is said to 'triumph'
or 'prevail' (7.1-9).[1] The implication, of course, is that such offenses
are also being recorded against the readers, and that they would do
well to avoid these things. The other list of offenses stands in the midst
of a description of the torment of souls in Hades (10.1-14) and the
implication is, again, obvious—if one wishes to avoid such condemnation, one should take care to obey God's law.

We have observed that the theme of blessedness or condemnation is
used to reinforce exhortations throughout the Jewish apocalypses.
Some writings, of course, are more explicit in this regard than others.
Yet the connection of blessedness or condemnation and exhortation is
certainly a major feature in these writings. It is interesting, as well, to
note how the motif of the heavenly book(s) functions within this
complex of ideas to strengthen the impact of the appeal. It is, of
course, not always found in association with the threat of imminent
judgment or the theme of blessedness or condemnation. At times it is

---

1. The Coptic has taken over quite literally the Greek χειρόγραφον; see James,
Apocryphal New Testament, p. 534, and Himmelfarb, *Tours of Hell*, p. 149.

associated with consolation (e.g. *4 Ezra* 6.20; *2 Bar.* 24.1-2).[1] Yet in a significant number of passages the motif of the heavenly book(s) is part of the larger theme of eschatological judgment.

2. *Admonitions/Rebukes of the Unrighteous*

I have focused up to now in this chapter on the function of revelation in the apocalypticists' understanding vis-à-vis the righteous: to stimulate the upright to obey the commandments of God. There is, however, another dimension to the message in (at least) one these writings: the admonition or rebuke of the unrighteous with the goal of leading them to repentance and salvation. It is my intent here to explore this feature further to see if it is represented in the apocalypses more generally.

To date, it is only in *1 Enoch* that revelation has been recognized as having a purpose with regard to the ungodly. The work of George Nickelsburg is especially significant here, for of late he has argued that there is an openness to outsiders in the *Epistle of Enoch*.[2] The underlying point of view is expressed in the Apocalypse of Weeks:

> Then after that in the ninth week the righteous judgment shall be revealed to the whole world [4QEn⁸ reads 'for all the children of the whole earth']. All the deeds of the sinners shall depart from upon the whole earth, and be written off for eternal destruction; and all people shall direct their sight to the path of uprightness (91.14).[3]

As was noted earlier, it is the revelation of the Apocalypse of Weeks that provides the basis for the Woes, Exhortations and explicit revelatory formulae that are present in this section and that speak so powerfully to the reader. So the prediction of revelation to the whole

---

1. Rau (p. 315) notes that in these passages the motif of the Book of Deeds guarantees or assures the coming release of God's people from the domination of sinners.

2. Nickelsburg, 'Epistle of Enoch', pp. 343-45; *idem*, 'Revealed Wisdom', pp. 76-77. This is a decided change of perspective vis-à-vis Nickelsburg's earlier studies on this section of *1 Enoch*; *idem*, *Resurrection*, pp. 112-30, esp. 128; *idem*, 'Riches, the Rich, and God's Judgment in 1 Enoch 92–105 and the Gospel according to Luke', *NTS* 25 (1978–79), esp. p. 332.

3. I have basically followed the translation of Charles, *Book of Enoch*, p. 268. Cf. VanderKam ('Apocalypse of Weeks', p. 519), who notes the parallels between the *judgments* of weeks two and nine; and Isaac, p. 73; *contra* Dexinger, *Zehnwochenapokalypse*, p. 179 ('rechte Satzung'), and Nickelsburg, 'Epistle of Enoch', pp. 340-41. Nickelsburg's argument with regard to the function vis-à-vis outsiders is much stronger, of course, if we follow the alternative reading.

world—including Gentiles—is an important indicator that the author's concerns are broader than one might initially expect. This impression is confirmed when we consider other statements in the Epistle, at least in its present form:

> Then the wise people shall see, and the sons of the earth shall give heed to all the words of this book. They shall know that their wealth shall not be able to save them at the place where their sins shall collapse (100.6).

> In those days, he says, the Lord will be patient and cause the children of the earth to hear. Reveal to them with your wisdom, for you are their guides; and (you are) a reward upon the whole earth (105.1).

It is clear that the author of the Epistle expected at least some of 'the children of the earth' to read his work and receive its message, and so come to to enjoy the blessings of salvation.[1] And Nickelsburg has pointed out that this kind of openness to the salvation of the Gentiles is evident as well in the Book of the Watchers and the second dream vision (90.37-38).[2]

It should not be surprising that there was at least some attention given by Jewish apocalyptic writers to the repentance and salvation of the ungodly. Many apocalyptists, if not all, wrote with a prophetic consciousness, and it is not the nature of a prophet to refrain from calling to repentance the rebellious within Israel—even, at times, the wicked among the Gentiles. Furthermore, as Münchow notes, there is in the apocalypses overall more emphasis on the acts of the ungodly and their negative consequences than there is on the deeds of the righteous and their just reward.[3] Indeed, predictions of judgment and woe have a significance for the godly. Yet the fate of the unrighteous. I would insist, was also a concern of the apocalyptists, and they sought to call them to repentance and obedience.

Several of the Jewish apocalypses are notable in that while they offer little or no hope to Gentiles, they demonstrate a deep concern for Israel to repent, to obey Torah, and to enjoy the salvific blessings that are their due. In *Jubilees* the author is faced with a crisis of dis-

---

1. Nickelsburg, 'Epistle of Enoch', p. 344.
2. Nickelsburg, 'Revealed Wisdom', pp. 76-77.
3. Münchow, pp. 126-27, though Münchow himself argues that predictions of judgment and woe no longer have their original function but now stand as words of salvation for the righteous, so that it is not 'sinners' who are addressed but only the righteous. Cf. Rössler, p. 77, though he draws no conclusions with regard to audience.

obedience in Israel, and so calls his nation to submit themselves to his revealed interpretation of the law. In *4 Ezra*, the seer is instructed to 'reprove the people' on the basis of the revelation he received (14.13, 20), and there are many indications that their present moral state is less than satisfactory.[1] Furthermore, in ch. 9 it is stressed that possession of the law is not sufficient for salvation unless it is accompanied by obedience (vv. 33-37); and that while repentance is possible in the present, such opportunities would be closed in the future (v. 11).

In *2 Baruch*, interestingly, the audience becomes wider and wider, with first 'the righteous', then the people 'from the greatest to the least', and, finally, 'all of Jewry' being addressed.[2] It is reasonable to suppose that the last two groups included both the righteous and the unrighteous of Israel, and so some exhortation to repentance and obedience is implied. Indeed, the author of *2 Baruch* is concerned to show that salvation and damnation cut through the heart of the Jewish community. Many Jews have chosen the darkness of Adam and will receive judgment (so ch. 18). Yet even Gentiles who flee under the wings of the God of Israel will be saved (41.3-5).[3] Thus while the author's concern is not primarily to call the unrighteous of Israel and sinners among the Gentiles to repentance, he seems not at all closed to such a ministry.

Also instructive in this regard are the Similitudes of Enoch. For while the primary goal of this work is to provide encouragement to 'the righteous and elect' who are suffering at the hands of ungodly kings and rulers, this is not the writer's only concern. A broader range of interests is evident in the references to a group whose character and fate appears to be ambiguous—i.e. those who are referred to as 'the children of the people' or 'those who dwell upon the earth'. It is apparent that the righteous ones and the angels in heaven take an interest in the welfare of this group (39.5; 40.6-7), though in other passages they are presented in a negative light. Of this group it is said that they have rejected wisdom, and so iniquity dwells among them

---

1. See 14.31, as well as many statements in the opening dialogues, with regard to the small number of the saved.
2. See Murphy (pp. 11-29), who analyzes the structure of the work along these lines.
3. One should not, however, overlook the nationalistic emphasis that appears as well in this work. There are some notable words of vengeance (e.g. 82.1-9), though it is clearly stated that Gentiles who have not oppressed Israel can be saved (72.4-6; 42.5).

'like rain in a desert, like dew on a thirsty land' (42.1-3); they have
been led astray by the armies of Azazel (54.6; 69.1-15),[1] and so
commit deeds characteristic of 'the sinners' (53.1-2; 54.9-10). Consequently, judgment is predicted for them.

Nevertheless, this is not the whole story with regard to the author's
perspective on this group. In contrast to 'the sinners' for whom there
is no hope of salvation,[2] the way for this group is by no means closed.
In fact, the Lord of the Spirits will utilize the revelation of the
blessedness of the righteous and the condemnation of the wicked at the
end of time to lead 'the others' to repentance and salvation:

> He heaped evil upon the sinners; but the righteous ones shall be victorious in
> the name of the Lord of the Spirits. *He will cause the others to see this so that
> they may repent and forsake the deeds of their hands.* There shall not be
> honor unto them in the name of the Lord of the Spirits. But through his name
> they shall be saved, and the Lord of the Spirits shall have mercy upon them,
> for his mercy is considerable. He is righteous in his judgment and in the glory
> that is before him. Oppression cannot survive his judgment; and *the unrepen-
> tant in his presence shall perish. The Lord of the Spirits has said that from
> henceforth he will not have mercy on them* (50.2-5).

Hence there is, both in the present and even up to the eschatological
revelation of blessedness and condemnation, an opportunity for this
group of people to repent and be saved.

This group of repentant people includes repentant Israelites, of
course, though the reference in 48.4 to the Son of Man as 'the light of
the Gentiles' suggests that it should be seen as being much broader.
There is a point, however, after which the unrepentant are condemned
together with 'the sinners' and thus eliminated, so that

> All those who dwell upon the earth shall fall and worship before him; they
> shall glorify, bless, and sing the name of the Lord of the Spirits (48.5).

The author's goal is reached on the day in which 'the children of the
elect and the holy ones [will descend] from the high heaven and their

---

1. Note that in the former verse it is 'those who dwell upon the earth' who are led
astray, while in the latter passage it is said that the angels misled 'the children of the
people'. While 'the children of the people' could refer to Israel as a whole, there is no
indication in the Similitudes that this is in fact the case. The expressions are used
interchangeably to refer to humanity in general.

2. This is not surprising since they are described as those 'who deny the name of
the Lord of the Spirits'; see 38.1-3; 41.2,8; 45.2-3, 6; 46.4-8; 48.8-10; 53.2-7;
54.1-3; 60.1-6; 62; 63; 67.

seed will become one with the children of the people'. So the statement at the beginning of the Similitudes is no mere rhetorical device; the work is indeed directed not only to the righteous, but also to the ungodly, both in Israel and among the Gentiles. As Enoch says: 'Three things were imparted to me; and I began to recount them *to those who dwell upon the earth*' (37.5).

Not all of the apocalypses are as clear in this regard as the Similitudes of Enoch. Yet with the exception of *3 Baruch*, all of these writings give some indication that they are concerned not only with the righteous but also with the unrighteous. The Book of Daniel is concerned with the instruction of the Jewish people as a whole,[1] and there were presumably some among them who were unrighteous. Nevertheless, an even broader concern is suggested in the confessions of Nebuchadnezzar (3.28–4.3, 34-37) and Darius (6.26-27), as well as in Daniel's call to repentance (4.25-27). Likewise, in the *Apocalypse of Abraham* it is probable that Abraham's example (chs. 1–7, in contrast to the behavior of his father Terah; cf. 26.3) is paradigmatic for those who desire to experience the salvation of which this work speaks.[2] In both of the above cases, of course, the appeal is by no means explicit. Yet such features are nonetheless striking, particularly in view of the concern for the walk of the unrighteous that is evident in other Jewish apocalypses.

Much the same can be found in apocalypses that stem from the Jewish Diaspora. Of course, some concern with respect to reaching the Gentiles is implied by the manner in which the authors of these writings play down distinctively Jewish requirements and stress those laws held in common with the Gentiles. Yet there are other features that also merit our attention and are instructive for our purposes. In *2 Enoch*, for example, it is said of Methusalam that he

---

1. One thinks specifically of the 'wise' (*maśkîlîm*) who stand behind at least the final form of the book of Daniel. These 'people of the holy ones' clearly came to think of themselves as the 'true Israel'; so R.R. Wilson, 'From Prophecy to Apocalyptic: Reflections on the Shape of Israelite Religion', *Semeia* 21 (1981), p. 93. Even here, however, their role would seem to include instruction of the people with the goal of leading them to understanding, steadfastness and obedience (Dan. 11.33-34; 12.3). It is likely, then, that the Book of Daniel was addressed to a wider audience within Israel.

2. An eschatological concern for the salvation of the Gentiles is clearly implied in 29.11, but it is possible that this section is a later (Christian?) addition; see Nickelsburg, *Jewish Literature, p.* 306 n. 32.

stood at the head of the altar and at the head of all the people from that day onward. In 492 he explored the earth, and he sought out all those who had believed in the Lord. And those who had apostatized he corrected them and converted them. And there was not found one person turning himself away from the Lord during all the days that Methusalam lived.[1]

A similar concern is evident in the *Testament of Abraham*, where God says, 'But I made the world, and I do not want to destroy any one of them; but *I delay the death of the sinner until he should convert and live*' (10.14 [rec. A]; 12.13 [rec. B]). It was, in fact, Abraham's quickness to judge sinners that was his sin. But when he repented, God restored those who were destroyed through his actions. In the *Testament of Abraham* there is no distinction between Jews and Gentiles. The atoning efficacy of repentance and premature death apply equally to all (see 14.10-15 [rec. A]). The way is open for sinners to repent, regardless of their ancestry.

Perhaps even clearer is the *Apocalypse of Zephaniah*, where the two explicit descriptions of the torment of sinners are accompanied by statements that emphasize the importance of timely repentance. In the Sahidic fragment (ln. 6) it is said, ' "This is [a] soul which was found in its lawlessness." And before it attained to repenting it was [vi]sited, and taken out of its body.' Similarly, in the second trumpet scene in the Akhmimic text we read, 'And I said to him, "Then do they not have repentance here?" He said, "Yes". I said, "How long?" He said to me, "Until the day when the Lord will judge" ' (10.10-11).[2] So here humanity is treated on an individual basis; each person is called to repentance and obedience regardless of whether he is a Jew or a Gentile.

The function of admonition and rebuke for the unrighteous is present in virtually all of the Jewish apocalypses. Admittedly, with the possible exception of *Jubilees*, it is by no means a primary function. Almost always it takes second place to the encouragement and exhortation of the righteous. In several cases, as noted, it is clearly the revelation of the event and consequences of coming judgment that strengthens the admonition or rebuke, though in some writings such a

---

1. *2 En.* 70.1. This quotation is from the shorter recension, though the longer recension is more suggestive with its statement that Methusalam 'taught all the earth and all his own people'. Cf. two other passages in the longer recension that suggest an interest in Gentiles, 48.7 and 64.5.

2. See esp. Wintermute ('Apocalypse of Zephaniah', p. 502) who also discusses the problem of the identification of the fragments and the Akhmimic manuscript.

correlation of revelation and exhortation is difficult to identify with any degree of certainty. Still, it is clear that the description 'conventicle literature' is problematic when applied to these writings.[1] Certainly the authors of at least some of these works may have belonged to such groups. But their concerns as writers were much broader. Their audience, while primarily composed of the righteous, also included the unrighteous in Israel—and, in certain cases, those among the Gentiles as well.

Conclusion

This analysis of the materials, selective as it has been forced to be, arrives at the conclusion that the exhortations of the apocalyptists take a variety of forms depending on the particular setting of the works. In most cases they are oriented in some way toward the commands and requirements of the Mosaic law. Of specific concern in a number of these writings are various calendrical matters, with the nature and intensity of these calendrical concerns varying from writing to writing. As well, in several writings a secondary function of admonition vis-à-vis the ungodly also appears. In every case, however, the revelation of the eschatological judgment and its consequences are the primary supports for the exhortations and admonitions, with these supports being strengthened in several texts by the motif of the heavenly book(s) of deeds.

Such a perspective on obedience and its relation to coming judgment is highly relevant for understanding the problem that occasioned Paul's letter to the church at Colossae. It is, therefore, to the investigation of that situation that I now turn in Part II of this study.

---

1. Vielhauer (p. 598) locates the origin of apocalyptic in 'those eschatologically-excited circles which were forced more and more by the theocracy into a kind of conventicle existence'. He is, of course, building on the arguments of Plöger, *Theocracy*.

PART II

THE SOTERIOLOGY OF COLOSSIANS

Chapter 5

Having sketched out the major features of the ascetic-mystical piety of Jewish apocalypticism in Part I of this study, my goal in Part II is to study the soteriology of Colossians—in particular, to reconstruct the error that threatened the church at Colossae and to explore how Paul utilized the themes of revelation and redemption in confronting it.

The reconstruction of the Colossian error is, of course, a matter that demands the utmost caution, especially in view of the fact that portraits of the error are both numerous and varied. Differing conclusions are due, in large measure, to differing methodologies. The immediate concern of many, for example, is to assign the Colossian error a place in the history of religions.[1] So they begin with an interpretation of certain key terms and phrases, which then set the framework for the remaining discussion. Especially significant for researchers who adopt this kind of approach are such terms and phrases as πλήρωμα (1.19; 2.9), σοφία (esp. 2.3, 23), γνῶσις (2.3) and τὰ στοιχεῖα τοῦ κόσμου (2.8, 20). Furthermore, most of those who take this approach make little distinction between passages that are directly polemical in nature and those that are more expositional.[2] Other researchers, however, proceed very differently, being keenly aware of the dangers of reconstructions based primarily on isolated terms and phrases, especially those that can be interpreted against a number of possible backgrounds.[3] And some have voiced the need to

1. For example, Bornkamm (p. 123) writes, 'If we succeed in assigning the details and the whole to a place in the history of religions, then we shall have attained the desired degree of certainty and avoided the suspicion of vague combinations and hypotheses'.
2. For example, Bornkamm (pp. 123-25) bases much of his initial discussion of the error on the use of the term πλήρωμα in the hymn (1.19) as well as in the subsequent exposition (2.9).

exercise caution in the use of passages not directly polemical, at least in the early stages of research.[1]

There is, in fact, little agreement in scholarly circles today with regard to a proper methodology in the reconstruction of the Colossian error and the setting forth of Paul's teaching in opposition to it. Yet rigorous controls are necessary in these areas. It is appropriate, therefore, that I sketch out in some detail my methodology before turning in the following chapters to a treatment of the Colossian error and Paul's response.

1. *Epistolary Analysis*

Important for the task in hand is the need to consider the various types of materials contained in Colossians. Particularly helpful here are the insights that can be gained from epistolary analysis. I am indebted to George Cannon for including a detailed epistolary analysis of Colossians in his 1983 study of traditional material in Colossians.[2] I accept Cannon's epistolary outline for Colossians; and without including his supporting argumentation, I reproduce it as follows:

I. Salutation 1.1, 2

II. Thanksgiving 1.3-23
   A. Εὐχαριστῶ Period 1.3-8
   B. Intercession 1.9-11
   C. Closing (marked by liturgical materials and eschatological themes) 1.12-23

III. Letter Body 1.24–4.1
   A. Body Opening 1.24–2.5
   B. Body Middle 2.6–4.1
   C. Body Closing 4.2-9

IV. Letter Closing 4.10-18
   A. Greetings 4.10-17
   B. 'Signature' Statement 4.18a
   C. Benediction 4.18b

---

3. E. Percy (*Die Probleme der Kolosser- und Epheserbriefe* [Lund: Gleerup, 1946], pp. 137-38) is especially instructive at this point. He defers comment on τὰ στοιχεῖα τοῦ κόσμου until he has considered other data, since this phrase is subject to divergent interpretations. Cf. Francis, 'Christological Argument', p. 193.

1. Schweizer, pp. 126-27, esp. with regard to 2.9-15; see also Percy, pp. 137-38, and Kehl, p. 366.

2. See Cannon, pp. 136-66. This portion of Cannon's study fills a significant gap since most epistolary analyses deal only with the undisputed letters of Paul.

For present purposes, the Letter Body of 1.24–4.1 is the most significant section of Colossians, since it is in this portion of the letter that Paul approaches the problem facing the church most directly. I shall, therefore, give primary attention to this section, though it is also both necessary and helpful to consider the ways in which the author's concerns are telegraphed in the Thanksgiving and summed up in the Letter Closing.

The Colossian Thanksgiving (1.3-23) telegraphs Paul's concerns in a way that is critical for my purposes. In 1.13-14 he brings together the ideas of 'forgiveness' and 'redemption'. The implied relation between the two concepts is unclear in these verses. Yet the manner in which they are brought together in the Thanksgiving is critical for a proper interpretation of 2.13-15, where Paul elaborates on the relation between the two blessings alluded to in 1.13-14. Discussion of these passages is reserved for Chapter 8, where I shall consider in detail 1.12-14 and 2.9-15 as Paul's expositional response to the Colossian error.

The Colossian Thanksgiving is also helpful in that it contains the hymn of 1.15-20. Since modern studies on Colossians focus so much attention on these verses in their effort to understand the letter, we should expect to find a variety of themes from these verses picked up in the Body of the letter. This is, however, not the case, as I shall discuss in Chapter 7 when we consider Paul's expositional response to the error in terms of the theme 'Revelation in Christ'.

Moving now to the Body of Colossians, the distinction between the Body Opening and the Body Middle, which was suggested by White in his study of this section of a Pauline letter,[1] is of great importance for my analysis. The Body Opening (1.24–2.5), which is introduced by a Joy Expression (νῦν χαίρω ἐν τοῖς παθήμασιν. . .),[2] functions in a number of ways: (1) to demonstrate philophronesis,[3] (2) to signal that the writer's purpose is polemical (2.4-5), and (3) to assert Paul's apostolic authority, thus establishing his right to address the situation in the Colossian church.[4] It does not provide a detailed description or

---

1. J.L. White, 'Introductory Formulae in the Body of the Pauline Letter', *JBL* 90 (1971), pp. 91-97, and *idem, The Form and Function of the Body of the Greek Letter* (2nd edn; Missoula, MT: Scholars Press, 1972), pp. 73-151.

2. Cf. White, 'Introductory Formulae', pp. 95-96; Cannon, pp. 151-52.

3. Cannon, pp. 152-53.

4. On the presence and function of the 'apostolic parousia', see R.W. Funk, 'The Apostolic Parousia: Form and Significance', in *Christian History and Interpretation:*

analysis of the error that threatened the church. In fact, the writer's references in this section to the error at Colossae are only of a general nature and tell us more about his perspective on the situation than they do about the error itself.[1]

It is true, of course, that 2.2-3 contains significant allusions to doctrine, and also true that these statements provide a basis for the writer's general warning in 2.4. Nevertheless, the relationship between the doctrine espoused and the warning given is ambiguous, and so a discussion of the significance of these verses is best reserved for Chapter 7. It is, in fact, only in light of a framework established on the basis of more direct statements that we can interpret such evidence with any degree of accuracy or confidence. Consequently, we do well to focus our attention elsewhere, at least for the moment.

Significantly more fruitful for the reconstruction of the Colossian error is the study of the Body Middle (2.6–4.1). Here again White's analysis is particularly helpful, especially in that he distinguishes between two parts of a Body Middle in Paul's letters. The first section is 'a tightly organized theological argument', while the second is 'the place where the principles espoused in the preceding are concretized'.[2] Such a pattern is clearly evident in Colossians, where 2.9-15 is highly theological and 2.16–3.4 contains the practical application of the theological argument (i.e. polemic against the errorists)—which is then 'further developed by the use of traditional *paraenesis* in 3.4–4.1 (the vice and virtue catalogues and the *Haustafel*)'.[3] The references to the error in 2.16–4.1 (especially in 2.16-23) are both direct and concrete, and therefore comprise the most significant data for our purposes.

Less relevant for present purposes is the Letter Closing (4.10-18). It is interesting to note, however, that the content of Epaphras's prayer,

---

Studies Presented to John Knox (ed. W.R. Farmer, C.F.D. Moule and R.R. Niebuhr; Cambridge: Cambridge University Press, 1967), pp. 249-69. Cf. T.Y. Mullins, 'Visit Talk in New Testament Letters', *CBQ* 35 (1973), pp. 350-58; also Cannon (pp. 153-54), who notes that this feature occurs early in the letter (as well as in its usual place near the end) because the author had not founded the church, and so needed to establish his authority early on.

1. See 2.4, Τοῦτο λέγω, ἵνα μηδεὶς ὑμᾶς παραλογίζηται ἐν πιθανολογίᾳ. All that is implied here is that the errorists were attempting to persuade the Colossians of the truth of a system of beliefs or practices that the writer believes to be false; cf. Lohse, p. 83; R.P. Martin, *Colossians and Philemon* (Grand Rapids: Eerdmans, 1981), p. 76.

2. White, *Form and Function*, pp. 96-97; cf. Cannon, pp. 156-58.

3. Cannon, p. 156.

ἵνα σταθῆτε τέλειοι καὶ πεπληροφορημένοι ἐν παντὶ θελήματι
τοῦ θεοῦ (v. 12), seems to summarize several of Paul's concerns that
surface earlier in the letter.[1] Such data can be useful once the framework of reconstruction is established on the basis of more secure
evidence.

2. *Polemical and Expositional Distinctions*

Also of importance methodologically are distinctions that must be
made between polemical material and expositional material. Several
considerations point to this distinction as offering a necessary control
for our study. First, the precise nature of the logical connections
between polemic (e.g. 2.8, 16-23) and exposition (e.g. 2.9-15) are
difficult to determine without at least a general framework of thought
drawn from sections that are directly polemical. It is, of course, possible that teachings affirmed within the more expositional passages are
also largely antithetical to the system of belief advocated by the errorists, and this is frequently assumed by many scholars. Yet one must
also allow that relationships could be more subtle—that, for example,
an exposition could simply contain teachings that are, at least in the
mind of Paul, incompatible with the beliefs and practices of the errorists.[2] In this case, the teachings of an expositional section of Colossians
may or may not correspond inversely to certain deviations in the system of the errorists. Furthermore, even if we determine that a direct
correlation exists between certain items of the exposition and the
polemic itself, there is the problem of determining the extent to which
other items in the teaching bear such a relationship. This problem is
especially significant in view of the fact that 2.9-15 contains
'traditional imagery used in abundant measure', so much so that sev-

---

1. τέλειοι, cf. 1.28; πεπληροφορημένοι, cf. 1.9, 10, 25; 2.10; ἐν παντὶ
θελήματι θεοῦ, cf. 1.9. According to F. Zeilinger, 'Die Träger der apostolischen
Tradition im Kolosserbrief', in *Jesus in der Verkündigung der Kirche* (ed. A. Fuchs;
Freistadt: Plöchl, 1976), p. 182, 'Paulus spricht, betet und präsentiert sich den
Kolossern in der Gestalt des Epaphras'.
2. J.M.G. Barclay ('Mirror-Reading a Polemical Letter: Galatians as a Test Case',
JSNT 31 [1987], p. 84) writes: 'If Paul makes an *assertion*, we may assume that, *at
least*, those to whom he writes may be in danger of overlooking what he asserts, and
at most, someone has explicitly denied it; in between those two extremes there is a
range of feasible suggestions, including the possibility that his audience have forgotten what he now reminds them about'.

eral scholars have argued for a traditional form being embedded in this section.[1]

It is obvious, therefore, that a simple 'mirror reading' of the Colossian letter, with no clear distinctions made between polemic and exposition, is a dangerous procedure. It is my contention that a reconstruction must begin with the section of the letter that is directly polemical, i.e. 2.16-23. Furthermore, I would argue that it is only after a working hypothesis based on the material in this passage has been developed that we can turn our attention to the expositional sections. In this way I establish some controls in my study and greatly reduce the possibility of reconstructing the Colossian situation in a way that bears no relationship to the historical phenomenon itself.

3. Direct Descriptions and Indirect References

There is also the need to distinguish between two varieties of polemical materials if a proper methodology for the reconstruction is to be established.[2] First, and most significant for my purposes, are direct descriptions of the position of the errorists. I include in this category certain probable citations from the errorists themselves, such as μὴ ἅψῃ μηδὲ γεύσῃ μηδὲ θίγῃς (2.21),[3] as well as descriptions of their practices, such as κρινέτω ἐν βρώσει καὶ ἐν πόσει ἢ ἐν μέρει ἑορτῆς ἢ νεομηνίας ἢ σαββάτων (2.16). Second, and at times significant for our purposes as well, are indirect references to the position of the errorists, which include the many polemically colored references to

1. E.g. Lohse, pp. 106-107. On the question of a traditional form in this section, see below, Chapter 8, §2.b.

2. I am indebted here to Kehl, p. 366, albeit with certain modifications.

3. My analysis, however, does not depend on the identification of certain words and phrases as 'direct echoes of the opponents' vocabulary'. As Barclay (p. 82) notes: 'Such an exercise depends on: (a) Paul's knowledge of the exact vocabulary used by his opponents; (b) Paul's willingness to re-use this vocabulary either ironically or in some attempt to redefine it; (c) our ability to discern where Paul is echoing his opponents' language; and (d) our ability to reconstruct the meaning that they originally gave to it. Such is our uncertainty surrounding each of these assumptions that I regard the results of such exercise as of very limited value. They should certainly not be used as the cornerstone of any theory, as has all too often been done in recent scholarship on Galatians.' My use of μὴ ἅψῃ μηδὲ γεύσῃ μηδὲ θίγῃς, however, does not depend on its being a direct citation of the errorists, though I tend to regard it as such. For even if it is not a direct citation, it yields insights into the specific prohibitions of the Colossian errorists—insights that are confirmed by statements in 2.16.

the error, such as εἰκῇ φυσιούμενος ὑπὸ τοῦ νοὸς τῆς σαρκὸς αὐτοῦ (2.18). Of these two types of data, the first is clearly the more objective and must be given priority in historical reconstruction. While indirect references can be useful in certain cases, one must be on guard not to interpret every Pauline characterization as an objective description of the beliefs and practices of the errorists at Colossae.[1] Paul writes from his own perspective, and the errorists themselves, no doubt, would have utilized very different language in describing their own faith and practices.

Distinctions between direct description and indirect reference are, of course, disputed. As a working model, I propose the following—organized in terms of the topics highlighted in Part I of this study and compressed somewhat in light of the reduced scope of the material in the letter to the Colossians:

Practices Associated with Revelatory Experiences

Direct Description
    ἐν βρώσει καὶ ἐν πόσει. . . (2.16)
    μὴ ἅψῃ μηδὲ γεύσῃ μηδὲ θίγῃς (2.21)
    ἐν. . . ταπεινοφροσύνῃ καὶ ἀφειδίᾳ σώματος (2.23)

Indirect Reference
    οὐκ ἐν τιμῇ τινι πρὸς πλησμονὴν τῆς σαρκός (2.23)

The Media of Revelation

Direct Description
    ἃ ἑόρακεν ἐμβατεύων (2.18)

The Content of Revelation

Direct Description
    θέλων ἐν ταπεινοφροσύνῃ καὶ θρησκείᾳ τῶν ἀγγέλων, ἃ
    ἑόρακεν ἐμβατεύων (2.18)

---

1. I do not wish to underestimate the distortion effects of polemic, yet I assume throughout that Paul has not wholly misrepresented the position of the Colossian errorists. Otherwise, my only recourse in this matter is agnosticism. Similarly, I must assume that Paul understood at least the main contours of the Colossian error. What Barclay (p. 76) writes concerning Galatians is equally true for Colossians: 'If Galatians is our only evidence for what the opponents believed, and if, in writing Galatians, Paul laboured under a major misapprehension about them, our search for the real opponents must be abortive'.

The Function of Revelation

Direct Description

Μὴ οὖν τις ὑμᾶς κρινέτω ἐν βρώσει καὶ ἐν πόσει ἢ ἐν μέρει
ἑορτῆς ἢ νεομηνίας ἢ σαββάτων (2.16)
μηδεὶς ὑμᾶς καταβραβευέτω. . . (2.18)

Indirect Reference

Τοῦτο λέγω, ἵνα μηδεὶς ὑμᾶς παραλογίζηται ἐν
πιθανολογίᾳ. . . (2.4)
Βλέπετε μή τις ὑμᾶς ἔσται ὁ συλαγωγῶν. . . (2.8)

Other Relevant Texts

Direct Description (Possible)

ἅτινά ἐστιν λόγον μὲν ἔχοντα σοφίας ἐν ἐθελοθρησκίᾳ. . .
(2.23)

Indirect Reference

. . . διὰ τῆς φιλοσοφίας καὶ κενῆς ἀπάτης κατὰ τὴν
παράδοσιν τῶν ἀνθρώπων, κατὰ τὰ στοιχεῖα τοῦ κόσμου
καὶ οὐ κατὰ Χριστόν (2.8)

ἅ ἐστιν σκιὰ τῶν μελλόντων, τὸ δὲ σῶμα τοῦ Χριστοῦ (2.17)

εἰκῆ φυσιούμενος ὑπὸ τοῦ νοὸς τῆς σαρκὸς αὐτοῦ (2.18)

καὶ οὐ κρατῶν τὴν κεφαλήν. . . (2.19)

ἅ ἐστιν πάντα εἰς φθορὰν τῇ ἀποχρήσει (2.22)

κατὰ τὰ ἐντάλματα καὶ διδασκαλίας τῶν ἀνθρώπων (2.22)

οὐκ ἐν τιμῇ τινι πρὸς πλησμονὴν τῆς σαρκός (2.23).

As was noted above, distinctions between direct description and indirect reference can be disputed. Detailed exegesis is necessary at each point, and that I shall attempt to set out in the following chapter. In some cases, of course, the balance of exegetical probability could fall either way. For example, a major point of dispute is whether τὰ στοιχεῖα τοῦ κόσμου of 2.8, 20 directly echoes the errorists' position, or, as I argue, is an indirect reference to their views. Disputed data such as this should be left, I believe, until other evidence is sifted and evaluated, so that we have a more developed framework to guide us in their interpretation. In most cases, however, the distinction between direct description and indirect reference is both obvious and helpful to our analysis.

4. *Logical and Thematic Structures*

My discussion of methodology to this point has identified certain data in Col. 2.16-23 as the most secure basis for a preliminary reconstruction of the Colossian error. After establishing this framework, we can investigate certain indirect references to the error with a view to understanding their significance in the argument of Colossians. We can also move to the expositional sections in order to determine what they reveal as to the nature of the Colossian error, and to understand their function in the argument of the letter.

It is here that the letter's logical and thematic structures are helpful. For it is clear that the baptismal theology set forth in 2.9-15 stands as the foundation for the writer's polemic. This is true whether we consider the general 'responsibility statements' of 2.6-8 or the more detailed and specific polemic of 2.16-23. With regard to 2.6-8, the fact that the theological section of 2.9-15 is introduced by ὅτι indicates that the warnings of the preceding verses find their logical basis in the exposition that follows. The connection between 2.9-15 and 2.16-23, however, is even more explicit. The polemic begins with the words, μὴ οὖν τις ὑμᾶς κρινέτω (2.16), the conjunction οὖν indicating that the passage it introduces contains inferences from the doctrinal teachings presented in vv. 9-15. This connection is further strengthened in 2.20 and 3.1, where the concept of dying and rising with Christ is picked up from v. 12 and used as the basis for the exhortations that follow.[1] What is striking in this passage, in fact, is that the direct polemic of 2.16ff. is based throughout on the theological exposition of 2.9-15.

Also important is the much shorter christological exposition in Col. 2.2b-3, for its connection to the warning of 2.4-5 is evident as well (v. 4: Τοῦτο λέγω, ἵνα μηδεὶς ὑμᾶς παραλογίζηται ἐν πιθανο-λογίᾳ.[2] In fact, the relationship between exposition and warning in Col. 2.2b-5 is analogous to that which exists between the exposition of 2.9-15 and the detailed polemic of 2.16ff. In both cases, Paul's exposition undergirds his polemical statements, providing the logical basis for his attempts to persuade the Christians at Colossae. For this

---

1. The οὖν in 3.1 makes this more explicit; cf. 2.20 where this has been added in some manuscripts (e.g. א², vg^mss, sy^h), thus making explicit the parallel nature of 2.20 and 3.1 and their dependence on 2.12.

2. For detailed argumentation in support of the view that ἵνα is used here retrospectively, see below.

reason, Col. 2.2b-3 and 2.9-15 are important blocks of material for my analysis. Once I have established a preliminary reconstruction of the Colossian error based on the direct descriptions of Col. 2.16-23, I shall consider the relation that exists between these supporting expositions and the error itself. This investigation should help us gain a fuller understanding of the error as well as greater insight into the meaning and function of Paul's exposition.

Conclusion

The methodology described in the preceding pages takes us through the evidence of Colossians step by step, beginning with direct descriptions of the Colossian error in Col. 2.16-23, then moving to indirect references and supporting blocks of exposition. Finally, of course, we can summarize and apply our results to the letter as a whole. This methodology may seem cumbersome. Nevertheless, I believe that it provides necessary controls for a difficult study. And so I attempt, in the following chapter, to reconstruct the error that occasioned Paul's letter to the Colossians.

Chapter 6

THE COLOSSIAN ERROR

I turn now to a preliminary reconstruction of the problem facing the church at Colossae. The discussion follows the outline suggested in Chapter 5, which in logical development parallels the discussion of revelation in Jewish apocalypticism in Part I. It is, however, primarily with the data in the Colossian letter itself that I am here concerned.

1. *The Achievement of Revelatory Experiences*

The most obvious starting point for a discussion of the Colossian error is with the warning of Col. 2.16, Μὴ οὖν τις ὑμᾶς κρινέτω ἐν βρώσει καὶ ἐν πόσει... Here it seems clear that the Colossian errorists had introduced requirements that, in some way, impinged on the normal activities of eating and drinking. These words do not in themselves, however, indicate the specific nature of such regulations, i.e. whether they had to do with a partial or a complete fasting, or eating and drinking only certain types of food. That fasting (whether partial or complete) is envisaged is suggested by μηδὲ γεύσῃ of 2.21, and scholars are unanimous in viewing fasting as a feature of the Colossian error.[1]

Further insight into the errorists can be gained from the words ταπεινοφροσύνῃ καὶ ἀφειδίᾳ σώματος of 2.23. We are indebted to

1. The background of the fasting advocated by the errorists has generated much discussion. Lähnemann (p. 135) argues that the prohibition concerning drink lacks a clear Jewish precedent; also Percy, p. 140. One must not, however, overlook the stringent regulations associated with the Nazirite vow; so O'Brien, p. 138, and Bruce, *Colossians* (1984), p. 114. S. Lyonnet, 'Paul's Adversaries in Colossae', in *Conflict* (pp. 151-52) refers to practices of dietary abstinence at Qumran as well as to John the Baptist and his disciples (Mt. 9.14; 11.18; Mk 1.6; Lk. 1.15). See also the many parallels in Schweizer, p. 155, as well as the discussion above in Chapter 2, & 2.b.

Fred Francis for a detailed study of ταπεινοφροσύνη, a term generally regarded as a technical term of the errorists themselves since it occurs twice in a negative sense in 2.16-23 as well as in its usual positive sense in the paraenesis that follows (3.12; cf. Acts 20.19; Eph. 4.2; Phil. 2.3 and 1 Pet. 5.5). Francis's research suggests that while the term includes fasting, it is, in fact, much broader than that, encompassing a whole range of bodily disciplines. To quote Francis:

> Ταπεινοφρόνησις in Tertullian is a broader term than fasting. It might well be translated 'rigor of devotion'; it encompasses fasting, abstinence, and stations—a discipline not unlike prison! In Hermas the value of fasting is contingent upon first keeping oneself from every evil word, every evil desire, and purifying the heart from the vanities of the world. So in Colossians ταπεινοφροσύνη is bound up with regulations of much broader effect than fasting.[1]

Many recent scholars have followed Francis here,[2] and I believe for good reason. Such an interpretation is consistent with the reference to food and drink in 2.16, the prohibition μηδὲ γεύσῃ in 2.21 and the reference (closely associated with the term ταπεινοφροσύνη) to ἀφειδίᾳ σώματος in 2.23. Also, the fact that ταπεινοφροσύνη is associated with ἃ ἑόρακεν ἐμβατεύων in 2.18 tells in favor of this interpretation, since ταπεινοφροσύνη, when used in this sense, is often associated with the pursuit of visions and other revelatory experiences.[3]

---

1. Francis, 'Humility and Angelic Worship', p. 168; cf. *idem*, 'Re-examination', pp. 28-31. The parallels are Tertullian, *De ieiunio adversus psychicos*, 12.2; 13.4; 16.4-6; Hermas, *Sim.* 5, 3, 7; *Vis.* 3, 10, 6. It is also significant that in the LXX ταπεινοῦν and ταπείνωσις can refer to the use of sackcloth and ashes and an abject posture; see Isa. 58 and Ps. 34(35).13-14.

2. See H.E. Lona, *Die Eschatologie im Kolosser- und Epheserbrief* (Würzburg: Echter Verlag, 1984), pp. 200-201, as well as O'Brien, p. 142. Some writers, however, misunderstand Francis, thinking that they disagree with him when they suggest that ταπεινοφροσύνη is necessarily broader than fasting; so Lohse, p. 118, R.P. Martin, p. 93, and J. Gnilka, *Der Kolosserbrief* (Freiburg: Herder, 1980), p. 149. In fact, they agree with him precisely. For those who mention only fasting in their explanation of ταπεινοφροσύνη, see Percy, pp. 147-49; C.F.D. Moule, p. 104; J.L. Houlden, *Paul's Letters from Prison* (Harmondsworth: Penguin, 1970), p. 197; Gunther, pp. 95-96; G.B. Caird, *Paul's Letters from Prison* (Oxford: Oxford University Press, 1976), p. 198, and Lincoln, p. 11; cf. W. Grundmann, 'ταπεινός, κτλ.', *TDNT*, VIII, p. 22.

3. Francis, 'Re-Examination', pp. 30-38; *idem*, 'Humility and Angelic Worship', pp. 168-71. Francis's parallels stem not only from Hermas, Tertullian and the Jewish apocalypses, but also include Philo and the *Corpus Hermeticum*; cf., in sup-

That the Colossian error involved fasting seems secure enough. The question remains, however, as to what other tenets were held by the errorists. Some have discerned, particularly in the words μὴ ἅψῃ of 2.21, a reference to abstention from sexual intercourse as being a requirement of the errorists.[1] And such a prohibition was not uncommon in the ancient world, especially in connection with visions and other forms of revelation. Yet ἅ ἐστιν πάντα εἰς φθορὰν τῇ ἀποχρήσει of 2.22 seems to suggest that the prohibitions in 2.21 refer only to restrictions governing food and drink.[2] It is, of course, impossible to deny that the Colossian errorists advocated abstinence from sexual intercourse, since such is well within the range of meaning possible for ταπεινοφροσύνη καὶ ἀφειδίᾳ σώματος. We have, however, no firm evidence from Colossians itself to indicate that this was, in fact, the case. In all probability, some features of ταπεινοφροσύνῃ καὶ ἀφειδίᾳ σώματος advocated at Colossae are simply not mentioned explicitly in the Colossian letter. This seems

port, J. Behm, 'νῆστις, κτλ.', *TDNT*, IV, p. 926; Lincoln, p. 111, and O'Brien, p. 142.

1. So R. Leaney, 'Colossians ii.21-23. (The use of πρός)', *ExpTim* 64 (1952–53), p. 92; Gunther, pp. 113-14. This interpretation is also mentioned as a possibility by BAGD, pp. 102-103. Cf. the many parallels of ἅπτεσθαι to denote intercourse in Schweizer, p. 166. Also, θιγγάνειν refers in certain passages to sexual intercourse; see LSJ, p. 801, and Lona, p. 227. Francis ('Re-examination', pp. 159-60; *idem*, 'Visionary Discipline', p. 73) argues that μὴ ἅψῃ alludes to the proscription of sexual relations in Exod. 19.15. Francis's argument is based almost entirely on the fact that ἅπτεσθαι and θιγγάνειν occur together in Exod. 19.12. This suggests, in his view, that visionary reflection on Exod. 19 stands behind the prohibitions of Col. 2.21. Yet in the Exodus passage it is not ἅπτεσθαι that refers to sexual intercourse, but rather προσέρχεσθαι!

2. So Lohse, p. 123; Schweizer, pp. 166-67; O'Brien, p. 150, and Bruce, *Colossians* (1984), p. 127; cf. Lightfoot, p. 204. Francis ('Re-Examination', pp. 160-64) argues that the relative clause ἅ ἐστιν πάντα εἰς φθορὰν τῇ ἀποχρήσει of 2.22a refers not to the unexpressed objects of the decrees, but to the decrees themselves, and so is consistent with the interpretation of the first prohibition as referring to sexual matters. Yet while his study of ἀπόχρησις demonstrates that 'misuse' is a possible translation, it is not at all clear that it has this meaning here. The translation 'use' is far more common. Furthermore, his analysis drives a wedge between μὴ ἅψῃ, μηδὲ γεύσῃ and μηδὲ θίγῃς in 2.21; for Francis argues that while 'the first two decrees are preparatory for visionary experience, the third has to do with its realization' (p. 160). Francis's interpretation here, however, is unlikely in view of the fact that ἅπτεσθαι and θιγγάνειν are generally synonymous, even in Exod. 19.12 (LXX); see also their synonymous usage in the passages cited by Lightfoot, p. 203.

probable in view of (1) the broad meaning of these terms, and (2) the fact that the congregation addressed was well aware of the details of the praxis, and so did not need to have them spelled out. Given the nature of the situation, no comprehensive description of the errorists' praxis was required—nor, probably, would such have been helpful. Paul's addressees knew what was involved. All we can say with any degree of confidence is that restrictions involving food and drink were a part of the ταπεινοφροσύνῃ καὶ ἀφειδί σώματος of the Colossian errorists.

One additional matter is also relevant in connection with the practices that were associated with revelation in the Colossian error. For in addition to fasting, the writer also mentions certain requirements related to sacred Jewish festivals in 2.16, Μὴ οὖν τις κρινέτω. . . ἐν μέρει ἑορτῆς ἢ νεομηνίας ἢ σαββάτων. These regulations will be treated in detail in our discussion of the function of revelation at Colossae. Nevertheless, as noted earlier in Chapter 2, it is to those who faithfully obey the law—including the observance of sacred days and festivals—that revelation is granted in Jewish apocalypticism. So it is important to note here, even though the matter will be treated more extensively later, that there is some overlap between those practices associated with revelation and the redemptive function of the revelations that are received.

2. *Media of Revelation*

Significant for present purposes are the words ἃ ἑόρακεν ἐμβατεύων of 2.18. Here, of course, we face an interpretive challenge of the highest order. Many earlier commentators, in fact, have felt compelled to resort to conjectural emendation in order to come up with any meaningful interpretation.[1] Fortunately, however, recent interpreters have attempted to make sense of the text as it stands, and in so doing have presented several plausible solutions to this exegetical dilemma.

The interpretive problems of the text are both lexical and syntactical. First, the meaning of the participle ἐμβατεύων has generated considerable discussion, and recent studies have yet to settle on one of several possibilities. Second, the relationship of the participle to the

---

1. For surveys of various suggested emendations, see C.F.D. Moule, pp. 105-106; Lohse, p. 119; Bruce, *Colossians* (1984), pp. 120-22.

preceding words ἃ ἑόρακεν is also a matter of concern, though on this issue the discussion seems to be making some progress. Both of these matters are crucial for an understanding of the media of revelation practiced at Colossae, as well as for the discussion of the content of revelation that follows.

Quite independently, Martin Dibelius and William Ramsay, on the basis of inscriptions from the sanctuary of Apollo at Claros,[1] argued that the verb ἐμβατεύειν was a technical term associated with initiation into a mystery cult. Dibelius argued at some length that the experience of the θεοπρόποι in Claros, referred to by the technical expression ἐπιτελεῖν μυστήρια, actually consisted of two parts: μυηθέντες or παραλαβὼν τὰ μυστήρια (receiving the mysteries) and the *Epoptia* or ἐμβατεύειν (entering the inner shrine). In his view, 'ἐμβατεύειν would be a technical designation of the mystery proper, legitimate participation in which was rendered possible by the *muesis* (or the παραλαμβάνειν τὰ μυστήρια)'.[2] So we should recognize in Col. 2.18 'einen kultischen Terminus' of the mysteries.[3] And it is on this basis that Dibelius argued that the errorists were Christians who sought 'initiation into mysteries already transformed in a gnostic direction'.[4]

Dibelius's interpretation of ἐμβατεύειν has won considerable support, even among scholars who take issue with other details in his general reconstruction of the Colossian error.[5] There are, however,

---

1. This was argued first in the 1912 edition of Dibelius's commentary on Colossians; cf. *idem*, 'Isis Initiation', pp. 61-121 (first published in German in 1917). W.M. Ramsay's contribution on this issue is often overlooked; see 'Ancient Mysteries and their Relation to St. Paul', *Athenaeum*, Jan 25, 1913, pp. 106-107, and *The Teaching of Paul in Terms of the Present Day* (London: Hodder & Stoughton, 1913), pp. 286-304. The inscriptions from Claros had, of course, been only recently published.

2. Dibelius, 'Isis Initiation', pp. 86-87.

3. Dibelius, 'Isis Initiation', pp. 86-87.

4. Dibelius, 'Isis Initiation', p. 92.

5. Cf. E.F. Scott, *The Epistle of Paul to the Colossians, to Philemon, and to the Ephesians* (London: Hodder & Stoughton, 1930), p. 55; S. Eitrem, 'ΕΜΒΑΤΕΥΩ. Note sur Col. 2,18', *ST* 2 (1948), pp. 90-94; Lohse, p. 120; Lähnemann, p. 138; R.P. Martin, pp. 94-95, and Argall, pp. 14-15. Bornkamm ('Heresy', p. 140) speaks of 'Dibelius' proof that ἐμβατεύειν is a term from the mysteries', but cannot decide whether it 'suggests the cultic act of "entering" the sanctuary, or whether, more likely, the word has the more general meaning, "investigate"'. Cf. Lähnemann, p. 86, and Lona, pp. 210-11. S. Lyonnet ('L'Epître aux Colossiens [Col 2,18] et les mystères d'Apollon Clarien', *Bib* 43 [1962], p. 435) and Houlden

several problems with Dibelius's interpretation of ἐμβατεύειν. Of primary concern is the fact that ἐμβατεύειν is found in this technical sense only in connection with μυεῖσθαι or παραλαμβάνειν τὰ μυστήρια.[1] Furthermore, in addition to pointing out the second-century dates of the Clarian inscriptions, Francis has even questioned whether ἐμβατεύειν was a technical term in those inscriptions.[2] It is rather, in his opinion, one of a number of terms used to refer to entrance into a chamber at the oracle shrine in order to present oneself for consultation.[3] So Francis concludes that while initiation is clear in the Clarian inscriptions, the verb ἐμβατεύειν, on its own, by no means signals the climax of that experience.[4]

Another interpretation of ἐμβατεύειν proposed by some is that the verb means 'to examine' or 'to investigate'.[5] That ἐμβατεύειν can be used in this sense is certain (cf. 2 Macc. 2.30; Philo, *De plant.* 80), yet the syntax of the clause points toward a different solution—that the

(p. 198) see this as a technical term of the mysteries, but argue that the writer is using irony at this point; Paul used the term 'afin de mieux stigmatiser l'erreur de ceux qu'il combat' (Lyonnet, p. 435).

1. A.D. Nock, 'The Vocabulary of the New Testament', *JBL* 52 (1933), pp. 132-33; H. Preisker, 'ἐμβατεύω', *TDNT*, II, pp. 535-36; E. Lohmeyer, *Die Briefe an die Philipper, an die Kolosser und an Philemon* (Göttingen: Vandenhoeck & Ruprecht, 1953), p. 124. Lohse (p. 120) argues, however, that 'when a catch-word-like phrase is quoted, it is not surprising that no other terms of the language of the mysteries appear in the context and that a sanctuary is not mentioned specifically'. His point is well taken, though the case in favor of the this view would be much stronger if ἐμβατεύειν referred in the inscriptions to initiation itself or if the writer of Colossians mentioned it in connection with the usual terms for initiation.

2. Francis, 'Background of EMBATEYEIN', pp. 197-207; cf. *idem*, 'Re-examination', pp. 39-47.

3. On the various terms used for entering in order to consult the oracle, see Francis, 'Background of EMBATEYEIN', pp. 201, 206. Most common are verbs meaning 'to go down', presumably into subterranean grottos. Other verbs that imply 'entering' at ground level are παρελθεῖν (Strabo, *Geog.* 17. 1, 43) and παρεῖναι (Pausanias, *Descript.* 10. 24, 5). The second-century AD rhetorician Aristides and the fourth-century sophist Himerius, both of whom were familiar with the Clarian Apollo, used ἐμβατεύειν in other non-technical senses; see Francis, 'Background of EMBATEYEIN', p. 203.

4. Francis, 'Re-examination', p. 41: 'The fact that the same verb for initiation appears both with and without *embateuein* suggests that the latter is not constitutive of the former. The proposition that *embateuein* is a second, higher initiation is sheer guess work, having no foundation in the inscriptions.'

5. Cf. Preisker, pp. 535-36; Lohmeyer, *Kolosser*, p. 124. See also Lyonnet, 'Col 2,18 et les mystères', p. 435, though with a somewhat sarcastic reference to mystery initiation at Claros.

term refers to a visionary entrance into heaven. This suggestion was mentioned as a possibility by A.D. Nock in 1933.[1] It was Fred Francis, however, who argued this position in detail in his 1965 dissertation,[2] and his views seem to have won the day.[3]

That ἐμβατεύων refers to a visionary entrance into heaven can be supported along two different lines of evidence. First, the term is found in the OT (Josh. 19.49, 51 [LXX]) and the hellenistic papyri in the sense of 'entering into possession of something', and so moves easily into the notion of 'entering heaven in order to possess oneself of salvation, a portion in the Lord'.[4] Second, in the Jewish apocalyptic writings the concept of entrance into heaven is frequently associated with ideas of ascetic preparation, revelatory visions and the worship of angels—and in a manner that corresponds closely to the data from Colossians.[5] Both of these lines of evidence are important. Yet it is as we consider the syntax of Col. 2.18 that the advantages of such an interpretation become particularly evident.

Two issues are critical in the syntax of 2.18. Most easily resolved is whether ἃ ἑόρακεν ἐμβατεύων stands on its own as a participial clause, or is to be seen as a part of the pejorative reference to the attitude of the errorists in the following clause, εἰκῆ φυσιούμενος ὑπὸ τοῦ νοὸς τῆς σαρκὸς αὐτοῦ. The former view has much to

---

1. Nock, p. 133, though he settles on the translation 'entering at length upon the tale of what he has seen (in a vision)'.

2. Francis, 'Re-examination', pp. 39-76; cf. *idem*, 'Visionary Discipline', pp. 76-77; 'Humility and Angelic Worship', pp. 171-76, and 'Background of EMBATEYEIN', pp. 197-99.

3. Cf. Bandstra, 'Colossian Errorists', p. 331; Evans, p. 198; O'Brien, p. 145; Schweizer, p. 161; Rowland, 'Apocalyptic Visions', p. 76; Yates, p. 14. Cf. Carr, pp. 68-69; also Lincoln, pp. 112-13, who seems to favor this approach, yet says that ἐμβατεύειν could be a technical term associated with the mysteries.

4. Francis ('Background of EMBATEYEIN', p. 199) writes, 'Joshua's use of ἐμβατεύειν in the allotting of tribal inheritances certainly bridges to Colossians through the *Testament of Levi*. *T. Levi* 2.10, 12; 4.2, 5.1-2 specifically relate Levi's portion and service to the Lord to heavenly entrance.' This interpretation is in line with the verb's basic meaning 'to enter', yet represents a development vis-à-vis Francis's earlier studies. Cf. also N. Hugedé (*Commentaire de l'Epître aux Colossiens* [Genève: Labor et Fides, 1968], pp. 150-51) who does not mention Francis's work.

5. See Chapters 2–3 above. Of course, the verb ἐμβατεύειν is not found in any of these sources; many of the apocalypses are preserved in languages other than Greek. According to Evans (p. 198), who cites a private communication from Francis, Nils Dahl has found the verb in the sense 'entering heaven' in Greek fragments of Cicero. I have not myself, however, seen this reference.

commend it, especially since the meaning of the adverb fits perfectly with the sense of the participial clause that follows.[1] Furthermore, it is confirmed by the analysis of the other major syntactical problem in this verse.

A couple of approaches are possible with regard to the relationship between the expression ἃ ἑόρακεν and the participle ἐμβατεύων. One treats the relative pronoun as the object of ἐμβατεύων.[2] This view is possible from a grammatical perspective. The structure of the passage, however, seems to point to another conclusion, as is evident from a simple outline of vv. 16-18:

Μὴ οὖν τις ὑμᾶς κρινέτω
   ἐν βρώσει καὶ ἐν πόσει ἢ ἐν μέρει ἑορτῆς ἢ νεομηνίας ἢ σαββάτων
    ἅ ἐστιν σκιὰ τῶν μελλόντων, τὸ δὲ σῶμα τοῦ Χριστοῦ.
μηδεὶς ὑμᾶς καταβραβευέτω
   θέλων ἐν ταπεινοφροσύνῃ καὶ θρησκείᾳ τῶν ἀγγέλων,
    ἃ ἑόρακεν ἐμβατεύων...

The relationship between the clauses in vv. 16-17 is clear enough. Ἐν βρώσει of 16b introduces a list of matters that Christians at Colossae are not to allow the errorists to judge them about (so 16a),[3] with that list summed up by the neuter relative pronoun of v. 17 and evaluated negatively.[4] The relationship between ideas in v. 18 is initially less clear than in the previous two verses. Yet the grammatical relationships in v. 18 run in a somewhat parallel fashion.[5] The relative clause

---

1. Cf. BAGD, p. 222. This arrangement is followed by virtually all modern scholars. See in opposition, however, A. Fridrichsen, 'θελων Col 2,18', *ZNW* 21 (1922), pp. 135-37 ('Grundlos eingebildet. . . wegen dessen, was er geschaut hat bei seiner Einweihung'); cf. *Syntax*, p. 246, and BDF, 154. Percy, p. 172, objects with regard to this construction 'dass sie ohne Analogie in der griechischen Literatur sein dürfte'.

2. So Dibelius, 'Isis Initiation', p. 87; cf. H.A.W. Meyer, *Critical and Exegetical Hand-Book to the Epistles to the Philippians and Colossians, and to Philemon* (trans. J. C. Moore, rev. and ed. W.P. Dickson; New York: Funk & Wagnalls, 1885), p. 319. Also among more recent commentators, cf. Hugedé, p. 151, and W. Hendriksen, *Philippians, Colossians and Philemon* (Grand Rapids: Baker, 1979), p. 127.

3. This is made even clearer by the words ἐν μέρει; cf. BAGD, p. 506, for parallels.

4. It is impossible to say with any degree of confidence whether the first part of v. 16c incorporates slogans of the errorists or is merely a part of the author's negative evaluation (an indirect reference).

5. Cf. F. Zeilinger, *Der Erstgeborene der Schöpfung* (Vienna: Herder, 1974), p. 57.

refers back to the words ταπεινοφροσύνῃ καὶ θρησκείᾳ τῶν ἀγγέλων and the neuter pronoun sums up these ideas. So the participle ἐμβατεύων functions as a temporal modifier, suggesting that the vision of the humility and worship of angels took place at a time of entrance.[1] Such a view of these verses has the advantage of allowing the clauses of v. 18 to function in a manner parallel to those of vv. 16-17.

Though there are lexical and syntactical difficulties associated with 2.18, certain factors are suggested with regard to the mode of revelation advocated by the Colossian errorists. The interpretation of ἐμβατεύειν to mean 'entering (heaven)' brings to mind the notion of heavenly ascent, with attendant visions suggested by the words ἃ ἑόρακεν. Such an experience was widespread in the ancient world. It is, however, impossible to determine the history of religions connection on the basis of this data alone. For this, we must turn to the next area of concern, namely the content of revelation.

3. *The Content of Revelation*

The primary exegetical data having to do with the content of revelation among the errorists at Colossae are the words ἐν ταπεινοφροσύνῃ καὶ θρησκείᾳ τῶν ἀγγέλων of 2.18. Apart from their immediate context, these words, of course, are subject to diverse interpretations. Dominant among modern authorities, in spite of their many other points of disagreement, is the view that both parts of this phrase represent some attitude or action on the part of the errorists. So it is argued that θρησκείᾳ τῶν ἀγγέλων refers in some way to the veneration of angels, while ταπεινοφροσύνῃ specifies the religious requirements necessary to placate such beings.[2] A close grammatical

---

1. This is the majority view among recent scholars, regardless of their interpretation of ἐμβατεύειν. For those who treat the verb as a technical term of the mysteries, see Lohse, pp. 118-19; Gnilka, p. 151. For those who view it as having to do with an ascent into heaven, see Lincoln, p. 112; Evans, pp. 197-98; O'Brien, p. 143; Schweizer, pp. 161-62; Rowland, 'Apocalyptic Visions', pp. 74-76, and Bruce, *Colossians* (1984), p. 117.

2. There are, of course, a number of variations even within this common interpretive approach. Many writers maintain that there was an actual cult of angels at Colossae: e.g. Dibelius–Greeven, p. 35; Bornkamm, 'Heresy', p. 128, and G. Kittel, 'ἄγγελος, κτλ.', *TDNT*, I, p. 86. Others attempt to soften the force of θρησκείᾳ by treating these words as a pejorative characterization introduced by the author rather than an objective description of the practices of the errorists; so Percy, pp. 168-69;

study of 2.18, however, suggests that such a view is incorrect—that these terms do not refer to the actions of the errorists or of other human figures, but to the activities of the angels themselves. On this interpretation, the words ἐν ταπεινοφροσύνῃ καὶ θρησκεᾳ τῶν ἀγγέλων not only provide additional information about the error but also reinforce the interpretation of ἐμβατεύων suggested above, and so point to Jewish apocalypticism as a relevant background for understanding the problems facing the church at Colossae.

It is important in an analysis of 2.16-18 to recall that the structure of the passage suggests that the relative pronoun ἅ refers back to the ideas of humility and angelic worship, and so implies that these elements were the objects of the visions (ἑόρακεν). Such an arrangement of clauses and ideas is widely accepted; indeed, it is the dominant view in recent studies. Often overlooked, however, are the implications of this understanding for the interpretation of θρησκείᾳ τῶν ἀγγέλων. The usual explanation, that τῶν ἀγγέλων is an objective genitive, makes very little sense in the context of v. 18, for one cannot speak in any meaningful way of visions of the worship (by Christians?) of angelic beings.[1] On the other hand, the interpretation of θρησκείᾳ τῶν ἀγγέλων as a subjective genitive is meaningful in context, especially against the background of Jewish apocalypticism.[2] For, as was set out in some detail in Chapter 3, apocalyptic visions often climaxed in a vision of the throne and in worship that is offered by the angelic hosts surrounding it. Assuming the rendering of ἐμβατεύων suggested above, then the sense of the text would be that the angelic worship is

---

C. Masson, *L'Epitre de Saint Paul aux Colossiens* (Paris: Delachaux & Niestlé, 1950), p. 134; Hugedé, pp. 148-49; Lyonnet, 'Paul's Adversaries', pp. 149-50, and, recently, P. Benoit, 'The "plérôma" in Colossians and Ephesians', *SEÅ* 49 (1984), pp. 152-53. Along similar lines see J.B. McClellan, 'Colossians II.18: A Criticism of the Revised Version and an Exposition', *Expositor*, series 7, 9 (1910), pp. 385-98.

1. Cf. Evans, pp. 197-98; Rowland, 'Apocalyptic Visions', p. 75. The difficulties facing interpreters who insist on reading θρησκείᾳ τῶν ἀγγέλων as an objective genitive are considerable. Lohse (p. 117) translates 'as he has had visions of them during the mystery rites'. He does not, however, discuss the syntactical problem that his rendering creates; cf. Gnilka, p. 151. One could perhaps argue that it was the need for believers to worship angelic beings that was the object of visions. Such a view, however, introduces concepts not in the text, and so is unlikely.

2. Francis, 'Re-Interpretation', p. 85; Evans, pp. 197-98, and Rowland, 'Apocalyptic Visions', p. 75.

the object of these visions that occurred when the seer entered the heavenly realm.

While the relation between θρησκείᾳ τῶν ἀγγέλων and the relative clause that follows is readily explicable, the function of ταπεινο-φροσύνη has generated some diversity of opinion. Two indicators, however, suggest that the term parallels θρησκείᾳ τῶν ἀγγέλων both in meaning and in terms of its relation to the following relative clause. First, the use of the neuter relative pronoun implies that the reference is to the 'whole idea' of the preceding clause (including ταπεινο-φροσύη) rather than to any single term.[1] Second, the non-repetition of the preposition ἐν before θρησκείᾳ tells in favor of the view that the following genitive (τῶν ἀγγέλων) applies to ταπεινοφροσύνη as well as to θρησκείᾳ (cf. the parallel in 2.22, κατὰ τὰ ἐντάλματα καὶ διδασκαλίας τῶν ἀνθρώπων).[2]

In light of this data, the simplest conclusion is that the visions of the errorists included 'humility and worship performed by angels'. The reference in 2.18 is thus to actions performed by angelic beings and not by the errorists themselves. Nevertheless, the reference to ταπεινοφροσύνη καὶ ἀφειδίᾳ σώματος in conjunction with ἐθελο-θρησκίᾳ in 2.23 suggests that the errorists sought to emulate the behavior of the heavenly beings in their own religious practices.[3]

1. See *Idiom Book*, p. 130, where Moule cites Eph. 5.5 and 1 Jn 2.8 (possibly) as examples of this usage; cf. Rowland, 'Apocalyptic Visions', p. 76 (citing Col. 2.26 and 3.6 as parallels).

2. According to Turner, *Syntax*, p. 275, 1 Corinthians and Romans contain twenty-four opportunities for repetition of the preposition before two or more phrases connected by καί, and in fourteen cases the preposition is actually repeated. Thus there is somewhat of a preference for repetition in these letters. In Ephesians, however, the repetition occurs in only six out of sixteen possible occurrences. Cf. BDF, 479(1).

3. Cf., however, E. Schweizer, 'Christ in the Letter to the Colossians', *RevExp* 70 (1973), p. 452: 'in verse 23 a Greek word which means literally a self-chosen worship [i.e., ἐθελοθρησκία] takes up the phrase of the worship of angels in a kind of caricature and declares that this is actually no worship of angels, but a worship rendered by men to angels. Therefore, v. 18 must mean a worship rendered by men to angels.' This argument was voiced earlier by Lohse, p. 119; cf. R.P. Martin, p. 94, who views it as a 'fatal objection' to the interpretation of θρησκείᾳ τῶν ἀγγέλων as a subjective genitive. Nevertheless, ἐθελοθρησκεία does not specify in this text a cult performed by men. As W.A. Meeks ('In One Body: The Unity of Humankind in Colossians and Ephesians', in *God's Christ and His People* [ed. J. Jervell and W.A. Meeks; Oslo: Universitetsforlaget, 1977], p. 218) writes, 'Granted that the unique word ἐθελοθρησκεία is a parody of the phrase used in 2.18, why could not the author be saying, by Schweizer's own logic, "This is actu-

In spite of a paucity of data regarding the content of the revelatory visions enjoyed by the errorists at Colossae, it is possible to arrive at a reasonable construction based on the syntax of 2.18. One cannot, of course, speak of 'proof', since the evidence is by no means abundant and we are forced to tackle difficult grammatical issues in setting out any proposed reconstruction. Nevertheless, the analysis suggested above accounts for the grammar and syntax of the text in a manner preferable to alternative interpretations, and it avoids the subjectivism associated with conjectural emendation.

My thesis is not that the content of revelation at Colossae was limited to visionary experiences of the *Merkabah* and the heavenly liturgy. In fact, if there is a connection between Jewish apocalypticism and the outlook and practices of the Colossian errorists, then we would expect to find significant variety in the revelation received. There is, of course, no direct evidence in the text of Colossians to suggest that this was, in fact, the case. Yet this supposition is rendered likely by our analysis of another important topic, namely the function of revelation among the errorists at Colossae.

4. *The Function of Revelation*

Highly significant for an understanding of the function of revelation at Colossae are the verbs κρινέτω of 2.16 and καταβραβευέτω of 2.18. The meaning of the former is straightforward enough, for linked with the object ὑμᾶς it certainly implies that one person or group was passing judgment on or condemning another person or group.[1] In context, this can only mean that the stance of the opponents—possibly also their sympathizers among the Colossian Christians—was one of judgment toward those who were disinclined to follow their beliefs and/or practices. A similar situation is implied by the term καταβραβευέτω (v. 18). This is true regardless of whether one lays stress on the athletic metaphor underlying the verb (i.e. 'to deprive' or

---

ally no worship copied from and authorized by angels, but a worship invented by men"?' Cf. O'Brien, p. 143.

1. See BAGD, p. 452; cf. O'Brien, p. 138. In this context it is likely that the use of the present imperative with μὴ is a prohibition against the continuation of action already in progress, rather than a general durative command. On the usual distinction between the present imperative and aorist subjunctive in prohibitions, see *Syntax*, pp. 74-78.

'to disqualify')[1] or treats the compound as roughly equivalent, though somewhat sharper in tone, to κρινέτω in v. 16.[2] If with a majority of modern interpreters we lay stress on the athletic metaphor underlying the verb, then the object of deprivation or disqualification lies close at hand—τὴν μερίδα τοῦ κλήρου τῶν ἁγίων ἐν τῷ φωτί (1.12). This is, however, not direct evidence, so detailed consideration of this point must await the further discussion in Chapter 8.

When we consider the related question of the basis for this attitude of judgment, the data are equally unambiguous. The verb κρινέτω is followed immediately by the words ἐν βρώσει καὶ ἐν πόσει ἢ ἐν μέρει ἑορτῆς ἢ νεομηνίας ἢ σαββάτων, and there is little doubt that these represent some of the major issues that stood as the basis for the condemnation of Colossian believers on the part of the errorists. Two areas of concern are evident in this text: (1) the consumption of food and drink, and (2) the observance of Jewish holy days and festivals.

The words ἐν βρώσει καὶ ἐν πόσει are, in themselves, subject to diverse interpretations, and one cannot draw conclusions with a high degree of confidence on these data alone. Nevertheless, in view of the fact that ταπεινοφροσύνη is used in v. 23 in conjunction with ἀφειδίᾳ σώματος, and this in a context that obviously refers to actions the errorists sought to impose on others, it is probable that the concern in v. 16 is with abstinence from certain kinds of food and drink. As noted above, such practices were believed to facilitate the experience of revelatory visions. So it is probable that the errorists sought to lead Christians at Colossae into the same types of experiences in which they themselves 'took delight'.[3]

---

1. Bruce (*Colossians* [1984], p. 117) summarizes the data as follows: 'The compound . . . means "give an unfavorable ruling"' on a competitor in some athletic contest, the ruling being given by the umpire (βραβεύς). In all passages quoted for the use of the compound it conveys the idea of depriving something which he or she would otherwise have possessed, such as an opportunity to compete (hence RSV "disqualify") or a prize. . .'; cf. E. Stauffer, 'βραβεύω, βραβεῖον', *TDNT*, I, pp. 637-38. Among writers who lay stress on this background are T.K. Abbott, *A Critical and Exegetical Commentary on the Epistles to the Ephesians and to the Colossians* (Edinburgh: T. & T. Clark, 1897), p. 266, and Evans, 'Colossian Mystics', p. 195.

2. See Percy, pp. 144-45 (with parallels); Dibelius–Greeven, p. 34; Lohmeyer, *Kolosser*; p. 123; Lähnemann, p. 138, and O'Brien, p. 141, 'with many modern commentators'.

3. Following the vast majority of modern authorities, I interpret the words θέλων ἐν (v. 18) as a Septuagintalism meaning 'to delight in' or 'to take pleasure in'; see

The other group of concerns expressed in v. 16 conforms to 'a stylized three-fold formula used from the prophetic period down into post-biblical literature'.[1] The sequence ἑορτή... νεομηνία... σάββατον is found in numerous passages from the OT (1 Chron. 23.31; 2 Chron. 2.4; 8.13; 31.3; Ezek. 45.17; Neh. 10.33; Hos. 2.11; cf. Num. 28–29; Isa. 1.13-14; Ezek. 46.4-11), the OT Apocrypha (1 Esdr. 5.52; Jdt. 8.6), the OT pseudepigrapha (*1 En.* 82.7; *Jub.* 1.10, 14; 2.9-10; 6.34-38; 23.19), and Qumran (1QM 2.4-6).[2] It is neither an *ad hoc* list of items chosen at random nor a summary of certain special days that must be observed, though interest in the calendar is evident enough. Rather, it refers to the whole complex of Jewish sacrificial worship,[3] the observance of which constituted evidence of obedience to God's law and stood as a sign of Israel's election among the nations.[4] And this, it seems, was an important basis on which the errorists leveled their accusations against the Colossian believers.

It is difficult to make a firm judgment on the relation between these two areas of concern based solely on the data of Colossians. It is possible that matters of sacrificial worship were viewed as parallel to issues of food and drink, with both being prerequisites for entering into the experience of angelic worship and enjoying the vision of the throne of God. On the other hand, we must also reckon with the possibility that the inclusion of matters pertaining to sacrificial worship has to do simply with religious obligations necessary if one was to avoid condemnation at the last judgment, and so are unrelated to attaining visions of heavenly ascent—except, of course, as sacrificial worship was seen to undergird the exhortations to obedience. If, however, I am correct in making use of the background of Jewish apocalypticism, then both perspectives could be operative. For obedience to the requirements of sacrificial worship, as well as the observance of fasts, could have been a prerequisite for heavenly ascent

G. Schrenk, 'θέλω, θέλημα, θέλησις', *TDNT*, III, p. 45, as well as Percy, pp. 145-47; C.F.D. Moule, p. 104; Lohse, p. 118, and Schweizer, p. 158. Relevant here are Ps. 111.1 (LXX) and *T. Asher* 1.6. For the adverbial interpretation of θέλων, see Fridrichsen, pp. 135-37, and Dibelius–Greeven, p. 34.

1. Francis, 'Visionary Discipline', pp. 78-79.
2. Esp. helpful is the discussion of parallels in the OT, OT Apocrypha, OT Pseudepigrapha and Qumran by P. Giem, 'SABBATON in Col 2.16', *AUSS* 19 (1981), pp. 198-206. The order varies in several of these texts, while in two cases the sequence is missing one of the elements.
3. See Francis, 'Re-examination', pp. 172-76.
4. O'Brien, p. 139.

as well as a religious requirement founded on the revelations associated with these experiences. Such appears to have been the case among the Jewish apocalyptists. And their writings on this matter yield a cohesive framework of thought for understanding the function of revelation at Colossae.

5. Τὰ στοιχεῖα τοῦ κόσμου

Many treatments of the Colossian error lay stress on the phrase κατὰ τὰ στοιχεῖα τοῦ κόσμου of 2.8 and the words εἰ ἀπεθάνετε σὺν Χριστῷ ἀπὸ τῶν στοιχείων τοῦ κόσμου of 2.20 as critical for the process of reconstruction. Since I have approached the question in a different manner, treating these texts as only secondary evidence for discerning the error at Colossae, some discussion of the issues involved is appropriate.

The exegesis of the στοιχεῖα passages in Colossians (as well as in Galatians) has generated a significant amount of discussion.[1] Andrew Bandstra lists three fundamental interpretations that have been argued in the nineteenth and twentieth centuries: (1) the 'principial' interpretation, (2) the 'cosmological' interpretation, and (3) the 'personalized-cosmological' interpretation. Some variation is evident among writers that embrace each interpretation, but Bandstra's categories are useful nonetheless.

The 'principial' interpretation received wide support among the fathers,[2] and was commonly held through the nineteenth century.[3] It finds support in several modern discussions, though it is clearly a minority viewpoint.[4] It builds on the usage, well attested in both the

---

1. For a survey of research, see Bandstra, *Law and the Elements*, pp. 5-30; cf. L.L. Belleville, '"Under Law": Structural Analysis and the Pauline Concept of Law in Galatians 3.21–4.11', *JSNT* 26 (1986), pp. 65-66 (with notes).

2. These include Clement of Alexandria, Origen, Tertullian and Jerome; see Bandstra, *Law and the Elements*, pp. 5-12.

3. E.g. W.M.L. de Wette, *Kurze Erklärung der Briefe an die Colosser, an Philemon, an die Ephesier und Philipper* (2nd edn; Leipzig: Weidmann, 1847), pp. 43-44; B. Weiss, *Biblical Theology of the New Testament* (trans. from the 3rd German edn; Edinburgh: T. & T. Clark, 1882), I, pp. 358, 372-73; Lightfoot, p. 180, and Abbott, p. 247. De Wette (p. 44) refers to this as 'the usual interpretation'.

4. E.g. E.D. Burton, *A Critical and Exegetical Commentary on the Epistle to the Galatians* (Edinburgh: T. & T. Clark, 1921), pp. 215-16; W.L. Knox (*St. Paul and the Church of the Gentiles* [Cambridge: Cambridge University Press, 1939], pp. 108-109, 140-41) who believes that the term also hints at bondage to the planets;

classical and hellenistic periods, of στοιχεῖα as referring to the elementary principles or rudimentary ideas of a particular subject or field of study.[1] In this interpretation, Paul uses the phrase τὰ στοιχεῖα τοῦ κόσμου in a pejorative sense in order to combat the Colossian errorists. For all their claims to superior knowledge, they were really taking a step backwards in their beliefs and practices, to the religious ABCs of the world (cf. Heb. 5.12).

The 'cosmological' interpretation is founded on extensive lexical evidence—the most extensive, in fact, of the three viewpoints.[2] It was dominant in the writings of the early fathers and is still represented today, though its popularity has diminished.[3] In this view τὰ στοιχεῖα τοῦ κόσμου refers to the basic components that make up the material world (i.e. earth, water, air and fire), though its meaning also extends to the planets and the stars. In explication of this position, it is usually argued that the errorists worshiped the 'elements', or that the errorists sought purification through fasting, and so on, in order to gain freedom from the lower elements and to ascend to the highest divine element.

Most recent interpreters adopt some form of the 'personalized-cosmological' interpretation. There are several variations on this approach. Some have identified the στοιχεῖα as the angels that served

R.M. Grant, 'Like Children', *HTR* 39 (1946), pp. 71-73; Masson, p. 123; C.F.D. Moule, pp. 90-92; H. Ridderbos, *Paul: An Outline of His Theology* (trans. J.R. de Witt; Grand Rapids: Eerdmans, 1975), p. 149, and Carr, pp. 75-76.

1. For a survey of the evidence, see G. Delling, 'στοιχεῖον', *TDNT*, VI, pp. 678-79; also, J. Blinzler, 'Lexikalisches zu dem Terminus τὰ στοιχεῖα τοῦ κόσμου', in *Studiorum Paulinorum Congressus Internationalis Catholicus 1961* (Rome: Pontificio Istituto Biblico, 1963), II, pp. 429-43.

2. For examples, see Delling, 'στοιχεῖον', pp. 672-78. Cf. W. Wink (*Naming the Powers* [Philadelphia: Fortress Press, 1984], p. 69) who finds that fifty-four of eighty-five occurrences of στοιχεῖα in Philo refer to the elements of nature.

3. Among the early fathers, Hilary of Poitiers, Chrysostom, Theodore of Mopsuestia, Victorinus and Augustine held to various forms of the 'cosmological' interpretation; see Bandstra, *Law and the Elements*, pp. 5-12. In the twentieth century, see T. Zahn, *Einleitung in das Neue Testament* (2nd edn; Leipzig: Deichert, 1900), I, pp. 335-36; N. Kehl, *Der Christushymnus im Kolosserbrief* (Stuttgart: Katholisches Bibelwerk, 1967), pp. 139-61; E. Schweizer, 'Die "Elemente der Welt" Gal 4,3.9; Kol 2,8.20' in *Verborum Veritas: Festschrift für Gustav Stahlin* (ed. O. Bücher and K. Haacker; Wuppertal: Brockhaus, 1970), pp. 245-59; also *idem*, 'Slaves of the Elements and Worshipers of Angels: Gal 4.3, 9 and Col 2.8, 18, 20', *JBL* 107 (1988), pp. 455-68.

as mediators of the law,[1] while most argue that the term refers to astral or spiritual powers associated with the planetary bodies that exert control over humans.[2] In this view, the requirements of the Colossian errorists were imposed 'for the sake of "the elements of the universe", who direct the course of the stars and thus also prescribe minutely the order of the calendar'.[3]

Many writers today embrace the 'personalized-cosmological' interpretation of τὰ στοιχεῖα τοῦ κόσμου in Colossians for three reasons: (1) they interpret θρησκείᾳ τῶν ἀγγέλων of 2.18 as an objective genitive, and so argue that a cult of angels threatened the congregation at Colossae; (2) they assume that αἱ ἀρχαὶ καὶ αἱ ἐξουσίαι, mentioned at several points in Colossians, are the angels who were worshiped; and (3) they assume an identification between these powers and τὰ στοιχεῖα τοῦ κόσμου of 2.8, 20.[4] We must, however, beware of this line of argumentation, since the interpretation of θρησκείᾳ τῶν ἀγγέλων as an objective genitive is questionable (we must reserve judgment as to the nature and function of the spiritual forces in Colossians until later in our study) and since many of the references to αἱ ἀρχαὶ καὶ αἱ ἐξουσίαι are in expositional sections of the letter (the concern is here with passages that are polemical).

The evidence for the interpretation of τὰ στοιχεῖα τοῦ κόσμου is both lexical and contextual. The lexical evidence supports the

---

1. Percy, pp. 160-67; cf. B. Reicke, 'The Law and this World according to Paul', *JBL* 70 (1951), pp. 261-63; Bruce, *Colossians* (1984), pp. 99-100.

2. E.g. G.H.C. Macgregor, 'Principalities and Powers: The Cosmic Background of Saint Paul's Thought', *NTS* 1 (1954), pp. 21-22; J. Gewiess, 'Die apologetische Methode des Apostels Paulus im Kampf gegen die Irrlehre in Kolossä', *BibLeb* 3 (1962), pp. 260-61; H.-M. Schenke, 'Der Widerstreit gnostischer und kirchlicher Christologie im Spiegel des Kolosserbriefes', *ZTK* 61 (1964), pp. 393-99; H. Schlier, *Der Brief an die Galater* (4th edn; Göttingen: Vandenhoeck & Ruprecht, 1965), pp. 190-93; Bornkamm, 'Heresy', pp. 123-24; Lohse, pp. 98-99; R.P. Martin, p. 14; H.-F. Weiss, 'Gnostische Motive und antignostische Polemik im Kolosser- und im Epheserbrief', in *Gnosis und Neuen Testament* (ed. K.-W. Tröger; Gütersloh: Gütersloher Verlagshaus, 1973), p. 313; H.D. Betz, *Galatians* (Philadelphia: Fortress Press, 1979), p. 205; B.H. Brinsmead, *Galatians—Dialogical Response to Opponents* (Chico, CA: Scholars Press, 1982), pp. 120-27.

3. Lohse, p. 115; cf. Lohmeyer, *Kolosser*, p. 122.

4. See e.g. Bornkamm ('Heresy', pp. 123-24) and Brinsmead (p. 123), who assume the identification of τὰ στοιχεῖα τοῦ κόσμου with the spiritual powers. Brinsmead (p. 123) writes, 'In 2.8 and 2.20 these ἀρχαί, ἐξουσίαι, and ἄγγελοι are summed up as στοιχεῖα τοῦ κόσμου'. Supporting argumentation for this identification is wholly lacking.

'principial' interpretation and the 'cosmological' interpretation, with the majority of occurrences of στοιχεῖα having a physical reference. The 'personalized-cosmological' interpretation lacks early lexical support. In fact, the earliest extant use of στοιχεῖα to refer to 'astral spirits' is *T. Sol.* 8.2, and this work is usually dated to the third century AD.[1] This evidence is not, in itself, decisive against the 'personalized-cosmological' interpretation, however, since (1) the amount of literature we possess from the NT period is relatively limited,[2] and (2) the association between the heavenly bodies and angelic figures antedates the NT.[3] Still, it is one factor that must be considered in determining the meaning of τὰ στοῖχεια τοῦ κόσμου.

The contextual evidence is more suggestive with regard to the meaning of the phrase, at least in Colossians. The clearest of the two στοιχεῖα passages in Colossians is 2.8, so it is appropriate that we begin with this verse. Here Paul first warns believers at Colossae against being 'taken captive' (συλαγωγῶν). He then specifies the means by which the errorists were attempting to lead them astray, spelling out those means by the use of two genitives governed by the preposition διά and two accusatives governed by the preposition κατά. It is, of course, difficult to tell whether the shift in prepositions is significant, though probably the first two governed by διά lay stress on the manner in which the errorists were attempting to 'take them captive'[4] while the latter two governed by κατά carry the idea of correspondence as well as source.[5]

1. For a survey of suggested dates for the Testament of Solomon and the evidence supporting them, see D.C. Duling, 'Testament of Solomon', *OTP*, I, pp. 940-43. The question is complicated by theories suggesting that the work has undergone a lengthy process of redaction.

2. G.B. Caird (*The Language and Imagery of the Bible* [Philadelphia: Westminster Press, 1980], p. 239) argues that the lack of early lexical evidence is not a strong argument against this position, since 'the volume of literature surviving from antiquity is not so large as to preclude the possibility that the New Testament may preserve the earliest example of a well-established usage'.

3. See e.g. the Astronomical Book of *1 Enoch*.

4. On this use of διά with the genitive, see BAGD, p. 180. Cf. Lohse, p. 94, 'It is said clearly, however, by what means these people intend to carry through their plan to ensnare the community: "through philosophy"'. See also O'Brien, p. 109.

5. The notion of conformity or correspondence is widely attested for κατά (see BAGD, p. 407), while the idea of source is derived from the obvious meaning of the phrase κατὰ τὴν παράδοσιν τῶν ἀνθρώπων; cf. O'Brien, p. 110.

The parallelism of the phrases in 2.8 is often seen as being suggestive for the interpretation of τὰ στοιχεῖα τοῦ κόσμου. Several proponents of the 'personalized-cosmological' interpretation point out that κατὰ τὰ στοιχεῖα τοῦ κόσμου stands in direct contrast to οὐ κατὰ Χριστόν, and so requires—or, at least, suggests—a personal interpretation for στοιχεῖα. Furthermore, it is maintained that this antithesis points to the primary nature of the phrase, reflecting the terminology of the errorists rather than simply Paul's words in characterizing the Colossian 'philosophy'.[1]

The argument from the antithesis between κατὰ τὰ στοιχεῖα τοῦ κόσμου and οὐ κατὰ Χριστόν may be valid if we take these phrases in isolation from the rest of v. 8. Yet it is clear that οὐ κατὰ Χριστόν is antithetical not only to κατὰ τὰ στοιχεῖα τοῦ κόσμου, but also to κατὰ τὴν παράδοσιν τῶν ἀνθρώπων—possibly, as well, to the whole of the verse following συλαγωγῶν.[2] So this antithetical relationship, far from suggesting a personalized interpretation of τὰ στοιχεῖα τοῦ κόσμου, may actually tell against such a view, for the previous items in the sequence are by no means personal in their meaning.[3]

Furthermore, the first three descriptions of 2.8 are clearly indirect references rather than direct descriptions, for in each case 'St. Paul is placing the boasted wisdom of his opponents in a contemptuous light'.[4] For all its persuasive polish, he argues, the 'philosophy' that they propose is really 'empty deceit'; in spite of its claims to superior, heavenly revelation, it actually reflects 'the traditions of men'. That leaves us, then, with only the disputed wording κατὰ τὰ στοιχεῖα τοῦ κόσμου καὶ οὐ κατὰ Χριστόν.

Several points can be made regarding the interpretation of the στοιχεῖα phrase itself. First, it would be confusing to introduce in so abrupt a fashion the terminology of the errorists into a sequence

---

1. E.g. Lohse, p. 99: 'This meaning of the term "elements of the universe" which is determined by syncretistic concepts is doubtless present in the sharply formulated antithesis: "according to the elements of the universe and not according to Christ". Consequently, "elements of the universe" cannot be taken as an expression that the author of Col has chosen to discredit that philosophy as a man-made tradition. . . Rather "elements of the universe" must have played a special role in the teaching of the "philosophers".' Cf. Brinsmead, p. 291.
2. So Lightfoot, p. 181.
3. See Carr, p. 75.
4. C.F.D. Moule, p. 90.

loaded with Paul's contemptuous and depreciatory references to the error. This seems obvious.[1] Therefore, the interpretation of τὰ στοιχεῖα τοῦ κόσμου as a Pauline characterization of the error is to be preferred. Second, the parallelism between κατὰ τὴν παράδοσιν τῶν ἀνθρώπων and κατὰ τὰ στοιχεῖα τοῦ κόσμου is important— the two phrases being grammatically parallel: both consist of κατά + definite article (accusative) + noun (accusative) + definite article (genitive) + noun (genitive). The only difference, grammatically speaking, is that τὴν παράδοσιν is singular, whereas τὰ στοιχεῖα is plural.

Of the proposed interpretations of τὰ στοιχεῖα τοῦ κόσμου in 2.8, only the 'principial' interpretation allows this parallelism to extend to the meaning and argumentative function of the two phrases as well. Both phrases would then attack the claims of the error in parallel fashion: in spite of its claims to superior, heavenly revelation, it actually reflects 'the traditions of men'; in spite of its claims to lift the 'worshipers of angels' to a higher level of spirituality and blessing, the 'philosophy' of the errorists is really nothing more than 'the elementary principles of the world'—in other words, the religious ABCs of this world. The Colossian error, therefore, rather than leading believers toward maturity, was actually a step backward toward spiritual infancy.

So I conclude that the 'principial' interpretation of τὰ στοιχεῖα τοῦ κόσμου in 2.8 is to be preferred over other interpretations on both lexical and contextual grounds. Of these two lines of evidence, the contextual argument is the more significant, since only this interpretation allows τὰ στοιχεῖα τοῦ κόσμου its proper function within the series of Paul's contemptuous references to the error—references that stand together in antithesis to οὐ κατὰ Χριστόν.

A similar conclusion is in order regarding the meaning of τὰ στοιχεῖα τοῦ κόσμου in 2.20. For in context, death σὺν Χριστῷ ἀπὸ τῶν στοιχείων τοῦ κόσμου is clearly linked to the Christian's freedom from various ascetic practices (τί . . . δογματίζεσθε; μὴ ἅψῃ μηδὲ γεύσῃ μηδὲ θίγῃς). On its own, this linkage neither establishes nor refutes a particular interpretation of τὰ στοιχεῖα τοῦ

---

1. *Contra* Brinsmead (p. 291) who seems to miss this point entirely. In fact, he writes, 'After adapting so many terms of the opposition to his own purposes. . . , the author of Colossians would not be likely to crown his rebuttal with a phrase that had been suddenly introduced into the debate out of the blue'.

κόσμου. It merely suggests a close relationship between τὰ στοιχεῖα and the regulations of the Colossian errorists. Still, I conclude that the data pertinent to 2.20 are most easily interpreted in light of the exegesis of 2.8 above, which passage contains the more suggestive reference to τὰ στοιχεῖα τοῦ κόσμου.

Therefore the two occurrences of the phrase τὰ στοιχεῖα τοῦ κόσμου should not be used as primary evidence in the reconstruction of the Colossian error. Both lexical and contextual data point to them as 'indirect' or secondary references to the error rather than primary descriptions. They reveal, I believe, more about Paul's perception of the error than they tell us about the Colossian error itself.

Conclusion

Using the methodological controls set out in Chapter 5, my preliminary analysis indicates that the Colossian error is strikingly similar to the ascetic-mystical piety of Jewish Apocalypticism. The errorists sought out heavenly ascents by means of various ascetic practices involving abstinence from eating and drinking, as well as careful observance of the Jewish festivals. These experiences of heavenly ascent climaxed in a vision of the throne and in worship offered by the angelic hosts surrounding it. It seems that these visions also pointed to the importance of observing the Jewish festivals, probably as evidence of submission to the law of God. These visionary experiences provided the basis for the errorists' judgments, by which they attempted to move the Colossian Christians to obedience and true Christian piety, as they understood it.

I have arrived at a preliminary reconstruction of the Colossian error based on the direct descriptions of 2.16-23, then argued my interpretation of two important indirect references to the error (τὰ στοιχεῖα τοῦ κόσμου in 2.8, 20). Now we are ready to turn our attention to the supporting expositional passages in Chapters 7 and 8.

Chapter 7

REVELATION IN CHRIST

Paul's response to the Colossian error focuses on the theme of revelation in Christ. Two passages in this regard are critical, 1.15-20 and 2.1-5. Other texts are related and will be considered after dealing with these two primary passages in the letter.

1. The Hymn of 1.15-20

That 1.15-20 is hymnic in form is a given in NT scholarship. The major question regarding this passage has to do with authorship: was this material written prior to and independently of the letter to the Colossians by someone other than Paul, and simply taken over by him? Or was it written by Paul himself, either before writing Colossians and then included in the letter or as part of the composition of Colossians? A majority of scholars today believe that 1.15-20 was written both independently of the Colossian letter and by someone other than Paul—though there are also some who hold that the hymn is indeed Pauline.[1] Precise determination of the history of this hymnic

---

1. For the majority position, see, for example, Lohse, p. 42; also Schweizer (*Colossians*, p. 55) who writes, 'It is no longer a matter for dispute that we have in these verses a hymn which has been taken over by the author'. For the minority viewpoint, see, for example, W.G. Kümmel (*Introduction to the New Testament* [trans. H.C. Kee, rev. edn; Nashville, Abingdon Press, 1975], p. 343), who claims that 'the author of Col himself has formed the hymn, utilizing traditional material', and L.R. Helyer, 'Colossians 1.15-20: Pre-Pauline or Pauline?', *JETS* 26 (1983), pp. 167-79. Several mediating positions have also been offered: A. Feuillet (*Le Christ sagesse de Dieu d'après les épitres pauliniennes* [Paris: Gabalda, 1966], pp. 246-73) suggests that Paul wrote the hymn at an earlier time and then utilized it in the composition of Colossians, while P. Benoit ('L'hymne christologique de Col 1,15-20', in *Christianity, Judaism and Other Greco-Roman Cults* [ed. J. Neusner; Leiden: Brill, 1975], pp. 254-60) argues that Paul received the first strophe from another, but adapted and completed it by composing a second strophe.

material, however, impacts this study very little, since presumably it has Paul's imprimatur, whether taken over (in whole or in part) from another or written (in whole or in part) directly by him. The fact that this material comes to us with Paul's imprimatur, however it originated, is rendered all the more probable when it is observed that these verses lay the foundation for several points in the argument of ch. 2 (cf., e.g., 1.16 and 2.10; 1.18 and 2.19; 1.19 and 2.9).[1] Consequently, we are justified in viewing the teaching of 1.15-20 as part of Paul's response to the situation at Colossae.[2]

Of particular significance, especially in view of the 'wisdom Christology' of 2.2-3, are those features of the hymn that appear to be derived from hellenistic-Jewish Wisdom speculation.[3] The opening

---

1. On the hymnic piece as being integral to the argument of Colossians, with serious dislocation occurring if it is removed, see O.A. Piper, 'The Saviour's Eternal Work', *Int* 3 (1949), p. 290; J.G. Gibbs, *Creation and Redemption* (Leiden: Brill, 1971), p. 101; P.T. O'Brien, 'Col. 1.20 and the Reconciliation of All Things', *RTR* 33 (1974), p. 50.

2. Of course, there may be features in 1.15-20 not directly relevant to Paul's response, particularly if the material was simply taken over as a unit from another source. On the other hand, any Pauline additions or 'corrections' to the original hymn, if such could be identified with any degree of confidence, would be highly relevant. There is, however, little agreement with regard to the form of the original hymn or the extent of Paul's additions. For a summary of opinions on the location and extent of the additions, see Benoit, 'L'hymne christologique', p. 238. It is also possible that terms or phrases have been omitted from the text of the hymn, though this is by nature impossible to prove; cf. T.E. Pollard, 'Colossians 1.12-20: A Reconsideration', *NTS* 27 (1981), pp. 572-73. In addition to the speculative nature of such work, J.C. O'Neill ('The Source of the Christology in Colossians', *NTS* 26 [1979], pp. 88-89) calls into question the legitimacy of all attempts to reconstruct 'a settled piece of liturgy'. For these reasons, I shall focus here on the present form of the hymn in the context of Col. 1; so W. McCown, 'The Hymnic Structure of Colossians 1.15-20', *EQ* 51 (1979), pp. 156-62.

3. R.P. Martin (p. 65) speaks of the 'emerging consensus' with respect to the background of 1.15-20—that it is best understood against the background of hellenistic Judaism. The view of E. Käsemann ('A Primitive Christian Baptismal Liturgy', in *Essays on New Testament Themes* [trans. W.J. Montague; Naperville, IL: Allenson, 1964], pp. 149-68), that the hymn is best understood in light of the gnostic myth of the *Urmensch*, has been ably critiqued by numerous writers and commentators; see N. Kehl, *Der Christushymnus im Kolosserbrief* (Stuttgart: Katholisches Bibelwerk, 1967), pp. 78-81, 87, 104; Lohse, p. 45; R.P. Martin, p. 65, and O'Brien, *Colossians*, pp. 37-38; cf., however, Wilckens, pp. 200-202. Also, the interpretation suggested by C.F. Burney ('Christ as the ΑΡΧΗ of Creation', *JTS* 27 [1926], pp. 160-77), that 1.15 is a Rabbinic meditative exposition on Gen. 1.1 in light of Prov. 8.22, which properly directs attention to the wisdom tradi-

statement, ὅς ἐστιν εἰκὼν τοῦ θεοῦ τοῦ ἀοράτου, πρωτότοκος πάσης κτίσεως (1.15a), closely parallels the teaching of several 'wisdom' passages. In Wis. 7.26 the description of wisdom is significant: ἀπαύγασμα γάρ ἐστιν φωτὸς ἀιδίου καὶ ἔσοπτρον ἀκηλίωτον τῆς τοῦ θεοῦ ἐνεργείας καὶ εἰκὼν τῆς ἀγαθότητος αὐτοῦ (cf. Philo, *Leg. All.* 1.43). It is clear that we have here a conceptual as well as a verbal parallel, since the emphasis in both Wisdom and the Colossian hymn is on wisdom's revelatory character.[1] Several conceptual parallels to the description of Christ as πρωτότοκος πάσης κτίσεως (1.15b; cf. also v. 17) are extant as well, for the antiquity of wisdom vis-à-vis the creation of the world is clearly affirmed in such writings as Prov. 8.22; Sir. 1.4; 24.9; and Wis. 9.9[2]—though in context it is probable that 'Christ's pre-existence is primarily a symbol of his pre-eminence'.[3]

With regard to Christ as Creator in 1.16, wisdom is closely associated with the events of creation in Prov. 8.22; Sir. 1.4; 24.9; and Wis. 9.9 (the passages cited above). Yet the parallel is even closer when we observe that wisdom plays a role in creation itself.[4] The Book of

tion, is inadequate as an explanation of the whole of vv. 15-17; see the criticisms in J. Jervell, *Imago Dei* (Göttingen: Vandenhoeck & Ruprecht, 1960), pp. 200-201, and H.J. Gabathuler, *Jesus Christus. Haupt der Kirche–Haupt der Welt* (Zurich: Zwingli, 1965), pp. 26-29. Cf., however, W.D. Davies, *Paul and Rabbinic Judaism* (Philadelphia: Fortress Press, 1980), pp. 150-52, E. Larsson, *Christus als Vorbild* (trans. B. Steiner; Lund: Gleerup, 1962), pp. 190-96; F. Manns, 'Col. 1,15-20: midrash chrétien de Gen. 1,1', *RSR* 53 (1979), pp. 100-10; and Pollard, pp. 572-75. On hellenistic Judaism as the conceptual background for the hymn, see, in addition to the commentators listed above, Feuillet, pp. 189-91. By adopting this terminology, however, I do not mean to drive a wedge sharply between 'Palestinian' and 'hellenistic' Judaism. Such a position is no longer tenable; see I.H. Marshall, 'Palestinian and Hellenistic Christianity: Some Critical Comments', *NTS* 19 (1973), pp. 271-87, and Hengel.

1. C.K. Barrett, *From First Adam to Last* (London: Black, 1962), p. 86; cf. Feuillet, pp. 173-74, and Gibbs, p. 102. Yet there may be an implied reference to Gen. 1.26-27 as well, in which case the 'dominion' of the 'image' could be in view. This meaning would be consistent with the context, where the supremacy of Christ is in view; see P. Beasley-Murray, 'Colossians 1.15-20: An Early Christian Hymn Celebrating the Lordship of Christ', in *Pauline Studies* (ed. D.A. Hagner and M.J. Harris; Exeter: Paternoster, 1980), pp. 170-71.

2. For a thorough discussion of parallels, see Feuillet, pp. 175-91.

3. P. Beasley-Murray, p. 171. On the use of πρωτότοκος to indicate sovereignty of rank in the LXX, see Gibbs, p. 103.

4. See A. Feuillet, 'La création de l'univers "dans le Christ" d'après l'Epître aux Colossiens', *NTS* 12 (1965), pp. 1-9.

Wisdom is most explicit in this regard, for not only is wisdom called τεχνῖτις ('craftswoman') but she is also spoken of as τὰ πάντα ἐργαζομένης (8.5-6). Proverbs gives a similar role to wisdom in 3.19 (Yahweh founded the earth 'in wisdom' (בחכמה); LXX: ὁ θεὸς τῇ σοφίᾳ ἐθεμελίωσεν τὴν γῆν), and possibly in 8.30 depending on the translation of אמון.[1] Such a view of wisdom accounts for Paul's statement in 1.16 that 'all things were created ἐν αὐτῷ and δι' αὐτοῦ'. The claim that 'all things were created εἰς αὐτόν', however, goes beyond anything found in the Wisdom writings.[2] And no direct parallels have been found between τὰ πάντα ἐν αὐτῷ συνέστηκεν of 1.17b and Wisdom. Many writers have proposed that Paul borrowed from popular Stoic philosophy at this point. Yet in Wis. 1.7 the πνεῦμα κυρίου is referred to as τὸ συνέχον τὰ πάντα, and in this writing the concepts of 'wisdom' and 'spirit' are closely related, if not identified (see 9.17).

The ascription to Christ of characteristics attributable to Wisdom in the 'cosmological' section of the hymn (vv. 15-17) seems obvious enough. It is not easy, however, to determine what purpose Paul had for including this material—or, for that matter, for including the hymn as a whole. Many assume that Paul was confronting a system of thought that explicitly undermined Christ's supreme role in creation or redemption. This is a possible conclusion. But is it consistent with the evidence?

It is helpful at this point to observe the manner and extent to which Paul picks up the terms and concepts from 1.15-20 in the polemical sections that follow. As mentioned earlier, several references to terms and concepts contained in the hymn are present in subsequent verses.[3]

---

1. For a survey of interpretations of this term, see H.P. Ruger, ' "Amôn—Pflegekind." Zur Auslegungsgeschichte von Prov 8.30a', in *Übersetzung und Deutung* (Nijkerk: Callenbach, 1977), pp. 154-63.

2. Eltester (*Εἰκών in the New Testament* [Berlin: de Gruyter, 1958], pp. 142-43) finds no parallels to the λόγος in Philo, to the αἰών in *Corp. Herm.* 11, or to the κόσμος in *Corp. Herm.* 12; cf. Lohse, p. 52, and R.P. Martin, p. 58. In spite of the importance of hellenistic Jewish Wisdom speculation as a background to several important terms and phrases, Helyer (p. 175) is correct when he writes, 'As a comprehensive explanation for the background of the hymn, the Wisdom speculation hypothesis is inadequate'.

3. See H. Löwe, 'Bekenntnis, Apostelamt und Kirche im Kolosserbrief', in *Kirche: Festschrift für Günther Bornkamm* (ed. D. Lührmann and G. Strecker; Tübingen: Mohr, 1980), pp. 308-309, for a helpful analysis of these references. Cf. H. Merklein, 'Paulinische Theologie in der Rezeption des Kolosser- und Epheser-

A case in point is the theme of reconciliation (1.20) that is continued and developed in 1.21-23, albeit with an emphasis on personal soteriology. Since reconciliation in 1.20 encompasses τὰ πάντα, the defeat of the powers in 2.13-15 is probably not to be seen as a willing reconciliation accepted by the powers but a peace imposed on them by a superior force.[1] Another clear reference back to the hymn is found in 2.19 where Paul uses κεφαλή in an ecclesiological sense (cf. 1.18), arguing that the errorists' preoccupation with ascetic-mystical practices and the observance of legal requirements hinders their relationship to the church's head, Jesus Christ. And it is only through its connection with the head that the body truly grows and prospers.

The primary text in which terms and concepts of the hymn are picked up and developed is 2.9-10. This text introduces a major expositional section (2.9-15) that supports the polemical admonitions of 2.8 and 2.16-23.[2] Lohse calls 2.9 'an explanatory repetition of 1.19',[3] and rightly so. For in both verses it is said that 'the πλήρωμα dwells (κατοικέω) in Christ', though τῆς θεότητος is added in 2.9 to clarify the nature of this πλήρωμα. In 2.10 the relative clause ὅς ἐστιν ἡ κεφαλὴ πάσης ἀρχῆς καὶ ἐξουσίας is loosely connected to the preceding clause and seems to sum up the message of the hymn, especially vv. 15-17. Since Christ is now revealed as 'head' of the spiritual powers, they are no longer able to call into question the redemption that he has obtained for those who are 'in Christ'.

The paucity of references to the hymn in the polemical and expositional sections of ch. 2, however, is somewhat surprising, especially in light of the attention 1.15-20 has received in traditional analyses of the situation at Colossae. Our survey of these polemical and expositional texts uncovered nothing to suggest that the errorists denied Christ's supreme role in creation, for statements as to his role in creation occur at no point subsequent to the hymn of 1.15-20. Also, when Christ's position as head over the spiritual forces is mentioned (2.9), the context has to do with the greatness of his redemption for those who are 'in Christ'. So it seems that teaching as to Christ's headship functions to undergird Paul's soteriological argument, without

---

briefes', in *Paulus in den neutestamentlichen Spätschriften* (ed. K. Kertelge; Freiburg: Herder, 1981), pp. 52-53.

1. Cf. O'Brien, 'Col 1.20', pp. 45-53. *Contra* W. Michaelis, *Versöhnung des Alls* (Bern: Siloah, 1950).
2. See Chapter 5. § 4..
3. Lohse, p. 99.

necessarily implying that the errorists explicitly denigrated the position of Christ by viewing him as simply one of many spiritual powers.

The bottom line in Paul's argument appears to be this: that Christ is ἡ κεφαλὴ πάσης ἀρχῆς καὶ ἐξουσίας—that is, that he existed before them; that they were created 'in him', 'through him' and 'for him'; that he now sustains and upholds their existence, and so, that they must submit to his redemptive purpose for believers. Spiritual forces can never denigrate by any pronouncements of judgment on believers the redemption that has been accomplished through the death of Christ. Christ's death is sufficient to ensure the full salvation of all believers, apart from any ascetic-mystical experiences or the observance of legal requirements.

Many of the specific points made in the hymn are passed over in the polemical and expositional sections of Colossians 2. It is possible, therefore, that Paul's purpose in citing the hymn was more general than is usually assumed. As we have observed, much that is said in the 'cosmological' section supports the simple contention that Christ is the 'head' of the spiritual forces. Also, the fact that the πλήρωμα dwells in Christ undergirds Paul's soteriological claims in 2.10-15, as will be explained further in what follows.

2. The Development and Application of the Hymn's Teaching in 2.1-5

The hymn of 1.15-20, indeed, supports the statements of 2.9-10. Yet it is also possible that the hymn was cited in order to lay the foundation for the exposition of 2.2-3, since at least some of Paul's readers would have recognized the portrait of Christ in 1.15-20 as being akin to that of personified Wisdom in hellenistic Judaism. This function for the incorporated hymn is difficult to establish with certainty. Yet it seems probable that the portrait of Christ in terms of Wisdom categories (1.15-20) and the explicit identification of Christ with Wisdom (2.2-3) reinforce each other, so providing a more effective opposition to the error than either could have provided alone.

a. The Referent of τοῦτο λέγω in v. 4

To treat 2.1-5, it is best to begin by a determination of the force of τοῦτο λέγω, ἵνα μηδεὶς ὑμᾶς παραλογίζηται ἐν πιθανολογίᾳ in v. 4. More specifically, we must determine whether the words τοῦτο λέγω, ἵνα are to be understood prospectively (i.e. ἵνα used in an imperatival sense) or retrospectively (i.e. a telic ἵνα).

There are substantial reasons for adopting the latter view. These were set forth by Bandstra and have been echoed by others.[1] The alleged parallels for a prospective use in Gal. 3.17 and 1 Cor. 1.12 do not have ἵνα following τοῦτο λέγω, and so are not true parallels. Much better is Jn 5.34, where ταῦτα λέγω ἵνα is clearly retrospective. There is, in fact, no example of an imperatival ἵνα following τοῦτο λέγω in the NT. Furthermore, the γάρ of v. 5 is more difficult to explain when the ἵνα is taken imperatively, since v. 5 picks up the thought of v. 1 and so binds 2.1-5 together. Therefore, ἵνα should be understood here in a telic sense, even though some continue to interpret this clause prospectively.[2]

If we take such a stance, 2.1-3 (esp. vv. 2-3), then, functions as the logical basis for the polemic of 2.4. This does not mean that the errorists necessarily denied what Paul says in vv. 2-3, though they may have. Rather, all that need be affirmed is that the exposition of vv. 2-3 in some way undermines the position of the errorists and so provides the logical basis for the warning of v. 4.

b. *The 'Wisdom-Christology' of vv. 2-3*
In 2.1 Paul indicates that he is deeply concerned for believers at Colossae, and then in 2.2-3 he states the content of his desire for them:

ἵνα παρακληθῶσιν αἱ καρδίαι αὐτῶν συμβιβασθέντες ἐν ἀγάπῃ καὶ εἰς πᾶν πλοῦτος τῆς πληροφορίας τῆς συνέσεως, εἰς ἐπίγνωσιν τοῦ

---

1. Bandstra, 'Colossian Errorists', pp. 339-40, followed by O'Brien, *Colossians*, p. 97; cf. Abbott, p. 242; Dibelius–Greeven, p. 26; Lohse, p. 83, and Gnilka, p. 113. Cannon (pp. 152-55) argues on the basis of epistolary analysis that 1.24–2.5 is the 'body opening' of Colossians, and that these verses are bound together by the 'apostolic parousia'; *contra* P. Lamarche ('Structure de l'épître aux Colossiens', *Bib* 56 [1975], p. 458), who introduces a break between 2.3 and 2.4 on the basis of thematic and logical analysis—though he recognizes the transitional character of vv. 4-5 and notes, 'Les versets 4 et 5 sont influencés par ce qui précède'.

2. E.g. C.J. Bjerkelund, *Parakalô: Form, Funktion und Sinn der parakalô-Sätze in den paulinischen Briefen* (Oslo: Universitetsforlaget, 1967), p. 182; Bruce, *Colossians* (1984), p. 92. Bjerkelund (p. 182), however, notes correctly, 'Nicht die Danksagung als solche legt den Grund für die nachfolgende Aufforderung, sondern ihr christologischer Inhalt'. Thus, even on his view, the exhortation of 2.4 is based on the christological teaching of the preceding section.

μυστηρίου τοῦ θεοῦ, Χριστοῦ, ἐν ᾧ εἰσιν πάντες οἱ θησαυροὶ τῆς σοφίας καὶ γνώσεως ἀπόκρυφοι.

Two points are suggestive as we examine this statement. First, it is clear that in Christ are hidden 'all the treasures of wisdom and knowledge';[1] second, that the repetition of clauses beginning with εἰς indicates that Paul is identifying the attainment of 'the full riches of complete understanding' with 'the knowledge of the mystery of God, namely, Christ'.[2] It is helpful to consider these items individually.

In his 1974 article, Andrew Bandstra referred to a number of parallels in *2 Baruch* to the words οἱ θησαυροὶ τῆς σοφίας καὶ γνώσεως of Col. 2.3. Especially important for my purposes is *2 Bar.* 54.13, 'And the treasures of wisdom beneath Thy throne hast Thou prepared', as well as 44.14, which says that those who shall receive the inheritance have 'acquired for themselves treasures of wisdom'. The verbal similarity of these texts to Col. 2.3 is striking, especially in view of the fact that such a phrase is rare in Greek, hellenistic-Jewish and early Christian sources.[3] Yet concepts which would give rise to such a phrase pervade the thought-world of Jewish apocalypticism. For as we observed earlier, the notion that wisdom is hidden for this age in the heavenly sphere recurs constantly in Jewish apocalyptic literature, and in a number of these texts the Throne is the center of such heavenly wisdom.[4] Furthermore, the importance of obtaining this wisdom through heavenly ascent or the teaching of one who has

---

1. The relative proximity of Χριστοῦ to ἐν ᾧ makes this a more logical referent than τοῦ μυστηρίου τοῦ θεοῦ; so Lightfoot, p. 173; E.F. Scott, p. 37; C.F.D. Moule, p. 86; Lohse, p. 82; R.P. Martin, pp. 85-86; Gnilka, p. 111; Schweizer, *Colossians*, pp. 117-18; O'Brien, *Colossians*, p. 95, and Bruce, *Colossians* (1984), p. 91; *contra* Abbott, p. 241, and Hugedé, p. 103.

2. The variants in this text are numerous. I follow here the reading that has the best external support and that best explains the development of the other readings. For a thorough review and evaluation of the evidence, see P. Benoit, 'Colossiens 2.2-3', in *The New Testament Age: Essays in Honor of Bo Reicke* (ed. W.C. Weinrich; Macon, GA: Mercer University Press, 1984), I, pp. 41-51; cf. Lohse, pp. 81-82, and B.M. Metzger, *A Textual Commentary on the Greek New Testament* (London: United Bible Societies, 1975), p. 622.

3. Cf. Bandstra, 'Colossian Errorists', p. 341.

4. See above, Chapter 2, § 1.c. More specific in this regard is the Similitudes of Enoch, where the 'fountain of righteousness' (closely associated with the divine Throne and the Elect One) stands as the locus and source of wisdom (48.1; 49.1; 51.3). Cf. Wis. 9.4. With regard to the Qumran materials, see D. Flusser and S. Safrai, 'The Essene Doctrine of Hypostasis and Rabbi Meir', *Immanuel* 14 (1982), pp. 47-57.

experienced such revelation is commonplace in these writings. Only those who give their attention to such wisdom will incline themselves to a proper obedience and enjoy participation in the eschatological salvation.

Paul's second point closely complements his first. For in identifying the attainment of 'the full riches of complete understanding' with 'the knowledge of the mystery of God, namely, Christ', Paul not only identifies 'the mystery of God' with Christ, but also suggests that those who know Christ have no need of further revelation in this present age. They have already attained 'the full riches of complete understanding' simply on the basis of their faith in Christ. The revelatory practices of the errorists, therefore, are pointless because of the fullness of revelation given to all those who are 'in Christ'. Thus it is imperative that Christians focus their attention on Christ himself instead of on mystical practices, since in Christ 'are hidden all the treasures of wisdom and knowledge'.[1]

The christological statement of 2.2-3 clearly provides the basis for the polemic that follows. This is not to say that the errorists explicitly denied Paul's teaching in these verses. Rather, Paul's point is that the fullness of God's revelation 'in Christ' as telegraphed in 1.15-20 and described in 2.2-3 leaves little room for ascetic-mystical practices. Still, these passage by no means exhaust the theme of revelation in Colossians. Other passages are significant as well and so merit our attention.

3. *'Knowledge' and Growth in Christ in 1.9-14*

In light of our reconstruction of the Colossian error and our analysis of the 'wisdom christology' of 2.2-3, it is helpful to examine 1.9-14 with regard to its teaching on the relationship between 'knowledge'

---

1. F.W. Beare ('The Epistle to the Colossians', in *The Interpreter's Bible* [ed. G.A. Buttrick; New York and Nashville: Abingdon Press, 1955], IX, p. 186) writes, 'We are bound to ask why this emphasis is laid on the "hidden" nature of these stores of truth, when we should expect rather the affirmation that in Christ these things are revealed'. Yet the point is that it is only to those who are 'in Christ' that such things are revealed—and even these must 'seek the things above, where Christ is seated at the right hand of God'. So there is clearly room for Christians to increase or grow in their knowledge of Christ. The point, however, is that they must seek him directly and apart from mystical practices. Conversely, see Davies, *Paul*, p. 173, and F. Hauck, 'θησαυρός, θησαυρίζω', *TDNT*, III, p. 138.

and growth 'in Christ'. The sequence of thought in these verses is clear. Paul prays for Christians at Colossae, referring to their progress in matters of faith, hope and love.[1] The content of his prayer is stated in the ἵνα clause of v. 9b: ἵνα πληρωθῆτε τὴν ἐπίγνωσιν τοῦ θελήματος αὐτοῦ ἐν πάσῃ σοφίᾳ καὶ συνέσει πνευματικῇ. Paul thus directs his prayer toward the goal of revelation. It is not, however, some esoteric body of information that he desires for the Colossians, but a knowledge of God's will that comes from the Spirit.[2]

Paul's prayer does not end with this request of v. 9, for he moves in v. 10 to explain the goal of this knowledge: περιπατῆσαι ἀξίως τοῦ κυρίου εἰς πᾶσαν ἀρεσκείαν. It is not enough simply to know the will of God. One must also be willing to obey it. Only in this way can a person live a life that is worthy of and pleasing to the Lord. In the Jewish apocalypses, of course, revelation is not an end in itself, but is, rather, a means to a higher end, namely obedience to the will of God.[3] And such is Paul's desire for believers at Colossae.

Up through 1.10a there is no indication of the specific content of the obedience that is the goal of Paul's prayer. All of this, however, changes in vv. 10b-12. For in these verses Paul indicates by means of four participial clauses what a life that is worthy of and pleasing to the Lord is all about. And here Paul's faith and practice differs in important respects from that of the Jewish apocalyptists. The first two

1. Hugedé (p. 38) notes that διὰ τοῦτο establishes a general connection to the preceding thanksgiving section; cf. Zeilinger, pp. 36-37. Gnilka (p. 40) specifies, correctly in my opinion, that the reference is primarily to v. 4.

2. Cf. Lohse, p. 27; Schweizer, *Colossians*, p. 41, and Gnilka, p. 40. The practical emphasis of ἐπίγνωσις in v. 9 is in accordance with the implications of the OT root ידע. Such a meaning is carried over into the Qumran writings, the LXX (translated γινώσκω or οἶδα), and a number of rabbinic texts; see B. Reicke, 'Da'at and Gnosis in Intertestamental Literature', in *Neotestamentica et Semitica* (ed. E.E. Ellis and M. Wilcox; Edinburgh: T. & T. Clark, 1969), pp. 245-55. We should not, however, stress here the intensive force of the compound ἐπίγνωσις. The compound form simply directs our attention to the object of one's knowledge, the will of God. See J.A. Robinson, *Commentary on Ephesians* (London: Macmillan, 1904; reprint edn, Grand Rapids: Kregel, 1979), pp. 248-54, and R.E. Picirelli, 'The Meaning of "Epignosis"', *EQ* 47 (1975), pp. 85-93; *contra* Lightfoot, pp. 137-38. The context is critical in defining the term here. It is a knowledge that comes ἐν πάσῃ σοφίᾳ καὶ συνέσει πνευματικῇ and is directed toward a life lived worthy of and pleasing to God.

3. On the Jewish flavor of these petitions, see E. Lohse, 'Christologie und Ethik im Kolosserbrief', in *Apophoreta: Festschrift für Ernst Haenchen* (ed. W. Eltester; Berlin: Töpelmann, 1964), p. 167.

clauses of vv. 10b-12 are reminiscent of Paul's statements with regard to the effects of the gospel in v. 6. Ἐν παντὶ ἔργῳ ἀγαθῷ καρπο-φοροῦντες is general in its thrust, while αὐξανόμενοι τῇ ἐπιγνώσει τοῦ θεοῦ emphasizes the blessing that comes to those whose lives are worthy of and pleasing to the Lord.[1] So Paul affirms an intimate connection between obedience to God's will and knowledge of God himself. In fact, Bruce is probably right to say that 'obedience to the knowledge of God which has already been received is a necessary and certain condition for the reception of further knowledge'.[2]

Paul continues his exposition on a 'worthy life' by focusing in v. 11 on the themes of 'power' and 'endurance'—ἐν πάσῃ δυνάμει δυνα-μούμενοι κατὰ τὸ κράτος τῆς δόξης αὐτοῦ εἰς πᾶσαν ὑπομονὴν καὶ μακροθυμίαν. His desire for the believers at Colossae is that they might experience God's power in all its fullness (notice the accumulation of words of similar value), though this empowering is for the specific goal characterized by 'patience' and 'endurance'.

Many commentators interpret 'patience' and 'endurance' in a general sense.[3] In view of the hortatory orientation of Paul's prayer, however, they are better understood against the background of the epistolary situation.[4] As Lohse correctly notes, ὑπομονή 'signifies the kind of 85
perseverance which is to be proven in battle by holding the position one has taken against all enemy attacks'.[5] So Paul's concern here is that the Colossians hold on to their faith in Christ, without

---

1. The first two clauses are thus chiastic in nature: complement + verb and verb + complement; so Hugedé, p. 42; O'Brien, *Colossians*, p. 23; and Bruce, *Colossians* (1984), p. 47. *Contra* Lightfoot, p. 139; Abbott, p. 203; Lohmeyer, *Kolosser*, p. 35; Lohse, p. 29; and Gnilka, p. 42. The latter group of commentators link καρποφοροῦντες and αὐξανόμενοι together so that the clause is rendered 'bearing fruit and increasing in every good work through the knowledge of God'.

2. Bruce, *Colossians* (1984), p. 47. Cf. K.G. Eckart, 'Exegetische Beobach-tungen zu Kol 1,9-20', *TV* 7 (1959), pp. 90-91, and K. Sullivan, 'Epignosis in the Epistles of St. Paul', in *Studiorum Paulinorum Congressus Internationalis Catholicus 1961* (Romae: Pontificio Istituto Biblico, 1963), II, p. 411. On this relationship between obedience to God's revealed will and the reception of further revelation in the Jewish apocalypses, see above, Chapter 2, § 2.a.

3. E.g. Lightfoot, p. 140; Abbott, pp. 204-205; E.F. Scott, p. 18; C.F.D. Moule, p. 54; Lohse, pp. 30-31.

4. So R.P. Martin, p. 53; O'Brien, *Colossians*, pp. 24-25.

5. Lohse, p. 30; cf. F. Hauck, 'μένω, κτλ.', *TDNT*, IV, pp. 581-83. Hauck also notes, however, that ὑπομένειν often takes on the meaning 'to wait on God' in the OT and certain other Jewish writings (*Hauck*, pp. 583-85).

compromising it through participation in the beliefs and practices of the errorists. The second term, μακροθυμίαν, is used in both the OT and NT in a general sense to refer to both the patience of God and that of his people.[1] Yet in this context a more specific meaning is probably in order—patience as one waits for the eschatological appearing of Christ with its attendant manifestation of the glory of those who are in Christ (3.3-4; cf. 1.5).[2]

The last participial clause of v. 12a introduces a theme that is developed in vv. 13-14. We will consider these verses at some length in Chapter 8. Suffice it here to note that thanksgiving assumes an important place in the Colossian letter (2.7; 3.15, 17; 4.2). Especially significant in this regard are the words περισσεύοντες ἐν εὐχαριστίᾳ in the exhortation of 2.6-7. The Colossians are to continue their Christian life in the same way they began when they received Christ Jesus: they are to 'walk in him'; to be rooted in him and built up in the faith καθὼς ἐδιδάχθητε; and they are to rejoice and be thankful for the blessings that are theirs through faith in Christ. Such is the position of believers that there is little need to seek salvation and maturity through either mystical experiences or legal obedience. Instead, one finds in 2.7, as in 1.12-14, that a major component of a worthy life—i.e. a life that is pleasing to God—is joy and thankfulness and appreciation for salvific blessings 'in Christ'.[3] The Colossian believers are already qualified to share in 'the inheritance of the saints in the kingdom of light' (1.12).[4]

In 1.9-14, therefore, Paul is concerned that believers at Colossae be filled with the knowledge of God's will, and this not for speculative purposes but in order that they might live properly. Yet Paul presents the issues in such a way as to motivate his readers to stand firm against

---

1. O'Brien, *Colossians*, pp. 24-25.
2. Schweizer, *Colossians*, pp. 44-45.
3. I take the words μετὰ χαρᾶς with the following clause rather than the former; so Abbott, p. 205; Lohse, p. 32, and O'Brien, *Colossians*, p. 25; *contra* Lightfoot, p. 140; C.F.D. Moule, p. 55, and Schweizer, *Colossians*, p. 44. This arrangement preserves the balance of the clauses in vv. 10-12; so Eckart, p. 93. Cf. Phil. 1.4.
4. Löwe (pp. 302-303) observes correctly, 'Vielleicht zeigt der Aufbau des Briefes schon in formaler Hinsicht, dass die Wortgruppe εὐχαριστεῖν, εὐχαριστία, εὐχάριστος in ihm durchweg einen präzisen Sinn hat, also nicht nur allgemein auf die Christen gebotene dankbare Haltung abhebt, sondern eine spezifische Äusserung des Glaubens bezeichnet: den in Worte gefassten Dank für das in der Taufe geschehene Werk der Erlösung und die Grösse des Erlösers, wie er in 1,12-20 formuliert worden ist'.

certain beliefs and practices of the errorists. First and foremost, knowledge of God's will in these verses is not assigned a saving function, as it is in Jewish apocalypticism. Rather, one is 'qualified' to receive the promised inheritance on the basis of faith in Christ (v. 12), with knowledge being simply a means of growth in experience (v. 10). Second, Paul suggests that knowledge comes not through ascents to heaven or visionary experiences; its true source is the Spirit (v. 9). Third, the motive for obedience is no longer the fear and expectation of judgment. Instead, one 'walks' in accordance with God's will in order to please him in every way (v. 10). Finally, a 'worthy walk' is one in which Christians rejoice and give thanks for the salvific blessings that are theirs in Christ (vv. 12-14), waiting patiently for the revelation of the fullness of their inheritance at Christ's appearing (v. 11). Such a pattern of thought leaves little room for Christians to participate in the mystical practices advocated by the Colossian errorists.

4. *The 'Mystery' and the Gospel in 1.24-29*

Another important passage that develops the theme of revelation in Christ is 1.24-29. Paul opens this text by making reference to his sufferings on behalf of Christians at Colossae (v. 24), and then proceeds to explain how these came about (vv. 25-29). A great deal of discussion has taken place as to the meaning of οἰκονομίαν in v. 25, which Paul uses as the major covering concept for all that he does. Some argue that it refers exclusively to Paul's apostolic office;[1] others, primarily on the basis of parallels in Ephesians (1.10; 3.9), that it refers to God's 'administration' or 'plan'.[2] The concepts are closely related, since an apostolic commission must be in accordance with God's plan and be concerned with proclaiming the content of that

---

1. So Dibelius–Greeven, p. 17; O. Michel, 'οἰκονομία', *TDNT*, V, pp. 151-53; Lohse, pp. 72-73; and Conzelmann, 'Kolosser', p. 188; cf. J. Reumann (' "Stewards of God"—Pre-Christian Religious Application of ΟΙΚΟΝΟΜΟΣ in Greek', *JBL* 77 [1958], pp. 339-49), who explains the term against the background of its use with already existing religious connotations in Greco-Roman life; and D. Lührmann, *Das Offenbarungsverständnis bei Paulus und in paulinischen Gemeinden* (Neukirchen-Vluyn: Neukirchener Verlag, 1965), p. 122.

2. So Lohmeyer, *Kolosser*, pp. 79-80; cf. O'Brien, *Colossians*, pp. 81-82, though he also acknowledges the former meaning in this context, albeit in a secondary sense.

administration (vv. 27c-29). Nevertheless, the words δοθεῖσάν μοι and the purpose of the οἰκονομίαν, viz. πληρῶσαι τὸν λόγον τοῦ θεοῦ, are far more appropriate if the term is understood to refer to Paul's apostolic commission and office.[1] Paul was called for the purpose of 'executing fully' his ministry of preaching the word of God.[2]

This apostolic 'word' is further described in v. 26: it is τὸ μυστήριον τὸ ἀποκεκρυμμένον ἀπὸ τῶν αἰώνων καὶ ἀπὸ τῶν γενεῶν—νῦν δὲ ἐφανερώθη τοῖς ἁγίοις αὐτοῦ. Probably, as Nils Dahl has argued, Paul utilizes here a pattern that belonged originally 'to discourses within the believing community unfolding the mystery and wisdom of God', which functioned to bring home to the hearers 'the eschatological newness and the heavenly riches of the revelation proclaimed in the gospel'.[3] The word of God is thus a 'mystery' in the sense that it was hidden until such a time as God was pleased to reveal it through the apostolic preaching.[4]

The Semitic flavor of μυστήριον is obvious in this context.[5] For the 'mystery' comes not only to initiates, as in the mystery religions

---

1. O'Brien (Colossians, p. 81) struggles to render the clause as follows: 'I am a minister according to the plan of God, the execution of which has been conferred upon me in that which concerns you'.

2. Cf. G. Delling, 'πλήρης, κτλ.', TDNT, VI, p. 297; see also Col. 4.17.

3. N.A. Dahl, 'Form-Critical Observations on Early Christian Preaching', in Jesus in the Memory of the Early Church (Minneapolis: Augsburg, 1976), p. 32; cf. R. Bultmann, Theology of the New Testament (trans. K. Grobel; New York: Scribner's, 1951), I, pp. 105-106, and G. Bornkamm, 'Die Hoffnung im Kolosserbrief', in Studien zum Neuen Testament und zur Patristik (Berlin: Akademie Verlag, 1961), p. 58. H. Conzelmann (1 Corinthians [trans. J.W. Leitch; Philadelphia: Fortress Press, 1975], p. 58) argues that this pattern resulted from school activity surrounding Paul, while Lührmann, Offenbarungsverständnis, pp. 113-40, maintains that Paul took over a model already in existence. In either case, there is no need to posit with E.P. Sanders ('Literary Dependence in Colossians', JBL 85 [1966], pp. 39-40) that this passage was formed through literary conflation from 1 Cor. 2.7, Rom. 16.25-26 and Rom. 9.23-24.

4. I interpret the phrase ἀπὸ τῶν αἰώνων καὶ ἀπὸ τῶν γενεῶν in a temporal sense; so Lohse, p. 74; Schweizer, Colossians, p. 108; and Gnilka, p. 101; contra Dibelius–Greeven (p. 17) and E.F. Scott (p. 33), who take it to refer to the principalities and powers who are denied access to the mystery (cf. 1 Cor. 2.8). Cf. Hugedé (p. 93), who sees in αἰώνων spiritual powers and in γενεῶν the generations of humans; also Bornkamm, 'Hoffnung', pp. 58-61.

5. Cf. R.E. Brown, The Semitic Background of the Term 'Mystery' in the New Testament (Philadelphia: Fortress Press, 1968), pp. 52-56. See also Benoit, 'Qumran and the New Testament', pp. 23-24, and J. Coppens, '"Mystery" in the

where the uninitiated 'are denied both access to the sacred actions and knowledge of them'.[1] Rather, it comes first to the apostle and then to those who hear and respond to his message. As O'Brien comments, the ἅγιοι

> are not some select group of initiates, but are those who have heard and received the word of God, for it is in the effective preaching and teaching of the gospel that the revelation of the mystery takes place (cf. 1 Cor. 2.1, 7; 4.1; Eph. 3.8, 9; 6.19).[2]

It is not until v. 27 that the content of the 'mystery' is stated explicitly. The first part of the verse repeats much of what Paul has already said in v. 26. In the latter part, however, Paul makes two additional points. First, he emphasizes the glorious nature of the 'mystery' (τί τὸ πλοῦτος τῆς δόξης τοῦ μυστηρίου); then he defines the primary recipients of the 'mystery' (ἐν τοῖς ἔθνεσιν).[3] This latter reference is significant in view of the fact that the definition of the 'mystery' follows immediately: ὅ ἐστιν Χριστὸς ἐν ὑμῖν [i.e. 'in you Gentiles'], ἡ ἐλπὶς τῆς δόξης.[4]

Theology of Saint Paul and its Parallels at Qumran', in *Paul and Qumran*, pp. 132-58.

1. G. Bornkamm, 'μυστήριον', *TDNT*, IV, p. 804. On p. 816, Bornkamm discusses the differences between the apocalyptic concept of 'mystery' and its use in the mystery cults and Gnosticism.

2. O'Brien, *Colossians*, p. 85. The context indicates that, contrary to Lührmann (p. 122), Paul is the apostolic *Offenbarungsmittler* in this text as well as in the undisputed letters; so S. Kim, *The Origin of Paul's Gospel* (2nd edn; Tübingen: Mohr, 1984), p. 82; cf. L. Cerfaux, *The Spiritual Journey of Saint Paul* (trans. J.C. Guinness; New York: Sheed & Ward, 1968), pp. 194-95. 'The mystery' is thus broader than 'the gospel' in the terminology of Colossians, and is best defined as the worldwide preaching of Christ by the apostle; see Merklein, pp. 28-29. Nevertheless, Col. 1.5, 23 suggest that the gospel does not have 'eine untergeordnete Funktion' in Colossians; *contra* Merklein, pp. 28-29.

3. For a different view of the syntax of this verse, see W.P. Bowers, 'A Note on Colossians 1.27a', in *Current Issues in Biblical and Patristic Interpretation* (ed. G.F. Hawthorne; Grand Rapids: Eerdmans, 1975), pp. 110-14.

4. Commentators are divided over the translation of the preposition ἐν in this clause. Some interpret it in line with ἐν τοῖς ἔθνεσιν, and so translate 'among you [Gentiles]'; so Abbott, p. 235; C.F.D. Moule, p. 285; Lohse, pp. 75-76; and Gnilka, p. 102. Others render it as 'in you', often stressing the mystical union between Christ and his followers; so Dibelius–Greeven, p. 17; Bornkamm, 'μυστήριον', p. 820; Conzelmann, 'Kolosser', p. 188; and O'Brien, *Colossians*, p. 87. We must question, however, whether Paul here introduces a distinction between Christ living among his people (who are, after all, his 'body'; cf. 2.19) and Christ indwelling his people, individually and collectively. Hugedé (p. 95) is prob-

This definition of the mystery is significant from a polemical perspective. For through it Paul affirms that it is not on the basis of ascetic observances or mystical experiences or legal obediences that individuals participate in the glorious hope of the revelation of Christ from the heavenly realm. Rather, it is simply by means of a present union with Christ through faith that men and women come to anticipate their future union with Christ at his coming in glory.[1]

Paul closes this section of the letter in vv. 28-29 by describing his ministry, as well as that of Timothy, Epaphras and his other fellow-workers (note the plural ἡμεῖς). Four points are made with respect to this work. First, it is primarily a ministry of proclamation. The use of the verb καταγγέλλω is significant, for, as Lohse observes, 'in the primitive Christian language it practically became a technical term for missionary preaching'.[2] Second, Christ is the object of the proclamation. As O'Brien writes, 'the Christ who is "proclaimed" is the one at the centre of God's mystery, i.e. Christ in you (Gentiles). He is the sum and substance of Paul's message.'[3] Third, the scope of the proclamation is universal, viz. to reach πάντα ἄνθρωπον with the proclamation of Christ. Regardless of one's view on the precise nature of the problem at Colossae, it is obvious that the threefold repetition of πάντα ἄνθρωπον is an attempt to counter the pride and exclusivism of the errorists (cf. 2.18-19, 23). The 'mystery' is revealed through Paul's missionary preaching to all who will receive it; it is not reserved for any sort of spiritual elite. Finally, Paul's goal, which he

---

ably correct when he writes, '»En vous« pourrait aussi convenir, à condition d'être compris non pas dans le sens d'une mystique individuelle, mais au sens de la vie communautaire. C'est dans l'Eglise que le Christ agit'; cf. Cannon, p. 213.

1. Kim (p. 82) notes 'a shift in emphasis in defining the mystery from 1 Cor 2.1ff. through Col 1.24ff. to Eph 3.1ff.' In 1 Cor. 2 it refers generally to 'God's plan of salvation embodied in Christ', while in Col. 1 it is specifically 'God's plan that makes the Gentiles participants in salvation'. This latter idea is made more explicit in Eph. 3. It is possible that this shift is related to the polemical concerns of Paul in writing to the Colossians.

2. Lohse, pp. 76-77; see also J. Schniewind, 'καταγγέλλω', *TDNT*, I, pp. 70-72, and Gnilka, p. 103. The verb occurs in the NT only in Paul (6×) and in Acts (11×). The object of the proclamation is variously presented as 'Christ' (Acts 17.3; Phil. 1.17-18), 'the mystery' (1 Cor. 2.1), 'the gospel' (1 Cor. 9.14), 'the word of God' (Acts 13.5; 15.36; 17.13), 'the way of salvation' (Acts 16.17), 'forgiveness of sins' (Acts 13.38), 'the Lord's death' (1 Cor. 11.26), and 'in Jesus the resurrection of the dead' (Acts 4.2). Regardless of differences in terminology, however, the verb refers in each case to missionary preaching.

3. O'Brien, *Colossians*, p. 87.

desires to reach through his preaching and teaching ministry, is summed up in the words ἵνα παραστήσωμεν πάντα ἄνθρωπον τέλειον ἐν Χριστῷ.

The interpretation of this final clause is a matter of some importance if we are to understand properly Paul's response to the situation at Colossae. Much discussion has taken place as to the meaning of τέλειος, and rightly so. Nevertheless, the broad range of meaning possible for this term means that caution is in order if we are to understand correctly Paul's goal in ministry.[1] Since Lightfoot most interpreters have understood τέλειος against the background of its use in the hellenistic world, where it 'often designated a man who was deemed worthy of special experiences of the divine by means of an appropriation of "spirit" (πνεῦμα) or by initiation into mysteries'.[2] Yet others have pointed to the Semitic background of the word.[3] It occurs some twenty times in the LXX and usually is the translation of שלם and תמים. In OT Greek, therefore, τέλειος means: (a) moral righteousness (associated with obedience to God's will and God's law; Deut. 18.13; 3 Kgs [LXX] 8.61; 11.4, 10; 15.3, 14; 1 Chron. 28.9; Sir. 44.17; cf. *T. Jud.* 23.5), (b) cultic purity (Exod. 12.5), and (c) 'perfection' in association with the reception of wisdom (Wis. 9.6).

The Qumran texts build on OT usage, using תמים to denote faultless obedience to the divine commands as developed and interpreted by the sect.[4] Such 'perfection' was possible only because they had received a revelation of the divine 'mysteries'.[5] There is some tension between the outlook of 1QS 1–9, where 'perfection of way' (the quality of the תמימי דרך) is required for membership in the community and consequently for salvation, and a number of statements in 1QH and 1QS 10–11 that set forth the viewpoint that 'perfection of way' is not of human

---

1. For a survey of the various contexts in which the word appears in the ancient world, see P.J. Du Plessis, *ΤΕΛΕΙΟΣ. The Idea of Perfection in the New Testament* (Kampen: Kok, 1959), pp. 36-121.

2. Lohse, *Colossians*, p. 78; cf. Lightfoot, p. 170. On τέλειος in Greek philosophy, see G. Delling, 'τέλος, κτλ.', *TDNT*, VIII, pp. 869-72, and for parallels in the mystery religions, see Dibelius–Greeven, p. 18, and the literature cited in BAGD, p. 809.

3. Cf. Bornkamm, 'Kolosser', p. 88; Gnilka, p. 104; O'Brien, *Colossians*, p. 89; and Schweizer, *Colossians*, p. 111.

4. Cf. Delling, 'τέλος', p. 73.

5. Cf. B. Rigaux, 'Révélation des mystères et perfection à Qumran et dans le Nouveau Testament', *NTS* 4 (1958), pp. 237-62.

origin and can only be established through God's power and grace.[1] Nevertheless, the meaning of the term in these writings remains clear: it denotes complete obedience to the commands of the law as interpreted by divine revelation, and it stands as the basic requirement for membership in the community and participation in the eschatological salvation.

In light of its range of possible meanings, the context of its use in 1.28 is critical to a proper understanding of τέλειος here. Most important is the use of the verb παραστῆσαι, which could refer to the presentation of a sacrifice or to the presentation of a person before a court (see 2 Cor. 4.14; 11.2; Rom. 14.10; Eph. 5.27; cf. Acts 23.33).[2] The immediate context makes a decision between a cultic or a legal sense difficult. It is helpful, however, to observe that the verb occurs earlier in v. 22, where it is stated that the purpose of Christ's reconciling work is παραστῆσαι ὑμᾶς ἁγίους καὶ ἀμώμους καὶ ἀνεγκλήτους κατενώπιον αὐτοῦ. Since the term is probably used with a similar meaning in both of these two passages, we may use the statement of v. 22 to illuminate that of v. 28, provided we do not violate the immediate context.

The first two adjectives of 1.22 are used to describe an unblemished sacrificial victim (Exod. 29.27-28; Heb. 9.14; 1 Pet. 1.19). The third, however, points in a different direction, and so must temper our interpretation of the other two. Ἀνέγκλητος refers to someone against whom no accusation can be brought, a person 'above reproach' or 'blameless'. It can refer in a general way to one's conduct (1 Tim. 3.10; Tit. 1.6-7).[3] But in 1 Cor. 1.8 it is used in a judicial sense to refer to one's status before God at the last judgment, for there Paul expresses his wish that the Lord βεβαιώσει ὑμᾶς ἕως τέλους ἀνεγκλήτους ἐν τῇ ἡμέρᾳ τοῦ κυρίου ἡμῶν Ἰησοῦ Χριστοῦ.[4]

---

1. Cf. Sanders, *Paul*, pp. 287-98. Sanders is certainly correct in his observation that the difference in emphasis is due, at least in part, to the difference in literary type (p. 292). Nevertheless, we must question his synthesis of the two viewpoints, that 'the principal point of the punishment for deeds but reward by mercy theme is that, while man can forfeit salvation by transgression, he can never be sufficiently deserving to earn it by obedience'. This appears to be merely another example of Sanders's attempt to reduce the variety of perspectives in Second Temple Judaism to a single pattern, that of 'covenantal nomism'.

2. For parallels, see Lohse, *Colossians*, p. 65; *contra* Lohmeyer (*Kolosser*, p. 88), who insists that the verb always has an eschatological interpretation.

3. For confirmation of this usage in the papyri, see MM, pp. 40-41.

4. Cf. W. Grundmann, 'ἀνέγκλητος', *TDNT*, I, pp. 356-57.

Furthermore, the words κατενώπιον αὐτοῦ are paralleled in Jude 24 with clear reference to one's appearance before God at the last judgment: τῷ δὲ δυναμένῳ φυλάξαι ὑμᾶς ἀπταίστους καὶ στῆσαι κατενώπιον τῆς δόξης αὐτοῦ ἀμώμους ἐν ἀγαλλιάσει (cf. *1 En.* 104.1).

The clustering of language appropriate to the setting of the last judgment in v. 22 suggests that this is the proper referent not only for this verse, but also for the purpose clause of v. 28.[1] Such an interpretation is consistent with the eschatological flavor of the passage, especially if we understand the sufferings connected with Paul's ministry (v. 24) to refer to the 'messianic woes'. On this view, Paul's attention is directed toward the end as he seeks through his ministry to 'fill up what is lacking' in the sufferings of the Messiah, and so to hasten his coming.[2]

So here in 1.28 Paul states his desire to present every person before God as τέλειος, which in context means free from blame or accusation

---

1. So Abbott, pp. 226-27; E.F. Scott, pp. 28, 35; J. Dupont, *Gnosis: La connaissance religieuse dans le épitres de Saint Paul* (Louvain: E. Nauwelaerts, 1949), p. 498; H.-L. Parisius, 'Über die forensische Deutungsmöglichkeit des paulinischen ἐν Χριστῷ', *ZNW* 49 (1958), p. 287; H. Hegermann, *Die Vorstellung vom Schöpfungsmittler im hellenistischen Judentum und Urchristentum* (Berlin: Akademie Verlag, 1961), pp. 194-96; R.P. Martin, pp. 67-68; O'Brien, *Colossians*, pp. 68-69, 89-90; Bruce, *Colossians* (1984), pp. 79, 87-88; *contra* Lightfoot (pp. 162-63, 170), who interprets the verb in both verses with regard to the presentation of a sacrificial victim; cf. C.F.D. Moule, pp. 22, 85, and Schweizer, *Colossians*, pp. 93, 111-12, who interpret the reference in v. 22 in sacrificial terms, yet take παραστήσωμεν in v. 28 more generally. See also Meeks, 'In One Body', p. 219: 'The metaphor is probably not sacrificial despite some similarities to Rom. 12.1, but drawn from the notion of the (eschatological) marriage of the restored Israel to God . . . But the thought that all must "present themselves" before God's judgment seat (Rom. 14.10) also echoes in this passage.' Lohse (p. 65) acknowledges that the language used here refers to the divine court, but denies that the temporal reference is primarily to the future day of the Lord. As he says, the language expresses 'that the Christians' present lives are lived in God's presence'; cf. similarly Hugedé, p. 82, and Gnilka, p. 104. The suggestion of D.M. Stanley (*Christ's Resurrection in Pauline Soteriology* [Rome: Pontificio Istituto Biblico, 1961], pp. 209, 211), that Paul refers here to 'the presentation of the Colossian church in the Eucharistic liturgy', is improbable.

2. See R.J. Bauckham, 'Colossians 1.24 Again: The Apocalyptic Motif', *EQ* 47 (1975), pp. 168-70; cf. Lohse, p. 71, and O'Brien, *Colossians*, pp. 78-80. See also Löwe, p. 313.

at the last judgment.[1] Of particular importance here is that one achieves this goal not on the basis of ascetic-mystical experiences or legal observances, but because one is 'in Christ'—because one has received the apostolic preaching, has responded to it, and is seeking to live in accordance with that message.

Conclusion

The most important feature of the theme of revelation in Colossians is that Christ is its focal point. This is indicated, first, by ascribing characteristics of personified wisdom to Christ in the hymnic section 1.15-20, and then by a direct reference to Christ as the locus of saving wisdom in 2.2-3. C.F.D. Moule correctly observes:

> That in Christ are hidden away all (God's) stores of wisdom and knowledge, is an overwhelmingly impressive way of saying once more what has already been noted as implied by other phrases—namely, that Christ has become to Christians all that the Wisdom of God was, according to the Wisdom Literature [and, I would add, the Jewish Apocalypses], and more still.[2]

The implication for the church at Colossae was that the preoccupation of the errorists with ascetic-mystical practices was mistaken, for it turned Christians' attention away from Christ, the true locus of saving wisdom.

Building on the centrality of Christ, Paul also stresses the importance of preaching the gospel and a response of faith. These emphases becomes evident when one observes that the letter refers to revelation in two senses. First, there is the revelation of the 'mystery', the gospel, which itself points to incorporation into Christ as the condition of salvation (1.12-14, 25-29). Second, there is the revelation of God's will to those who are already 'in Christ', that they might live in a manner that is worthy of and pleasing to the Lord who saved them. Consequently, there is room for growth in the Christian life, and Paul teaches and exhorts toward that end. But a major facet of such progress toward maturity is a sense of thankfulness for the redemption that is theirs, not on the basis of ascetic-mystical piety, but on the

---

1. For broader conceptual parallels to this idea, see 1 Thess. 3.13; 5.23; Phil. 1.10.
2. C.F.D. Moule, p. 86.

condition of being 'in Christ'.[1] It is only through incorporation into Jesus Christ that they will be found 'blameless' at the revelation of his glory.

1. In this sense I agree with N.A. Dahl, 'Anamnesis: Memory and Commemoration in Early Christianity', in *Jesus in the Memory of the Early Church*, p. 16: 'I would say that for the early Christians, knowledge was an anamnesis, a recollection of the gnosis given to all those who have believed in the gospel, received baptism, and been incorporated into the church. . . Clearly, there always remains a possibility of growing in knowledge; but this essentially signifies an ever growing assimilation and an ever more perfect application of what has been once for all received.'

Chapter 8

REDEMPTION IN CHRIST

Paul's argument that Christ is the locus of saving wisdom is an important foundation for his admonitions in 2.6-8. There is, however, a second pillar for Paul's admonitions that is equally significant, not only for the warnings of 2.6-8 but also for the lengthy polemic of 2.16-23. And it is to this subject that we must turn our attention in this section. For not only are those who are 'in Christ' partakers in a saving revelation, they also experience redemption from the dominion of spiritual forces.

This idea is first telegraphed in the thanksgiving period (in 1.12-14), and then is developed using specific images associated with the world of Jewish apocalypticism in 2.13-15. Obviously, 2.13-15 is of strategic importance in Paul's argument. The fact that it stands at the climax of the exposition that undergirds the polemic of 2.16-23 is evidence enough. Nevertheless, the significance of 2.13-15 in the argument of Colossians has not been explored in detail, probably due to the fact that this text is loaded with interpretive problems. Indeed, it is no exaggeration to say that this is one of the most difficult texts in all of Paul's writings. Still, we are helped in our interpretation by the way Paul signals his concerns in 1.12-14, as well as by his use of various images that are associated with Jewish apocalypticism.

In dealing with 2.13-15, it is appropriate that we turn our attention first to 1.12-14, since much there is foundational for 2.13-15. In both passages baptismal experience, forgiveness of sins, and redemption from spiritual forces play similar roles. This is striking in view of the fact that the language of 'forgiveness' has no great place in the Pauline corpus—in fact, apart from a very few exceptions, its absence is conspicuous.[1] Yet here in Colossians this relationship of baptism, forgive-

---

1. Apart from Colossians, divine forgiveness is mentioned only in Rom. 4.7 (an OT citation) and Eph. 1.7 and 4.32. Some include Rom. 3.25 (πάρεσις) as well.

ness and redemption is critical for a proper interpretation of both 1.12-14 and 2.13-15, as well as for a true understanding of Paul's overall argument.

1. *The Interpretation of 1.12-14*

In dealing with 1.12-14 we will consider first the question of traditional material, then the logical structure of the passage, and finally the meaning of significant terms and phrases. In conclusion we will summarize our results.

a. *The Presence of Traditional Material*

The fundamental interpretive problem pertaining to 1.12-14 is whether the passage relates primarily to what precedes it or what follows. On the former interpretation, which is also the traditional view, the introductory participle εὐχαριστοῦντες functions adverbially and parallels καρποφοροῦντες, αὐξανόμενοι and δυναμούμενοι in further defining περιπατῆσαι ἀξίως τοῦ κυρίου.[1] The latter view, which is more recent, breaks the thought at the beginning of v. 12. The development of this approach can be sketched out briefly as follows.

In 1913 Norden argued, on the basis of participial constructions and the accumulation of relative clauses, that the hymnic section began not with v. 15 but with τῷ ἱκανώσαντι of v. 12.[2] Later Käsemann, building on the observation of Lohmeyer that 'Paulus hat sonst an

---

The most common explanation for this paucity of occurrences has been that Paul preferred other terminology, since forgiveness implied only remission from past guilt and not deliverance from the present power of sin; see W.H.P. Hatch, 'The Pauline Idea of Forgiveness', in *Studies in Early Christianity* (ed. S.J. Case; New York: Century, 1928), pp. 344-45; cf. Bultmann, *Theology*, I, p. 287; L. Cerfaux, *Christ in the Theology of St. Paul* (trans. G. Webb and A. Walker; Freiburg: Herder, 1959), p. 142, and H. Conzelmann, *An Outline of the Theology of the New Testament* (trans. J. Bowden; London: SCM Press, 1969), p. 71. For a somewhat different perspective, see H. Ridderbos, *Paul: An Outline of His Theology* (trans. J.R. de Witt; Grand Rapids: Eerdmans, 1975), p. 165, and Sanders, *Paul*, p. 500.

1. This interpretation, while traditional, is still widely represented. E.g. P. Schubert, *Form and Function of the Pauline Thanksgivings* (Berlin: Töpelmann, 1939), p. 93; L.B. Radford, *The Epistle to the Colossians and the Epistle to Philemon* (London: Methuen, 1946), p. 161; C.F.D. Moule, p. 55; Gibbs, p. 101; and P.T. O'Brien, *Introductory Thanksgivings in the Letters of Paul* (Leiden: Brill, 1977), p. 73.

2. E. Norden, *Agnostos Theos* (Leipzig: Teubner, 1913), pp. 250-53.

keiner Stelle die Fürbitte selbst mit einem Dank oder der Aufforderung zum Danke geschlossen',[1] as well as the work of Bornkamm with
respect to the verb εὐχαριστέω,[2] argued that the hymn in vv. 15-20
had already undergone redaction when received by the author of
Colossians and that together with vv. 12-14 it made up a Christian
baptismal liturgy.[3] Käsemann attempted to trace the progress of the
hymn through three distinct life-settings: the pre-Christian composition of vv. 15-20; the redaction of the hymn so as to form a liturgical
piece that included what is now 1.12-20; and the adaptation and incorporation of this liturgy into Colossians at the time of composition.
Such a reconstruction is suggested not only by the use of
εὐχαριστοῦντες (which may be a technical term) at the beginning of
v. 12, the presence of participial constructions, and the accumulation
of relative clauses, but also by the occurrence of many features in
vv. 12-14 that appear to be not typically Pauline (e.g. the use of
ἱκανόω instead of Paul's usual καλέω, the occurrence of the term
μερίς, the use of οἱ ἅγιοι in a way that leads many to think that it
refers to angels, and the presence of the term βασιλεία).[4]

While Käsemann's analysis has certain advantages, there are also
significant problems connected with it that require consideration as
well. First, as Deichgräber has argued, vv. 12-14 are properly categorized as a 'Dankgebet', and so 'es liegt. . . eine ganz andere Gattung
vor als im folgenden Abschnitt'.[5] Whether or not one agrees completely with Deichgräber's description of these verses as 'ein ad hoc
formuliertes Prosagebet',[6] numerous differences can be noted between

---

1. Lohmeyer, *Kolosser*, p. 38.
2. G. Bornkamm, 'Das Bekenntnis im Hebräerbrief', reprinted in *Studien zu
Antike und Urchristentum* (Munich: Chr. Kaiser Verlag, 1963), pp. 196-97. He
argued that εὐχαριστοῦντες is a technical term introducing a liturgical confession of
Christ. Thus it would be appropriate to insert a semi-colon and quotation marks after
εὐχαριστοῦντες in v. 12. Unlike Käsemann, he located the confession within a
eucharistic context.
3. Käsemann, pp. 149-54, who is followed closely by B. Vawter, 'The Colossian Hymn and the Principle of Redaction', *CBQ* 33 (1971), pp. 62-81.
4. These peculiarities are conveniently listed and discussed in R. Deichgräber,
Gotteshymnus und Christushymnus in der frühen Christenheit (Göttingen: Vandenhoeck & Ruprecht, 1967), pp. 79-80.
5. Deichgräber, p. 145.
6. Note the criticisms of this position by Gnilka (p. 45), who argues that the
parallel passages, Eph. 1.3ff. and 1 Pet. 1.3ff., are eulogies rather than examples of
a 'Dankgebet für die Erlösung im Prosaform', and that the patristic parallels adduced
by Deichgräber 'fallen strukturell anders aus'.

this section and the hymn that follows: vv. 12-14 are in prose style, while vv. 15-20 are highly poetic; vv. 12-14 speak with reference to the congregation, yet vv. 15-20 are mostly cosmic in focus; vv. 12-14 are largely in the first person plural, while vv. 15-20 focus on the redeemer himself.[1] In light of these significant differences, it is difficult to imagine these two sections being linked together to form a 'Gemeindehomologie' or a 'Bekenntnis'.

A second problem with Käsemann's analysis relates to the awkward fact that the second person plural is used in v. 12, while the first person plural appears in v. 13.[2] Since the 'we-style' is a characteristic of confessional material, the case for Käsemann's view would be much stronger if the first person plural occurred throughout.[3]

Third, many scholars have rejected Bornkamm's view that εὐχαριστοῦντες is a technical term. The main objections to Bornkamm's view are (1) that this usage simply does not seem characteristic of the NT, and (2) that the author had available to him the verbs εὐλογέω and (ἐξ)ομολογέω, which more naturally express such a technical sense.[4]

Finally, we should mention that while vv. 12-14 contain many terms and concepts that seem not characteristically Pauline, it is likely that the reference to τὴν ἄφεσιν τῶν ἁμαρτιῶν in v. 14 comes, in fact, from the hand of the author of Colossians. 'Forgiveness', as we noted earlier, plays a major role in the argument of the Colossian letter, and it is difficult to believe that it occurs here simply because it is

1. These contrasts are taken from Conzelmann, 'Kolosser', pp. 135-36, though I have applied them with reference to vv. 12-14 as a whole. Contrast O'Brien (*Introductory Thanksgivings*, pp. 74-75), who regards the change from a prayer to a creed or hymn as 'almost imperceptible', and A.M. Hunter (*Paul and His Predecessors*, [London: SCM Press, 1961], p. 124), who states that the hymn of vv. 15-20 is 'unrelated to its context both before and after'.

2. That v. 12 must be taken together with vv. 13-14 is evident from the fact that the contrast between light and darkness is split between vv. 12 and 13; cf. Deichgräber, p. 79. Thus we must take issue with Lohmeyer (*Kolosser*, pp. 40-41), who created a break after v. 12.

3. Käsemann (p. 153) argued in favor of ἡμᾶς instead of ὑμᾶς in v. 12, following A C D G etc. over against ℵ B etc. Yet it is more likely that ὑμᾶς was brought into conformity with the person of v. 13 than that ὑμᾶς was changed so as to agree with the implicit subject of the passive participle δυναμούμενοι in v. 11; cf. Lohmeyer, *Kolosser*, p. 30; Deichgräber, p. 79; Gnilka, p. 44; and Metzger, *Textual Commentary*, p. 620.

4. The former objection is voiced by Gnilka, p. 45; both are mentioned by Deichgräber, p. 145, and O'Brien, *Introductory Thanksgivings*, pp. 73-74.

part of a larger confession. Rather, it is more likely that the writer himself purposely set in juxtaposition the ideas of divine forgiveness and redemption from the domination of blackmailing powers—a pattern that is developed further in 2.13-15, as we will see later.[1]

In short, the most reasonable option, we believe, is to understand 1.12-14 as a Pauline composition containing several traditional terms and images. That these images had their place within the context of baptism in the early Church is suggested by several characteristics of vv. 12-14: (1) the decisive nature of the transfer from one lordship to another, as suggested by the verbs ἱκανώσαντι, ἐρρύσατο and μετέστησεν; (2) the absolute contrast between light, for which God has qualified us, and darkness, from which we have been rescued; (3) the use of the genitives τοῦ υἱοῦ τῆς ἀγάπης αὐτοῦ with reference to the βασιλείαν (cf. the accounts of Jesus' baptism in Mt. 3.17; Mk 1.11, and Lk. 3.22);[2] and (4) the use of the concept τὴν ἄφεσιν τῶν ἁμαρτιῶν, which is closely associated with baptism in the traditions of the early Church (e.g. Mk 1.4; Lk. 3.3; Acts 2.38).[3] This clustering of terms and images, which are generally associated with baptism and not characteristically Pauline, is perhaps best regarded as resulting from the heightened emphasis that Paul gave to the Colossians' baptism in light of the doctrinal and practical challenges facing the Colossian church.

Such an understanding of 1.12-14 allows us to account for the clustering of traditional imagery while at the same time retaining the close connection of these verses to the previous section, as seems required because of the parallelism between εὐχαριστοῦντες and the three participles of 1.10-11.[4] So vv. 12-14 serve primarily to conclude

1. Of course, the expression 'the forgiveness of sins' might be understood as a Pauline addition to some pre-existing confession, but such a view cannot be argued with any degree of confidence.
2. Käsemann, pp. 159-60, though on his view these characteristics point toward the presence of a liturgical form; cf. R.P. Martin, p. 55.
3. R.P. Martin, p. 37. For other arguments pointing to a baptismal setting, see H. Halter, *Taufe und Ethos* (Freiburg: Herder, 1976), pp. 186, 603.
4. Several commentators have argued that εὐχαριστοῦντες has imperatival force in Col. 1.12; cf. Lohse, p. 32; R.P. Martin, p. 53; and Gnilka, p. 44. Lohse appeals to D. Daube ('Participle and Imperative in 1 Peter', in E. Selwyn, *The First Epistle of St. Peter* [London: Macmillan, 1946; reprint edn, Grand Rapids: Baker, 1981], pp. 467-88) to show that his interpretation, which is derived largely from form critical analysis, is grammatically justifiable. Nevertheless, the imperatival participle occurs when there is a *series* of ethical injunctions, as Daube argued; cf.

Paul's intercessory prayer rather than to introduce the hymn of vv. 15-20, though that is not to deny that their function is transitional as well.[1]

b. *The Logical Structure of the Passage*

While the question of traditional material and the relation of the passage to its immediate context are issues fraught with problems, the exegesis of 1.12-14 itself is fairly straightforward. Indeed, the logical structure of the passage is especially clear. Paul's desire is for the Colossian believers to offer thanks to the Father. So he provides a basis for thanksgiving by recounting the blessings God has graciously given them 'in Christ'.

First, in v. 12 he describes God's saving action by means of a participial clause beginning with ἱκανώσαντι. Then in v. 13 he shifts to a relative construction that opens with ὅς ἐρρύσατο. It seems clear that the relative clause (v. 13) functions as a further description of the transformation that takes place at baptism (described in v. 12).[2] This is so because the contrast between 'light' and 'darkness' is split between vv. 12 and 13,[3] the aorist tenses point to the same event, and the parallelism of clauses—as seen especially in the prepositional phrases that follow each verb (εἰς τὴν μερίδα, ἐκ τῆς ἐξουσίας and εἰς τὴν βασιλείαν)—points toward an interdependence of vv. 12 and 13.[4]

A further point with respect to internal structure relates to the function of the relative clause of v. 14, which is itself contained

O'Brien, *Introductory Thanksgivings*, p. 73; BDF, §468; *Idiom Book, pp.* 179-80, and *Biblical Greek,* pp. 129-30. Such a context is lacking in Col. 1.

1. O'Brien (*Introductory Thanksgivings*, pp. 62-104) is especially cautious at this point. He discusses the thanksgiving period of Colossians in a section dealing with 'thanksgiving and petitionary prayer conjoined' (noting the pattern 'thanksgiving–intercession–thanksgiving'). While recognizing that the form of the letter is somewhat deviant in this respect, he resists the temptation to attempt to bring its thanksgiving period into conformity with the other Pauline letters.

2. R. Schnackenburg, *God's Rule and Kingdom* (trans. J. Murray; New York: Herder, 1963), p. 298; Lohse, p. 36; R. P. Martin, p. 54; and O'Brien, *Introductory Thanksgivings*, pp. 96-97. Halter (p. 186) argues 'dass die folgenden Sätze [i.e. vv. 13-14] genauer erklären, was mit der "Teilhabe am Los der Heiligen im Lichte" gemeint ist'.

3. Schnackenburg, p. 298.

4. The parallelism within and between these verses is illustrated graphically by Zeilinger, pp. 38-39.

within the relative construction that commences at the beginning of v. 13. Clearly v. 14 is transitional, serving to link the soteriological discussion of vv. 12-13 (which centers on the saving action of the Father) with the cosmic description of vv. 15-20.[1] Hence, while its concerns are primarily soteriological (like vv. 12-13), v. 14 also indicates that the deliverance described in vv. 12-14 is found 'in the beloved Son'—who then is discussed at length in vv. 15-20.[2]

c. The Meaning of Significant Terms and Phrases

Having dealt with the relationship of 1.12-14 to its immediate context and investigated briefly its internal structure, it is now appropriate to inquire as to the meaning and significance of certain key terms and phrases in the passage.

In v. 12 we are met with Paul's statement that the Colossian believers had been qualified for or with respect to τὴν μερίδα τοῦ κλήρου τῶν ἁγίων.[3] Scholars have been unable to agree as to the precise relationship between these terms. Many view the construction as pleonastic, with κλήρου functioning appositionally (i.e. 'the portion which is the lot'),[4] while others understand κλήρου to be a partitive genitive and so translate 'a share in the inheritance'.[5] My preference is the latter, though the meaning is much the same in either case. The apostle is utilizing language familiar from the OT and from Qumran[6] to stress the participation of believers in the inheritance apportioned to the ἅγιοι. Thus as the tribes of Israel received their portion of the land of Canaan (Num. 26.52ff.; 34.2, 13), so Christian believers have come

---

1. On the redemptive setting of the cosmological hymn, see Pollard, p. 573.
2. It is interesting to note that ἐν ᾧ functions in 1.14 in much the same way as in 2.11, where it links the cosmological discussion of 2.9-10 with the catalogue of soteriological blessings listed in 2.11-15.
3. On the use of εἰς to denote reference to a person or thing, see BAGD, p. 230.
4. So Lightfoot, p. 141; Abbott, p. 206; W. Foerster, 'κλῆρος, κτλ.', *TDNT*, III, p. 763; O. Procksch, 'ἅγιος, κτλ.', *TDNT*, I, p. 107; and Schnackenburg, p. 299.
5. So A.L. Williams, *The Epistles of Paul the Apostle to the Colossians and to Philemon* (Cambridge: Cambridge University Press, 1907), p. 33; C.F.D. Moule, p. 55; O'Brien, *Introductory Thanksgivings*, p. 95; and BAGD, pp. 435, 505.
6. Similarities between the terms and concepts found in 1.12-14 and those in numerous documents from Qumran are widely recognized; see R.E. Murphy, *The Dead Sea Scrolls and the Bible* (Westminster, MD: Newman, 1956), pp. 92-93, and Lohse, 'Christologie und Ethik', pp. 165-66. For a summary of the parallel terms and ideas, as well as bibliography, see H. Braun, *Qumran und das Neue Testament* (Tübingen: Mohr, 1966), I, p. 226.

into an even greater heritage,[1] which is described by the words τῶν
ἁγίων ἐν τῷ φωτί.

The identification of the ἅγιοι in v. 12 has occasioned some debate
ever since parallels at Qumran have been recognized. Traditionally,
the word has been interpreted in its usual Pauline sense to mean
'saints' or 'believers'.[2] In light of the fact, however, that 'holy ones'
parallels 'the sons of heaven' in 1QS 11.7-8, a number of scholars prefer to understand ἅγιοι in Col. 1.12 as referring to angels rather than
humans.[3] Yet Pierre Benoit has pointed out places in the Qumran texts
where 'holy ones' is used in a way that is ambiguous—i.e. not referring exclusively either to the community or to angels, but seemingly
including both. And Benoit argues persuasively that such an ambiguity
is present in Col. 1.12.[4] So it seems that the emphasis of 1.12 is not on
the persons of the ἅγιοι but on two related characteristics: that they
are *holy* and that their inheritance has its place *in light*.

The parallels from Qumran, especially that of 1QS 11.7-8, suggest
that the local significance of the phrase ἐν τῷ φωτί points toward
communion with the 'Sons of Heaven', the 'heavenly throngs that
delight in God's glory'.[5] Here, it seems, Paul is making clear to the
Colossian believers that they have already been qualified to participate
in the life of those who enjoy the experience of God's holiness and
glory—that is, here, anticipating his polemic against θρησκεία τῶν
ἀγγέλων,[6] Paul declares that believers have already been prepared to
join the 'holy ones', who worship and praise in the light of the pres-

---

1. R.P. Martin, 'Reconciliation and Forgiveness in the Letter to the Colossians',
in *Reconciliation and Hope* [ed. R. Banks; Grand Rapids: Eerdmans, 1974], p. 106)
argues that a spiritualized interpretation of the 'appointed lot' was already present in
the OT (e.g. Ps. 15.5).

2. So Conzelmann, 'Kolosser', p. 135; C.F.D. Moule, p. 55; Procksch, p. 107;
and O'Brien, *Introductory Thanksgivings*, pp. 95-96; cf. Halter, p. 188. Caird
(p. 171) argues that the ἅγιοι are Jewish Christians.

3. Käsemann, p. 44; Deichgräber, p. 79; Lohse, p. 36; R.P. Martin, *Colossians*, p. 54; and Gnilka, p. 47. See also BAGD, p. 9.

4. P. Benoit, '"Ἅγιοι en Colossiens 1.12: hommes ou anges?', in *Paul and
Paulinism* (ed. M.D. Hooker and S.G. Wilson; London: SPCK, 1982), pp. 83-99.
Some years earlier Schnackenburg (p. 299), while indicating his preference for the
view that ἅγιοι refers to angels, added to this the comment that 'the just are not necessarily excluded'.

5. Cf. Schnackenburg, p. 299. This view seems preferable to that of Procksch
(p. 107), who understands φῶς to refer 'to the light of grace. . . rather than to that
of heavenly glory'.

6. Cf. R.P. Martin, *Colossians*, p. 54.

ence of God himself. The eschatology of this section is clearly inaugurated, for while Christians are already qualified for this heritage and experience intimate fellowship with the Father in this life, they also look forward to the revelation of τὴν ἐλπίδα τὴν ἀποκειμένην... ἐν τοῖς οὐρανοῖς (1.5) when they shall enjoy those rich blessings in full measure.

In v. 13 Paul further elaborates on God's salvific work by describing the 'transference' that took place at conversion (faith-baptism) from one sphere of authority to another. While the aorist tense appears throughout vv. 12-13, the verbs ἐρρύσατο and μετέστησεν in v. 13 lay further stress on the realized nature of this blessing.[1] The imagery provided by these two verbs is picturesque. Ῥύομαι is used to describe the deliverance of the Israelites from the Egyptians in preparation for their entrance into the land of Canaan (Exod. 14.30, LXX),[2] while μετατίθημι recalls nuances of 'the wholesale transportation of peoples..., of which the history of oriental monarchies supplied so many examples'.[3] Negatively, Paul reminds the Colossians that they have been delivered ἐκ τῆς ἐξουσίας τοῦ σκότους, and most see in these words something of a local sense. So the expression is generally interpreted to mean 'from the sphere of authority (or domain) of darkness'.[4]

The meaning of σκότους in v. 13 is illuminated by parallels in the NT and at Qumran. Luke presents Jesus in Lk. 22.53 as referring to the supernatural forces of evil marshalled against him as ἡ ἐξουσία

---

1. This is not to say that a clear distinction can be drawn between the 'qualification' of v. 12 and the 'rescue-transference' described in v. 13, as if the former thought was directed toward the future kingdom of God and the latter toward the believer's present experience of the kingdom of Christ. Such a distinction may be present elsewhere in Paul's writings, but in 1.12-14 the eschatological contrast between light and darkness is split between vv. 12 and 13—which fact points to the conclusion that all three verbs refer to the same event. Thus we must take issue with the analysis of C.H. Dodd, 'Matthew and Paul', in *New Testament Studies* (Manchester: Manchester University Press, 1953), p. 55.

2. Cf. R.P. Martin, 'Reconciliation and Forgiveness', p. 107.

3. Lightfoot, p. 141; also O'Brien, *Introductory Thanksgivings*, p. 98; *contra* Deichgräber, p. 80.

4. H. Conzelmann, 'σκότος, κτλ.', *TDNT*, VII, pp. 442, 447; Foerster, 567; Dibelius–Greeven, p. 9; Carr, p. 101; and Halter, p. 187. R. Yates ('Christ and the Powers of Evil in Colossians', in *Studia Biblica 1978: III. Papers on Paul and Other New Testament Writers* [ed. E.A. Livingstone; Sheffield: JSOT Press, 1980], p. 462) writes, 'Here "darkness" is used of that sinister sphere where the principalities and powers hold sway'.

τοῦ σκότους;[1] while in Acts 26.18 the Gentiles are τοῦ ἐπιστρέψαι ἀπὸ σκότους εἰς φῶς καὶ τῆς ἐξουσίας τοῦ σατανᾶ ἐπὶ τὸν θεόν. The Qumran texts point in much the same direction, for there the expression 'lot of darkness' or 'dominion of darkness' is synonymous with the lot or dominion 'of Belial' (1QS 1.18, 23-24; 2.5, 19; 1QM 1.1, 11; 14.9; 17.5-6).[2] In short, then, Paul is arguing that believers have already been delivered from the sphere of authority (or tyranny) of devilish spiritual powers, and so have little to fear from them.

This deliverance has a positive aspect as well, for believers are transferred εἰς τὴν βασιλείαν τοῦ υἱοῦ τῆς ἀγάπης αὐτοῦ. The parallel with ἐκ τῆς ἐξουσίας τοῦ σκότους suggests that βασιλείαν here also has the sense of 'sphere of power or authority',[3] though without the implication that Christians are released from one tyranni-cal dominion only to be made subject to another. Rather, those who enter this sphere receive almost indescribable blessings (cf. v. 12). Schnackenburg has elaborated on this point as follows:

> In giving them a share in 'the lot of the saints in light' God has snatched them from the realm of darkness. It is a genuine vocation which because of baptism (2.12) bestows on them even now real salvation, a share in the risen life of Christ and at least in a hidden sense (3.1-3) in his heavenly glory. This is the most likely meaning of the phrase 'into the kingdom of the Son of his love'.[4]

It goes without saying, then, that those who already have a share in the kingdom and glory of God's beloved Son should not—indeed, must not—allow themselves to be intimidated by inferior spiritual forces who are no longer able to wield their tyrannical power against them.

The description of salvation in vv. 12-13 is followed by the words of v. 14, which are especially significant for our purpose. Here Paul reminds his readers what they possess because of redemption 'in Christ'. The formula 'in Christ' likely includes both the instrumental sense (i.e. 'by him' or 'through him') and the local sense (i.e. 'in him').[5] There is some disagreement among scholars as to the meaning of τὴν ἀπολύτρωσιν in this verse. Some argue that it refers to redemption by means of the payment of a ransom-price (i.e. the death

1. Cf. Bruce, *Colossians* (1957), p. 189, and O'Brien, *Introductory Thanks-givings*, p. 98.
2. Cf. Conzelmann, 'σκότος', p. 432, and R.P. Martin, 'Reconciliation and Forgiveness', p. 107, both of whom refer to these parallels.
3. Cf. Lohse, p. 38.
4. Schnackenburg, p. 298.
5. Cf. E. Best, *One Body in Christ* (London: SPCK, 1955), pp. 5-6.

of Christ).[1] Others, however, pointing to the lack of explicit reference to a ransom-price and the fact that τὴν ἄφεσιν τῶν ἁμαρτιῶν stands in apposition to τὴν ἀπολύτρωσιν, argue that the notion of payment is absent here. On this latter view, the term stresses the emancipation of believers from the dominion of evil powers,[2] or their 'present enjoyment of eschatological benefits' rather than 'redemption in the substitutionary sense of the word'.[3]

Precise determination is certainly difficult. Yet the fact that the action implied by ἀπολύτρυσις is very close to that signified by ἐρρύσατο in v. 13 leaves one with the distinct impression that the terminology of v. 14 serves to 'make more explicit the theme of that verse' (i.e. v. 13).[4] Indeed, the thought of a ransom-price is not entirely absent from v. 14, particularly in light of the obvious connection between this section and 2.13-15 where the crucifixion of Christ is explicitly mentioned. Nevertheless, the primary emphasis of v. 14a is on the fact of emancipation rather than on the means by which it was brought about.[5] It appears, then, that v. 14a adds little to the themes developed in v. 13, with the exception that this deliverance is available in and through the person of God's beloved Son—who is described at length in the hymn that follows.

It is in v. 14b, however, that Paul introduces a new concept, τὴν ἄφεσιν τῶν ἁμαρτιῶν. A more precise statement of the relationship between this blessing and God's redemption will be explicated below. For now it is sufficient to note that τὴν ἄφεσιν τῶν ἁμαρτιῶν stands in apposition to τὴν ἀπολύτρωσιν. So there is an identification between the two blessings referred to in this passage, and this is an insight that is significant for our exegesis of 2.13-15.

What, then, is being said in 1.12-14? Paul here encourages an attitude of joy and thanksgiving for the blessings God has given Chris-

---

1. So L. Morris, *The Apostolic Preaching of the Cross* (Grand Rapids: Eerdmans, 1965), pp. 46-47; Bruce, *Colossians* (1970), pp. 190-91, and I.H. Marshall, 'The Development of the Concept of Redemption in the New Testament', in *Reconciliation and Hope*, pp. 164-65.

2. So D. Hill, *Greek Words and Hebrew Meanings* (Cambridge: Cambridge University Press, 1967), p. 74.

3. So D.E.H. Whiteley, 'St. Paul's Thought on the Atonement', *JTS* 8 (1957), p. 153.

4. Hill, p. 74.

5. While we are indebted to Morris for his detailed study of the λύτρον word group, we agree with Hill (p. 55) and Whiteley (p. 250) that the notion of divine redemption is not always accompanied by the idea of a ransom price.

tians. For God has qualified them to join the 'holy ones', who worship and praise in the light of the presence of God himself. So they have been redeemed from the tyranny of hostile spiritual forces. In some way this redemption is identified in this passage with the forgiveness of sins. The precise nature of this relationship, however, is here unclear. It is only as we examine the related passage, 2.13-15, that we are able to understand how redemption and forgiveness function together in the argument of Colossians.

2. *The Interpretation of 2.13-15*

The interpretation of 2.13-15 cannot be carried out on its own but must be done in light of 1.12-14. The thematic similarities between these two texts are striking. And more importantly, it seems clear that the writer is telescoping in the thanksgiving period of the letter the concerns he plans to develop in 2.13-15. Consequently, the comments of 1.12-14 are highly relevant to the interpretation of 2.13-15, as we will argue in what follows.

The history of interpretation of 2.13-15 has yielded diverse and contradictory results. Little progress has been made in recent years with respect to understanding the function of this passage in the broader context of the argument of Colossians. A different approach, therefore, seems warranted, especially if it can explain the purpose of both 1.12-14 and 2.13-15 in the argument of the letter.

a. *The Broader Setting of 2.13-15*
The first task in an investigation of 2.13-15 is to examine the broader setting of the passage. And here, it appears, the task is relatively straightforward.

Paul's warnings in 2.8 are followed by a ὅτι clause (v. 9), which is itself connected by καί to another clause (v. 10). So vv. 9 and 10 provide the foundation or support for the warnings given in v. 8.[1] It is important (1) to observe the relation that exists between these two clauses, and (2) to note the themes that are introduced. Clearly v. 9 is concerned with *ontological* Christology, regardless of whatever ideo-

---

1. The ὅτι is causal rather than recitative; see Deichgräber, p. 168, Lähnemann, p. 115, and O'Brien, *Colossians*, p. 111, as well as the discussion below of a hymn in vv. 9-15. *Contra* G. Schille, *Frühchristliche Hymnen* (Berlin: Evangelische Verlagsanstalt, 1965), p. 31.

logical background is posited for the difficult term πλήρωμα. Yet just
as clearly v. 10a is concerned with *functional* Christology: that 'in
Christ', and not through any legal practices or mystical experiences,
believers have been 'made complete'. These statements are not merely
juxtaposed; rather v. 10 is rooted and grounded in the teaching of
v. 9.

It is no accident that the noun πλήρωμα and the participle
πεπληρωμένοι occur in succession in these two verses.[1] For it is only
because 'all the fullness of deity' dwells in Christ that Christians can
be certain that they are 'made full' or 'made complete' in him. They
lack nothing because he lacks nothing. The fullness that resides in
Christ is, in a sense, imparted to those who are 'in him'. As Murray
Harris explains,

> it was only because God in all his fullness had chosen to dwell in Christ (Col.
> 1.19), only because there dwelt embodied in Christ the total plenitude of
> Deity (Col. 2.9), that reconciliation was accomplished. A functional christo-
> logy presupposes, and finds its ultimate basis in, an ontological christology.[2]

Since the Colossian believers have already been 'made complete', Paul
argues, they have no reason to seek 'fullness' in any other way.
Instead, they should focus their attention on their head, Jesus Christ
(cf. 2.19).[3]

The relative clause ὅς ἐστιν ἡ κεφαλὴ πάσης ἀρχῆς καὶ ἐξουσίας
of v. 10b reminds the readers of the teachings of the hymn in ch. 1—
that it was 'in Christ' that the spiritual powers were created (1.16) and
that 'in him' they are held together and sustained (1.17). But v. 10b
also prepares the reader for the teaching of 2.13-15—that Christ is
also the head of the powers because he has disarmed and subjugated
them through the cross. Consequently, since Christians have been
'made complete' through the one who is supreme over all spiritual
powers, any claims to the effect that the powers require obedience are
out of order. The head of the church is also the head of these powers,
and they must submit to his rule and authority.

1. R.P. Martin (*Colossians*, p. 80) observes that 'Paul is obviously making capi-
tal out of the word for "fullness": "fullness of life" answers to "fullness of deity"'.
2. M. Harris, 'Prepositions and Theology in the Greek New Testament',
NIDNTT, III, p. 1193; cf. O'Brien, *Colossians*, pp. 111-12.
3. Cf. Lohse, pp. 100-101. C.F.D. Moule (p. 94) argues that 'the phrase is
clearly an attack on the mistake evidently current at Colossae, of supposing that
"completeness" could not be found through Christ alone, but must be sought by
additional religious rites and beliefs'.

Verses 11-15, then, flesh out the teachings of v. 10,[1] by (1) giving examples of the various ways in which Christians have been 'made complete' through faith and baptism, and (2) celebrating Christ's victory over the spiritual forces of evil.[2] The climax of this section is the vivid description of the defeat of these powers in v. 15, which in turn becomes the immediate referent for the οὖν of v. 16 and so the basis for the polemic of vv. 16-23. Thus while 2.13-15 bears a special relationship to the admonitions that follow, the ὅτι of v. 9 suggests that the whole of 2.9-15 is foundational not only for vv. 16-23 but also for the warning of v. 8.

b. *The Presence of Traditional Material*

Several attempts have been made to isolate traditional material in Colossians 2. The most ambitious has been that of Schille, who argued that a hymn is embedded in vv. 9, 10b, 11b and most of 13b-15, with vv. 10a, 11a, c, 12, 13a and b, and ὃ ἦν ὑπεναντίον ἡμῖν of v. 14 being additions by the author of Colossians.[3] His reconstruction, however, has been severely criticized, especially by Deichgräber[4] and C. Burger.[5] And for the following reasons Schille's approach is widely seen to be untenable: (1) he ends up with an extremely fragmented text; (2) the form of v. 9, being thoroughly prosaic, does not signal the introduction of a hymn;[6] (3) he is forced to argue that a *Themezeile* precedes the first section, yet it has no evident connection with the rest of the hymn;[7] and (4) he loosens ἐν τῇ ἀπεκδύσει τοῦ σώματος τῆς σαρκός from its context in v. 11, where it makes good

---

1. Halter, p. 194: 'V. 11 konkretisiert das schon Erfüllt-Sein der Kolosser "in Christus"'.
2. On the connection between baptism and the triumph of Christ over evil powers in the NT, see O. Bücher, *Christus Exorcista: Dämonismus und Taufe im Neuen Testament* (Stuttgart: Kohlhammer, 1972), pp. 170-72. Bücher correctly observes that the baptismal material of 2.11-14 is sandwiched between the assertion of Christ's lordship over the powers (v. 10) and the proclamation of his victory over them (v. 15).
3. Schille, pp. 31-37.
4. Deichgräber, pp. 167-69.
5. C. Burger, *Schöpfung und Versöhnung* (Neukirchen-Vluyn: Neukirchener Verlag, 1975), pp. 79-114.
6. Deichgräber, p. 167.
7. Burger, p. 83.

sense, and connects it with v. 10b, where it is syntactically problematic since v. 10b has ἐστιν instead of ἐγένετο.[1]

Others have made more modest attempts at isolating traditional material in Colossians 2. Deichgräber considered it possible that hymnic material underlies vv. 13c-15,[2] and his view has been adopted with more conviction by Lohse who calls this postulated material 'a fragment of a confession formulated in hymnic phrases'.[3] In support, Lohse points to several pieces of evidence: (1) the introduction of the first person plural at v. 13; (2) the piling up of participles; and (3) the 'remarkably large number of uncommon words and expressions' in these verses—the NT *hapax legomena* being χειρόγραφον, προσηλοῦν and ἀπεκδύεσθαι, while the Pauline *hapax legomena* are ἐξαλείφειν, ὑπεναντίος and δειγματίζειν, with θριαμβεύειν found elsewhere in the NT only at 2 Cor. 2.14 and παραπτώματα used instead of Paul's usual term ἁμαρτία.[4]

Evidence such as that marshalled by Lohse indeed seems to point to the presence of a significant amount of traditional material in vv. 13c-15.[5] Yet it is necessary to bear in mind, as well, that *hapax legomena* tend to cluster in Paul's letters; furthermore, that the introduction of rare or unique images (such as χειρόγραφον and the triumphal imagery) often brings with it a number of unusual terms. The argument from the vocabulary of a passage, therefore, while significant, should not be regarded as sufficient of itself to establish the presence of traditional pre-Pauline material.

The situation is that since Deichgräber and Lohse, scholars have been unable to come to a consensus as to the precise nature and extent of traditional material in Colossians 2. Wengst argued on the basis of grammatical structure that vv. 13-15 are a continuous piece drawn from a baptismal liturgy,[6] while Martin limits the traditional material

---

1. Deichgräber, p. 167, followed here by Burger, p. 83.

2. Deichgräber, pp. 168-69.

3. Lohse, pp. 106-107; cf. his earlier study, 'Ein hymnisches Bekenntnis in Kol 2,13c-15', in *Mélanges Biblique* (ed. A. Descamps and A. de Halleux; Gembloux: Duculot, 1969), pp. 427-35.

4. Lohse, *Colossians*, p. 106.

5. One cannot simply dismiss the possibility of traditional material being present, as does J.D.G. Dunn (*Unity and Diversity in the New Testament* [London: SCM Press, 1977], p. 139), who regards this as a 'purple passage' of the writer himself.

6. K. Wengst, *Christologische Formeln und Lieder* (Gütersloh: Mohn, 1972), pp. 186-94.

to vv. 14-15[1] and Burger attributes a great deal of vv. 14-15 to the redactional work of the author of Colossians.[2] It seems fairly clear that a considerable amount of traditional imagery is utilized in vv. 13-15, but it is far less certain that a pre-Pauline composition itself is embedded in the text. Attempts to establish the parameters of such an embedded composition have led to varied and contradictory results.

The problem of whether v. 13 should be regarded as part of this hypothetical composition is particularly difficult. The grammatical structure of this verse is remarkably similar to that of vv. 14-15, which tells in favor of its inclusion. Yet at the same time the logical place to begin such a citation is not with v. 13a but with v. 13c, where the object switches awkwardly from the second to the first person plural.[3] If, however, we follow this line of reasoning and suppose that the traditional material begins at v. 13c, then the symmetry of the section is disturbed and a strong argument in favor of the inclusion of v. 13 with vv. 14-15 is negated. On the other hand, if we regard the whole of v. 13 as a part of the traditional composition on the basis of its grammatical structure, then the awkwardness of the change in person is left without adequate explanation.

In view of the number and gravity of problems involved, it seems prudent to take a cautious approach to 2.13-15 in this matter. Rather than trying to define precisely the limits of a hypothetical hymn, baptismal liturgy or confession, it is best simply to acknowledge, with Schweizer, that 'what we have here is traditional imagery used in abundant measure'.[4] In what follows, therefore, we will explore the 'referential background' of this traditional imagery, with the hope that such an investigation will provide an explanation for this clustering of non-Pauline words and images.

---

1. Martin, 'Reconciliation and Forgiveness', p. 116.
2. See Burger, Faltblatt III, for a visual presentation of his reconstructed *Urtext*.
3. The switch to the first person, however, may also occur at v. 13b since ἡμᾶς occurs in $\mathfrak{P}^{46}$, B and a number of lesser witnesses, and the presence of ὑμᾶς in א* A C K and others might be explained as the result of an attempt to bring the person into conformity with that of the pronoun occurring in v. 13a; see Lohmeyer, *Kolosser*, p. 101. Yet it is also possible to argue that ὑμᾶς is original, and that the switch to ἡμᾶς was made in order to bring the person in line with that of the pronoun ἡμῖν in v. 13c. Most authorities regard the balance of probability as tipped slightly in favor of the latter solution; cf. Lohse, *Colossians*, p. 108, and Metzger, *Textual Commentary*, p. 623.
4. Schweizer, *Colossians*, p. 136.

c. *The Referential Background of 2.13-15 as an Aid to Interpretation*
A number of interpreters have utilized the *Apocalypse of Zephaniah*
in support of seeing χειρόγραφον as a 'heavenly book'. To date, however, no one has considered the possibility that the relevant passages in
both Colossians and the *Apocalypse of Zephaniah* share a common
'referential background', namely the tradition of the judgment scene
that plays an important role in several of the Jewish apocalypses.[1] As
background for our present discussion, it is helpful to list again the
features associated with this tradition:

1. The angelic witnesses, both good and bad;
2. The heavenly book(s) of deeds;
3. The post-mortem judgment, which includes both the good and the
   evil;
4. The consequences of judgment, which includes the vindication of
   the righteous and the condemnation of the wicked.

My intention here is not to argue that a traditional composition is
embedded in 2.13-15, but rather to suggest that Paul writes at this
point with the judgment scene in mind. As we explore this suggestion
in what follows, it is important to recall two characteristics of the
traditional judgment scenes as found in the Jewish apocalypses. First,
not every passage that contains a judgment scene includes all of the
features of that traditional form. Second, the features associated with
the judgment tradition are sometimes not concentrated in a few verses,
but rather appear spread out in the broader context of a chapter or
two. And such phenomena of fluidity and dispersement are also what
we find in Colossians, particularly in Paul's telescoping of material in
1.12-14 and then elaborating on those same themes in 2.13-15.

1. *The Angelic Witnesses*. The logical place to begin an interpretation
of 2.13-15 with regard to the angelic witnesses is at v. 15. Several
difficult exegetical problems are present and the nature of the spiritual
powers mentioned there is anything but obvious. Yet the context and
parallel material of 1.12-14 provide some guidelines to keep us on
track. It is, however, necessary to approach the verse one step at a
time.

Of great significance in any analysis of the nature of 'the rulers and
authorities' in v. 15, as well as in the whole of Colossians, is the

---

1. See above, Chapter 3, §2.

meaning of the aorist participle ἀπεκδυσάμενος. It describes Christ's action vis-à-vis these spiritual powers and so provides an important clue as to their nature and function. The problem here, however, is to assess the significance of the middle voice. Is it to be identified as (1) a direct or reflexive middle, (2) an indirect or intensive middle, or (3) a middle that functions with active force?[1] The latter two possibilities are best considered together since the resulting translations are similar.

Several scholars prefer to render the participle in either an indirect or an active sense. On the former view, the force of the middle voice is to stress personal interest, so that the subject is viewed as acting 'for or on behalf of himself'.[2] The latter interpretation, however, is more popular,[3] though with respect to the significance of the participle within the context of the passage as a whole there is very little difference between these two views.

The decision to understand the participle in either an indirect or an active sense leads one to consider another problem of interpretation. For while it is clear that the basic meaning of ἀπεκδυσάμενος in either case is 'to strip someone or something',[4] the further question inevitably arises, 'Of what are they stripped?' Again, scholars are divided on the issue. Some regard this as an allusion to the practices of a royal court, where public officials may be degraded by being stripped of their honor.[5] Others suggest that the imagery is that of a battlefield, and that the participle refers to the disarming of defeated forces.[6] In either case, however, whether one accepts an indirect or an

---

1. Grammarians, of course, differ as to the labels they assign to these various functions, but the labels used here are widely recognized; cf. J.A. Brooks and C.L. Winbury, *Syntax of New Testament Greek* (Washington, DC: University Press of America, 1979), p. 101.

2. So H.C.G. Moule, pp. 107-108, and Bruce, *Colossians* (1957), p. 240.

3. So BDF, §316; *Biblical Greek*, p. 76; and BAGD, p. 83. Among commentators the position is represented by Abbott, p. 261; E.F. Scott, p. 48; Dibelius–Greeven, p. 32; Caird, p. 196; and Lohse, *Colossians*, p. 112.

4. Cf. *Biblical Greek*, p. 76, and Lohse, *Colossians*, p. 112.

5. So Lohmeyer, *Kolosser*, p. 119; H. Schlier, 'δείκνυμι, κτλ.', *TDNT*, II, p. 31; R.P. Martin, *Colossians*, p. 87; and Lohse, *Colossians*, p. 112.

6. So Abbott, p. 261; Dibelius–Greeven, p. 32; A. Oepke, 'δύω, κτλ.', *TDNT*, II, p. 319; Schweizer, *Colossians*, p. 151; F.F. Bruce, 'Christ as Conqueror and Reconciler', *BibSac* 141 (1984), p. 298; and BAGD, p. 83. E.F. Scott (p. 48) specifies that the powers are stripped of their armor.

active interpretation of ἀπεκδυσάμενος, it is clear that the object of the participle is τὰς ἀρχὰς καὶ τὰς ἐξουσίας.

Also fairly common is the view that the middle participle functions in a reflexive sense, though there is some disagreement with regard to the identification of the person(s) or object(s) that Christ, the assumed subject on this view, has stripped off from himself. Lightfoot and others, following the Greek fathers, understand τὰς ἀρχὰς καὶ τὰς ἐξουσίας as being those stripped off. In words often-quoted, Lightfoot wrote: 'The powers of evil, which had clung like a Nessus robe about His humanity, were torn off and cast aside forever'.[1] Alternatively, others have followed the Latin fathers, and so assume an unexpressed reference to τὴν σάρκα as that which Christ 'stripped off'.[2] This last suggestion is, however, in my opinion, untenable, for it requires the insertion of an idea (τὴν σάρκα) not found in the immediate context,[3] and it leaves ἀπεκδυσάμενος dangling in a way completely unlike other participles in the passage.

While there may be contextual support for the view that ἀπεκδυσάμενος functions in an indirect or active sense, the lexical data point in a very different direction. For the lexical data clearly suggest that the full middle force of the participle is preferable, especially since the use of the middle voice with active force is unsup-

---

1. Lightfoot, p. 190; cf. J. Rutherford, 'Note on Colossians ii.15', *ExpTim* 18 (1906–07), p. 566; R. Leivestad, *Christ the Conqueror* (London: SPCK, 1954), p. 103; D.E.H. Whiteley, *The Theology of St. Paul* (Philadelphia: Fortress Press, 1966), p. 30, and Yates, 'Christ and the Powers of Evil', p. 465. Williams (pp. 99-100) also takes this view, but identifies the powers not as evil forces but as 'those that attended Christ'.

2. So C.A.A. Scott, *Christianity According to St. Paul* (Cambridge: Cambridge University Press, 1927), p. 35; J.A.T. Robinson, *The Body* (London: SCM Press, 1952), p. 43; cf. Käsemann, p. 162, as well as Carr (p. 61), who renders the participle 'preparing himself' and sees in v. 15 a reference to the imagery of the Roman triumph, especially 'the putting-off of the old clothes of the victor and the putting-on of the ceremonial dress of a *triumphator*'. He understands Christ's battle dress to be his flesh. Carr's rendering of ἀπεκδυσάμενος, as well as his interpretation of ἐδειγμάτισεν and θριαμβεύσας, is consistent with his overall thesis, that the notion of Christ's victory over rebellious forces is foreign to Paul and his contemporaries. For a critique of Carr's thesis and his explanation of 2.15, see P.T. O'Brien, 'Principalities and Powers: Opponents of the Church', in *Biblical Interpretation and the Church* (ed. D.A. Carson; Nashville: Nelson, 1984), pp. 125-28, and C.E. Arnold, 'The "Exorcism" of Ephesians 6.12 in Recent Research', *JSNT* 30 (1987), pp. 71-87.

3. C.F.D. Moule (p. 96), however, is representative of those who find such a teaching in 2.11.

ported elsewhere for the verbs ἀποδύω, ἐκδύω and ἀπεκδύω,[1] and since the parallel middle participle of 3.9 obviously functions in a reflexive sense.

This line of argumentation, however, which at first seems rather straightforward, leads to problems when the subject of vv. 14-15 and the meaning of ἀπεκδυσάμενος are considered together. These two matters are clearly interrelated. Yet the evidence does not point in a single direction. On the one hand, since there is no indication of a change in subject, the evidence would seem to favor the view that God is the subject throughout vv. 13-15. Yet at the same time the lexical data, albeit limited,[2] point to the reflexive force of ἀπεκδυσάμενος.

The best approach to resolving this dilemma, at least on the surface, would seem to be one that allows God to function as subject and yet gives ἀπεκδυσάμενος its full middle force. Such an interpretation, however, is virtually impossible, since the idea of God stripping powers or flesh off himself is absurd and wholly unlike anything found elsewhere in Paul.[3] So because of the contradictory nature of the evidence presently available, most focus on one factor and minimize the other, either positing a 'semi-conscious' or 'illogical' transition from God to Christ as subject or appealing to the flexibility of κοινή Greek in using the middle voice at times where classical grammar would require an active form.

A clear solution seems impossible without further considerations being introduced. Research to date has led to a stalemate and commentators are hopelessly divided. It is, therefore, necessary to introduce evidence from our study of 1.12-14 in order to clarify issues here.

Though certain ambiguities remain in the interpretation of 1.12-14, one fact is certain: that redemption from the spiritual forces is closely tied in with the blessing of forgiveness received at conversion. In fact, one could argue on the basis of 1.14 that redemption consists of and/or comes about through the forgiveness of sins. This observation is critical in seeking to understand the meaning of the participle ἀπεκδυσάμενος, which serves as a kind of hinge between the theme of forgiveness (vv. 13b-14) and the action involving the spiritual powers

---

1. Cf. Williams, pp. 99-100, and C.F.D. Moule, p. 101.

2. Lightfoot (p. 189) is probably correct in his suggestion that Paul coined this compound verb especially for his purposes in Colossians; cf. MM, p. 56. This would, of course, explain the limited nature of the lexical data.

3. So Percy (p. 96) writes 'dass aber die Geistermächte als eine Gott umgebende Hülle gedacht sein sollten, ist ganz absurd'.

(v. 15). In view of the logical and thematic connections between these two passages, it may be posited that a correct interpretation of 2.13-15 would yield a similar relationship between the concepts of forgiveness and redemption as was observed in 1.12-14.

When one examines the text from this perspective, those interpretations that render the middle participle in a reflexive sense appear lacking. It has been said above that the view that Christ stripped off his flesh is improbable. Now it must also be said that the idea of Christ stripping powers off from himself is unsatisfactory as well, since it does not relate the action of the exposure of the powers back to the blessing of forgiveness. Far better are those translations that give to the middle participle (in spite of slight lexical evidence to the contrary) an indirect or an active sense. And best of all is the view that the participle refers to the disarming of defeated forces.[1] For if this view is adopted, then ἀπεκδυσάμενος gathers up the thoughts of vv. 13b-14 and applies them directly to τὰς ἀρχὰς καὶ τὰς ἐξουσίας.

It is logical to assume, on this view, that the action of disarming refers back to the wiping out and removal of the χειρόγραφον— which, as will be argued in detail in the next section, served formerly as the instrument by which the accusations of the spiritual forces acquired their condemning power. So when one appropriates at conversion the forgiveness spoken of in 2.13b-14, the weapon that might be used against him is removed and he is delivered from the tyranny of those accusing, devilish powers. Or in the language of 1.12-14, it is divine forgiveness that rescues believers from the sphere of authority of the spiritual powers and transfers us into the kingdom of God's beloved Son.[2]

Such an interpretation, of course, affects one's view as to the nature of the powers referred to in Colossians. The decision to render ἀπεκδυσάμενος as 'disarming' brought with it a commitment to see τὰς ἀρχὰς καὶ τὰς ἐξουσίας in a negative light. Such a view is consistent with the most likely interpretation of ἐδειγμάτισεν ἐν

---

1. W. Wink, *Naming the Powers* (Philadelphia: Fortress Press, 1984), p. 58, points out that the vanquished were stripped of their armaments and publicly disgraced in the Roman triumph. See Plutarch, *Triumph of Aemilius Paulus*, 32-34.

2. See K. Wengst, 'Versöhnung und Befreiung: Ein Aspekt des Themas "Schuld und Vergebung" im Lichte des Kolosserbriefes', *EvT* 36 (1976), pp. 20-22.

παρρησία,[1] as well as the interpretation of the adverbial participle θριαμβεύσας in 2.15.[2] Further evidence, however, is available from 1.12-14, which serves both to confirm and to clarify our conclusions as based on a study of 2.13-15.

In 1.13 the writer states plainly that God 'delivered us ἐκ τῆς ἐξουσίας τοῦ σκότους'. In light of the parallels elsewhere in the NT and at Qumran, there can be little doubt that this statement refers to God's action in rescuing believers from the authority of *evil* powers— i.e. from those forces that take their stand against God's people, whether militarily or judicially.[3] And if we are correct in our assessment of the relationship between 1.12-14 and 2.13-15, then τὰς ἀρχὰς καὶ τὰς ἐξουσίας in 2.15 are the same type of beings.

---

1. The verb δειγματίζειν is generally rendered 'to make public' or 'to bring to public notice', and refers especially to 'that which seeks concealment', so that it almost has the sense 'to expose'. See Schlier, p. 31. Since the military image of Roman triumph is clearly indicated by the adverbial participle θριαμβεύσας (see below), a pejorative sense seems most probable: 'to expose to shame or ridicule'.

2. R.B. Egan ('Lexical Evidence on Two Pauline Passages', *NovT* 19 [1977], pp. 41-43), on the basis of evidence from the papyri, Tatian's *Adversus Graecos*, and *Acta Pauli et Theclae*, argues that one possible meaning of the verb is 'to manifest, reveal or make known'. Thus he translates, 'Uncovering the principalities, He [i.e. God] displayed them openly, making them known in Him [i.e. Christ]'. On the evidence from the papyri, see MM, p. 293. In spite of this evidence, however, the most probable interpretation of θριαμβεύσας in this context is that it refers to the celebration of a military victory by driving the captives (designated by the accusative) before the victor's triumphal chariot. The lexical evidence favors such a view, which also fits well with the meaning of ἀπεκδυσάμενος and the statements in the parallel text in 1.12-14. See esp. L. Williamson, Jr, 'Led in Triumph', *Int* 22 (1968), pp. 317-32; also G. Delling, 'θριαμβεύω', *TDNT*, III, pp. 159-60; BAGD, p. 363, as well as most commentators. The suggestion of Carr (p. 63), that the image 'is of Christ leading his triumphant armies as they follow him crying "Io triumphe!"' is unlikely in view of the fact that such a rendering of θριαμβεύειν with the accusative is simply not a normal usage. If the verb here refers to a triumph (as I believe it does), then the spiritual powers are viewed as captives of the triumphant Christ.

3. In Lk. 22.53 Jesus refers to the supernatural forces of evil marshalled against him as ἡ ἐξουσία τοῦ σκότους, while in Acts 26.18 Paul describes the risen Lord as sending him to the Gentiles τοῦ ἐπιστρέψαι ἀπὸ σκότους εἰς φῶς καὶ τῆς ἐξουσίας τοῦ σατανᾶ ἐπὶ τὸν θεόν. The Qumran texts point in much the same direction, for there the expression 'lot' or 'dominion' of darkness is parallel to and interchangeable with that of 'of Belial' (1QS 1.18, 23-24; 2.5, 19; 1QM 1.1, 11; 14.9; 17.5-6). See H. Conzelmann, 'σκότος', p. 432, and R.P. Martin, 'Reconciliation and Forgiveness', p. 107.

2. *The Heavenly Book(s) of Deeds.* Interpretation of the term χειρόγραφον in 2.14 has generated a considerable amount of discussion down through the centuries.[1] A rather ingenious idea has recently been set forth by Wesley Carr, who argues with respect to the background of the term that 'it is difficult to find anything that fits more exactly than the penitential *stelae* of Phrygia and Lydia'.[2] Other scholars interpret the term in its common technical sense as signifying 'a certificate of debt' or 'a bond',[3] though there is disagreement as to the significance underlying the figure—that is, whether it refers to the fact of indebtedness,[4] to the Mosaic law,[5] or, more narrowly, to the requirements of the Colossian errorists.[6] There is, however, another interpretation that has received some attention in recent days and that

---

1. For a survey of the history of interpretation, see E.C. Best, *An Historical Study of the Exegesis of Colossians 2,14* (Rome: Pontificia Universitas Gregoriana, 1956). The view that χειρόγραφον represents a covenant made between Adam and the devil is regarded today as eccentric. See, for example, the comments of Leivested, p. 101; Bruce, *Colossians* (1957), p. 238; Lohse, *Colossians*, p. 108; Schweizer, *Colossians*, p. 148; and Carr, p. 53. Such a view was proposed by some of the Fathers and has been argued by G. Megas, 'Das χειρόγραφον Adams', *ZNW* 27 (1928), pp. 305-20, and Lohmeyer, *Kolosser*, p. 116.

2. Carr, p. 58. Carr lists three objections to this view: (1) that the actual term χειρόγραφον or its related noun is not found on a single *stele* (p. 55); (2) that the earliest example of such an inscription dates from AD 126 (p. 56); and (3) that it is absurd to speak of nailing a stone to the cross (p. 58). Carr's responses to these objections are unconvincing. Cf. Wink, p. 56.

3. So A. Deissmann, *Bible Studies* (trans. A. Grieve; Edinburgh: T. & T. Clark, 1901), p. 247, 'the technical signification bond, certificate of debt. . . is very common in the papyri'. Others who adopt this view are Leivested, p. 101; Bruce, *Colossians* (1957), p. 238; Lohse, *Colossians*, p. 108; C.F.D. Moule, p. 97; Conzelmann, 'Kolosser', p. 144; S. Lyonnet, *Sin, Redemption, and Sacrifice* (Rome: Biblical Institute Press, 1970), pp. 47-48; Yates, 'Christ and the Powers of Evil', p. 464; Schweizer, *Colossians*, p. 148; and BAGD, p. 880.

4. In Jewish thought sin leaves humans greatly indebted to God. See SB, III, p. 628 for references. On this view, it is not the Mosaic law that is abolished, but rather the debt that results from transgressions or a subscription to the ordinances of the law. See J.A.T. Robinson, p. 43; Bruce, *Colossians* (1957), p. 238; C.F.D. Moule, p. 98; Hugedé, pp. 133-36; Lohse, *Colossians*, p. 109; and R.P. Martin, *Colossians*, pp. 83-84.

5. Abbott (p. 255) argues that behind χειρόγραφον stands the Mosaic law, 'which being unfulfilled is analogous to an unpaid "note of hand"'. Others who have adopted this approach are Lightfoot, p. 187; H.C.G. Moule, p. 106; Williams, pp. 97-98; E.F. Scott, p. 46; Houlden, pp. 191-92; and Ridderbos, p. 212.

6. Wengst, 'Versöhnung und Befreiung', p. 21.

we must explore in detail, viz. the view that χειρόγραφον refers to a heavenly book or writing.

This latter interpretation has developed and evolved over time. Its express beginnings are to be found in a 1961 article by Oliva Blanchette,[1] who followed Jean Daniélou in proposing that behind Col. 2.14 lies a Jewish-Christian interpretation parallel to what can be found in the *Odes of Solomon* 23 and the *Gospel of Truth* 19.35–20.25.[2] Blanchette developed and modified Daniélou's insights, however, and identified χειρόγραφον with a 'celestial scroll'. In the context of 2.14, he argued, this scroll 'represents our body and our flesh which he [Christ] took upon himself, and in which our sins were condemned'. So by means of his crucifixion and fulfillment of the law, Christ wiped out the Christian's debt before God. Thus, Blanchette concluded, it is possible 'to arrive at a better understanding of St. Paul's thought' by combining in this way 'the classical exegesis' [i.e. that suggested by Abbott and others] and the Jewish Christian exegesis [i.e. that set forth by Daniélou]'.[3]

Blanchette's approach has received further elaboration in the work of Andrew Bandstra, although Bandstra differs from Blanchette in certain respects.[4] Bandstra differs in his overall approach to 2.14 in that he links the phrase τοῖς δόγμασιν with the following relative clause and identifies the δόγματα as the commandments of the Mosaic law,[5] whereas Blanchette connected these words with τὸ . . . χειρό-γραφον and interpreted them as referring to 'the evangelical dispensation'.[6] With reference to the χειρόγραφον itself, however, Bandstra agrees with Blanchette in understanding it to represent a 'celestial' or 'heavenly' book that is to be identified with our 'body of flesh and sin', though in Bandstra's opinion that heavenly book is presented by accusing spiritual forces and contains a record of humanity's sins. So the removal of this object 'from our midst' is closely related to the victory over τὰς ἀρχὰς καὶ τὰς ἐξουσίας described in v. 15. Bandstra summarizes the impact of this event as follows:

1. O.A. Blanchette, 'Does the Cheirographon of Col. 2,14 Represent Christ Himself?', *CBQ* 23 (1961), pp. 306-12.

2. On this Jewish-Christian exegesis, see R. Yates, 'Colossians and Gnosis', *JSNT* 27 (1986), pp. 59-62.

3. Blanchette, p. 312.

4. *Law and the Elements*, pp. 158-66.

5. Bandstra, pp. 158-68.

6. Blanchette, pp. 310-11.

Christ by taking our chirograph, or body of flesh and sin, and nailing it to the cross, destroyed the law's effect against us and, in so doing, exposed and left empty-handed the satanic accusers.[1]

Such an interpretation for χειρόγραφον in 2.14 has found support in an article by Herold Weiss,[2] a commentary by Ralph Martin,[3] and monographs by Andrew Lincoln and Walter Wink.[4] And, we believe, it has much to commend it. To date, however, it remains a minority viewpoint for two reasons. The first of these applies particularly to the interpretation proposed by Blanchette, who closely identified Christ with the heavenly writing. To quote Wesley Carr, 'the transition of thought from the Heavenly Book to Christ and thence to the abolition of the book is too severe; it makes impossible demands upon the reader'.[5] And Carr is right, though it is important to recognize that the identification of Christ with the heavenly book is not intrinsic to this interpretation of χειρόγραφον in 2.14. The second objection that is often made, however, is more significant, and relates directly to any variation on this view. For Bandstra and others rely heavily on the occurrence of χειρόγραφον in the *Apocalypse of Zephaniah* (where it is transliterated in the Coptic text), yet this evidence must stand up against the numerous places where the term bears the sense 'certificate of debt'.[6]

It is important, however, to note that the relevant passage in the *Apocalypse of Zephaniah* is no mere verbal parallel. Rather, the points of contact between *Apocalypse of Zephaniah* 7 and Col. 2.14-15 are numerous and significant: (1) the transliterated term χειρόγραφον appears a number of times in *Apocalypse of Zephaniah* 7 (vv. 1, 3, 4, 5, 6, 7, 8), and so must be considered important in that passage as it is in Col. 2.14; (2) divine mercy is expressed in *Apocalypse of Zephaniah* 7 through the 'wiping out' of this record of sins (v. 8), in much

---

1. *Law and the Elements*, p. 166.
2. 'The Law in the Epistle to the Colossians', *CBQ* 34 (1972), p. 302. Weiss agrees essentially with the analysis of Bandstra, though he is careful to note that the term δόγματα in 2.14 denotes 'the ascetic practices false teachers were imposing on the Colossian Christians' rather than the Jewish law (p. 304).
3. *Colossians*, p. 81.
4. *Paradise*, pp. 113-14, and Wink (p. 56), who combines this view with the interpretation of χειρόγραφον as an I.O.U. promissory note.
5. Carr, p. 54.
6. MM (p. 687) point out that the word is 'very common' in the papyri in this sense.

the same way that the χειρόγραφον is 'wiped out' (ἐξαλείψας) in Col. 2.14;[1] and (3) the 'wiping out' of the 'manuscript' leads in *Apocalypse of Zephaniah* 7, as in Col. 2.14-15, to the language of triumph with respect to the angelic figure who wielded the document:

> Then I arose and stood, and I saw a great angel before me saying to me, ' Triumph, prevail because you have prevailed and have triumphed over the accuser, and you have come up from Hades and the abyss. You will now cross over the crossing place' (v. 9).

Furthermore, (4) in spite of the break in the manuscript in the middle of *Apocalypse of Zephaniah* 7.11, it is evident that the mercy and forgiveness that was extended through the 'wiping out' of the 'manuscript', as well as the 'triumph' over the accuser that was closely associated with it, result in the seer's 'crossing over' into the realm of the 'righteous ones', both angelic (8.2-9.3) and human (9.4-5). So if we are correct in arguing that Col. 1.12-14 and 2.13-15 must be interpreted together, then this parallel from the *Apocalypse of Zephaniah* is significant for them both.

My interpretation of χειρόγραφον in 2.14 against the referential background of an apocalyptic judgment scene leads naturally to the question of the interpretation of τοῖς δόγμασιν in the same verse. Admittedly this is a difficult problem for the view espoused above, just as it is on any scheme of interpretation. It is, in fact, impossible to

---

1. We do not, of course, have the Greek text of the *Apocalypse of Zephaniah*, and the verb is not transliterated as in the case of the noun χειρόγραφον. So we cannot be entirely sure we have an exact verbal parallel, though this may be suggested by the fact that the same root is used in the Coptic version of the NT and in the *Apocalypse of Zephaniah*. At the very least, the Greek verbs were similar in meaning. Ἐξαλείφειν is widely used in at least three related senses. One of these is the occurrence of the verb in Num. 5.23 to refer to the literal washing or 'wiping away' of writing from a scroll. Another use is the reference to the 'wiping out' or 'blotting out' of sins or transgressions in Ps. 50[51].1, 9; Ps. 108[109].14; Isa. 43.25; Jer. 18.23; 2 Macc. 12.42. Such an action is often mentioned in connection with a reference to divine judgment. And while there is no obvious reference to a book in these texts, such a notion may be implicit in any or all of these passages. Finally, this verb is used to indicate the 'wiping out' of a name or names from 'the book of life' (Exod. 32.32-33; Ps. 68[69].28; cf. *1 En.* 108.3, though we lack the Greek text for this section) or 'the book of the discipline of mankind' (*Jub.* 36.10-11, without Greek text). The last group of parallels are especially important in view of the complex traditio-historical relationship between the 'book of life' and the 'book of sins', cf. Rau, pp. 332-36.

speak with certainty on the issue.[1] Nevertheless, we offer here several suggestions consistent with our overall approach to the passage as a whole.

With regard to syntax, it is probable that τοῖς δόγμασιν is to be taken with the preceding clause rather than the clause that follows. As Moule points out, to read τοῖς δόγμασιν with the clause that follows, as do Percy, Bandstra and Lohse,[2] simply commits 'too much violence to word order'.[3] Nevertheless, the meaning of the term δόγμα and the force of the dative, two concerns that are clearly interrelated, are problems we must address with caution.

A possible understanding of 2.14 that has been neglected by commentators, but one that makes good sense in light of an apocalyptic background, is based on the fact that the term δόγμα signifies in the LXX, the papyri, and the NT a decision imposed, which may include a judgment or decision as well as a command.[4] The former sense is evident in several passages in the Jewish apocalypses where it refers specifically to decrees of judgment, especially as they have been set forth by angelic figures (cf. *1 En.* 100.10; *Jub.* 39.6, though without the Greek text for these lines). In the Jewish apocalypses, such judg-

---

1. As Bruce (*Colossians* [1957], p. 237) says, 'the difficulties of construction and interpretation make it advisable to treat every reasonable suggestion with respect'.

2. Percy, p. 88; Bandstra, *Law and the Elements*, p. 158; Lohse, *Colossians*, p. 109.

3. *Idiom Book*, p. 45; cf. Abbott, p. 255. Percy (p. 88) produces numerous parallels in support of his view, including Jn 4.18; Acts 5.35; 19.4; Rom. 11.2, 31; 1 Cor. 14.9, 12; 15.36; 2 Cor. 2.4; 12.7; Col. 4.16. Concerning these Percy writes, 'besonders bei Paulus ist somit ein solche proleptische Stellung eines Ausdrucks vor dem Satze, zu dem er gehort, ein beliebtes Mittel, dem betreffenden Wort Nachdruck zu verleihen'. The problem, however, is that none of these parallels really applies to Col. 2.14.

4. See H.H. Esser, 'δόγμα', *NIDNTT*, I, pp. 330-31; also R. Kittel, 'δόγμα, δογματίζω', *TDNT*, II, pp. 230-31 for examples. On the papyri, see MM, p. 166. The term can also refer to a 'doctrine' or 'dogma' (see BAGD, p. 201, though Carr [p. 57] correctly points out that there is 'no evidence in the New Testament for such a sense for δόγμα), and it is on this basis that Blanchette and R. Kittel, following some of the Greek fathers and St Jerome, understand the word to refer to the 'evangelical ordinances'; see Blanchette, p. 310, and R. Kittel, 'δοκέω, κτλ.', *TDNT*, II, p. 231 (who also puts forth another possible meaning). Apart from these writers, however, this rendering has been rejected almost universally in modern times since there is a lack of NT lexical evidence and it is inappropriate contextually. Much the same can be said of the suggestion by Carr (p. 57) that δόγμασιν refers to 'personal decisions'.

ments were pronounced on the basis of one's obedience or disobedience as recorded in the heavenly book(s). So when applied to Col. 2.14, the text would read: 'wiping out the record of deeds that was against us (together) with the decrees', viz. the decrees of judgment set out on the basis of the content of the heavenly book(s). This rendering makes excellent sense contextually, for ὅ ἦν ὑπεναντίον ἡμῖν is no longer redundant[1] and the κρινέτω of v. 16 follows naturally—though, admittedly, on this view the connection with δογματίζεσθε of v. 20 is less immediate than would be the case if δόγμασιν referred to the regulations of the Colossian errorists.

An alternative approach, however, also merits consideration, namely that δόγμα refers to the regulations of the errorists at Colossae that find their basis in the Jewish law.[2] In this case τοῖς δόγμασιν is to be interpreted as a dative of reference, which leads to the translation 'wiping out the record of sins (or transgressions) with respect to the decrees'. Clearly, on such a view the decrees stand at the root of the condemnation and judgment, and it is violations of these regulations that are recorded in the heavenly book(s).

Both of these latter two interpretations are consistent with viewing 2.14-15 against the background of an apocalyptic judgment scene. And both work syntactically, whether or not we place a full stop before the

1. This interpretation also eliminates the need to force the interpretation of καθ' ἡμῶν so that it differs substantially in meaning from these words. For an example of this kind of interpretation, see Robinson (p. 43), who translates wiping out 'our *subscription to* the ordinances', which stood 'in our name [καθ' ἡμῶν]'; cf. *Idiom Book*, p. 45. Yet apart from its use in swearing and oaths in hellenistic Greek, the preposition κατά with the genitive simply does not occur with this sense in the NT or elsewhere, as far as I know; see Bruce, *Colossians* (1957), p. 237, and Carr, p. 54.

2. Along these lines, many interpreters argue that δόγμα refers here specifically to the commands of the Mosaic law (so R. Kittel, p. 231, as well as Abbott, p. 255; E.F. Scott, p. 46; Käsemann, p. 163; Bandstra, *Law and Elements*, p. 161; Houlden, pp. 191-92; Lohse, *Colossians*, p. 109; and BAGD, p. 201), while some mention natural law and religious customs as well (Lightfoot, p. 187; H.C.G. Moule, p. 106; and Williams, p. 97) and others define the ordinances as those which were imposed by the Colossian errorists. Conzelmann ('Kolosser', p. 144) stresses that the term applies both to the Mosaic law and the 'Heilsanweisungen' of the Gnostics; cf. also R.P. Martin, *Colossians*, pp. 84-85. Schweizer (*Colossians*, p. 116), on the other hand, understands δόγμασιν to refer to Pythagorean rules, which the errorists were putting on the same level as the commands of the OT. For the term 'decree' as indicative of the requirements of Jewish apocalypticism, see *Jub.* 49.8, 17.

words ὃ ἦν ὑπεναντίον ἡμῖν.[1] It is impossible to be dogmatic as to which is to be preferred. Yet the basic thrust of the verses is clear, particularly when interpreted in terms of the features of the judgment scenes of Jewish apocalypticism. In fact, it is our thesis that such a background accords well with the lexical and syntactical characteristics of this passage.

3. *The Post-Mortem Judgment, Which Includes Both the Good and the Evil.* Though I have already touched on certain matters that relate to the post-mortem judgment, it is important here to consider the statements of 2.15b-c in greater detail. Verse 15 does not contain a description of this event as we find it described in several of the Jewish apocalypses. Rather, Paul simply states the fact of judgment against the referential background of the eschatological judgment scene. Nevertheless, v. 15 contains certain images that parallel closely those found in the judgment scenes of Jewish apocalyptic writings, particularly those of the *Apocalypse of Zephaniah*.

Immediately following his statement regarding the disarming of the powers in v. 15a, Paul says: ἐδειγμάτισεν ἐν παρρησίᾳ, θριαμβεύσας αὐτοὺς ἐν αὐτῷ. The verb ἐδειγμάτισεν is generally rendered 'to make public' or 'to bring to public notice', and refers especially to 'that which seeks concealment, so that it almost has the sense of "to expose"'.[2] Yet some writers prefer a more pejorative sense in this verse, 'to expose to shame or ridicule'.[3] Apart from the broader context, either meaning is possible.[4]

---

1. Several interpreters place a full stop after τοῖς δόγμασιν, which leads one to render the relative ὅ as 'that which' and the following καί as ascensive; so Lohmeyer, pp. 101, 117-18, followed by R.P. Martin, 'Reconciliation and Forgiveness', p. 120. The main advantage of this punctuation is that it avoids overloading v. 14a unnecessarily. For parallels to this use of the relative pronoun, see Rom. 6.10, 1 Cor. 7.36 and Gal. 2.20, as well as Mt. 13.12, Mk 6.16 and Jn 6.14; cf. BAGD, p. 584, and BDF, §294 (5). See, however, the criticism of Wengst, p. 190.

2. Cf. Schlier, 'δείκνυμι', p. 31.

3. So Gnilka, p. 142.

4. *Contra* Egan (p. 53), who says concerning the latter rendering, 'This is a meaning which the compound παραδειγματίζω definitely has, but which is not really attested for δειγματίζω itself'. While this statement is true in general, one must reckon with the fact that δειγματίζω may bear the pejorative sense in Mt. 1.19 (though the compound verb is a fairly well attested variant), and that the noun δειγματίσμος appears in the papyri with the meaning 'public disgrace'; cf. BAGD, p. 172.

Closely related to this question is how we understand the participle θριαμβεύσας and its function with respect to τὰς ἀρχὰς καὶ τὰς ἐξουσίας. The interpretation of the verb to refer to a Roman triumph has held pride of place for many years, and is still accepted by most commentators. On this view, when the verb is followed by an accusative object (as in v. 15) it refers to the celebration of a military victory by driving the captives (designated by the accusative) before the victor's triumphal chariot.[1] Yet evidence from the papyri, Tatian's *Adversus Graecos*, and *Acta Pauli et Theclae* has led to the documentation of another plausible area of meaning, namely 'to manifest, reveal or make known'.[2] Egan, who interprets θριαμβεύσας in this manner in v. 15, translates the verse as follows, 'Uncovering the principalities, He (i.e. God) displayed them openly, making them known in Him (i.e. Christ)'. According to Egan, this approach has at least two major advantages over the traditional interpretation: (1) it 'goes a long way towards explaining. . . the use of the middle voice in ἀπεκδυσάμενος', and (2) it avoids attributing to the powers, who are said to have been created in Christ (1.15-16) and to have him as their head (2.10), a character that is hostile.[3]

Without the aid of additional data, we lack a firm basis for choosing between these interpretive options; hence we cannot determine with confidence on a merely lexical or syntactical basis the exact meaning of 2.15b-c. Fortunately, however, it is at this point that the close relationship of this text to 1.12-14 is suggestive. For in our analysis of 1.12-14, we argued that it was through the forgiveness of sins that believers experienced redemption and were transferred from the sphere of the authority of the powers of darkness. So, it may reasonably be argued, in 2.13-15 it is through the blessing of forgiveness (i.e. the wiping out of the χειρόγραφον), based on the death of Christ, that the powers are 'disarmed'. The clauses in 2.15b-c simply elaborate further the impact of this event with respect to the spiritual forces. Consistent with such an interpretation is the rendering of

1. See esp. Williamson, pp. 317-32; also Delling, 'θριαμβεύω', pp. 159-60, and BAGD, p. 363, as well as most commentators.
2. For evidence from the papyri, see MM, p. 293, and, more generally, Egan, pp. 41-43. Williamson (p. 327) found such a rendering attractive, but was unaware of the relatively early evidence for it.
3. Egan, p. 55. While the first advantage is difficult to understand, since Egan's rendering gives an active force to the middle participle, the second is more substantial.

ἐδειγμάτισεν as meaning that the powers are 'exposed', especially in their weak and powerless condition. Also consistent is the traditional interpretation of θριαμβεύσας as signifying the image of a Roman triumph. Thus the power of these forces has been broken—they no longer stand in their accusing function vis-à-vis believers in Christ.

It is obvious that this interpretation of Col. 1.12-14 and 2.13-15 leads to a negative portrayal of the powers mentioned in 2.15. Of course, these spiritual powers were hardly represented in this way by the Colossian errorists. This is rather Paul's interpretation of what they proposed. In the view of the errorists, the angelic witnesses were servants of God responsible to record the deeds of humans and to hold them accountable at the last judgment. But in Paul's mind a new era had dawned in the history of salvation with the death and resurrection of Christ. And with this new era came a new requirement for salvation. Christians are now qualified to enjoy all the blessings of heaven, not on the basis of legal observances or ascetic experiences, but simply because they are 'in Christ'. So when the powers accuse the Christians at Colossae and pronounce judgment on those who do not participate in ascetic-mystical practices or legal observances, they are acting in opposition to the decree of God himself. In the most basic sense, they are acting as 'the powers of darkness'. According to Paul, they have been disarmed, exposed and displayed openly in all their weakness and humiliation.[1]

A description of the post-mortem judgment scene, as we have said, is not given in 2.14-15, as it is in certain Jewish apocalypses. Nevertheless, references to the wiping out of the book of sins and the resultant triumph over the accuser suggest that Paul wrote against the referential background of just such an event—though, of course, he reinterpreted it by reference to the death of Christ. Such an experience of triumph at the eschatological judgment leads naturally to the resulting state or condition, namely the consequences of judgment.

4. *The Consequences of Judgment*. The consequences of judgment are not mentioned in 2.13-15. Nevertheless, it is at this point that the connection between this text and 1.12-14 is helpful once again. As we mentioned earlier in our discussion of 1.12-14, the consequence of

---

1. Paul thus makes use of the ambiguous nature of the שטן and the angelic witnesses in the OT and the Jewish apocalypses to turn his opponents' position on its head. See above, Chapter 3, §3.a.

judgment for Christians is summed up in v. 12: they are qualified to participate in τὴν μερίδα τοῦ κλήρου τῶν ἁγίων ἐν τῷ φωτί. So Paul's stress is on the vindication of the righteous rather than the condemnation of the wicked. This emphasis is in accord with the purpose of the argument, since Paul's design is not to call on the disobedient, by threat of judgment, to take up the commands of the law. Rather, he admonishes those who are 'in Christ' to hold to their heavenly blessings apart from any regulations that might be deemed necessary by others, whether in the congregation or without.

Conclusion

One facet of Paul's response to the error at Colossae was to highlight the redemptive blessings that believers have 'in Christ'. As a part of this tactic, he wrote against the referential background of the eschatological judgment scene present in several Jewish apocalypses. Condemnation of believers on the basis of the regulations of the errorists is, and should be, ineffective, since the basis for accusation at the last judgment (the record of their transgressions) has been removed.[1] Consequently, believers have nothing to fear from the accusing spiritual powers. Their future experience of the blessings of heaven is assured simply because they are 'in Christ'. Thus the polemic of 2.16-23 rests on a firm soteriological basis as elaborated in 2.9-15—a soteriological basis that was stated briefly in 1.12-14 and then unpacked in more detail in 2.13-15. And this polemic responds to terms and ideas used by the Colossian errorists in its imagery drawn from Jewish apocalypticism.

---

1. Paul thus utilizes imagery drawn from Jewish apocalypticism, but he turns it on its head. Instead of using the angelic witness(es) and the heavenly book(s) to move his audience toward faithful adherence to legal requirements, he uses these images to stress the freedom that belongs to those who are 'in Christ', thus encouraging the Christians at Colossae to continue to walk 'in him', apart from the regulations of the errorists.

CONCLUSION

1. *Situation and Response in Colossians*

My investigation of the ascetic-mystical piety of Jewish apocalypticism has yielded results that are significant for understanding both the problem at Colossae and Paul's response. The direct descriptions in the polemic of 2.16-23 suggest that the error corresponds to the practices associated with the reception of revelation in the Jewish apocalypses, as well as to the media of revelation, the content of revelation, and the functions of revelation described in these writings. Indeed, there appears to be a correspondence between the two religious systems, not only in certain particulars, but in their beliefs and practices as a whole.

This interpretation of the data found further support in Paul's admonitions in 2.1-5 and 2.9-15. For in 2.1-5 he undermines the errorists' insistence on the need for visionary ascent into the heavenly realm in order to gain insights into the heavenly mysteries. It is 'in Christ', Paul argues, that 'all the treasures of wisdom and knowledge' are hidden; and since believers at Colossae are 'in him', they can know 'the full riches of complete understanding' apart from ascetic-mystical practices and experiences.

Likewise in 2.9-15 Paul emphasizes the 'fullness' that belongs to these Christians. His 'catalogue of blessings' climaxes in vv. 13-15, where he celebrates Christ's victory over the accuser and his forces. Since the Colossian Christians' eschatological record of sins is wiped out and done away with, the apocalyptists' admonitions to obedience have lost their basis and power. The Colossians need not fear their threats of judgment or their warnings that those who differ in their practices will be 'disqualified' from salvific blessings. Rather, they must continue in their faith, 'established and firm, not moved from the hope held out in the gospel'. There is certainly room for growth in wisdom and obedience in the Christian life. Yet Christians' eschatological salvation is secure because they have been qualified 'to share in the inheritance of the saints in the kingdom of light'.

The direct descriptions of the practices of the Colossian errorists and the supporting expositional passages in the Colossian letter are mutually reinforcing: both point to Jewish apocalypticism as the religious movement most relevant for the study of Colossians. So we may describe the Colossian error as a type of Jewish/Gentile Christianity that was strongly oriented toward the ascetic-mystical piety of Jewish apocalypticism.[1] Still, there is much that we do not know about the situation at Colossae. Were the errorists themselves Jews or Jewish Christians? Or were they, like the majority of the Christians at Colossae, Gentiles who had been proselytized by Jews or Jewish Christians? What was their point of contact with the church at Colossae? Were other congregations in danger from their influence, as may be suggested by Col. 4.16? These and other questions must remain unanswered, simply because of the paucity and nature of the evidence.

2. *Implications for the Study of Colossians*

Significant as well are the implications of this analysis for understanding the eschatology of the Colossian letter. Many argue that there is here a fundamental difference in perspective between the undisputed letters of Paul and Colossians.[2] These writers find little emphasis in Colossians on the temporal dimension (i.e. the contrast between 'now' and 'then'). Rather, the important dimension is spatial, and the vertical axis (i.e. 'above' and 'below') is stressed throughout. References such as 3.4 ('When Christ, who is your life, appears, then you also will appear with him in glory') and 3.24 ('knowing that you will receive an inheritance from the Lord as a reward') demonstrate that the expectation of a future parousia has not receded altogether. Yet these do not express the essential viewpoint of the author, it is argued, since they are stereotyped expressions and occur within the paraenesis. The overriding emphasis in the letter is on the 'now' as opposed to the 'not

---

1. See R. Brown, 'Not Jewish Christianity and Gentile Christianity but Types of Jewish/Gentile Christianity', *CBQ* 45 (1983), pp. 74-79. Our study points to the existence of another type of Jewish/Gentile Christianity in addition to those categorized by Brown.

2. E.g. Bornkamm, 'Hoffnung', pp. 56-64; E. Lohse, 'Pauline Theology', pp. 216-17.

yet', and the fundamental perspective throughout is one of 'realized eschatology'.

There is much that is true in this kind of interpretation of Colossians, for there is certainly in the letter a shift in perspective vis-à-vis the undisputed letters. In Rom. 6.8, for example, the Christian is said to have died with Christ in the present, yet his resurrection remains a future hope ('Now if we died with Christ, we believe that we will also live with him'). And this stands in contrast to the perspective of Col. 2.12, 'In baptism you were buried with him and raised with him through your faith in the power of God, who raised him from the dead' (cf. 2.13; 3.1).[1] Such an emphasis on blessings already received is also found at several other points in the letter—e.g. God 'has qualified' the Colossians 'to share in the inheritance of the saints in the kingdom of light' (1.12); he 'has rescued' them from the dominion of darkness and brought them into the kingdom of the Son he loves (1.13); 'in Christ' they are also circumcised, in the putting off of their sinful nature (2.11); and in blotting out the record of their sins, Christ has already triumphed over the powers and authorities (2.14-15). All these blessings belong to the Colossian believers now because of their position 'in Christ'.

Still, two caveats are necessary in order to represent more adequately the eschatology of the Colossian letter. First, the contrast between the eschatology of Colossians and that of the undisputed letters appears to have been exaggerated. Several writers have argued this point already. On the one hand, these writers stress that the 'now' plays a much more significant role in several undisputed letters of Paul than many have been prepared to acknowledge. They point out, for example, that Rom. 6.8 is closely related, in the course of Paul's argument, to Rom. 6.11 ('In the same way, count yourselves dead to sin but alive to God in Christ Jesus'; cf. Rom. 8.10).[2] And this is clearly an admonition for the present, not the eschatological future. On the other hand, the 'not yet' appears several times in Colossians and its significance should not be minimized. There is simply no reason to believe that Paul would have taken over traditional eschatological formulae if they did not authentically reflect his own thoughts.[3]

---

1. See, e.g., Merklein, pp. 42-43, with extensive bibliographical notes.
2. Lincoln, pp. 131-32; also G.F. Wessels, 'The Eschatology of Colossians and Ephesians', *Neot* 21 (1987), pp. 186-87.
3. Wessels, pp. 197-99.

And so 3.4, 24 are important as well for understanding the teaching of the Colossian letter.

Indeed, as my analysis suggests, the horizontal dimension plays a much greater role in Colossians than is usually acknowledged. If I am correct in my interpretation of 1.22 and 1.28 as well as 1.12-14 and 2.13-15, then the eschatological judgment is a central issue in this letter. For the goal of Paul's ministry, toward which he struggles (1.29) and suffers (1.24), is to present everyone perfect (τέλειος) in Christ (1.28), i.e. 'holy', 'without blemish', and 'free from accusation' at the last judgment (1.22). And this will take place only as they continue to live 'in Christ', 'rooted and built up in him' and 'strengthened in the faith' as they were taught by their earliest preachers and teachers. For it is only 'in Christ' that believers participate in his victory over the powers and authorities and share in the eschatological forgiveness he has secured.

A second caveat is that the emphasis on blessings already obtained in several important passages of Colossians undoubtedly resulted from Paul's attempt to combat the perspective of the errorists. Here we must again recall the perspective of the Jewish apocalypses. For in these writings 'the things above' are hidden, but those who have obtained wisdom understand that the glory and the righteousness and the blessings of the heavenly realms will be revealed at the eschaton. There is thus a correspondence between 'the things above' and 'the things to come'. Yet it is only 'the wise'—those who understand the revelation and act on it through obedience to the standards that are revealed—who can expect to enjoy this blessedness at its revelation.

In order to combat this perspective Paul uses his typical method of 'outclassing his opponents on their own ground'.[1] The Colossians need not pursue the ascetic practices and legal observances advocated by the errorists (the revealed standards) because they have *already* been rescued 'from the dominion of darkness' and brought 'into the kingdom of the Son he loves', and so are 'qualified' to share in 'the inheritance of the saints in the kingdom of light' (1.12; i.e. 'the things above'). Hence the emphasis on realized eschatology in these passages. Yet the explanation of these statements in 2.13-15 focuses on the impact Christ's death and victory over the accusing powers will have at the eschatological judgment. Christians at Colossae have been qualified to receive their inheritance through faith in Christ, and this blessed state

---

1. H. Chadwick, 'All Things to All Men', *NTS* 1 (1955), p. 272.

exists even now in the heavenly realms. Yet they must wait to receive their inheritance at the revelation of their glory, when their participation in Christ's victory over the powers is realized.

This implied relation between participation in the blessedness of the heavenly realm and the blissful life of the age to come is thoroughly in accord with the thinking of the Jewish apocalyptists.[1] Still, there is a fundamental difference in the revealed standard for salvation. In Colossians it is faith in Christ, and not ascetic practices or legal observances, that guarantees the reception of mercy at the last judgment. Because the book of sins has been 'wiped out' through Christ's victory, and Christians now share in this victory through faith in Christ, they can look forward with anticipation to enjoying the fullness of God's eschatological salvation when Christ appears in glory.

---

1. On the 'heavenly dimension' in Paul as consistent with the perspective of Jewish apocalyptic, see Lincoln, *Paradise*, pp. 169-85. *Contra* Merklein, pp. 43-44.

BIBLIOGRAPHY

Abbott, T.K. *A Critical and Exegetical Commentary on the Epistles to the Ephesians and to the Colossians.* Edinburgh: T. & T. Clark, 1897.

Alexander, P. '3 (Hebrew Apocalypse of) Enoch.' In *OTP*, 1.223-315.

—'Comparing Merkavah Mysticism and Gnosticism: An Essay in Method.' *JJS* 35 (1984), 1-18.

Andersen, F.I. '2 (Slavonic Apocalypse of) Enoch.' In *OTP*, 1.91-221.

Arbesmann, P.R. 'Fasting and Prophecy in Pagan and Christian Antiquity.' *Trad* 7 (1949–51), 1-71.

Arbesmann, R. *Das Fasten bei den Griechen und Römern.* Berlin: Töpelmann, 1929.

Argall, R.A. 'The Source of a Religious Error in Colossae.' *CTJ* 22 (1987), 6-20.

Arnold, C.E. 'The "Exorcism" of Ephesians 6.12 in Recent Research.' *JSNT* 30 (1987), 71-87.

Aune, D. *Prophecy in Early Christianity and the Ancient Mediterranean World.* Grand Rapids: Eerdmans, 1983.

Baird, W. 'Visions, Revelation, and Ministry: Reflections on 2 Cor 12:1-5 and Gal 1:11-17.' *JBL* 104 (1985), 651-62.

Bandstra, A.J. *The Law and the Elements of the World.* Kampen: Kok, 1964.

—'Did the Colossian Errorists Need a Mediator?' In *New Dimensions in New Testament Study*, pp. 329-43. Edited by R.N. Longenecker and M.C. Tenney. Grand Rapids: Zondervan, 1974.

Barclay, J.M.G. 'Mirror-Reading a Polemical Letter: Galatians as a Test Case.' *JSNT* 31 (1987), 73-93.

Barrett, C.K. *From First Adam to Last.* London: Black, 1962.

Bauckham, R.J. 'Colossians 1:24 Again: The Apocalyptic Motif.' *EQ* 47 (1975), 168-170.

—'The Rise of Apocalyptic.' *Themelios* 3 (1978), 10-23.

—'The Apocalypses in the New Pseudepigrapha.' *JSNT* 26 (1986), 97-117.

Baumgarten, J.M. 'The Calendar in the Book of Jubilees and the Bible.' In *Studies in Qumran Law*, pp. 101-14. Edited by J.M. Baumgarten. Leiden: Brill, 1977.

Beale, G.K. *The Use of Daniel in Jewish Apocalyptic Literature and in the Revelation of St. John.* Lanham, MD: University Press of America, 1984.

Beare, F.W. 'The Epistle to the Colossians.' In *The Interpreter's Bible*, 11.131-241. Edited by G.A. Buttrick. New York and Nashville: Abingdon, 1955.

Beasley-Murray, G.R. *The Book of Revelation.* Grand Rapids: Eerdmans, 1981.

Beasley-Murray, P. 'Colossians 1:15-20: An Early Christian Hymn Celebrating the Lordship of Christ.' In *Pauline Studies*, pp. 169-83. Edited by D.A. Hagner and M.J. Harris. Exeter: Paternoster, 1980.

Becker, J. *Untersuchungen zur Entstehungsgeschichte der Testamente der Zwölf Patriarchen.* Leiden: Brill, 1970.

Beckwith, R.T. 'The Earliest Enoch Literature and its Calendar: Marks of their Origin, Date and Motivation.' *RevQ* 10 (1981), 365-403.

Beer, G. 'Das Buch Henoch.' In *APAT*, 2.217-310.

Behm, J. 'νῆστις, κτλ.' *TDNT* 4.924-35.

Belleville, L. ' "Under Law": Structural Analysis and the Pauline Concept of Law in Galatians 3.21–4.11.' *JSNT* 26 (1986), 53-78.

Benoit, P. 'Rapports littéraires entre les épîtres aux Colossiens et aux Ephésiens.' In *Neutestamentliche Aufsätze. Festschrift für Prof. Josef Schmid*, pp. 11-22. Edited by J. Blinzler, O. Kuss and F. Mussner. Regensburg: Friedrich Pustet, 1963.

—'Qumran and the New Testament.' In *Paul and Qumran*, pp. 1-30. Edited by J. Murphy-O'Connor. Chicago: Priory, 1968.

—'L'hymne christologique de Col I,15-20.' In *Christianity, Judaism and Other Greco-Roman Cults. Studies for Morton Smith*, pp. 226-63. Edited by J. Neusner. Leiden: Brill, 1975.

—' "Ἅγιοι en Colossiens 1.12: hommes ou anges?' In *Paul and Paulinism*, pp. 83-99. Edited by M.D. Hooker and S.G. Wilson. London: SPCK, 1982.

—'Colossiens 2:2-3.' In *The New Testament Age: Essays in Honor of Bo Reicke*, 1.41-51. Edited by W.C. Weinrich. Macon, GA: Mercer University Press, 1984.

—'The "πλήρωμα" in the Epistles to the Colossians and the Ephesians.' *SEÅ* 49 (1984), 136-58.

Berger, K. 'Das Buch der Jubiläen.' In *JSHRZ* 2.3, pp. 275-575.

Best, E. *One Body in Christ*. London: SPCK, 1955.

Best, E.C. *An Historical Study of the Exegesis of Colossians 2,14*. Rome: Pontificia Universitas Gregoriana, 1956.

Betz, H.D. 'On the Problem of the Religio-Historical Understanding of Apocalypticism.' *JTC* 6 (1969), 134-56.

—*Der Apostel Paulus und die sokratische Tradition*. Tübingen: Mohr, 1972.

—*Galatians*. Philadelphia: Fortress Press, 1979.

Bietenhard, H. *Die himmlische Welt im Urchristentum und Spätjudentum*. Tübingen: Mohr, 1951.

Bjerkelund, C.J. *Parakalô: Form, Funktion und Sinn der parakalô-Sätze in den paulinischen Briefen*. Oslo: Universitetsforlaget, 1967.

Black, M. 'The Tradition of Hasidaean-Essene Asceticism: Its Origins and Influence.' In *Aspects du Judéo-Christianisme. Colloque de Strasbourg*, pp. 19-33. Paris: Presses Universitaires de France, 1965.

—(ed.) *Apocalypsis Henochi Graece*. Leiden: Brill, 1970.

—*The Book of Enoch or I Enoch*. Leiden: Brill, 1985.

Blanchette, O.A. 'Does the Cheirographon of Col. 2,14 Represent Christ Himself?' *CBQ* 23 (1961), 306-12.

Blinzler, J. 'Lexikalisches zu dem Terminus τὰ στοιχεῖα τοῦ κόσμου bei Paulus.' In *Studiorum Paulorum Congressus 1961*, 2.429-43. Rome: Pontifical Biblical Institute, 1964.

Bücher, O. *Christus Exorcista: Dämonismus und Taufe im Neuen Testament*. Stuttgart: Kohlhammer, 1972.

Bogaert, P. *Apocalypse de Baruch, introduction, traduction du syriaque et commentaire*. 2 volumes. Paris: Editions du Cerf, 1969.

Bonwetsch, G.N. *Die Apokalypse Abrahams. Das Testament der vierzig Märtyrer*. Leipzig, 1897; reprint edn, Aalen: Scientia, 1972.

—*Die Bücher der Geheimnisse Henochs: Das sogenannte slavische Henochbuch.* Leipzig: Hinrichs, 1922.

Bornkamm, G. 'Die Hoffnung im Kolosserbriefe—zugleich ein Beitrag zur Frage der Echtheit des Briefes.' In *Studien zum Neuen Testament und zur Patristik. Festschrift für Erich Klostermann*, pp. 56-64. Edited by the Kommission für spätantike Religionsgeschichte. Berlin: Akademie-Verlag, 1961.

—'Das Bekenntnis im Hebräerbrief.' In his *Studien zu Antike und Urchristentum*, pp. 188-203. Munchen: Chr. Kaiser Verlag, 1963.

—'μυστήριον, μυέω.' *TDNT* 4.802-28.

—'The Heresy of Colossians.' In *Conflict at Colossae*, pp. 123-45. Edited by F.O. Francis and W.A. Meeks. Missoula, MT: Scholars Press, 1975.

Bousset, W. 'Die Himmelsreise der Seele.' *ARW* 4 (1901), 136-69, 229-73.

—*Die Offenbarung Johannis.* 6th edition. Göttingen: Vandenhoeck & Ruprecht, 1906.

Bousset, W. and Gressmann, H. *Die Religion des Judentums im späthellenistischen Zeitalter*, 4th edn, Tübingen: Mohr, 1966.

Bowers, W.P. 'A Note on Colossians 1:27a.' In *Current Issues in Biblical and Patristic Interpretation. Studies in Honor of Merrill C. Tenney*, pp. 110-14. Edited by G. Hawthorne. Grand Rapids: Eerdmans, 1975.

Bowker, J.W. ' "Merkabah" Visions and the Visions of Paul.' *JSS* 16 (1971), 157-73.

Box, G.H. 'IV Ezra.' In *APOT*, 2.542-624.

—*The Apocalypse of Ezra.* London: SPCK, 1917.

—*The Testament of Abraham.* Translated from the Greek text with introduction and notes. London: SPCK, 1927.

Box, G.H., and J.I. Landsman. *The Apocalypse of Abraham.* London: SPCK, 1918.

Brandenburger, E. *Adam und Christus: Exegetisch-religionsgeschichtliche Untersuchung zu Röm. 5.12-21.* Neukirchen: Neukirchener Verlag, 1962.

—*Die Verborgenheit Gottes im Weltgeschehen.* Zürich: Theologischer Verlag, 1981.

Braun, H. *Qumran und das Neue Testament.* Band 1. Tübingen: Mohr, 1966.

Breech, E. 'These Fragments I Have Shored Against my Ruins: the Form and Function of 4 Ezra.' *JBL* 92 (1973), 267-74.

Brinsmead, B.H. *Galatians—Dialogical Response to Opponents.* Chico, CA: Scholars Press, 1982.

Brooks, J.A., and C.L. Winbery. *Syntax of New Testament Greek.* Washington, DC: University Press of America, 1979.

Brown, R.E. *The Semitic Background of the Term 'Mystery' in the New Testament.* Philadelphia: Fortress Press, 1968.

—'Not Jewish Christianity and Gentile Christianity but Types of Jewish/Gentile Christianity.' *CBQ* 45 (1983), 74-79.

Bruce, F.F. *Paul: Apostle of the Heart Set Free.* Grand Rapids: Eerdmans, 1977.

—*The Epistles to the Colossians, to Philemon, and to the Ephesians.* Grand Rapids: Eerdmans, 1984.

—'Christ as Conqueror and Reconciler.' *BibSac* 141 (1984), 291-302.

Bruce, F.F., with E.K. Simpson. *Commentary on the Epistles to the Ephesians and Colossians.* Grand Rapids: Eerdmans, 1957.

Buck, C.H., and G. Taylor. *St. Paul: A Study of the Development of his Thought.* New York: Scribner's, 1969.

Bujard, W. *Stilanalytische Untersuchungen zum Kolosserbrief als Beitrag zur Methodik von Sprachvergleichen.* Göttingen: Vandenhoeck & Ruprecht, 1973.

Bultmann, R. *Theology of the New Testament.* 2 volumes. Translated by K. Grobel. New York: Scribner's, 1951.

—*Exegetica: Aufsätze zur Erforschung des Neuen Testaments.* Tübingen: Mohr, 1967.

Burger, C. *Schöpfung und Versöhnung.* Neukirchen-Vluyn: Neukirchener Verlag, 1975.

Burkitt, F.C. *Jewish and Christian Apocalypses.* London: Oxford University Press, 1914.

Burney, C.F. 'Christ as the ΑΡΧΗ of Creation (Prov. viii 22, Col. i 15-18, Rev. iii 14).' *JTS* 27 (1926), 160-77.

Burton, E.D. *A Critical and Exegetical Commentary on the Epistle to the Galatians.* Edinburgh: T. & T. Clark, 1921.

Caird, G.B. *Paul's Letters from Prison.* Oxford: Oxford University Press, 1976.

—*The Language and Imagery of the Bible.* Philadelphia: Westminster Press, 1980.

Cannon, G.E. *The Use of Traditional Materials in Colossians.* Macon, GA: Mercer University Press, 1983.

Carr, W. *Angels and Principalities.* Cambridge: Cambridge University Press, 1981.

Carson, H.M. *The Epistles of Paul to the Colossians and Philemon.* Grand Rapids: Eerdmans, 1960.

Cavallin, H.C.C. *Life After Death.* Lund: Gleerup, 1974.

—'Leben nach dem Tode im Spätjudentum und im frühen Christentum. I. Spätjudentum.' In *ANRW* II.19.1, pp. 240-345.

Cerfaux, L. *Christ in the Theology of Saint Paul.* Translated by G. Webb and A. Walker. Freiburg: Herder, 1959.

—'En faveur de l'authenticité des épîtres de la captivité.' *RechBib* 5 (1960), 60-71.

—*The Spiritual Journey of Saint Paul.* Translated by J.C. Guinness. New York: Sheed & Ward, 1968.

Chadwick, H. 'All Things to All Men.' *NTS* 1 (1955), 261-75.

Charles, R.H. *The Apocalypse of Baruch, translated from the Syriac.* London: Black, 1896.

—*The Book of Jubilees.* London: Black, 1902.

—*The Testaments of the Twelve Patriarchs.* London: Black, 1908.

—*The Book of Enoch.* Oxford: Clarendon Press, 1912.

—'Book of Enoch.' In *APOT*, 2.163-281.

—'II Baruch.' In *APOT*, 2.470-526.

—'The Book of Jubilees.' In *APOT*, 2.1-82.

—'The Testaments of the XII Patriarchs.' In *APOT* 2.282-367.

—*The Apocalypse of Baruch.* London: SPCK, 1917.

—*The Apocalypse of Baruch.* London: SPCK, 1929.

Charles, R.H., with an introduction by G.W. Buchanan. *Eschatology: The Doctrine of the Future Life in Israel, Judaism and Christianity.* New York: Schocken, 1963.

Charles, R.H., and W.R. Morfill. *The Books of the Secrets of Henoch.* Oxford: Clarendon Press, 1896.

Charlesworth, J.H. 'The SNTS Pseudepigrapha Seminars at Tübingen and Paris on the Books of Enoch.' *NTS* 25 (1979), 315-23.

—'A History of Pseudepigrapha Research: The Re-emerging Importance of the Pseudepigrapha.' In *ANRW*, II.19.1, pp. 54-88.

—*The Pseudepigrapha and Modern Research with a Supplement.* Chico, CA: Scholars Press, 1981.

—*The Old Testament Pseudepigrapha and the New Testament.* Cambridge: Cambridge University Press, 1985.

Chernus, I. *Mysticism in Rabbinic Judaism: Studies in the History of Midrash*. Berlin: de Gruyter, 1982.

Collins, A.Y. 'Numerical Symbolism in Jewish and Early Christian Apocalyptic Literature.' In *ANRW*, II.21.2, pp. 1221-87.

Collins, J.J. 'The Court-Tales in Daniel and the Development of Apocalyptic.' *JBL* 94 (1975), 218-34.

—'Jewish Apocalyptic against its Hellenistic Near Eastern Environment.' *BASOR* 220 (1975), 27-36.

—*The Apocalyptic Vision of the Book of Daniel*. Missoula, MT: Scholars Press, 1977.

—'Pseudonymity, Historical Reviews and the Genre of the Apocalypse of John.' *CBQ* 39 (1977), 329-43.

—'Introduction: Towards the Morphology of a Genre.' *Semeia* 14 (1979), 1-19.

—'The Jewish Apocalypses.' *Semeia* 14 (1979), 21-59.

—'The Heavenly Representative. The "Son of Man" in the Similitudes of Enoch.' In *Ideal Figures*, pp. 153-79.

—'The Apocalyptic Technique: Setting and Function in the Book of Watchers.' *CBQ* 44 (1982), 91-111.

—'The Genre Apocalypse in Hellenistic Judaism.' In *Apocalypticism*, pp. 531-48.

—'Apocalyptic Eschatology as the Transcendence of Death.' In *Visionaries*, pp. 61-84.

—*Between Athens and Jerusalem*. New York: Crossroad, 1983.

—*The Apocalyptic Imagination: An Introduction to the Jewish Matrix of Christianity*. New York: Crossroad, 1984.

—*Daniel, with an Introduction to Apocalyptic Literature*. Grand Rapids: Eerdmans, 1984.

—'Testaments.' In *JWSTP*, pp. 325-55.

—'Apocalyptic Literature.' In *Early Judaism and its Modern Interpreters*, pp. 345-70. Edited by R.A. Kraft and G.W.E. Nickelsburg. Philadelphia: Fortress Press, 1986.

Conzelmann, H. 'Der Brief an die Kolosser.' In *Die kleineren Briefe des Apostels Paulus*, pp. 130-54. Göttingen: Vandenhoeck & Ruprecht, 1962.

—'Paulus und die Weisheit.' *NTS* 12 (1965–66), 231-44.

—*An Outline of the Theology of the New Testament*. Translated by J. Bowden. London: SCM Press, 1969.

—'σκότος, κτλ.' *TDNT* 7.423-45.

—*1 Corinthians*. Translated by J.W. Leitch. Philadelphia: Fortress Press, 1975.

Coppens, J. ' "Mystery" in the Theology of Saint Paul and its Parallels at Qumran.' In *Paul and Qumran*, pp. 132-58. Edited by J. Murphy-O'Connor. Chicago: Priory, 1968.

Crenshaw, J.L. Review of *Wisdom in Israel*, by G. von Rad. *RelSRev* 2 (1976), 6-12.

Cross, F.M., Jr. *The Ancient Library of Qumran and Modern Biblical Studies*. New York: Doubleday, 1958.

Dahl, N.A. 'Anamnesis: Memory and Commemoration in Early Christianity.' In *Jesus in the Memory of the Early Church*, pp. 11-29. Minneapolis: Augsburg, 1976.

—'Form-Critical Observations on Early Christian Preaching.' In *Jesus in the Memory of the Early Church*, pp. 30-36. Minneapolis: Augsburg, 1976.

Daube, D. 'Participle and Imperative in 1 Peter.' In *The First Epistle of St. Peter*, by E.G. Selwyn. London: Macmillan, 1947; reprint edn, Grand Rapids: Baker, 1981.

Davenport, G.L. *The Eschatology of the Book of Jubilees*. Leiden: Brill, 1971.

Davies, P.R. 'Calendrical Change and Qumran Origins: An Assessment of VanderKam's Theory.' *CBQ* 45 (1983), 80-89.

Davies, W.D. *Torah in the Messianic Age and/or the Age to Come.* Philadelphia: Society of Biblical Literature, 1952.

—'Apocalyptic and Pharisaism.' In *Christian Origins and Judaism,* pp. 19-30. Edited by W.D. Davies. London: Darton, Longman & Todd, 1962.

—*Paul and Rabbinic Judaism.* Philadelphia: Fortress Press, 1980.

—'Paul and the Dead Sea Scrolls: Flesh and Spirit.' In *Christian Origins and Judaism,* pp. 145-77. Edited by W.D. Davies. London: Darton, Longman & Todd, 1962.

Dean-Otting, M. *Heavenly Journeys: A Study of the Motif in Hellenistic Jewish Literature.* Frankfurt: Lang, 1984.

Decock, P.B. 'Holy Ones, Sons of God, and the Transcendent Future of the Righteous in 1 Enoch and the New Testament.' *Neot* 17 (1983), 70-82.

Deichgräber, R. *Gotteshymnus in der frühen Christenheit.* Göttingen: Vandenhoeck & Ruprecht, 1967.

Deissmann, G.A. *Bible Studies.* Translated by A. Grieve. Edinburgh: T. & T. Clark, 1901.

Delcor, M. *Le Testament d'Abraham.* Leiden: Brill, 1973.

Delling, G. 'θριαμβεύω.' *TDNT* 3.159-60.

—'πλήρης, κτλ.' *TDNT* 6.283-311.

—'στοιχεῖον.' *TDNT* 7.670-87.

—'τέλος, κτλ.' *TDNT* 7.49-87.

Denis, A.-M. *Introduction aux pseudépigraphes grecs d'Ancien Testament.* Leiden: Brill, 1970.

De Wette, W.M.L. *Kurze Erklärung der Briefe an die Colosser, an Philemon, an die Epheser und Philipper.* 2nd edn. Leipzig: Weidmann, 1847.

Dexinger, F. *Das Buch Daniel und seine Probleme.* Stuttgart: Katholisches Bibelwerk, 1969.

—*Henochs Zehnwochenapokalypse und offene Probleme der Apokalyptikforschung.* Leiden: Brill, 1977.

Dibelius, M. 'The Isis Initiation in Apuleius and Related Initiatory Rites.' In *Conflict,* pp. 61-121.

Dibelius, M., and Greeven, H. *An die Kolosser, Epheser, an Philemon.* Tübingen: Mohr, 1953.

Dillmann, A. *Das Buch Henoch.* Leipzig: Fr. Chr. Wilh. Vogel, 1853.

Dodd, C.H. 'The Mind of Paul: II.' *BJRL* 18 (1934), 68-110.

—'Matthew and Paul.' In his *New Testament Studies,* pp. 53-66. Manchester: Manchester University Press, 1953.

Dodds, E.R. *The Greeks and the Irrational.* Berkeley: University of California Press, 1963.

Duling, D.C. 'Testament of Solomon.' *OTP* 1.935-87.

Dunn, J.D.G. *Unity and Diversity in the New Testament.* London: SCM Press, 1977.

Du Plessis, P.J. *ΤΕΛΕΙΟΣ. The Idea of Perfection in the New Testament.* Kampen: Kok, 1959.

Dupont, J. *Gnosis: La connaissance religieuse dans les épîtres de Saint Paul.* Louvain: Nauwelaerts, 1949.

Eckart, K.-G. 'Exegetische Beobachtungen.' *TV* 7 (1959–60), 87-106.

Egan, R.B. 'Lexical Evidence on Two Pauline Passages.' *NovT* 19 (1977), 34-62.

Ehrlich, E.L. *Der Traum im Alten Testament.* Berlin: Alfred Töpelmann, 1953.

Eissfeldt, O. *Einleitung in das Alte Testament.* 3rd edition. Tübingen: Mohr, 1964.

—*The Old Testament: An Introduction.* Translated by P.R. Ackroyd. Oxford: Blackwell, 1965.

Eitrem, S. 'EMBATEYΩ. Note sur Col. 2,18.' *ST* 2 (1948), 90-94.

Eliade, M. *Shamanism: Archaic Techniques of Ecstasy*. Princeton: Princeton University Press, 1964.

Eltester, F.W. *Eikon im Neuen Testament*. Berlin: de Gruyter, 1958.

Esser, H.H. 'δόγμα.' *NIDNTT* 1.330-31.

Evans, C. 'The Colossian Mystics.' *Bib* 63 (1982), 188-205.

Feuillet, A. 'La création de l'univers 'dans le Christ' d'après l'Epître aux Colossiens.' *NTS* 12 (1965–66), 1-9.

—*Le Christ sagesse de Dieu d'après les épitres pauliniennes*. Paris: J. Gabalda, 1966.

Fiddes, P.S. 'The Hiddenness of Wisdom in the Old Testament and Later Judaism.' PhD dissertation, Oxford University, 1976.

Fitzmyer, J.A. 'A Feature of Qumran Angelology and the New Testament.' *NTS* 4 (1957–58), 48-58.

Flusser, D. and Safrai, S. 'The Essene Doctrine of Hypostasis and Rabbi Meir.' *Immanuel* 14 (1982), 47-57.

Foerster, W. 'κλῆρος, κτλ.' *TDNT* 3.758-85.

—'Die Irrlehrer des Kolosserbriefes.' In *Studia Biblica et Semitica*, pp. 71 80. Edited by W.C. van Unnik and A.S. van der Woude. Wageningen: H. Veenman & Zonen, 1966.

Francis, F.O. 'A Re-examination of the Colossian Controversy.' PhD dissertation, Yale University, 1965.

—'Visionary Discipline and Scriptural Tradition at Colossae.' *LTQ* 2 (1967), 71-81.

—'Humility and Angelic Worship in Col 2:18.' In *Conflict*, pp. 163-95.

—'The Background of EMBATEYEIN (Col 2:18) in Legal Papyri and Oracle Inscriptions.' In *Conflict*, pp. 197-207.

—'The Christological Argument of Colossians.' In *God's Christ and His People*, pp. 192-208. Edited by J. Jervell and W.A. Meeks. Oslo: Universitetsforlaget, 1977.

Frey, J.B. 'Abraham (Apocalypse d').' In *DBSup*, 1.32.

Fridrichsen, A. 'θελων Col 2,18.' *ZNW* 21 (1922), 135-37.

Funk, R.W. 'The Apostolic Parousia: Form and Significance.' In *Christian History and Interpretation: Studies Presented to John Knox*, pp. 249-69. Edited by W.R. Farmer, C.F.D. Moule and R.R. Niebuhr. Cambridge: Cambridge University Press, 1967.

Gabathuler, H.J. *Jesus Christus. Haupt der Kirche–Haupt der Welt*. Zurich: Zwingli, 1965.

Gammie, J.G. 'The Classification, Stages of Growth, and Changing Intentions in the Book of Daniel.' *JBL* 95 (1976), 191-204.

—'Spatial and Ethical Dualism in Jewish Wisdom and Apocalyptic Literature.' *JBL* 93 (1974), 356-85.

Gaylord, H.E., Jr. '3 (Greek Apocalypse of) Baruch.' In *OTP*, 1.653-79.

Gewiess, J. 'Die apologetische Methode des Apostels Paulus im Kampf gegen die Irrlehre in Kolossä.' *BibLeb* 3 (1962) 258-70.

Gibbs, J.G. *Creation and Redemption*. Leiden: Brill, 1971.

Giem, P. 'SABBATON in Col 2:16.' *AUSS* 19 (1981), 198-206.

Ginzberg, L. 'Baruch, Apocalypse of (Greek).' In *JE*, 2.551.

Gnilka, J. *Der Kolosserbrief*. Freiburg: Herder, 1980.

Goudoever, J. van. *Biblical Calendars*. Leiden: Brill, 1961.

Grant, R.M. 'Like Children.' *HTR* 39 (1946), 71-73.

Greenfield, J.C. and Stone, M.E. 'The Enochic Pentateuch and the Date of the Similitudes.' *HTR* 70 (1977), 51-65.

Greenspahn, F.E. 'Why Prophecy Ceased.' *JBL* 108 (1989), 37-49.

Grelot, P. 'La géographie mythique d'Hénoch et ses sources orientales.' *RB* 65 (1958), 33-69.

Gruenwald, I. ' "Knowledge" and "Vision".' *IOS* 3 (1973), 63-107.

—'Jewish Apocalyptic Literature.' In *ANRW*, II.19.1, pp. 89-118.

—*Apocalyptic and Merkavah Mysticism*. Leiden: Brill, 1980.

—'Jewish Merkavah Mysticism and Gnosticism.' In *Studies in Jewish Mysticism*, pp. 41-55. Edited by J. Dan and F. Talmage. Cambridge, MA: Association for Jewish Studies, 1981.

Grundmann, W. 'ἀνέγκλητος.' *TDNT* 1.356-57.

—'ταπεινός, κτλ.' *TDNT* 8.1-26.

Gry, L. *Les dires prophétiques d'Esdras (IV. Esdras)*. 2 volumes. Paris: Paul Geuthner, 1938.

Gunkel, H. 'Das vierte Buch Esra.' In *APAT*, 2.331-401.

Gunther, J.J. *St. Paul's Opponents and their Background. A Study of Apocalyptic and Jewish Sectarian Teachings*. Leiden: Brill, 1973.

Hadot, J. 'La datation de l'apocalypse syriaque de Baruch.' *Semitica* 15 (1965), 79-95.

Hall, R.G. 'The "Christian Interpolation" in the Apocalypse of Abraham.' *JBL* 107 (1988), 107-12.

Halperin, D.J. *The Merkabah in Rabbinic Literature*. New Haven: American Oriental Society, 1980.

Halter, H. *Taufe und Ethos*. Freiburg: Herder, 1976.

Hanson, J.S. 'Dreams and Visions in the Greco-Roman World and Early Christianity.' In *ANRW*, II.23.2, pp. 1395-1427.

Hanson, P.D. *The Dawn of Apocalyptic*. Philadelphia: Fortress Press, 1979.

Harnack, A. *Geschichte der altchristlichen Literatur bis Eusebius*. 2nd edn. Leipzig: Hinrichs, 1958.

Harnisch, W. *Verhängnis und Verheissung der Geschichte*. Göttingen: Vandenhoeck & Ruprecht, 1969.

—'Der Prophet als Widerpart und Zeuge der Offenbarung. Erwägungen zur Interdependenz von Form und Sache im IV. Buch Esra.' In *Apocalypticism*, pp. 461-93.

Harris, M. 'Prepositions and Theology in the Greek New Testament.' In *NIDNTT* 3.1171-1215.

Harrison, R.K. *Introduction to the Old Testament*. Grand Rapids: Eerdmans, 1969.

Hartman, L. *Prophecy Interpreted*. Translated by N. Tomkinson. Uppsala: Gleerup, 1966.

—*Asking for a Meaning*. Lund: Gleerup, 1979.

Hatch, W.H.P. 'The Pauline Idea of Forgiveness.' In *Studies in Early Christianity*, pp. 335-49. Edited by S.J. Case. New York: Century, 1928.

Hauck, F. 'μῶμος, κτλ.' *TDNT* 4.829-31.

—'θησαυρός, θησαυρίζω.' *TDNT* 3.136-38.

—'μένω, κτλ.' *TDNT* 4.574-88.

Hayman, A.P. 'The Problem of Pseudonymity in the Ezra Apocalypse.' *JSJ* 6 (1975), 47-56.

Hegermann, H. *Die Vorstellung vom Schöpfungsmittler im hellenistischen Judentum und Urchristentum*. Berlin: Akademie Verlag, 1961.

Hellholm, D. 'The Problem of Apocalyptic Genre and the Apocalypse of John.' In *Society of Biblical Literature 1982 Seminar Papers*, pp. 157-98. Edited by K.H. Richards. Chico, CA: Scholars Press, 1982.

Helyer, L.R. 'Colossians 1:15-20: Pre-Pauline or Pauline?' *JETS* 26 (1983), 167-79.

Hendriksen, W. *Philippians, Colossians and Philemon.* Grand Rapids: Baker, 1979.

Hengel, M. *Judaism and Hellenism.* Translated by J. Bowden. Philadelphia: Fortress, 1974.

Herford, R.T. *Talmud and Apocrypha.* London: Soncino, 1933.

Herr, M.D. 'The Calendar.' In *The Jewish People in the First Century*, 2.834-64. Edited by S. Safrai and M. Stern. Philadelphia: Fortress Press, 1976.

Hill, D. *Greek Words and Hebrew Meanings.* Cambridge: Cambridge University Press, 1967.

Himmelfarb, M. *Tours of Hell: The Development and Transmission of an Apocalyptic Form in Jewish and Christian Literature.* Philadelphia: University of Pennsylvania Press, 1983.

—'From Prophecy to Apocalypse: The Book of the Watchers and Tours of Heaven.' In *Jewish Spirituality: From the Bible through the Middle Ages*, pp. 145-65. Edited by A. Green. New York: Crossroad, 1986.

Hindley, J.C. 'Toward a Date for the Similitudes of Enoch: An Historical Approach.' *NTS* 14 (1967–68), 551-65.

Hollander, H.W. and Jonge, M. de. *The Testaments of the Twelve Patriarchs: A Commentary.* Leiden. Brill, 1985.

Hooker, M.D. 'Were There False Teachers in Colossae?' In *Christ and Spirit in the New Testament*, pp. 315-31. Edited by B. Lindars and S.S. Smalley. Cambridge: Cambridge University Press, 1973.

Houlden, J.L. *Paul's Letters from Prison.* Harmondsworth: Penguin, 1970.

Hugedé, N. *Commentaire de l'Epître aux Colossiens.* Genève: Labor et Fides, 1968.

Hughes, H. Maldwyn. *The Ethics of Jewish Apocryphal Literature.* London: Robert Culley, n.d.

—'The Greek Apocalypse of Baruch or III Baruch.' In *APOT*, 2.527-41.

Hultgard, A. *L'eschatologie des Testaments des Douze Patriarches.* Uppsala: Almqvist & Wiksell, 1981.

Hunter, A.M. *Paul and His Predecessors.* London: SCM Press, 1961.

Hurtado, L.W. 'Revelation 4–5 in the Light of Jewish Apocalyptic Analogies.' *JSNT* 25 (1985), 105-24.

Isaac, E. '1 (Ethiopic Apocalypse of) Enoch.' In *OTP*, 1.5-89.

Jacob, E. 'Aux sources bibliques de l'apocalyptique.' In *Apocalypses et théologie de l'espérance*, pp. 43-62. Edited by L. Monloubou. Paris: Les Editions du Cerf, 1977.

James, M.R. *The Testament of Abraham: The Greek Text now First Edited with an Introduction and Notes.* Cambridge: Cambridge University Press, 1892.

—*Apocrypha Anecdota.* Cambridge: Cambridge University Press, 1897.

—*The Lost Apocrypha of the Old Testament.* London: Society for Promoting Christian Knowledge, 1920.

—*The Apocryphal New Testament.* Oxford: Clarendon Press, 1924.

Janssen, E. 'Testament Abrahams.' In *JSHRZ* 3.2, pp. 195-256.

Jaubert, A. *The Date of the Last Supper.* Translated by I. Rafferty. Staten Island, NY: Alba House, 1965.

Jervell, J. *Imago Dei: Gen 1,26f. im Spätjudentum, in der Gnosis und in den paulinischen Briefen.* Göttingen: Vandenhoeck & Ruprecht, 1960.

Johnson, A.R. *The Cultic Prophet in Ancient Israel.* Cardiff: University of Wales Press, 1962.

Jonge, M. de. *The Testaments of the Twelve Patriarchs: A Study of their Text, Composition and Origin.* Assen: Van Gorcum, 1953.

Kabisch, R. *Das vierte Buch Esra*. Göttingen: Vandenhoeck & Ruprecht, 1889.

Käsemann, E. 'A Primitive Christian Baptismal Liturgy.' In *Essays on New Testament Themes*, pp. 149-68. Translated by W.J. Montague. London: SCM Press, 1964.

Kaufmann, J. 'Apokalyptik.' In *EJ*, 2.1142-61.

Kee, H.C. 'Testaments of the Twelve Patriarchs.' In *OTP*, 1.775-828.

Kehl, N. *Der Christushymnus im Kolosserbrief*. Stuttgart: Katholisches Bibelwerk, 1967.

—'Erniedrigung und Erhöhung in Qumran und Kolossä.' *ZKT* 91 (1969), 364-94.

Kiley, M.C. 'Colossians as Pseudepigraphy.' PhD dissertation, Harvard University, 1983.

Kim, S. *The Origin of Paul's Gospel*. 2nd edn. Tübingen: Mohr, 1984.

Kittel, G. 'ἄγγελος, κτλ.' *TDNT* 1.74-87.

Kittel, R. 'δόγμα, δογματίζω.' *TDNT* 2.230-32.

—'δοκέω.' *TDNT* 2.232-33.

Klijn, A.F.J. 'The Sources and the Redaction of the Syriac Apocalypse of Baruch.' *JSJ* 1 (1970), 65-76.

—'Die syrische Baruch-Apokalypse.' *JSHRZ* 5.2, 107-91.

Knibb, M.A. 'The Date of the Parables of Enoch: A Critical Review.' *NTS* 25 (1979), 345-59.

—'Apocalyptic and Wisdom in 4 Ezra.' *JSJ* 13 (1982), 56-74.

—'Prophecy and the Emergence of the Jewish Apocalypses.' In *Israel's Prophetic Tradition*, pp. 155-80. Edited by R. Coggins, A. Phillips and M. Knibb. Cambridge: Cambridge University Press, 1982.

Knibb, M.A., with R.J. Coggins. *The First and Second Books of Esdras*. Cambridge: Cambridge University Press, 1979.

Knibb, M.A., in consultation with E. Ullendorff. *The Ethiopic Book of Enoch*. Oxford: Clarendon Press, 1978.

Knox, W.L. *St. Paul and the Church of the Gentiles*. Cambridge: Cambridge University Press, 1939.

Koch, K. *The Rediscovery of Apocalyptic*. Translated by M. Kohl. London: SCM Press, 1972.

—'Vom prophetischen zu apokalyptischen Visionsbericht.' In *Apocalypticism*, pp. 413-46.

Koep, L. *Das himmlische Buch in Antike und Christentum*. Bonn: Hanstein, 1952.

Koester, H. *Introduction to the New Testament*. 2 volumes. Philadelphia: Fortress Press, 1982.

Kohler, K. 'The Pre-Talmudic Haggada II C: The Apocalypse of Abraham and its Kindred.' *JQR* 7 (1895), 581-606.

Kraabel, A.T. 'The Roman Diaspora: Six Questionable Assumptions.' *JJS* 33 (1982), 445-64.

Krämer, H. *et al.* 'προφήτης, κτλ.' *TDNT* 6.781-861.

Kümmel, W.G. *Introduction to the New Testament*. Revised edn. Translated by H.C. Kee. Nashville: Abingdon, 1975.

Lacocque, A. *Le Livre de Daniel*. Neuchâtel: Delachaux et Niestlé, 1976.

Ladd, G.E. 'Why Not Prophetic-Apocalyptic?' *JBL* 76 (1956), 192-200.

Lähnemann, J. *Der Kolosserbrief: Komposition, Situation und Argumentation*. Gütersloh: Gütersloher Verlagshaus, 1971.

Lake, K. 'The Date of the Slavonic Enoch.' *HTR* 16 (1923), 397-98.

Lamarche, P. 'Structure de l'épître aux Colossiens.' *Bib* 56 (1975), 453-63.

Larsson, E. *Christus als Vorbild*. Translated by B. Steiner. Lund: Gleerup, 1962.

Leaney, A.R.C. '"Conformed to the Image of His Son" (Rom. VIII. 29).' *NTS* 10 (1963–64), 470-79.

Leaney, R. 'Col. ii.21-23 (the use of πρός).' *ExpTim* 64 (1952–53), 92.

Lebram, J.C.H. 'The Piety of the Jewish Apocalyptists.' In *Apocalypticism*, pp. 171-210.

Leivestad, R. *Christ the Conqueror*. London: SPCK, 1954.

Lenglet, A. 'La structure littéraire de Daniel 2–7.' *Bib* 53 (1972), 169-90.

Lentzen-Dies, F. 'Das Motiv der "Himmelsöffnung" in verschiedenen Gattungen der Umweltliteratur des Neuen Testaments.' *Bib* 50 (1969), 301-27.

Levison, J.R. '2 Apoc. Bar. 48:42–52:7 and the Apocalyptic Dimension of Colossians 3:1-6.' *JBL* 108 (1989), 93-108.

Licht, J. 'Abraham, Apocalypse of.' In *EJ*, 2.126-27.

Lightfoot, J.B. *Saint Paul's Epistles to the Colossians and to Philemon*. London: Macmillan & Co., 1879; reprint edn, Grand Rapids: Zondervan, 1959.

Limbeck, M. *Die Ordnung des Heils. Untersuchungen zum Gesetzesverständnis des Frühjudentums*. Düsseldorf: Patmos-Verlag, 1971.

Lincoln, A.T. *Paradise Now and Not Yet*. Cambridge: Cambridge University Press, 1981.

Lindblom, J. *Prophecy in Ancient Israel*. Oxford: Basil Blackwell, 1962.

—'Die Vorstellung vom Sprechen Jahwes zu den Menschen im Alten Testament.' *ZAW* 75 (1963), 263-88.

—*Gesichte und Offenbarungen*. Lund: Gleerup, 1968.

Lods, A. *Histoire de la littérature hébraïque et juive*. Paris: Payot, 1950.

Lohmeyer, E. 'Die Offenbarung des Johannes 1920–34.' *TRu* 7 (1935), 28-62.

Lohmeyer, E., with additional notes by W. Schmauch. *Die Briefe an die Philipper, an die Kolosser und an Philemon*. Göttingen: Vandenhoeck & Ruprecht, 1953.

Lohse, E. 'Christologie und Ethik im Kolosserbrief.' In *Apophoreta: Festschrift für Ernst Haenchen*, pp. 156-68. Edited by W. Eltester. Berlin: Töpelmann, 1964.

—'Pauline Theology in the Letter to the Colossians.' *NTS* 15 (1968–69), 211-20.

—'Ein hymnisches Bekenntnis in Kol 2,13c-15.' In *Mélanges Bibliques*, pp. 427-35. Edited by A. Descamps and R.P.A. de Halleux. Gembloux: Duculot, 1969.

—*Colossians and Philemon*. Translated by W.R. Poehlmann and R.J. Karris. Philadelphia: Fortress, 1971.

Lona, H.E. *Die Eschatologie im Kolosser- und Epheserbrief*. Würzburg: Echter Verlag, 1984.

Long, B.O. 'The Effect of Divination upon Israelite Literature.' *JBL* 92 (1973), 489-97.

Longenecker, R.N. 'Ancient Amanuenses and the Pauline Epistles.' In *New Dimensions in New Testament Study*, pp. 281-97. Edited by R.N. Longenecker and M.C. Tenney. Grand Rapids: Zondervan, 1974.

—'On the Form, Function, and Authority of the New Testament Letters.' In *Scripture and Truth*, pp. 101-14. Edited by D.A. Carson and J.D. Woodbridge. Grand Rapids: Zondervan, 1983.

Löwe, H. 'Bekenntnis, Apostelamt und Kirche im Kolosserbrief.' In *Kirche: Festschrift für Günther Bornkamm*, pp. 299-314. Edited by D. Lührmann and G. Strecker. Tübingen: Mohr, 1980.

Lowy, S. 'The Motivation of Fasting in Talmudic Literature.' *JJS* 9 (1958), 19-38.

Lührmann, D. *Das Offenbarungsverständnis bei Paulus und in paulinischen Gemeinden*. Neukirchen-Vluyn: Neukirchener Verlag, 1965.

Lyonnet, S. 'L'Epître aux Colossiens (Col 2,18) et les mystères d'Apollon Clarien.' *Bib* 43 (1962), 417-35.

—*Sin, Redemption, and Sacrifice*. Rome: Biblical Institute Press, 1970.

—'Paul's Adversaries in Colossae.' In *Conflict*, pp. 147-61.

McClellan, J.B. 'Colossians II.18: A Criticism of the Revised Version and an Exposition.' *Expositor*, series 7, 9 (1910), 385-98.

McCown, W. 'The Hymnic Structure of Colossians 1:15-20.' *EQ* 51 (1979), 156-62.

Macgregor, G.H.C. 'Principalities and Powers: The Cosmic Background of Saint Paul's Thought.' *NTS* 1 (1954), 17-28.

Mack, B.L. *Logos und Sophia*. Göttingen: Vandenhoeck & Ruprecht, 1973.

Maier, J. 'Die Sonne im religiösen Denken des antiken Judentums.' In *ANRW*, II.19.1, pp. 346-412.

Manns, F. 'Col. 1,15-20: midrash chrétien de Gen. 1,1.' *RSR* 53 (1979), 100-10.

Marshall, I.H. 'The Development of the Concept of Redemption in the New Testament.' In *Reconciliation and Hope*, pp. 153-69. Edited by R. Banks. Grand Rapids: Eerdmans, 1974.

—'Palestinian and Hellenistic Christianity: Some Critical Comments.' *NTS* 19 (1972–73), 271-87.

Martin, F. *Le Livre d' Hénoch*. Paris: Letouzey et Ané, 1906.

Martin, R.P. 'Reconciliation and Forgiveness in the Letter to the Colossians.' In *Reconciliation and Hope*, pp. 104-24. Edited by R. Banks. Grand Rapids: Eerdmans, 1974.

—*Colossians and Philemon*. Grand Rapids: Eerdmans, 1981.

Masson, C. *L'Epitre de Saint Paul aux Colossiens*. Paris: Delachaux & Niestlé, 1950.

Meeks, W.A. 'Moses as God and King.' In *Religions in Antiquity: Essays in Memory of Erwin Ramsdell Goodenough*, pp. 354-71. Edited by J. Neusner. Leiden: Brill, 1968.

—'In One Body: The Unity of Humankind in Colossians and Ephesians.' In *God's Christ and His People: Studies in Honour of Nils Alstrup Dahl*, pp. 209-21. Edited by J. Jervell and W.A. Meeks. Oslo: Universitetsforlaget, 1977.

—*The First Urban Christians*. New Haven: Yale University Press, 1983.

Megas, G. 'Das χειρόγραφον Adams.' *ZNW* 27 (1928), 305-20.

Merklein, H. 'Paulinische Theologie des in der Rezeption des Kolosser- und Epheserbriefes.' In *Paulus in den neutestamentlichen Spätschriften*, pp. 25-69. Edited by K. Kertelge. Freiburg: Herder, 1981.

Mertens, A. *Das Buch Daniel im Lichte der Texte vom Toten Meer*. Würzburg: Echter Verlag, 1971.

Metzger, B.M. *A Textual Commentary on the Greek New Testament*. London: United Bible Societies, 1975.

—'The Fourth Book of Ezra.' In *OTP*, 1.516-59.

Meyer, H.A.W. *Critical and Exegetical Hand-Book to the Epistles to the Philippians and Colossians, and to Philemon*. Translated by J.C. Moore. Revised and edited by W.P. Dickson. New York: Funk & Wagnalls, 1885.

Meyer, R. 'Zephanja-Apokalypse.' In *RGG*³ 6.1900-1901.

Michaelis, W. *Versöhnung des Alls*. Bern: Siloah, 1950.

Michel, O. 'οἶκος, κτλ.' *TDNT* 5.119-159.

Milik, J.T. *Ten Years of Discovery in the Wilderness of Judaea*. Translated by J. Strugnell. London: SCM Press, 1959.

Milik, J.T., with the collaboration of M. Black. *The Books of Enoch. Aramaic Fragments of Qumran Cave 4*. Oxford: Clarendon Press, 1976.

Mitchell, H.C. *A Critical and Exegetical Commentary on Haggai and Zechariah*. Edinburgh: T. & T. Clark, 1912.

Montgomery, J.A. *A Critical and Exegetical Commentary on the Book of Daniel*. Edinburgh: T. & T. Clark, 1927.

Morris, L. *The Apostolic Preaching of the Cross*. Grand Rapids: Eerdmans, 1965.

Moule, C.F.D. *The Epistles to the Colossians and to Philemon*. Cambridge: Cambridge University Press, 1957.

Moule, H.C.G. *The Epistles to the Colossians and to Philemon*. Cambridge: Cambridge University Press, 1894.

Müller, H.-P. 'Mantische Weisheit und Apokalyptik.' In *Congress Volume, Uppsala, 1971*, pp. 268-93. Leiden: Brill, 1972.

Münchow, C. *Ethik und Eschatologie: Ein Beitrag zum Verständnis der frühjüdischen Apokalyptik*. Göttingen: Vandenhoeck & Ruprecht, 1982.

Mullins, T.Y. 'Visit Talk in New Testament Letters.' *CBQ* 35 (1973), 350-58.

Mundle, W. 'Das religiöse Problem des IV. Esrabuches.' *ZAW* 47 (1929), 222-49.

Murphy, F.J. *The Structure and Meaning of Second Baruch*. Atlanta: Scholars Press, 1985.

Murphy, R.E. *The Dead Sea Scrolls and the Bible*. Westminster, MD: Newman, 1956.

Murray, R. ' "Disaffected Judaism" and Early Christianity: Some Predisposing Factors.' In *'To See Ourselves as Others See Us': Christians, Jews, 'Others' in Late Antiquity*, pp. 263-81. Edited by J. Neusner and E.S. Frerichs. Chico, CA: Scholars Press, 1985.

Myer, R. 'Abraham-Apokalypse.' In *RGG³* 1.72.

Myers, J.M. *I and II Esdras*. Garden City, NY: Doubleday, 1974.

Neugebauer, O. *The 'Astronomical' Chapters of the Ethiopic Book of Enoch (72–82). Translation and Commentary*. Copenhagen: Munksgaard, 1981.

Neusner, J. *A Life of Johanan Ben Zakkai*. Leiden: Brill, 1970.

Newsom, C.A. 'The Development of 1 Enoch 6–19: Cosmology and Judgment.' *CBQ* 42 (1980), 310-29.

—*Songs of the Sabbath Sacrifice: A Critical Edition*. Atlanta: Scholars Press, 1985.

—'Merkabah Exegesis in the Qumran Sabbath Shirot.' *JJS* 38 (1987), 11-30.

Nickelsburg, G.W.E., Jr. *Resurrection, Immortality, and Eternal Life in Intertestamental Judaism*. Cambridge, MA: Harvard University Press, 1972.

—'Narrative Traditions in the Paraleipomena of Jeremiah and 2 Baruch.' *CBQ* 35 (1973), 60-68.

—'Eschatology in the Testament of Abraham: A Study of the Judgment Scene in the Two Recensions.' In *Studies on the Testament of Abraham*, pp. 23-64. Edited by G.W.E. Nickelsburg. Missoula, MT: Scholars Press, 1976.

—'The Apocalyptic Message of 1 Enoch 92–105.' *CBQ* 39 (1977), 309-28.

—Review of *The Books of Enoch: Aramaic Fragments of Qumrân Cave 4*, by J.T. Milik. *CBQ* 40 (1978), 411-19.

—'Enoch, Levi, and Peter: Recipients of Revelation in Upper Galilee.' *JBL* 100 (1981), 575-600.

—*Jewish Literature Between the Bible and the Mishnah*. Philadelphia: Fortress Press, 1981.

—'The Epistle of Enoch and the Qumran Literature.' *JJS* 33 (1982), 333-48.

—'The Bible Rewritten and Expanded.' In *JWSTP*, pp. 89-156. Edited by M.E. Stone. Assen: Van Gorcum, 1984.

—'Revealed Wisdom as a Criterion for Inclusion and Exclusion: From Jewish Sectarianism to Early Christianity.' In *'To See Ourselves as Others See Us': Christians, Jews, 'Others' in Late Antiquity*, pp. 73-81. Edited by J. Neusner and E.S Frerichs. Chico, CA: Scholars Press, 1985.

Nicholson, E.W. 'Apocalyptic.' In *Tradition and Interpretation*, pp. 189-213. Edited by G.W. Anderson. Oxford: Clarendon Press, 1979.

Niditch, S. 'The Visionary.' In *Ideal Figures*, pp. 153-79.

—*The Symbolic Vision in Biblical Tradition*. Chico, CA: Scholars Press, 1983.

Nissen, A. 'Tora und Geschichte im Spätjudentum.' *NovT* 9 (1967), 241-77.

Nock, A.D. 'The Vocabulary of the New Testament.' *JBL* 52 (1933), 131-39.

Nötscher, F. 'Himmlische Bücher und Schicksalglaube in Qumran.' In *Vom Alten zum Neuen Testament*, pp. 72-79. Edited by F. Nötscher. Bonn: Hanstein, 1962.

Noll, S.F. 'Angelology in the Qumran Texts.' PhD dissertation, Manchester University, 1979.

Norden, E. *Agnostos Theos*. Leipzig: Teubner, 1913.

O'Brien, P.T. 'Col. 1:20 and the Reconciliation of All Things.' *RTR* 33 (1974), 45-53.

—*Introductory Thanksgivings in the Letters of Paul*. Leiden: Brill, 1977.

—*Colossians and Philemon*. Waco, TX: Word, 1982.

—'Principalities and Powers: Opponents of the Church.' In *Biblical Interpretation and the Church*, pp. 110-50. Edited by D.A. Carson. Nashville: Thomas Nelson, 1984.

Odeberg, H., with a prolegomenon by J.C. Greenfield. *3 Enoch or The Hebrew Book of Enoch*. New York: Ktav, 1973.

Oepke, A. 'δύω, κτλ.' *TDNT* 2.318-21.

—'ἔκστασις, ἐξίστημι.' *TDNT* 2.449-60.

Oesterley, W.O.E. *II Esdras*. London: Methuen, 1933.

—*The Jews and Judaism during the Greek Period: The Background of Christianity*. London: SPCK, 1941.

Olbricht, T.H. 'Colossians and Gnostic Theology.' *ResQ* 14 (1971), 65-79.

O'Neill, J.C. 'The Source of the Christology in Colossians.' *NTS* 26 (1979–80), 87-100.

Parisius, H.-L. 'Über die forensische Deutungsmöglichkeit des paulinischen ἐν Χριστῷ.' *ZNW* 49 (1958), 285-88.

Percy, E. *Die Probleme der Kolosser- und Epheserbriefe*. Lund: Gleerup, 1946.

Philonenko, M. *Les interpolations chrétiennes des Testaments des Douze Patriarches et les manuscrits de Qoumrân*. Paris: Presses Universitaires de France, 1960.

Philonenko-Sayar, B. and M. Philonenko. 'Die Apokalypse Abrahams.' In *JSHRZ*, 5.5, pp. 415-60.

Picard, J.-C. *Apocalypsis Baruchi Graece*. Leiden: Brill, 1967.

—'Observations sur l'Apocalypse Grecque de Baruch.' *Semitica* 20 (1970), 77-103.

Picirelli, R.E. 'The Meaning of "Epignosis".' *EQ* 47 (1975), 85-93.

Piper, O.A. 'The Saviour's Eternal Work.' *Int* 3 (1949), 286-98.

Plöger, O. *Das Buch Daniel*. Gütersloh: Mohn, 1965.

—*Theocracy and Eschatology*. Translated by S. Rudman. Oxford: Blackwell, 1968.

Pollard, T.E. 'Colossians 1.12-20: A Reconsideration.' *NTS* 27 (1981), 572-83.

Porton, G.G. 'Diversity in Postbiblical Judaism.' In *Early Judaism and its Modern Interpreters*, pp. 57-80. Edited by R.A. Kraft and G.W.E. Nickelsburg. Philadelphia: Fortress Press, 1986.

Preisker, H. 'ἐμβατεύω.' *TDNT* 2.535-36.

Procksch, O., and Kuhn, K.G. 'ἅγιος, κτλ.' *TDNT* 1.88-115.

Rad, G. von. *Theologie des Alten Testaments*. Volume 2. Munich: Chr. Kaiser Verlag, 1960.

Rad, G. von, and W. Foerster. 'διαβάλλω, διάβολος.' *TDNT* 2.71-81.

Radford, L.B. *The Epistle to the Colossians and the Epistle to Philemon.* London: Methuen, 1931.

Ramsay, W.M. 'Ancient Mysteries and their Relation to St. Paul.' *Athenaeum* (1913), 106-107.

—*The Teaching of Paul in Terms of the Present Day.* London: Hodder & Stoughton, 1913.

Rau, E. 'Kosmologie, Eschatologie und die Lehrautorität Henochs: Traditions- und form-geschichtliche Untersuchungen zum äth. Henochbuch und zu verwandten Schriften.' Unpublished Doctoral Dissertation, Hamburg, 1974.

Reicke, B. 'The Law and this World according to Paul.' *JBL* 70 (1951), 259-76.

—'Da'at and Gnosis in Intertestamental Literature.' In *Neotestamentica et Semitica: Studies in Honour of Matthew Black*, pp. 245-55. Edited by E.E. Ellis and M. Wilcox. Edinburgh: T. & T. Clark, 1969.

Reid, S.B. '1 Enoch: The Rising Elite of the Apocalyptic Movement.' In *Society of Biblical Literature 1983 Seminar Papers*, pp. 147-56. Edited by K.H. Richards. Chico, CA: Scholars Press, 1983.

Reumann, J. 'Stewards of God—Pre-Christian Religious Application of ΟΙΚΟΝΟΜΟΣ In Greek.' *JBL* 77 (1958), 339-49.

Ridderbos, H. *Paul: An Outline of His Theology.* Translated by J.R. de Witt. Grand Rapids: Eerdmans, 1975.

Rigaux, B. 'Révélation des mystères et perfection à Qumran et dans le Nouveau Testament.' *NTS* 4 (1957–58), 237-62.

Robinson, H.W. 'The Council of Yahweh.' *JTS* 45 (1944), 151-57.

Robinson, J.A. *Commentary on Ephesians.* London: Macmillan, 1904; reprint edn, Grand Rapids: Kregel, 1979.

Robinson, J.A.T. *The Body.* London: SCM Press, 1952.

Rössler, D. *Gesetz und Geschichte, Untersuchungen zur Theologie der jüdischen Apokalyptik und der pharisäischen Orthodoxie.* 2nd edn. Neukirchen: Neukirchener Verlag, 1960.

Roller, O. *Das Formular der paulinischen Briefe.* Stuttgart: Kohlhammer, 1933.

Rost, L. *Einleitung in die alttestamentlichen Apokryphen und Pseudepigraphen einschliesslich der grossen Qumran-Handschriften.* Heidelberg: Quelle & Meyer, 1971.

Rowland, C. 'The Influence of the First Chapter of Ezekiel on Judaism and Early Christianity.' PhD dissertation, Cambridge University, 1975.

—*The Open Heaven.* London: SPCK, 1982.

—'Apocalyptic Visions and the Exaltation of Christ in the Letter to the Colossians.' *JSNT* 19 (1983), 73-83.

—*Christian Origins.* London: SPCK, 1985.

Rowley, H.H. 'The Unity of the Book of Daniel.' In *The Servant of the Lord and other Essays on the Old Testament*, pp. 249-80. Oxford: Blackwell, 1965.

Rubinkiewicz, R. 'La vision de l'histoire dans l'Apocalypse d'Abraham.' In *ANRW*, II.19.1, pp. 137-51.

—'Les sémitismes dans l'Apocalypse d'Abraham.' *FO* 21 (1980), 141-48.

—'Apocalypse of Abraham.' In *OTP*, 1.681-705.

Rubinstein, A. 'Hebraisms in the Slavonic "Apocalypse of Abraham".' *JJS* 4 (1953), 108-15.

—'Hebraisms in the "Apocalypse of Abraham".' *JJS* 5 (1954), 132-35.

—'Observations on the Slavonic Book of Enoch.' *JJS* 13 (1962), 1-21.

Ruger, H.P. ' "Amôn—Pflegekind." Zur Auslegungsgeschichte von Prov. 8:30a.' In *Übersetzung und Deutung*, pp. 154-63. Edited by D. Barthélemy *et al.* Nijkerk: F. Callenbach, 1977.

Russell, D.S. *The Method and Message of Jewish Apocalyptic.* Philadelphia: Fortress Press, 1964.

Rutherford, J. 'Note on Colossians ii.15.' *ExpT* 18 (1906–1907), 565-66.

Ryssel, V. 'Die syrische Baruchapokalypse.' In *APAT*, 2.404-46.

—'Die griechische Baruchapokalypse.' In *APAT*, 2.446-57.

Sabatier, A. 'L'apocalypse juive et la philosophie de l'histoire.' *REJ* 14 (1900), lxiv-lxxxvi.

Saldarini, J. 'Apocalypses and "Apocalyptic" in Rabbinic Literature and Mysticism.' *Semeia* 14 (1979), 187-205.

Sanders, E.P. 'Literary Dependence in Colossians.' *JBL* 85 (1966), 28-45.

—*Paul and Palestinian Judaism.* Philadelphia: Fortress Press, 1977.

—'The Genre of Palestinian Jewish Apocalypses.' In *Apocalypticism*, pp. 447-59.

—'Testament of Abraham.' In *OTP*, 1.871-902.

Sappington, T.J. 'The Factor of Function in Defining Jewish Apocalyptic Literature.' *JSP* (forthcoming).

Satran, D. 'Daniel: Seer, Philosopher, Holy Man.' In *Ideal Figures*, pp. 33-48.

Saunders, E.W. 'The Colossian Heresy and Qumran Theology.' In *Studies in the History and Text of the New Testament*, pp. 133-45. Edited by B.L. Daniels and M.J. Suggs. Salt Lake City: University of Utah Press, 1967.

Sayler, G.B. *Have the Promises Failed? A Literary Analysis of 2 Baruch.* Chico, CA: Scholars Press, 1984.

Schäfer, P. 'New Testament and Hekhalot Literature: The Journey into Heaven in Paul and in Merkavah Mysticism.' *JJS* 35 (1984), 19-35.

—*Rivalität zwischen Engeln und Menschen.* Berlin: de Gruyter, 1975.

Schenk, W. 'Der Kolosserbrief in der neueren Forschung (1945–1985).' In *ANRW*, II.25.4, pp. 3327-64.

Schenke, H.-M. 'Der Widerstreit gnostischer und kirchlicher Christologie im Spiegel des Kolosserbriefes.' *ZTK* 61 (1964), 391-403.

Schille, G. *Frühchristliche Hymnen.* Berlin: Evangelische Verlagsantalt, 1965.

Schlier, H. *Der Brief an die Galater.* 4th edn. Göttingen: Vandenhoeck & Ruprecht, 1965.

—'δείκνυμι, κτλ.' *TDNT* 2.25-33.

Schmidt, F. 'Le Testament d'Abraham: Introduction, édition de la recension courte, traduction et notes.' 2 volumes. Unpublished doctoral dissertation, Université des Sciences Humaines de Strasbourg, 1971.

—'The Two Recensions of the Testament of Abraham: In Which Direction Did the Transformation Take Place?' In *Studies on the Testament of Abraham*, pp. 65-83. Edited by G.W.E. Nickelsburg. Missoula, MT: Scholars Press, 1976.

Schmidt, J.M. *Die jüdische Apokalyptik.* Neukirchen-Vluyn: Neukirchener Verlag, 1969.

Schmidt, N. 'The Two Recensions of Slavonic Enoch.' *JAOS* 41 (1921), 307-12.

Schmithals, W. *The Apocalyptic Movement.* Translated by J.E. Steely. Nashville: Abingdon, 1975.

Schnackenburg, R. *God's Rule and Kingdom.* Translated by J. Murray. New York: Herder, 1963.

Schneider, C. *Die Erlebnisechtheit der Apocalypse des Johannes.* Leipzig: Dörffling & Franke, 1930.

Schniewind, J. 'ἀγγελία, κτλ.' *TDNT* 1.56-73.

Scholem, G.G. *Major Trends in Jewish Mysticism*. London: Thames & Hudson, 1955.

—'Die Lehre vom "Gerechten" in der jüdischen Mystik.' *Eranos-Jahrbuch* 27 (1958), 237-97.

—*Jewish Gnosticism, Merkabah Mysticism and Talmudic Tradition*. New York: The Jewish Theological Seminary of America, 1960.

Schreiner, J. *Alttestamentlich-jüdische Apokalyptik*. München: Kösel, 1969.

—'Das 4. Buch Esra.' In *JSHRZ* 5.4, 291-412.

Schrenk, G. 'βίβλος, βιβλίον.' *TDNT* 1.615-20.

—'θέλω, θέλημα, θέλησις.' *TDNT* 3.44-62.

Schubert, K. 'Versuchung oder Versucher? Der Teufel als Begriff oder Person in den biblischen und ausserbiblischen Texten.' *Bibel und Liturgie* 50 (1977), 104-13.

Schubert, P. *Form and Function of the Pauline Thanksgivings*. Berlin: Töpelmann, 1939.

Schürer, E. Review of *Die Apokalypse des Elias, eine unbekannte Apokalypse und Bruchstücke der Sophonias-Apokalypse*, by G. Steindorff. *TLZ* 24 (1899), 4-8.

Schweizer, E. 'Die "Elemente der Welt" Gal 4,3.9; Kol 2,8.20.' In *Verborum Veritas: Festschrift für Gustav Stählin*, pp. 245-59. Edited by O. Böcher and K Haacker. Wuppertal: Theologischer Verlag, 1970.

—'Christ in the Letter to the Colossians.' *RevExp* 70 (1973), 451-67.

—'The Letter to the Colossians—Neither Pauline nor Post-Pauline?' In *Pluralisme et oecuménisme en recherches théologiques: mélanges offerts au R.P. Dockx*, pp. 3-16. Edited by Y. Congar *et al*. Paris: Duculot, 1976.

—*The Letter to the Colossians*. Translated by A. Chester. Minneapolis: Augsburg, 1982.

—'Slaves of the Elements and Worshipers of Angels: Gal 4:3, 9 and Col 2:8, 18, 20.' *JBL* 107 (1988), 455-68.

Scott, C.A.A. *Christianity According to St. Paul*. Cambridge: Cambridge University Press, 1927.

Scott, E.F. *The Epistle of Paul to the Colossians, to Philemon, and to the Ephesians*. London: Hodder & Stoughton, 1930.

Scott, R.B.Y. 'Isaiah 21.1-10: The Inside of a Prophet's Mind.' *VT* 2 (1952), 278-82.

Segal, A.F. 'Heavenly Ascent in Hellenistic Judaism, Early Christianity and their Environment.' In *ANRW*, II.23.2, pp. 1333-94.

—'Paul and Ecstasy.' In *Society of Biblical Literature 1986 Seminar Papers*, pp. 555-80. Edited by K.H. Richards. Atlanta: Scholars Press, 1986.

—*The Other Judaisms of Late Antiquity*. Atlanta: Scholars Press, 1987.

Sjöberg, E. *Der Menschensohn im äthiopischen Henochbuch*. Lund: Gleerup, 1946.

Slingerland, H.D. *The Testaments of the Twelve Patriarchs: A Critical History of Research*. Missoula, MT: Scholars Press, 1977.

Smith, M. 'Observations on Hekalot Rabbati.' In *Biblical and Other Studies*, pp. 142-60. Edited by A. Altmann. Cambridge, MA: Harvard University Press, 1963.

—*Clement of Alexandria and a Secret Gospel of Mark*. Cambridge, MA: Harvard University Press, 1973.

Stanley, D.M. *Christ's Resurrection in Pauline Soteriology*. Rome: Pontifical Biblical Institute, 1961.

Stauffer, E. 'βραβεύω, βραβεῖον.' *TDNT* 1.637-39.

Steck, O.H. *Israel und das gewaltsame Geschick der Propheten*. Neukirchen-Vluyn: Neukirchener Verlag, 1967.

Steindorff, G. *Die Apokalypse des Elias, eine unbekannte Apokalypse und Bruchstücke des Sophonias-Apokalypse*. Leipzig: Hinrichs, 1899.

Stone, M.E. 'Apocalyptic—Vision or Hallucination.' *Milla Wa-Milla. The Australian Bulletin of Comparative Religion* 14 (1974), 47-56.

—'Lists of Revealed Things in the Apocalyptic Literature.' In *Magnalia Dei: The Mighty Acts of God*, pp. 414-52. Edited by F.M. Cross *et al.* Garden City, NY: Doubleday, 1976.

—'The Book of Enoch and Judaism in the Third Century B.C.E.' *CBQ* 40 (1978), 479-92.

—*Scriptures, Sects and Visions.* Philadelphia: Fortress Press, 1980.

—'Reactions to Destructions of the Second Temple: Theology, Perception and Conversion.' *JSJ* 12 (1981), 195-204.

—'Enoch and Apocalyptic Origins.' In *Visionaries*, pp. 92-100.

—'Apocalyptic Literature.' In *JWSTP*, pp. 383-441.

—'Enoch, Aramaic Levi and Sectarian Origins.' *JSJ* 19 (1988), 159-70.

Sullivan, K. 'Epignosis in the Epistles of St. Paul.' In *Studiorum Paulinorum Congressus Internationalis Catholicus 1961*, 2.405-16. Rome: Pontifical Biblical Institute, 1963.

Suter, D.W. 'Apocalyptic Patterns in the Similitudes of Enoch.' In *Society of Biblical Literature 1978 Seminar Papers*, 1.1-13. Edited by P.J. Achtemeier. Missoula, MT: Scholars Press, 1978.

—'Fallen Angel, Fallen Priest: The Problem of Family Purity in 1 Enoch 6–16.' *HUCA* 50 (1979), 115-35.

—*Tradition and Composition in the Parables of Enoch.* Missoula, MT: Scholars Press, 1979.

—'Weighed in the Balance: The Similitudes of Enoch in Recent Discussion.' *RSR* 7 (1981), 217-21.

Testuz, M. *Les idées religieuses du livre des Jubilés.* Genève: Librairie E. Droz, 1960.

Thompson, A.L. *Responsibility for Evil in the Theodicy of IV Ezra.* Missoula, MT: Scholars Press, 1977.

Thompson, G.H.P. *The Letters of Paul to the Ephesians, to the Colossians and to Philemon.* Cambridge: Cambridge University Press, 1967.

Tigchelaar, E.J.C. 'More on Apocalyptic and Apocalypses.' *JSJ* 18 (1987), 137-44.

Turner, N. 'The "Testament of Abraham": Problems in Biblical Greek.' *NTS* 1 (1954–55), 219-23.

Uhlig, S. 'Das äthiopische Henochbuch.' In *JSHRZ*, 5.6, pp. 463-780.

Unnik, W.C. van. 'Die "geöffneten Himmel" in der Offenbarungsvision des Apokryphons des Johannes.' In *Apophoreta: Festschrift für Ernst Haenchen*, pp. 269-80. Edited by W. Eltester. Berlin: Töpelmann, 1964.

Vaillant, A. *Le Livre des Secrets d'Hénoch.* Paris: Institut d'études Slaves, 1976.

VanderKam, J.C. *Textual and Historical Studies in the Book of Jubilees.* Missoula, MT: Scholars Press, 1977.

—'The Origin, Character and Early History of the 364-Day Calendar: A Reassessment of Jaubert's Hypotheses.' *CBQ* 41 (1979), 390-411.

—'The 364-Day Calendar in the Enochic Literature.' In *Society of Biblical Literature 1983 Seminar Papers*, pp. 157-65. Edited by K.H. Richards. Chico, CA: Scholars Press, 1983.

—*Enoch and the Growth of an Apocalyptic Tradition.* Washington, DC: The Catholic Biblical Association of America, 1984.

—'Studies in the Apocalypse of Weeks (1 Enoch 93:1-10; 91:11-17).' *CBQ* 46 (1984), 511-23.

Vawter, B. 'Apocalyptic: Its Relation to Prophecy.' *CBQ* 22 (1960), 33-46.

—'The Colossian Hymn and the Principle of Redaction.' *CBQ* 33 (1971), 62-81.

Vielhauer, P. 'Apocalypses and Related Subjects.' In *New Testament Apocrypha*, 2.581-607. Edited by E. Hennecke and W. Schneemelcher. Philadelphia: Westminster Press, 1965.

Villiers, P.G.R. de. 'Revealing the Secrets. Wisdom and the World in the Similitudes of Enoch.' *Neot* 17 (1983), 50-68.

Volkmar, G. *Das vierte Buch Esra und apokalyptische Geheimnisse überhaupt*. Zürich: Meyer & Zeller, 1858.

Volz, P. *Die Eschatologie der jüdischen Gemeinde im neutestamentlichen Zeitalter*. Tübingen: Mohr, 1934.

Vries, S. de. 'Observations on Quantitative and Qualitative Time in Wisdom and Apocalyptic.' In *Israelite Wisdom: Festschrift for Samuel Terrien*, pp. 263-76. Edited by J.G. Gammie *et al*. Missoula, MT: Scholars Press, 1978.

Weinel, H. 'Die spätere christliche Apokalyptik.' In *EYXAPIΣTHPION: Studien zur Religion und Literatur des Alten und Neuen Testaments, für Hermann Gunkel*, 2.141-73. Edited by H. Schmidt. Göttingen: Vandenhoeck & Ruprecht, 1923.

Weiss, B. *Biblical Theology of the New Testament*. Translated from the 3rd German edn. Edinburgh: T. & T. Clark, 1882.

Weiss, H. 'The Law in the Epistle to the Colossians.' *CBQ* 34 (1972), 294-314.

Weiss, H.-F. 'Gnostische Motive und antignostische Polemik im Kolosser- und im Epheserbrief.' In *Gnosis und Neues Testament*, 311-24. Edited by K.-W. Tröger. Gütersloh: Gütersloher Verlagshaus, 1973.

Wengst, K. *Christologische Formeln und Lieder*. Gütersloh: Mohn, 1972.

Wessels, G.F. 'The Eschatology of Colossians and Ephesians.' *Neot* 21 (1987), 183-202.

White, J.L. 'Introductory Formulae in the Body of the Pauline Letter.' *JBL* 90 (1971), 91-97.

—*The Form and Function of the Body of the Greek Letter*. 2nd edn. Missoula, MT: Scholars Press, 1972.

Whiteley, D.E.H. 'St. Paul's Thought on the Atonement.' *JTS* ns (1957), 240-55.

—*The Theology of St. Paul*. Philadelphia: Fortress Press, 1966.

Widengren, G. *Literary and Psychological Aspects of the Hebrew Prophets*. Uppsala: Lundqvist, 1948.

Wilckens, U. *Weisheit und Torheit: Eine exegetisch-religionsgeschichtliche Untersuchungen zu 1.Kor 1 und 2*. Tübingen: Mohr, 1959.

Wilder, A.N. *Eschatology and Ethics*. Revised edn. New York: Harper, 1950.

Willi-Plein, I. 'Das Geheimnis der Apokalyptik.' *VT* 27 (1977), 62-81.

Williams, A.L. *The Epistles of Paul the Apostle to the Colossians and to Philemon*. Cambridge: Cambridge University Press, 1907.

Williamson, L., Jr. 'Led in Triumph.' *Int* 22 (1968), 317-32.

Wilson, R.R. *Prophecy and Society in Ancient Israel*. Philadelphia: Fortress Press, 1980.

—'From Prophecy to Apocalyptic: Reflections on the Shape of Israelite Religion.' *Semeia* 21 (1981), 79-95.

Wink, W. *Naming the Powers*. Philadelphia: Fortress Press, 1984.

Wintermute, O.S. 'Apocalypse of Zephaniah.' In *OTP*, 1.497-515.

—'Jubilees.' In *OTP*, 2.35-142.

Yates, R. 'Christ and the Powers of Evil in Colossians.' In *Studia Biblica 1978: III. Papers on Paul and Other New Testament Writers*, pp. 461-68. Edited by E.A. Livingstone. Sheffield: JSOT Press, 1980.

—' "The Worship of Angels" (Col 2:18).' *ExpTim* 97 (1985), 12-15.

—'Colossians and Gnosis.' *JSNT* 27 (1986), 49-68.

Young, B.H. 'The Ascension Motif of 2 Corinthians 12 in Jewish, Christian and Gnostic Texts.' *GTJ* 9 (1988), 73-103.

Zahn, T. *Einleitung in das Neue Testament.* 2nd edn. Leipzig: Deichert, 1900.

Zeilinger, F. *Der Erstgeborene der Schöpfung. Untersuchungen zur Formalstruktur und Theologie des Kolosserbriefes.* Vienna: Herder, 1974.

—'Die Träger der apostolischen Tradition im Kolosserbrief.' In *Jesus in der Verkündigung der Kirche*, pp. 175-93. Edited by A. Fuchs. Freistadt: Plöchl, 1976.

Ziegler, M. *Engel und Dämon im Lichte der Bibel, mit Einschluss des ausserkanonischen Schrifttums.* Zurich: Origo, 1957.

Zimmerli, W. 'Visionary Experience in Jeremiah.' In *Israel's Prophetic Tradition: Essays in Honour of Peter R. Ackroyd*, pp. 95-118. Edited by R. Coggins, A. Phillips and M. Knibb. Cambridge: Cambridge University Press, 1982.

INDEXES

INDEX OF BIBLICAL REFERENCES

OLD TESTAMENT

NEW TESTAMENT

72–82	29, 32, 57, 60, 87, 121	89.76	56	98.14-16	120
		90	98, 104	99.1-2	79
		90.6-7	61	99.3-5	79
72–80	56	90.9-27	105	99.3	104
72.1	75	90.9-16	33	99.10	120, 125
73–74	121	90.14	56	99.11-16	79
74.2	75	90.17	34, 98, 104	99.16	98
75.1-3	121			100.1-3	79
75.3	75	90.20	98, 104	100.4-6	79
75.4	75	90.21	100	100.6	132
79.6	75	90.34-35	61	100.7-9	79
80–81	32	90.37-38	132	100.10-13	79
80.1	75	91–105	34, 79, 103, 120	102.1-3	79
80.2–82.3	32			103.5-8	79
81	32	91	34	104.1	97, 102, 104, 189
81.1-2	125	91.3-11	125		
81.1	75	91.10	61	104.2	109
81.2	103	91.14	131	104.4	109
81.4	103, 121	91.17	110	104.5	104
81.5–82.3	121, 125	91.18-19	125	104.7	98, 104
81.5-6	125	92–105	80	104.9-10	120
82	32, 121	92	34	105	34
82.1-3	125	92.1	34, 63	105.1	132
82.1-2	61	93	34	106–107	34
82.4-8	121, 125	93.1-3	79	108	34, 79, 103, 120
82.4-7	121	93.2	75		
82.4	121, 125	93.10	61	108.3	102, 217
82.5	121	93.11-14	60		
82.7	75	94.1-5	125	*2 Enoch*	
83–90	33, 69, 72	94.3-4	125	1.2-3	68
83–84	33	94.6-8	79	1.3-5	75
83.2-5	72	95.4-7	79	1.6-10	68
83.2	69	96.4-8	79	1.6-7	75
83.7-9	72	96.7-8	104	3.1-3	75
84.2-4	33	96.7	103, 104	7.3 (rec J)	98
84.6	33	97.3-6	79	8–10	126
85–90	33, 72	97.5-7	104	8	92
89	98	97.8	104	8.1–9.1	126
89.32-33	61	98.1-8	104	8.1-8	81
89.41	61	98.1	104	8.8	93
89.51-54	61	98.4	104	9.1	118
89.59-67	56	98.6-8	104	9.1 (rec A)	93, 126
89.61-65	98	98.6	104	10.1-6	126
89.61-62	104	98.7-8	98	16.5	36
89.64	104	98.8–99.5	104	17.1	93
89.70-71	104	98.9-16	79	18.2 (rec A)	93
89.74	61	98.9-10	120	18.3	98
89.76-77	104	98.9	79	18.7	98

JOURNAL FOR THE STUDY OF THE NEW TESTAMENT

Supplement Series